Shutdown

ADAM TOOZE

Shutdown

How Covid Shook the World's Economy

ALLEN LANE
an imprint of
PENGUIN BOOKS

ALLEN LANE

UK | USA | Canada | Ireland | Australia
India | New Zealand | South Africa

Allen Lane is part of the Penguin Random House group of companies
whose addresses can be found at global.penguinrandomhouse.com

Penguin
Random House
UK

First published in the United States of America by Viking 2021
First published in Great Britain in Allen Lane 2021
001

Copyright © Adam Tooze, 2021

The moral right of the author has been asserted

Printed and bound in Great Britain by Clays Ltd, Elcograf S.p.A.

The authorized representative in the EEA is Penguin Random House Ireland,
Morrison Chambers, 32 Nassau Street, Dublin D02 YH68

A CIP catalogue record for this book is available from the British Library

Hardback ISBN: 978–0–241–48587–3
Trade Paperback ISBN: 978–0–241–50177–1

www.greenpenguin.co.uk

Penguin Random House is committed to a
sustainable future for our business, our readers
and our planet. This book is made from Forest
Stewardship Council® certified paper.

For our traveling friends.

Contents

Acknowledgments

This book wasn't planned. I am even more grateful than usual to Sarah Chalfant and James Pullen, of the Wylie Agency, who rallied behind the idea of doing a "2020 book," and to Wendy Wolf and Simon Winder, my U.S. and UK editors, for making *Shutdown* happen. It has been an unusually rapid and intense collaboration. Thanks to Terezia Cicel and the entire production team for getting it done. A special thank-you to Detlef Felken of Beck, with whom this is my first book.

Graham Weaver was invaluable in helping me finish the manuscript on time. I would not be able to manage my digital life without the support of Kate Marsh. I am deeply in their debt.

2020 was a year of furious debate and discussion. Twitter buddies too numerous to mention will recognize moments of wonky ping-pong in the following pages, none more so than the phenomenon that goes by the name of Albert Pinto, aka @70sBachchan.

At *Foreign Policy*, my editor, Cameron Abadi, has been an ideal collaborator and sounding board. Thank you, Jonathan Tepperman, for taking me on. Thank you to Jonathan Shainin, Yohann Koshy, and David Wolf at *The Guardian*, Paul Myerscough at the *London Review of Books*, and Henning Meyer and Robin Wilson at SocialEurope.com.

As the manuscript emerged, I was lucky once again to have the intellectual comradeship of a group of friends to whom, over the years, I have accumulated intellectual debts I can no longer sensibly enumerate. To have Matt Inniss, Ted Fertik, Stefan Eich, Nick Mulder, Barnaby Raine, and Grey Anderson as first readers is truly a privilege. They will see the imprint of their comments all over this book. I am particularly indebted to Daniela Gabor for her indispensable technical guidance on several key chapters, given incisively and at short notice. If this book adds something to the collective project of critical microfinance, Daniela deserves most of the credit.

All year I have learned from workshops and seminars organized by Joerg Haas at the Heinrich Boell Stiftung in the context of the Transformative Responses project. The online central banking salon orchestrated by Leah Downey and Stefan Eich has been a joy. It has been a treat to talk with Paul Tucker. Keith Breckenridge brought together a remarkable group of colleagues for three online seminars based around WiSER, the Wits Institute for Social and Economic Research, University of the Witwatersrand. Thank you to Jakob Vogel, my old Berlin friend, for a great seminar at the Centre Marc Bloch. Martijn Konings convened a super panel at Sydney University for the Wheelwright Lecture. I gained a huge amount from an ad hoc roundtable with Vera Songwe and Bartholomew Armah of UN-ECA. Josh Younger has educated me about bond markets and Lev Menand about the Fed. Megan Greene has taught me about dual interest rates. Robin Brooks and the team at the IIF are an essential source of data and analysis. The graphics in this book bear their imprint.

For fascinating conversation across the year, I would like to thank, in no particular order, Eric Levitz, Gilliant Tett, David Pilling, Gideon Rachman, Michael Pettis, Robert Harris, Georg Diez, Karin Pettersson, Joe Weisenthal, Tracey Alloway, Nathan Tankus, Benjamin Braun, Mark Sobel, Rohan Grey, Alex Doherty, Mark Schieritz, Menaka Doshi, Brad Setser, Ezra Klein, Elisabeth von Thadden, Ben Judah, Matt Klein, Jordan Schneider, Helen Thompson, David Runciman, Hugo Scott-Gall, Lisa Splanemann, Eric Graydon, David Wallace-Wells, Aaron Bastani, Lee Vinsel, Kaiser Kuo, Noah Smith, Ian Bremmer, Wolfgang Schmidt, Ole Funke, Moritz Schularick, David Beckworth, Christian Odendahl, Ewald Engelen, John Authers, Luis Garicano.

I happened to be on leave in the first half of 2020, for which I am grateful to Columbia University. At the time, Adam Kosto was serving as departmental chair. I would like to express my sincere gratitude to him for what he did for our department. Adam is not just a fabulous scholar. He is an extraordinary academic leader: cheerful, determined, clearheaded, focused on the stuff that should ground an academic department—ideas and books. We need people like Adam. We are lucky if we find them in the right place at the right time.

The 2020 shock went deep, touching practically everyone in the world in their everyday lives, disrupting life plans and the delicate arrangement of our family lives. Every one of my books for the last twenty years has been entwined with the stages of my daughter Edie's growing up. This is the first I have written about a shock that touched her life, along with my own and that of everyone we know and care about. One of the ways I felt the shock most deeply was through Edie, as a parent. I'll never forget the hasty evacuation of her dorm room and the weird, becalmed weeks that followed. The year was miserable for so many young people all over the world. A year spent in lockdown is an irreplaceable loss. You can't get your second year of college back. I am deeply impressed by how Edie and her peers have made the best of it.

As for my own coping, I owe a huge debt to two therapists, Dr. Donald Moss and Dr. Montie Mills Meehan. Though life coaching is the very least of what good therapy does for you, I am not at all sure I would have been able to write this book without them. I am very fortunate that I did not have to try.

The worst thing in 2020 was to be alone. I never was. There were swarms of friends and family in countless Zoom calls. Kudos to my cousin Jamie for pulling the extended Wynn-Tooze clan together. Great to reconnect with James Thompson and Max Jones. There were memorable chats with Paul Solman, David Edgerton, Hans Kundnani, and Danilo Scholz.

But as we have learned, there is nothing like actually seeing people in the flesh. Practically every day there were our dog friends "on the hill" in Riverside Park, to share both muddy and sunny mornings, the questions of life, and the progress of this book. A shout goes out to the dog gang—Jim and Merrill, Simon and Meredith, Terry and Adrian, Arisa, Ali, and above all, Michelle Lehrman, our pod buddy—and to the joyful, carefree creatures that bring us together—Yan Yan, Effi, Rocket, Betty Boo, Iro, Keila, Apollo, and our very own Ruby, aka "the heart stealer," our endlessly hilarious, adorable companion.

And then there was the weekly ritual of socially distanced dinner parties with Simon and Jane—paced out in feet with full protective PPE and no sharing of dishes or utensils—in the hallway opposite the elevator on the seventh floor of our apartment building. The warmth of everyday friendships saw us through some bad times in New York City. I am glad that we stayed. But it was intense. We needed to get away. Stays with our dear friends Brent Donovan, Isabel Barzun and Gavin Parfit, and Janet and Ed Wood offered respite and delightful company.

I lived this year with Dana Conley, from start to finish, not something we normally get to say. Dana read and commented meticulously on practically every page of the manuscript, but above all, Dana inspired. The travel industry was the most direct casualty of the shutdown. It has been profoundly impressive to be by her side as she faced the crisis, day after day, working with colleagues all over the world to put their lives on hold, coping collectively with unemployment, loss of income, anxiety, and shock. To imagine this happening not just to us, but to everyone we know in Dana's world of travel—to Julian and Sophie, Lionel and Dominique, Tim and Tek and Robert and Seph; from the UK to France, Italy, Tanzania, and Cambodia; in hotels, restaurants, wine cellars, game reserves, and tourist sites—was dizzying. Even more impressive has been watching Dana as she brought that community back together online, showcasing talents, adding new friends—here's to you, Ross and Craig—opening up conversations that stretched around the globe. I've seen Dana's energy, enthusiasm, kindness, and charm work its magic in very many places. The extraordinary thing in 2020 was to see that sense of shared enjoyment and sociability reflected back again, this time from dozens of Zoom screens—virtual, but unmistakably real. It is to the spirit of that community, brought to life by Dana, my extraordinary spouse, that this book is dedicated.

INTRODUCTION

I f one word could sum up the experience of 2020, it would be disbelief. Between Xi Jinping's public acknowledgment of the coronavirus outbreak on January 20, 2020, and Joseph Biden's inauguration as the 46th president of the United States precisely a year later on January 20, 2021, the world was shaken by a disease that in the space of twelve months killed more than 2.2 million people and rendered tens of millions severely ill. As of the end of April 2021, when this book went to press, the global death toll exceeded 3.2 million. The danger it posed disrupted the daily routine of virtually everyone on the planet, stopped much of public life, closed schools, separated families, interrupted travel both within and between countries, and upended the world economy. To contain the fallout, government support for households, businesses, and markets took on dimensions not seen outside wartime. It was not just by far the sharpest economic recession experienced since World War II, it was qualitatively unique. Never before had there been a collective decision, however haphazard and uneven, to shut large parts of the world's economy down. It was, as the International Monetary Fund (IMF) put it, "a crisis like no other."[1]

The virus was the trigger. But even before we knew what would hit us, there was every reason to think that 2020 might be tumultuous. The conflict between China and the United States was boiling up.[2] A "new Cold War" was in the air. Global growth had slowed seriously in 2019. The IMF worried about the destabilizing effect that geopolitical tension might have on a world economy piled high with debt.[3] Economists cooked up new statistical indicators to track the uncertainty that was dogging investment.[4] The data strongly suggested that the source of the trouble was in the White House.[5] America's 45th president, Donald Trump, had succeeded in turning himself into an unhealthy global obsession. He was up for reelection in November and seemed bent on discrediting the electoral process even if it yielded a win. Not for nothing, the slogan of the 2020 edition of the Munich Security Conference—the Davos for national security types—was "Westlessness."[6]

Apart from the worries about Washington, the clock on the interminable Brexit negotiations was running out. Even more alarming for Europe as 2020 began was the prospect of a new refugee crisis.[7] In the background lurked both the threat of a final grisly escalation in Syria's civil war and the chronic problem of underdevelopment. The only way to remedy that was to energize investment and growth in the global south. The flow of capital, however, was both unstable and unequal. At the end of 2019, half the lowest income borrowers in sub-Saharan Africa were already approaching debt distress.[8]

And more growth was not a panacea. It brought more environmental pressure. The year 2020 was set to be a decisive one in the politics of climate. The twenty-sixth UN Climate Change Conference, also known as COP26, was scheduled to meet in Glasgow in November 2020, only days after the U.S. election.[9] It would mark the fifth anniversary of the Paris climate agreement. If Trump was to win, which at the start of the year seemed a distinct possibility, the future of the planet would hang in the balance.

The pervasive sense of risk and anxiety that hung around the world economy was a remarkable reversal. Not so long before, the West's apparent triumph in the Cold War, the rise of market finance, the miracles of information technology, and the widening orbit of economic growth all together appeared to cement the capitalist economy as the all-conquering driver of modern history.[10] In the 1990s, the answer to most political questions had seemed simple: "It's the economy, stupid."[11] As economic growth transformed the lives of billions, there was, Margaret Thatcher liked to say, "no alternative." That is, there was no alternative to an order based on privatization, light-touch regulation, and the freedom of movement of capital and goods. As recently as 2005, Britain's centrist prime minister Tony Blair could declare that to argue about globalization made as much sense as arguing about whether autumn should follow summer.[12]

By 2020, both globalization and the seasons were very much in question. The economy had morphed from being the answer to being the question. The obvious retort to "It's the economy, stupid," was "Whose economy?" or "Which economy?" or even "What's the economy?" A series of deep crises beginning in Asia in the late 1990s and moving to the Atlantic financial system in 2008, the eurozone in 2010, and global commodity producers in 2014 had shaken confidence in market economics.[13] All those crises had been overcome, but by government spending and central bank interventions that drove a coach and horses through firmly held precepts about "small government" and "independent" central banks. And who benefited? Whereas profits were private, losses were socialized. The crises had been brought on by speculation. The scale of the interventions necessary to stabilize them had been historic. Yet the wealth of the global elite continued to expand. Who could be surprised, it was now commonplace to ask, if surging inequality led to populist disruption?[14] What many Brexit and Trump voters wanted was "their" national economy back.

Meanwhile, China's spectacular ascent robbed the economy of its innocence in another sense. It was no longer clear that the great gods of growth were on the side of the West. That, it turned out, disturbed an important assumption underpinning the Washington consensus. Soon America would no longer be number one. In fact, it was increasingly clear that the gods, at least as represented by the nature goddess Gaia, were at odds with economic growth full stop.[15] Climate change, which had once been a preoccupation of the environmental movement alone, became an emblem for a wider imbalance between nature and humanity. Talk of "Green Deals" and of the energy transitions was everywhere.

And then, in January 2020, the news broke from Beijing. China was facing a full-blown epidemic of a novel coronavirus. It was by that point already worse than the SARS outbreak, which in 2003 had sent shivers down the spine. This was the natural "blowback" that environmental campaigners had long warned us about, but whereas climate change caused us to stretch our minds to a planetary scale and set a timetable in terms of decades, the virus was microscopic and all-pervasive and was moving at a pace of days and weeks. It affected not glaciers and ocean tides, but our bodies. It was carried on our breath. It would put not just individual national economies but the world's economy in question.

The virus that would by January 2020 be labeled SARS-CoV-2 was not a black swan, a radically unexpected, unlikely event. It was a gray rhino, a risk that has become so taken for granted that it is underestimated.[16] As it emerged from the shadows, the gray rhino SARS-CoV-2 had the look about it of a catastrophe foretold. It was precisely the kind of highly contagious, flu-like infection that virologists had predicted. It came from one of the

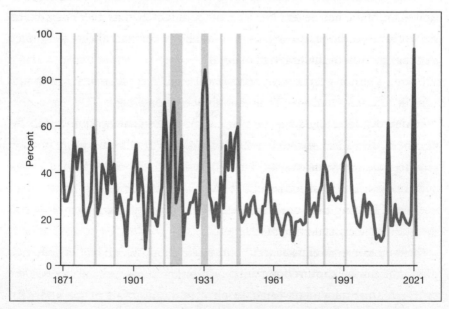

Forecasting global disaster, June 2020: The proportion of economies with an annual contraction in per capita GDP. Shaded areas refer to global recessions. Data for 2020–21 are forecasts.

A. Kose and N. Sugarawa, "Understanding the Depth of the 2020 Global Recession in 5 Charts," *World Bank Blogs*, June 15, 2020.

places they expected it to come from—the region of dense interaction between wildlife, agriculture, and urban populations sprawled across East Asia.[17] It spread, predictably, through the channels of global transport and communication. It had, frankly, been a while coming.

There has been much debate in economics about the "China shock"— the impact on Western labor markets of globalization and the sudden rise in imports from China in the early 2000s.[18] SARS-CoV-2 was a "China shock" with a vengeance. Back to the days of the Silk Road, infectious diseases had traveled east to west across Eurasia. In earlier times, the spread had been limited by the slow pace of travel. In the age of sail, those who carried diseases tended to die en route. In 2020 the coronavirus moved at the speed of the jet and the high-speed train. Wuhan in 2020 was an affluent metropolis of recent migrants. Half the population would leave the city to celebrate Chinese New Year. SARS-CoV-2 took only a matter of weeks to spread from Wuhan around China and to much of the rest of the world.

One year later, the world was reeling. In the historic record of modern capitalism, there has never been a moment in which close to 95 percent of the world's economies suffered a simultaneous contraction in per capita GDP, as they did in the first half of 2020.

Over 3 billion adults were furloughed from their jobs or struggled to work from home.[19] Close to 1.6 billion young people had their education interrupted.[20] Quite apart from the unprecedented disruption to family life, the World Bank estimated that the loss of lifetime earnings due to human capital forgone may run to $10 trillion.[21] The fact that the world collectively willed that shutdown makes this utterly unlike any previous recession. Tracing out who made the decisions where and under which conditions is a crucial task for this book.

It was, as we all experienced, a disruption that went far beyond anything that can be captured in statistics of gross domestic product (GDP), trade, and unemployment. Most people had never suffered such a serious interruption to their everyday life. It caused stress, depression, and mental anguish. By the end of 2020, the largest part of scientific research on Covid-19 was dedicated to mental health.[22]

The experience of crisis depended on your location and nationality. In the UK and the United States, 2020 was experienced not just as a public health emergency or a major recession, but as the culmination of a period of escalating national crisis, summarized by the words "Trump" and "Brexit." How could countries that once boasted of global hegemony and that were undisputed leaders in matters of public health fail so badly to manage the disease? It must reflect a deeper malaise.[23] Perhaps it was their common enthusiasm for neoliberalism? Or the culmination of a process of decline stretching over many decades. Or the insularity of their political cultures?[24]

In the EU, "polycrisis" is a term that has come into use in the last decade. European Commission president Jean-Claude Juncker borrowed the idea from the French theorist of complexity Edgar Morin.[25] Juncker used it to capture the convergence between 2010 and 2016 of the eurozone crisis, the conflict in Ukraine, the refugee crisis, Brexit, and the Europe-wide upsurge in nationalist populism.[26]

Polycrisis neatly captures the coincidence of different crises but it doesn't tell us much about how they interact.[27] In January 2019, China's president Xi Jinping gave a widely remarked speech on the duty of Chinese Communist Party (CCP) cadres to anticipate both black swan and gray rhino risks.[28] That summer, *Study Times* and *Qiushi*, the two journals through which the CCP communicates doctrinal statements to its more intellectual cadres, published an essay by Chen Yixin that elaborated on Xi's aphoristic observations.[29] Chen is a protégé of Xi Jinping and would be chosen during the coronavirus crisis to lead the party's cleanup operation in Hubei province.[30] In his 2019 essay Chen put the question: How did risks combine? How did economic and financial risks morph into political and social risks? How did "cyberspace risks" brew up to become "actual social risks"? How did external risks become internalized?

To understand how polycrises develop, Chen suggested that China's security officials should focus on six major effects.

As China moved to the center of the world stage they should guard against "backflow" from interactions with the outside world.

At the same time, they should be alert to the convergence of what might appear to be superficially distinct threats into a single new threat.

Differences between inside and outside and between new and old could easily become blurred.

Apart from convergence, one also had to contend with the "layering effect," in which "interest group demands from different communities overlap with one another to create layered social problems: current problems with historical problems, tangible interest problems with ideological problems, political problems with nonpolitical problems; all intersecting and interfering with one another."

As communication was becoming easier around the world, "linkage effects" could result. Communities could "call out to one another across distances, and mutually reinforce one another. . . ."

The internet did not just enable backflow and linkage, it also enabled the sudden amplification of news. The CCP had to reckon, Chen warned, with the "magnifier effect" in which "any small thing can become a . . . whirl-pool; a few rumors . . . can easily produce a 'storm in a teacup' and abruptly produce a real-life 'tornado' in society."

Finally, there was the "induction effect," by which problems in one region indirectly incited sympathetic reaction and imitation in another region, often feeding off preexisting unresolved problems.[31]

Though presented in the wooden style of the Chinese Communist Party, Chen's list has an uncanny fit with the experience of 2020. The virus was an example of backflow on a huge scale, from the Chinese countryside to the city of Wuhan, from Wuhan to the rest of the world. Politicians in the West, as much as in China, struggled with convergence, layering, and linkage. The Black Lives Matter protest movement was a giant demonstration of the power of magnification and induction, generating resonances around the globe.[32]

Indeed, if you ignore its original context, Chen's checklist for the party cadres could even be read as a guide to our private lives, a self-help manual for the corona crisis. How many families, how many couples, how many of us confined and isolated by quarantine were proof against magnification and induction effects? It could feel at times as though the invisible threat of the virus was stressing the weakest parts of our personalities and our most intimate relationships.

———

There have been far more lethal pandemics. What was dramatically new about coronavirus in 2020 was the scale of the response. And that begs a question. As the *Financial Times*'s chief economic commentator Martin Wolf put it,

> Why . . . has the economic damage of such a comparatively mild pandemic been so huge? The answer is: because it could be. Prosperous people can easily dispense with a large proportion of their normal daily expenditures, while their governments can support affected people and businesses on a huge scale. . . . The response to the pandemic is a reflection of economic possibilities and social values today, at least in rich countries.[33]

In fact, one of the striking things about 2020 is that poor and middle-income countries were willing to pay a huge price too. By early April, the vast majority of the world outside China, where it had already been contained, was involved in an unprecedented effort to stop the virus. As a haggard-looking Lenín Moreno, president of Ecuador, one of the hardest-hit countries, put it: "This is the real first world war. . . . The other world wars were localised in [some] continents with very little participation from other continents...but this affects everyone. It is not localised. It is not a war from which you can escape."[34]

If it was a war that you could not escape, it was nevertheless a war that you had to choose to fight. And it is that which truly warrants describing 2020 as a crisis. In its original sense, crisis or *krisis* (in Greek) describes a critical turning point in the course of a disease. It is associated with the word *krinein*, which means to separate, decide, or judge, from which we derive "critic" and "criterion," the standard of judgment.[35] It therefore seems a doubly apt phrase to describe the impact of a virus, which forced on people, on organizations, on governments at every level, all over the world, a series of huge and profoundly difficult choices.

Lockdown is the phrase that has come into common use to describe our collective reaction. The very word is contentious. Lockdown suggests compulsion. Before 2020 it was a term associated with collective punishment in prisons. There were moments and places where that is a fitting description for the response to COVID. In Delhi, in Durban, and in Paris, armed police patrolled the streets, took names and numbers, and punished those who were violating curfews.[36] In the Dominican Republic, an astonishing 85,000 people, almost 1 percent of the population, were arrested for violating the lockdown.[37]

Even if no violence was involved, a government-mandated closure of all eateries and bars could feel repressive to their owners and clients. But if we trace the broader course of events and, in particular, if we focus, as this book does, on the economic reaction to the pandemic, lockdown seems a one-sided way of describing the reaction to the coronavirus. Mobility fell precipitately, well before government orders were issued. The flight to safety in financial markets began in late February. There was no jailer slamming the door and turning the key. Investors were running for cover. Consumers were staying at home. Businesses were closing or shifting to homework. Garment workers in Bangladesh were locked out of their workplaces before they were ordered to stay at home. Sometimes government actions followed private decisions. Sometimes they anticipated them. By mid-March, the whole world was acting under the constraint of mutual observation and emulation. Shutting down became the norm. Those who were outside national territorial space, like hundreds of thousands of seafarers, found themselves banished to a floating limbo.

The point of using the term "shutdown" is to hold open the question of who decided what, where, and how and who imposed what on whom. Resisting the term "lockdown" is not to imply that the process was voluntary or a matter of individual free will, as it certainly was neither. The aim of this book is to trace the interaction in the economic sphere between constrained choices being made under conditions of huge uncertainty at different levels all across the world, from main streets to central banks, from families to factories, from favelas to traders hunched frantically over improvised workstations in suburban basements. Decisions were driven by fear or by scientific predictions. They were required by government orders or social convention. But they could also be motivated by the movement of hundreds of billions of dollars impelled by tiny, flickering variations in interest rates.

The widespread adoption of the term "lockdown" is an index of how contentious the politics of the virus would turn out to be. Societies, communities, families quarreled bitterly over face masks, social distancing, and quarantine. The stakes often seemed and sometimes were existential. It was hard to tell one from the other. The entire experience was an example on the grandest scale of what the German sociologist Ulrich Beck in the 1980s dubbed "risk society."[38] As a result of the development of modern society, we found ourselves collectively haunted by an unseen threat, visible only to science, a risk that remained abstract and immaterial until you fell sick and the unlucky ones found themselves slowly drowning in the fluid accumulating in their lungs.

One way to react to such a situation of risk is to retreat into denial. That may work. It would be naive to imagine otherwise. Many pervasive diseases and social ills, including many that cause loss of life on a large scale, are ignored and naturalized, treated as "facts of life." With regard to the largest environmental risks, notably climate change, one might say that our normal mode of operation is denial and willful ignorance on a grand scale.[39] Even urgent, life-and-death medical emergencies like pandemics are filtered by politics and power. Faced with the coronavirus, some would clearly have preferred a strategy of denial. That involves a gamble. It risks sudden, scandalous politicization. The pros and cons were weighed up over and over again. Often the advocates of "toughing it out" liked to proclaim themselves the defenders of common sense and realism, only to find that their sangfroid was more convincing in theory than in practice.

Facing up to the pandemic was what the vast majority of people all over the world tried to do. But the problem, as Beck pointed out, is that getting to grips with modern macro risks is easier said than done.[40] It requires agreement on what the risk is, which entangles the science in our arguments and taxes the rest of us with the uncertainty of the science.[41] It also requires self-reflexive critical engagement with our own behavior and with the social order to which it belongs. It requires a willingness to contend with political choices, choices about resource distribution and priorities at every level. That runs up against the prevalent desire of the last forty years to avoid precisely that, to depoliticize, to use markets or the law to avoid such decisions.[42] This is the basic thrust behind what is known as neoliberalism, or the market revolution—to depoliticize distributional issues, including the very unequal consequences of societal risks, whether those be due to structural change in the global division of labor, environmental damage, or disease.[43]

Coronavirus glaringly exposed our institutional lack of preparation, what Beck called our "organized irresponsibility." It revealed the weakness of basic apparatuses of state administration, like up-to-date registers of citizens and government databases. To face the crisis, we needed a society that gave far greater priority to care.[44] Loud calls issued from unlikely places for a "new social contract" that would properly value essential workers and take account of the risks generated by the globalized lifestyles enjoyed by the most fortunate.[45] Like the programs for a Green New Deal that had emerged repeatedly since the beginning of the millennium, such grand designs were intended to inspire.[46] They were intended to mobilize. They begged the question of power. If there was to be a new social contract, who would make it?

There was a strange aftertaste to many of the calls for grand social reform in 2020. As the coronavirus crisis overtook us, the left wing on both sides of the Atlantic, at least that part that had been fired up by Jeremy Corbyn and Bernie Sanders, was going down to defeat. The promise of a radicalized and reenergized left, organized around the idea of the Green New Deal, seemed to dissipate amid the pandemic. It fell to governments mainly of the center and the right to meet the crisis. They were a strange assortment. Jair Bolsonaro in Brazil and Donald Trump in the United States experimented with denial. For them climate skepticism and virus skepticism went hand in hand. In Mexico, the notionally left-wing government of Andrés Manuel López Obrador also pursued a maverick path, refusing to take drastic action. Nationalist strongmen like Rodrigo Duterte in the Philippines, Narendra Modi in India, Vladimir Putin in Russia, and Recep Tayyip Erdoğan in Turkey did not deny the virus, but relied on their patriotic appeal and bullying tactics to see them through. It was the managerial centrist types who were under most pressure. Figures like Nancy Pelosi and Chuck Schumer in the United States, or Sebastián Piñera in Chile, Cyril Ramaphosa in South Africa, Emmanuel Macron, Angela Merkel, Ursula von der Leyen, and their ilk in Europe. They accepted the science. Denial was not an option. They were desperate to demonstrate that they were better than the "populists." To meet the crisis, very middle-of-the-road politicians ended up doing very radical things. Most of it was improvisation and compromise, but insofar as they managed to put a programmatic gloss on their responses—whether in the form of the EU's Next Generation program or Biden's Build Back Better program in 2020—it came from the repertoire of green modernization, sustainable development, and the Green New Deal.

The result was a bitter historic irony. Even as the advocates of the Green New Deal went down to political defeat, 2020 resoundingly confirmed the realism of their diagnosis. It was the Green New Deal that had squarely addressed the urgency of huge environmental challenges and linked it to questions of extreme social inequality. It was the Green New Deal that had insisted that in meeting these challenges, democracies could not allow themselves to be hamstrung by conservative fiscal and monetary doctrines inherited from the bygone battles of the 1970s and discredited by the financial crisis of 2008. It was the Green New Deal that had mobilized energetic, engaged, future-oriented, young citizens on whom democracy, if it was to have a hopeful future, clearly depended. The Green New Deal had also, of course, demanded that rather than endlessly patching a system that produced and reproduced inequality, instability, and crisis, it should be radically reformed. That was challenging for centrists. But one of the attractions of a crisis was that questions of the long-term future could be set aside. The year 2020 was all about survival.

The immediate economic policy response to the coronavirus shock drew directly on the lessons of 2008. Fiscal policy was even larger and more prompt. Central bank interventions were even more spectacular. If one married the two in one's mind—fiscal and monetary policy together—it confirmed the essential insights of economic doctrines once advocated by radical Keynesians and made newly fashionable by doctrines like Modern Monetary Theory (MMT).[47] State finances are not limited like those of a household. If a monetary sovereign treats the question of how to organize financing as anything more than a technical matter, that is itself a political choice. As John Maynard Keynes once reminded his readers in the midst of World War II: "Anything we can actually do we can afford."[48] The real challenge, the truly political question, was to agree what we wanted to do and to figure out how to do it.

Experiments in economic policy in 2020 were not confined to the rich countries. Enabled by the abundance of dollars unleashed by the Fed but drawing on decades of experience with fluctuating global capital flows, many emerging market governments displayed remarkable initiative in response to the crisis. They put to work a toolkit of policies that enabled them to hedge the risks of global financial integration.[49] Ironically, unlike in 2008, China's greater success in virus control left its economic policy looking relatively conservative. Those countries like Mexico and India, where the pandemic spread rapidly but governments failed to respond with large-scale economic policy, looked increasingly out of step with the times. The year would witness the head-turning spectacle of the IMF scolding a notionally left-wing Mexican government for failing to run a large enough budget deficit.[50]

It was hard to avoid the sense that a turning point had been reached. Was this, finally, the death of the orthodoxy that had prevailed in economic policy since the 1980s? Was this the death knell of neoliberalism?[51] As a coherent ideology of government, perhaps. The idea that the natural envelope of economic activity could be ignored or left to markets to regulate was clearly out of touch with reality. So too was the idea that markets could self-regulate in relation to all conceivable social and economic shocks. Even more urgently than in 2008, survival dictated interventions on a scale last seen in World War II.

All this left doctrinaire economists gasping for breath. That in itself is not surprising. The orthodox understanding of economic policy was always unrealistic. As a practice of power, neoliberalism had always been radically pragmatic. Its real history was that of a series of state interventions in the interests of capital accumulation, including the forceful deployment of state violence to bulldoze opposition.[52] Whatever the doctrinal twists and turns, the social realities with which the market revolution had been entwined since the 1970s—the entrenched influence of wealth over politics, the law and the media, the disempowerment of workers—all perdured. And what historic force was it that was bursting the dikes of the neoliberal order? The story we will be tracing in this book is not that of a revival of class struggle or of a radical populist challenge. What did the damage was a plague unleashed by heedless global growth and the massive flywheel of financial accumulation.[53]

In 2008, the crisis had been brought on by the overexpansion of the banks and the excesses of mortgage securitization. In 2020, the coronavirus hit the financial system from the outside, but the fragility that this shock exposed was internally generated. This time it was not banks that were the weak link, but the asset markets themselves. The shock went to the very heart of the system, the market for American Treasuries, the supposedly safe assets on which the entire pyramid of credit is based. If that had melted down, it would have taken the rest of the world with it. By the third week of March 2020, the City of London and Europe too were in crisis. Once again, the Fed, the U.S. Treasury, and Congress cobbled together a patchwork of interventions that effectively backstopped a large part of the private credit system. The effect radiated through the dollar-based financial system to the rest of the world. What was at stake was the survival of a global network of market-based finance that Daniela Gabor has aptly dubbed the Wall Street consensus.[54]

The scale of stabilizing interventions in 2020 was impressive. It confirmed the basic insistence of the Green New Deal that if the will was there, democratic states did have the tools they needed to exercise control over the economy. This was, however, a double-edged realization, because if these interventions were an assertion of sovereign power, they were crisis driven.[55] As in 2008, they served the interests of those who had the most to lose. This time, not just individual banks but entire markets were declared too big to fail.[56] To break that cycle of crisis and stabilizing and to make economic policy into a true exercise in democratic sovereignty would require root and branch reform. That would require a real power shift, and the odds were stacked against that.

The market revolution of the 1970s was no doubt a revolution in economic ideas, but it was far more than that. The war on inflation waged by Thatcher and Reagan was a comprehensive campaign against a threat of social upheaval, which they saw as coming from without and from within. It had the ferocity that it did because in the 1970s and early 1980s, class conflict in Europe, Asia, and the United States was still framed by the global struggles of decolonization and the Cold War.[57] The conservative campaign was all the more urgent because the collapse of the Bretton Woods system between 1971 and 1973 unfastened money from gold and opened the door to expansive economic policy. What threatened was not the decorous Keynesianism of the postwar era, but something far more radical. Containing that risk required redrawing the boundaries of state and society. In that battle, the most decisive institutional move was to insulate control of money from democratic politics, placing it under the authority of independent central banks. As MIT's Rudiger Dornbusch, one of the most influential economists of his generation, put it in 2000, the "past 20 years, the very rise of independent central banks, is all about getting priorities right, getting rid of democratic money which is always short-sighted, bad money."[58]

This has a bitter implication. If central banks since 2008 have massively expanded their remit, it was out of necessity, to contain the instability of the financial system. But that was politically possible—indeed, it could be done with no fanfare whatsoever—because the battles of the 1970s and 1980s had been won. The threat that haunted Dornbusch's generation had evaporated. Democracy was no longer the menace that it had been in neoliberalism's years of struggle. Within the sphere of economic policy, that expressed itself in the startling realization that there was no risk of inflation. For all the centrist hand-wringing about "populism," class antagonism was enfeebled, wage pressure was minimal, strikes nonexistent.

The massive economic policy interventions of 2020, like those of 2008, were Janus-faced. On the one hand, their scale exploded the bounds of neoliberal restraint and their economic logic confirmed the basic diagnosis of interventionist macroeconomics back to Keynes. They could not but appear as harbingers of a new regime beyond neoliberalism. On the other hand, these interventions were made from the top down. They were politically thinkable only because there was no challenge from the left and their urgency was impelled by the need to stabilize the financial system. And they delivered. Over the course of 2020, household net worth in the United States increased by more than $15 trillion. Overwhelmingly that benefited the top 1 percent, who owned almost 40 percent of all stocks.[59] The top 10 percent, between them, owned 84 percent.

If this was indeed a "new social contract," it was an alarmingly one-sided affair. Nevertheless, it would be wrong to see in the response to the 2020 crisis nothing more than escalating plunder. Centrists who were fighting for their political lives could not ignore the massive force of the social and economic crisis. The threat from the nationalist right wing was serious. The appeal for more social solidarity for a restoration of the national economy had real resonance. Despite being in a minority, the "green" political movement was increasingly a force to be reckoned with.[60] While the right wing played on powerful emotions, the strategic analysis offered by the advocates of the Green New Deal was on point, and intelligent centrists knew it. The leadership of the EU or the Democratic Party in the United States might not have the stomach for structural reform, but they grasped the interconnection between modernity, the environment, the unbalanced and unstable growth of the economy, and inequality. The facts were, after all, so stark that it took an act of will to ignore them. So 2020 was a moment not just of plunder, but of reformist experimentation. In response to the threat of social crisis, new modes of welfare provision were tried out in Europe, in the United States, and in many emerging market economies. And in search of a positive agenda, centrists embraced environmental policy and the issue of climate change as never before. Contrary to the fear that Covid-19 would distract from other priorities, the political economy of the Green New Deal went mainstream. "Green Growth," "Build Back Better," "Green Deal"—the slogans varied, but they all expressed green modernization as the common centrist response to the crisis.[61]

———

The year 2020 exposed how dependent economic activity was on the stability of its natural environment. A tiny virus mutation in a microbe could threaten the entire world's economy. It also exposed how in extremis, the entire monetary and financial system could be directed toward supporting markets and livelihoods, thus forcing the question of who was supported and how. Both shocks tore down partitions that were fundamental to the political economy of the last half century, lines that divided the economy from nature, economics from social policy and from politics per se. On top of that, there was a third shift, which in 2020 completed the dissolution of the framing assumptions of the era of neoliberalism: the rise of China.

According to the best available science, it was not surprising that the virus came out of China. Rapid zoonotic mutation was the predictable result of biological, social, and economic conditions in the Hubei region. To call this a natural process obscured the degree to which it was driven by economic and social factors, but there were always those who thought there was more to it than that. One of the more plausible alternative theories was the view that the virus had escaped from a Chinese biological research establishment.[62] It would thus be a Chernobyl-style incident, but on a global scale and better covered up, very much an example of risk society but an instance of attempted mastery of nature gone wrong as opposed to the negligent production of dangerous side effects. More alarmist was the view that the virus originated in a biological warfare program and that Beijing allowed it to spread deliberately with a view to destabilizing Western societies.[63] Beijing added to the speculation by resisting all attempts to conduct an independent international inquiry and allowing conspiratorial counternarratives of its own to circulate.[64] In any case, whichever interpretation one espoused, these theories were about more than the virus and where it came from. They were interpretations of globalization and the rise of China. This entanglement of anxieties was new.

When in 2005 Tony Blair scoffed at critics of globalization, it was their fears that he mocked. He contrasted their parochial anxieties to the affirmative modernizing energy of Asian nations, for which globalization offered a bright horizon. The global security threats that Blair recognized were Islamic terrorism and Saddam Hussein's weapons of mass destruction. They were nasty. If they were in fact real, they might cause mass casualties. They were symptoms of globalization gone rogue. But for all their violence, they had no hope of actually changing the status quo. Therein precisely lay their suicidal, otherworldly irrationality. In the decade after 2008, it was that confidence in the robustness of the status quo that was lost.

Resurgent Russia, replenished by global exports of oil and gas, was the first to expose globalization's geopolitical innocence. Russia's challenge was limited. China's was not. The Obama administration made its "pivot to Asia" in 2011.[65] In December 2017 the United States issued its new National Security Strategy that for the first time designated the Indo-Pacific as the decisive arena of great power competition.[66] In March 2019, the EU issued a strategy document to the same effect.[67] In 2020 the French and German foreign offices followed suit.[68] The UK, meanwhile, performed an extraordinary about-face, from celebrating a new "golden era" of Sino-UK relations in 2015 to deploying an aircraft carrier to the South China Sea.[69]

The military logic was familiar. All great powers are rivals, or at least so the "realist" logic goes. In the case of China, there was the added factor of ideology. In 2021 the CCP did something its Soviet counterpart never got to do: it celebrated its centenary. Beijing made no secret of its adherence to an ideological heritage that ran by way of Marx and Engels to Lenin, Stalin, and Mao. Xi Jinping could hardly have been more emphatic about the need to cleave to this tradition and no clearer in his condemnation of Mikhail Gorbachev for losing hold of the Soviet Union's ideological compass.[70] So the "new" Cold War was really the "old" Cold War revived, the Cold War in Asia, the one that the West had in fact never won.

There were, however, two spectacular differences dividing old from new. The first was the economy. China was the threat that it was as the result of the greatest economic boom in world history. That had hurt some workers in the West in manufacturing, but businesses and consumers across the Western world and beyond had profited immensely from

China's development and stood to profit even more in future. That created a quandary. A revived Cold War with China made sense from every vantage point except "the economy, stupid."

The second fundamental novelty was the global environmental problem and the role of economic growth in accelerating it. When global climate politics first emerged in its modern form in the 1990s, it was under the sign of the unipolar moment. The United States was the largest and most recalcitrant polluter. China was poor and its emissions barely figured in the global balance. By 2020, China emitted more carbon dioxide than the United States and Europe put together, and the gap was set to widen at least for another decade. One could no more envision a solution to the climate problem without China than one could imagine a response to the risk of emerging infectious diseases. China was the most powerful incubator of both.

The green modernizers of the EU resolved this double dilemma in their strategic documents by defining China all at the same time as a systemic rival, a strategic competitor, and a partner in dealing with climate change. The Trump administration made life easier for itself by denying the climate problem. But Washington too was impaled on the horns of the economic dilemma, between ideological denunciation of Beijing, strategic calculation, long-term corporate investment, and the president's desire to strike a quick deal. This was an unstable combination, and in 2020 it tipped. Despite the Phase I trade deal that the president had been keen to celebrate at the start of the year, by the summer, strategic competition and ideological denunciation trumped economic interest. China was redefined as a threat to the United States, both strategically and economically. It had taken American jobs and had illegally appropriated billions in American intellectual property for the benefit of a hostile regime.[71] In reaction, the intelligence, security, and judicial branches of the American government declared economic war on China. They deliberately set out to sabotage the development of China's high-tech sector, the heart of any modern economy.

It was to a degree accidental that this escalation took place when it did. China's rise was a long-term world historic shift, to which everyone in the world would eventually have to respond. But Beijing's success in handling the coronavirus and the assertiveness that unleashed were a red flag to the Trump administration. Furthermore, the superheated atmosphere of the American election generated powerful amplification and induction effects—to use Chen's somewhat euphemistic vocabulary. The Trump team not only blamed China for the virus, they extended the culture war they were unleashing at home to China's American collaborators. Added to which, by the summer of 2020, it was increasingly undeniable that something else was going on. There was something deeply wrong with America.

It was not the first moment of modern American malaise. President Carter would become notorious for an address he gave to the American nation on that very topic in the summer of 1979, amid the fallout from the Iranian revolution and the second energy crisis.[72] One of the promises of the 1980s market revolution was that Ronald Reagan's "morning in America" would heave the country out of its slump, just as Thatcher promised to do for Britain. Donald Trump, the party boy of 1980s Manhattan, was the living embodiment of that new era of swagger. But Trump also personified the ugly truth about that moment, which is that the market revolution left a large part of American society behind. America's continued global strength in finance, tech, and military power rested on domestic feet of clay. As Covid-19 painfully exposed, the U.S. health system was ramshackle and its domestic social safety net left tens of millions at risk of poverty. If Xi's "China dream" came through 2020 intact, the same cannot be said for its American counterpart.

The general crisis of neoliberalism in 2020 thus had a specific and traumatic significance for America and for one part of the American political spectrum in particular. The vision of American government crafted by successive Democratic administrations starting with Woodrow Wilson and FDR gave American liberals tools with which to respond to the coronavirus challenge. Even the new generation of American radicals led by Alexandria Ocasio-Cortez could find things to like about the New Deal.[73] By contrast, the Republican Party and its nationalist and conservative constituencies suffered in 2020 what can best be described as an existential crisis, with profoundly damaging consequences for the American government, for the American Constitution, and for America's relations with the wider world. This culminated in the extraordinary period between November 3, 2020, and January 6, 2021, in which Trump refused to concede defeat, a large part of the Republican Party actively supported an effort to overturn the election, the social crisis and the pandemic were left unattended to, and finally, on January 6, the president and other leading figures in his party encouraged a mob invasion of the Capitol.

For good reason, this raises deep concerns about the future of American democracy. And there are elements on the far right of American politics that can fairly be described as fascistoid.[74] But two basic elements were missing from the original fascist equation in America in 2020. One is total war. Americans remember the Civil War and imagine future civil wars to come. They have recently engaged in expeditionary wars that have blown back on American society in militarized policing and paramilitary fantasies.[75] But total war reconfigures society in quite a different way. It constitutes a mass body, not the individualized commandos of 2020.

The other missing ingredient in the classic fascist equation, which is more central to this book, is social antagonism, a threat, whether imagined or real, to the social and economic status quo. As the constitutional storm clouds gathered in 2020, American business aligned massively and squarely against Trump. Nor, as we shall see, were the major voices of corporate America afraid to spell out the business case for doing so, including shareholder value, the problems of running companies with politically divided workforces, the economic importance of the rule of law, and astonishingly, the losses in sales to be expected in the event of a civil war. This alignment of money with democracy in the United States in 2020 should be reassuring, up to a point. But consider for a second an alternative scenario. What if the virus had arrived in the United States a few weeks sooner, the spreading pandemic had rallied mass support for Bernie Sanders and his call for universal health care, and the Democratic primaries had swept an avowed socialist to the head of the ticket rather than Joe Biden?[76] It is not difficult to imagine a scenario in which the full weight of American business was thrown the other way, for all the same reasons, backing Trump so as to ensure that Sanders was not elected.[77] And what if Sanders had in fact won a majority? Then we would have had a true test of the American Constitution and the loyalty of the most powerful social interests to it.

Seeing 2020 as a comprehensive crisis of the neoliberal era—with regard to its environmental envelope, its domestic social, economic, and political underpinnings, and the international order—helps us find our historical bearings. Seen in those terms, the coronavirus crisis marks the end of an arc whose origin is to be found in the 1970s. It might also be seen as the first comprehensive crisis of the age of the Anthropocene to come—an era defined by the blowback from our unbalanced relationship to nature.[78]

But rather than trying prematurely to sketch the continuities of that half century of history, or attempting to project speculatively into the future, this book stays, as far as possible, in the moment itself. We will work backward and forward as the need for context arises, but the focus will be squarely on the chain of events between the outbreak of the virus in January 2020 and the inauguration of Joe Biden.

These tight chronological limits are a deliberate choice. It is a way of making tractable the tension between past and present that defines what it means to write history. It is also a personal strategy for coping with the intellectual and psychological stresses of a moment that was otherwise overwhelming.

As it did to billions of other people around the world, the coronavirus forced me to change my plans. I began the year working on a book about the history of energy policy, tracing the political economy of carbon back to the era of the oil crises, mapping a prehistory of the Green New Deal. Like so many others, I had become preoccupied with the Anthropocene, a transformation driven by capitalist economic growth that puts in question the very separation between natural and human history.[79]

In February, as the virus was spreading silently around the world, I was traveling in East Africa, immersed for the first time in the history of the continent. Out of the corner of my eye, I noticed the unfamiliar health checks at airports, but like most people I was oblivious to the drama that was about to unfold. It was only when I was on the way back, on Friday, March 6, in the cavernous halls of Istanbul's new airport, that the scale of the mounting panic began to dawn on me. Travelers from every part of the world were sporting masks of all shapes and sizes. They were novel, ill-fitting, impossible on a long flight.

That weekend in New York, while I was in a haze of jet lag, all hell broke loose. The virus was now driving a giant economic contraction. I suddenly found myself fielding a wave of questions from journalists prodding me to help them understand what was looking like a rerun of *Crashed*, my book about the financial crises of 2008.

Crashed was itself a history that had been overtaken by events. I had set out to write a ten-year anniversary book and ended up, in the wake of Brexit and Trump's victory, in the middle of a crisis that refused to end. At the time, a wise friend joked that I was laying myself open to the demand to write a never-ending new edition. In March 2020 I felt the full force of his point. As stock prices and bond markets plummeted, as dysfunction in repo markets hit the headlines and central bank swap lines were once again on the agenda, the *Crashed* narrative was catching up with me.

By April, I found the pressure of facing the present on a minute-by-minute basis while thinking about the energy policies of Jimmy Carter to be too much. I surrendered to the immediate flow of events.

2020 turned out to be history with a capital *H*, something quite different from anything we had ever seen before. This book is therefore even more contemporary than *Crashed*. Somewhat paradoxically, this makes the risk of "missing the moment" even more hair-raising. Any effort to cast a narrative frame over the tumult we are still living through is bound to be partial and subject to revision. But if we are to make sense of events around us, it is a risk we have to take. The one comfort is that in this endeavor we are not alone. The year 2020 was nothing if not a year of talking to each other, of storytelling, argument, and analysis.

A narrative of this kind may be premature, but in projecting an interpretation, making an intellectual wager, right or wrong, you gain something precious: a deeper understanding of what is really entailed by the proposition that every true history is contemporary history.[80] Indeed, in light of 2020, Benedetto Croce's insight takes on a new meaning. A discussion of the climate crisis—the historical transformation of nature and its implications for our history—written from the safety of an Upper West Side apartment could seem remote. The Anthropocene remained an abstract intellectual proposition. The coronavirus crisis has stripped even the most sheltered of us of that illusion.

Part I

DISEASE X

Chapter 1

ORGANIZED
IRRESPONSIBILITY

Skeptics—and there have been skeptics from the start—like to point out that the remarkable thing about the Covid crisis is that we turned something ordinary into a global crisis. No matter what we do, people die, and the same people die of Covid as die normally—old people with preexisting conditions. In a normal year, those people die of flu and pneumonia. Outside the privileged core of the rich world, millions of people die of infectious diseases like malaria, tuberculosis, and HIV. And yet "life goes on." Severe acute respiratory syndrome coronavirus 2 (SARS-CoV-2) was, by the standards of historic plagues, not very lethal. What was unprecedented was the reaction. All over the world, public life shut down, and so too did large parts of commerce and the regular flow of business. All over the world this massive interruption of normality stirred, in various degrees, incomprehension, indignation, resistance, noncompliance, and protest. One need not sympathize with the politics of the objectors to acknowledge the historical force of their point. In a new and remarkable fashion, a medical challenge became a much wider crisis. Explaining how this might have happened not as the result of effete and overly protective political culture or as the result of a deliberate policy of repression, but as a result of structural tensions within early twenty-first-century societies, will help set the stage for understanding the crisis of 2020.

It is true that old people die, but what matters is how many and at what rate and from which causes. At any given moment, this rank order of mortality can be described in terms of a matrix of probabilities that has evolved over time and is held in place by medical possibilities, health economics, and the pattern of social advantage and disadvantage.

Table 1: Causes of Death

	Total deaths		Communicable, maternal, neonatal, and nutritional diseases (%)		Noncommunicable diseases (%)		Injury (%)	
	m	m	%	%	%	%	%	%
	1990	2017	1990	2017	1990	2017	1990	2017
Western Europe	3.86	4.16	4	5	90	91	6	4
United States	2.14	2.86	6	5	87	89	7	7
Latin America and Caribbean	2.36	3.39	28	12	57	76	15	13
China	8.14	10.45	17	3	72	89	11	7
India	8.38	9.91	51	27	40	63	9	10
Sub-Saharan Africa	6.77	7.48	69	58	24	34	7	7
World	4.65	5.59	33	19	58	73	9	8

https://ourworldindata.org/causes-of-death

Seen globally, the story of the last decades is one of considerable advance in reducing death from diseases of poverty—communicable, maternal, neonatal, and nutritional diseases. Nevertheless, it remains true that poor people and people in low-income countries die soonest and of the most preventable conditions. In a low-income country like Nigeria, where life expectancy at birth is fifty-five, 68 percent of deaths are due to diseases of poverty. In Germany, where life expectancy is eighty-one, that share is 3.5 percent; in the UK, 6.8. The United States is in-between. In 2017, health spending per capita in high-income countries was 49 times greater in purchasing power parity terms than in low-income countries.[1]

Within rich countries, there are appalling disparities in infant and maternal mortality and overall life expectancy along lines of race and class. Epidemics of drug use in disadvantaged and marginalized populations, asthma, and lead poisoning go unaddressed. In Germany, 27 percent of men in the lowest income class die before the age of sixty-five, compared to 14 percent for the highest income group. For women, the disparities are only slightly less stark.[2] In the country's two-class health insurance system, the life expectancy of the 11 percent in private insurance is four years longer than those in the public system.[3] In the United States, commonly described as the richest country in the world, according to a study of 2009, 45,000 people died for lack of health insurance.[4] People in low-income census tracts in the United States are twice as likely as those in high-income areas to be hospitalized with flu, to require intensive care, and to die of it.[5] The difference is starkest for poor people over the age of sixty-five.

It would be too much to say that these probabilities enjoy general acceptance. They are, on their face, a scandal. They give the lie to any idea that our collective priority is keeping people alive, but as stark as these differences are, the ratios are at least familiar. The probabilities change, but only gradually and generally only in a favorable direction. The crucial point, as far as the coronavirus crisis is concerned, is that as 2020 began, the only infectious diseases that still plagued the average citizen in a country above the high middle-income threshold were lower respiratory tract infections and the flu, and they were generally dangerous only to those of advanced age. In the United States, only 2.5 percent of all deaths in a normal year were attributed specifically to influenza and pneumonia. Adding all lower respiratory tract infections brought the share to 10 percent of all deaths.[6] Together they accounted for 80 percent of deaths from infectious disease. HIV/AIDS and diarrheal disease, notably *C. difficile*, made up the rest. SARS-CoV-2 shook the confidence in those probabilities.

The conquest of major infectious diseases was one of the great triumphs of the era after 1945. It was a historic achievement on a par with the end of famine, universal literacy, running water, or birth control. Increased life expectancy is the secret sauce behind economic growth.[7] It is marvelous to consume more. It's even better if you live decades longer to enjoy it. By one estimate, if we properly factored in the greater longevity achieved over the course of the twentieth century, it would double our estimate of the growth in the American standard of living.[8] By the 1970s, as the final victory over smallpox and polio came within grasp, these triumphs spawned the idea of the epidemiologic transition.[9] Infectious diseases would be consigned to the past.

The advances were greatest in the rich Western countries. But achieving the epidemiologic transition was a common aspiration of modernity. It was as relevant to the Soviet Union and Communist China as it was to the West.[10] Indeed, as a collectivist project led by public agencies, it suited their political vision better than that of the West. Embattled Cuba, with its hardy public health system and outsize program of global medical assistance, is a dramatic demonstration of this point. For the Communist regimes, there was no contradiction between sacrificing tens of millions of lives for the advance of socialism, coercive birth control campaigns like China's one-child policy, and a massive collective effort to save lives and conquer infectious disease.

But as momentous as it was, almost at the moment of its triumph in the 1970s, the conquest of infectious disease began to be hedged by doubt. Influenza remained unconquered. It is both ubiquitous and easily underestimated as a cause of death. It accounts for a surge in mortality from all causes that occurs on a regular annual basis.[11] This is normalized because many of these deaths are attributed to other, more immediate causes such as pneumonia and heart attacks. Influenza is highly contagious and there is no interval between infection and infectivity, which means that testing and quarantine are hopeless. It mutates rapidly, so vaccination will be at best partially effective. The one saving grace is its low lethality.

The same could not be said for some of the new infectious diseases that specialists began to tangle with in the 1970s. The nightmarish Ebola virus was identified in 1976, AIDS in 1981. In the West, HIV/AIDS remained confined to stigmatized minority populations. In sub-Saharan Africa, it became a generational crisis of young heterosexual people, and above all, women.[12] By 2020, HIV/AIDS had claimed 33 million lives. Somewhere around 690,000 would die of the disease in 2020.[13] As far as infectious diseases were concerned, it turned out, we were far from having reached the end of history.

Indeed, as scientists explored disease mutation and circulation, the picture that emerged was one of a precarious balance. Modern science, technology, medicine, and economic development might be giving us greater ability to fight disease, but those same forces were also contributing to the generation of new disease threats.[14] The emerging infectious diseases paradigm, proposed by scientists from the 1970s onward, was, like the models of climate change and earth systems ecology that emerged at the same moment, a profound critique of our modern way of life, our economy, and the social system built on it.[15] Our use of land across the globe, relentless incursions into the remaining wilderness, the industrial farming of pigs and chickens, our giant conurbations, the extraordinary global mobility of the jet age, the profligate, commercially motivated use of antibiotics, the irresponsible circulation of fake news about vaccines—all these forces combined to create a disease environment that was not safer, but increasingly dangerous. It was no doubt true that all these factors had been present to a greater or lesser extent for at least two millennia. The sophisticated urban communities of the Roman empire had already been prey to pandemics sweeping across Eurasia. But the late twentieth century, for all its medical prowess and newfound affluence, was seeing a dramatic escalation of threat potential. We were, whether we recognized it or not, involved in an arms race.

This was a profound diagnosis of the threats generated by our modern way of life. There are groups led by the anti-vaxxers who dispute its logic. But they are fringe elements. It is not the warning of emerging infectious diseases as such that has proven controversial. It is our willingness to follow through on its implications. If the experts tell us that our modern economic and social system is systematically generating disease risk, what do we do about it?

To address the problem at its source would require a comprehensive effort to map potential viral threats combined with systematic control of land use and a dramatic change to industrial farming.[16] Such a transformation would mean confronting interests that range from giant global agro-industrial firms to Asian poultry magnates, corrupt city officials in Southern China, and hardscrabble farmers in some of the poorer places in the world.[17] The drift of higher-income diets toward more meat and dairy products would have to be reversed. Unsurprisingly, the actual policy response falls far short. Health officials undertake efforts to impose hygiene regulations on factory farming and to tidy up wild meat markets. There are local and sporadic bans on the hunting of "bushmeat." But the more fundamental drivers of emerging infectious diseases remain unaddressed.

At the global level we have organizations like the World Health Organization (WHO), in which thousands of highly professional, motivated, and well-intentioned individuals from all over the world fight the good fight. But as a global health agency for a rapidly developing globe inhabited by 7.8 billion people, the WHO is a Potemkin village. For the two years 2018–2019, the WHO's approved program budget was no more than $4.4 billion, less than that of a single big city hospital.[18] The WHO's funding is cobbled together from a hodgepodge of sources, including national governments, private charities, the World Bank, and big pharma. In 2019, among its largest donors, the Gates Foundation ranks alongside the national governments of the United States and the UK and ahead of Germany. The venerable Rotary International contributed as much, if not more, than the governments of either China or France. Altogether, the WHO can muster no more than 30 cents per year in spending for every person on the planet.

The WHO's dependence on its donors shapes what it does. Campaigns for disease eradication such as polio are high on its agenda. The WHO plays a key role in monitoring the flux of diseases around the world. It is a technical business. It is also highly political. The two essential preoccupations of international health regulation back to its earliest days in the first half of the nineteenth century were the Western fear of disease spreading from east to west and the interest of advocates of free trade to limit the use of onerous public health regulation such as lengthy quarantines.[19] The idea was to ensure that plagues did not become an excuse for shutting off commerce.

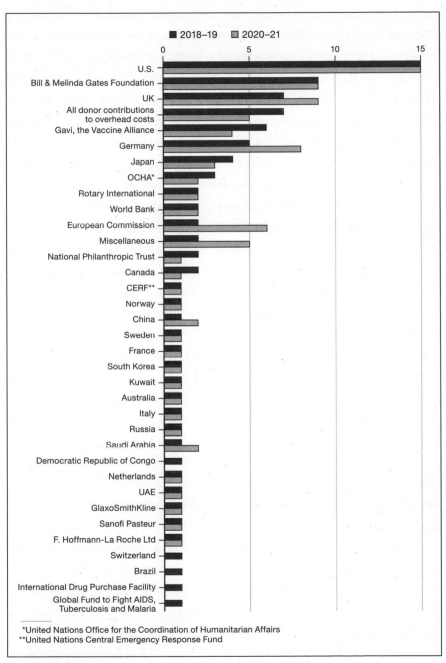

Funding for WHO representing total contributions by contributor as of June 30, 2020 (%)

WHO, via A. Gross and J. Pickard, "Johnson to Boost WHO Backing with £571m Vaccine Pledge," *Financial Times*, September 25, 2020.

Those twin tensions still haunt the WHO. In its efforts to coordinate a global public health response, it is caught between the fear of antagonizing states by labeling them as sources of infection, its professional desire to take early and decisive action, and the backlash that it will face if it triggers what turn out to be costly and unnecessary limitations on movement and trade. After the global panic triggered by the appearance of plague in Surat, India, in 1994 and the blanket shutdown of travel during the SARS crisis in 2003, there was a push at the WHO to adopt a more cautious approach to travel restrictions.[20] Likewise after the anticlimax of the 2009 swine flu epidemic, the WHO faced a vociferous campaign accusing some of its officials of artificially inflating the market for expensive vaccines.[21] To manage these hugely difficult choices on a precarious shoestring budget was a recipe for disaster.[22]

The British economist Lord Nicholas Stern once remarked that climate change results from history's greatest market failure—the failure to attach a price to the costs of CO_2 emissions.[23] If this is true, then as the coronavirus crisis of 2020 demonstrates, the failure to build adequate defenses against global pandemics must be a close second. Even the best-funded global public health infrastructure cannot offer guarantees, but as 2020 began, the disproportion between pandemic risk and the investment in global public health was nothing short of grotesque.

To talk in terms of "market failure" understates the force of the point. What is at stake in the response to pandemic threats is not just a vast amount of economic value. What is at stake are basic questions of social order and political legitimacy.

If it were the case that governments could simply ignore epidemic threats they had done too little to forestall, if life could simply continue in the face of a sudden surge in deaths, then the underinvestment in public health would have a cynical rationale. But in fact one of the foundations of the modern state is the promise to protect life. Not by accident, the frontispiece to Thomas Hobbes's *Leviathan* features plague doctors.[24] Given this basic understanding, for a modern state to allow a dangerous pandemic to run through a country unchecked would require a bold strategy of depoliticization, or at the very least, a gradual process of "hardening" of public attitudes. In 2020, the idea that Covid was "just the flu" turned out to be a harder sell than its advocates imagined.

Rather than ignoring the pandemic threat, in recent decades governments around the world have equipped themselves with specialist departments that prepare for biomedical catastrophe.[25] They think like the military. Their assumption is not that the threat can actually be overcome—the faith that infectious diseases can be tamed is the conceit of sunny-minded public health campaigners. The job of the pandemic specialists is to prepare for a threat that will never go away and is, if anything, increasing in seriousness. Ominously, since the 1990s, "preparedness" has become the mission of more and more branches of government all over the world.

It is an intensely serious but also grimly futile business. The potential risks are vast. We can all too easily imagine a global outbreak of an Ebola-like disease, or a highly infectious influenza with the lethality of the Spanish flu. But at the same time, there is no willingness to make structural changes to our food chain or transport system to reduce risk or even to invest in an adequate public health system. Little wonder, therefore, that a global inventory of pandemic preparedness in 2019 found literally every government in the world wanting.[26] It is a classic instance of what Ulrich Beck called "organized irresponsibility."[27] And it harbors within it the potential for not just economic and social damage but political crisis.

In the face of a sudden and unexpected threat to life, publicly accountable authorities cannot in fact be indifferent. They scramble to respond to the disease. Indeed, their reaction has, in principle, no limit. At the height of the epidemic in New York State, Governor Cuomo could boldly declare: "How much is a human life worth? . . . To me, I say the cost of a human life, a human life is priceless."[28] Despite the evident unreality of such a statement, no one was eager to contradict him.

In public discourse—as distinct from the actual practice of daily life, the actual distribution of life chances, the actual probability of death—life and death are not commensurate with other priorities. If forced to rank order, we put life and death in a different class. The prospect of any death, let alone mass death, easily brings public and political debate to a halt. A shock like a pandemic jolts us into action. But even the normal, pre-pandemic matrix of life and death is politically unstable. Shot through as it is with scandalous inequalities, the common order of death is accepted as such, so long as it does not need to be justified. If dragged into the daylight and subject to sustained challenge, it is evidently indefensible. There was thus a deep logic to the coincidence of the pandemic with the huge political upheaval of Black Lives Matter over the summer of 2020. As the movement so powerfully demonstrated, a single life taken illegitimately can trigger a giant political movement. When a death becomes a martyrdom, it has huge force.

Black Lives Matter fed off a deep well of historic injustice. It tied the present to the past. It linked the killing on May 25, 2020, to centuries of injustice that preceded it. That was powerful, and all the more so because in the context of a runaway pandemic, anger and indignation over the past were compounded by fear of the future.[29] In light of the inequities of 2020, how many more Black Americans would become victims of violence, discrimination, and poverty?

Political responsibility is measured against forward-looking projections, forecasts, and warnings of what is to come.[30] The greater the future threat, the greater the responsibility. There are good reasons that states have often passed laws against fortune-tellers and prophets of doom.[31] It is not just that their methods are suspect. Their predictions right or wrong are apt to endanger the public peace of mind. And yet, in the twenty-first century, there are no laws against social scientists and epidemiologists predicting catastrophe. Indeed, those wielding power and money cling to whatever foresight they can offer.

In early 2020, we did not know how many people of any race would succumb to Covid-19. What we did know were the alarming mortality rates of SARS in 2003 and the novel MERS that emerged in 2012. When the early data out of China and Italy were run through the models of epidemiological teams, such as the one at Imperial College London, they foretold a death toll from Covid-19 running to many millions.[32] Even governments notionally committed to a hard-boiled approach found those kinds of numbers hard to ignore.

At moments of stress, when we envision the possibility of catastrophe, the sheer scale of modern society is awe inspiring. Were 1 percent of Americans to die as a result of a virus, that would be 3.3 million people, more than twice the number killed in all of America's wars since the foundation of the republic. One percent of Europe's population would be 5 to 6 million, matching the benchmark of the Holocaust. One percent of the world's population would be 78 million, more than all the casualties of World War I and World War II put together. If the same percentage of the world's current population were to die of Covid as died of Spanish flu in 1918–19, the death toll would come to over 200 million people. The world in the twenty-first century is a very big place. Its sheer scale made public health officials haggard in 2020.

The determined skeptic will press on. You say lives matter. That, you say, justifies the shutdowns whatever the cost, but how much do lives matter?

It clearly isn't the case that life is sacred and non-negotiable. Not only do social statistics tell us that millions die all over the world, including in the rich world, due to neglect and lack of treatment, but many modern bureaucracies weigh the probabilities and costs of life and death as a matter of course in apportioning resources. Every day, all over the world, workers are exposed to deadly risks to save their employers extra expense. When we cost out the development of drugs or of workplace safety measures, the allocation of hospital beds, or the value of pollution reduction, we place a number on the value of life.

The incorporation of death into an economic calculus is both inescapable and, like its incorporation into politics, unstable and contentious. As two prominent economists carefully observe: "Although putting a value on a given human life is impossible, economists have developed the technique of valuing 'statistical lives'; that is, measuring how much it is worth to people to reduce their risk of mortality or morbidity."[33] In the United States, surveys regularly find that workers are willing to take a pay cut of approximately $1,000 to reduce the probability of death in their workplace by 1 in 10,000. The implication, according to the economists' logic, is that in a large firm with 10,000 staff, the workforce would be willing to pay $10 million to save one life. This is how the so-called Value of a Statistical Life (VSL) is derived. The figure of $10 million is accepted by the U.S. Department of Health and Human Services (HHS), the U.S. Environmental Protection Agency, and the U.S. Department of Transportation. The World Bank in its cost-benefit exercises uses a VSL of $3.8 million. The rich-country OECD grouping applies a figure of $3.6 million to Europeans.[34]

The methodology has profound limitations. The VSL is not what anyone would pay to save their life if they had an unlimited budget. Nor is what we would actually pay from limited means. It is a collective measure derived from incremental low-cost choices. VSL estimates remain in use for want of anything better. They have the virtue of being simple and egalitarian. What is more, without being outlandish, VSLs in the $3 million to $10 million range are large enough to really matter. If you combine those values with the right forecasting model, you easily arrive at impressive results. Assume, for instance, that preventative measures were able to save the lives of 1 million people, no more than a third of 1 percent of the American population, the economic benefit would be in the order of $10 trillion, half of America's total GDP ahead of the crisis. Even if we ignore the societal impact of a million deaths, ten trillion dollars are a compelling motive for action.

VSLs are also, however, a fudge. They treat a healthy young person and an eighty-year-old with multiple chronic conditions as equivalent. By assuming that all lives have the same value, they ignore what, as far as coronavirus was concerned, was the basic problem. It killed mainly old people, and as one leading expert observes: the "appropriate" VSL for those over the age of sixty-five is "very uncertain."[35] The subject matter becomes even more explosive when one factors in wealth and income. Elderly people with wealth put a high price on extending their lives. They account for the vast majority of the huge health expenditures of rich societies, but should the value they place on extending their lives by a few years serve as the basis for policy measures that disproportionately harm younger people with much lower incomes? How on earth is one to arbitrate such choices?

In making decisions about the allocation of scarce medical resources, some health systems use broader measures of the quality of life. Britain's National Institute for Health and Care Excellence uses Quality-Adjusted Life Years, or QALYS, as a basis on which to evaluate drug procurement and treatments in the National Health Service. But the scope of those life-and-death decisions is limited. The choices are made between specific alternatives, behind closed doors, and not in a moment of general crisis, in the full glare of media attention.[36] Imagine for a second extending a similar calculus to the entire collective response to the coronavirus. The question is this: What was the remaining value of the lives of mainly elderly patients who might be saved by a sudden and massive shutdown, and the suffering avoided for those who develop a lingering form of Covid affliction, weighed against the cost to the 1.6 billion young people whose education was disrupted and the hundreds of millions who lost their jobs and the tens of millions who would go hungry as a result of worldwide economic disruption?

It is a contentious, unpalatable, and crude question. To take it seriously, one would need to factor in the systemic ramifications of an unchecked pandemic—the collective trauma, the institutional damage, the potential for long-term health effects, and the risk of mutation, to name just a few aspects. In any case, some calculation of this kind is the basis on which an "economic" critique of the Covid response is founded. It insists, as unpalatable as it may be, on the reality of a trade-off, and there is, after all, a familiar language in which such a trade-off can be couched.

In the last week of March 2020, Lieutenant Governor Dan Patrick of Texas gained a brief moment of celebrity when he told Fox News that he was willing to take a chance on his survival as a senior citizen for the good of the economy. He went on to add that he thought "there are lots of grandparents out there in this country who feel the same way . . . No one reached out to me and said, as a senior citizen, are you willing to take a chance on your survival in exchange for keeping the America that all Americans love for your children and grandchildren? And if that's the exchange, I'm all in."[37] In a similar spirit, Chinese TV featured elderly Covid patients making patriotic salutes from their hospital beds. By accepting isolation and the likelihood of a lonely death, they were doing their bit for the cause.

The temptation is to dismiss Chinese TV as propaganda and Patrick as a heedless advocate for Texas business interests, who advocated a strategy of personal self-isolation from the comfortable surroundings of his well-upholstered suburban home. But before we sweep them aside, it is worth lingering on the strong emotional and social themes embedded in such appeals. The idea of "dying for the economy" is evidently grotesque, but accepting the risk of death for one's nation or for one's family is the bedrock of conventional conceptions of state and society. The basic logic of war is that a minority, usually men of fighting age, are put in harm's way for the collective good. In total war, that risk extends to the entire population. The economy is not incidental but absolutely central to the struggle. What makes sense of the trade-off are the ideas of belonging and existential collective threat. The losses—whether they be on the field of battle, the supply lines, or the home front—are borne with stoicism. What we owe our heroes is that their lives are not sacrificed in vain and that we remember them.

In fact, precisely this rhetoric of risk, sacrifice, and honor was widely mobilized in 2020, but on a selective basis. Throughout the crisis, health care workers were exposed to what were in some cases very considerable hazards. Those newly classified as "essential workers," which included warehouse workers, grocery delivery teams, and bus drivers, also took elevated risks. Drugstores and pharmacies celebrated their cashiers as heroes. They were acknowledged as "serving on the front line" of the fight. And, at least in the case of the health workers, they were honored. Many cities held evening rituals—cheering or banging on pots—to express their appreciation.

What 2020 revealed, however, was that in most places where there was open public debate, the language of stoicism, heroism, and sacrifice was not elastic. Young mothers, working as nurses without adequate PPE, taking risks to intubate eighty-year-old patients fighting for their lives, were rightly celebrated as heroes. But it was difficult to extend the logic. Should the schools on which the same nurse relied for childcare be expected to continue normally, even if this involved an elevated risk for teachers and staff? Should meat packers risk their lives to keep hamburger in the food chain? How much self-restraint should young people be expected to exercise to protect their grandparents? What the unfamiliar and mysterious new threat exposed is that we did not know who owed what to whom. We struggled to decide how to decide.[38]

It would be historically naive to imagine that such questions have ever been easy to answer. Many retrospective accounts of collective solidarity of World War II are egregiously sugarcoated.[39] The first total war of the twentieth century, World War I, produced revolutionary upheaval around the world. Coronavirus did not produce such drama. The dissension and disunity, however, were real enough. The difficulty of finding a language to encompass complex societal trade-offs and to order them in a sensible and agreeable fashion led to fights, misunderstandings, inhumane rhetoric, accusations, and institutional chaos.

In any case, as the virus struck in early 2020, there was little time for deliberation. What overrode any strategic trade-offs and cost-benefit calculations was the threat that an unknown disease would cause mass death and institutional breakdown. Those fears were encapsulated in images from the hospitals of Wuhan, from Bergamo in Italy, from Queens, New York City, and from the streets of Guayaquil in Ecuador. ICUs at breaking point, panic-stricken patients, the horror of triage, mortuaries running out of cold storage, dead bodies laid out in makeshift coffins in the street—it was a collage of nightmares.

What was immediately at stake were not wider collective trade-offs but the functioning of those institutions that we rely on to bring some degree of control to critical moments of life and death. As initial efforts to contain the virus broke down, the essential rationale of pandemic policy was to protect the health care system. That is what "flattening the curve" was about.[40] If we could not stop the disease, if the same number of people were eventually going to get sick regardless of what we did, the critical thing was to ensure that they did not all get sick at once, so that the hospital system could continue to function and save lives. Ultimately, the aim was to minimize death; to do that, the critical thing to do was to protect the intensive care units from overloading.

Hospitals are clearly pivotal to the apparatus of medicine, to the management of disease, life, and death.[41] They are also part of the defining structures of modernity. The French thinker Michel Foucault famously aligned hospitals with asylums, prisons, barracks, factories, and schools as an array of institutions that, by the early nineteenth century, formed the matrix for liberal visions both of individual freedom and collective order.[42] In the contemporary world, one might want to add other great containers of modern life such as offices, shopping malls, hotels, casinos, amusement parks, and sports arenas. And as well as static infrastructure, we would also need to think of highly organized modern conveyances such as subways, railways, and aircraft—all the places where we stand in line, where we are scanned and surveilled, where we move as a herd.

The risk of infection put all these basic containers of modern life under a massive collective pressure. Reopen schools, restaurants, malls, and arenas, and you feared your hospitals collapsing. On the other hand, stopping their functioning was extremely disruptive. Indeed, the end of regular traffic in those places *was* the disruption. Shutting the doors of the big institutional complexes brought life as we know it to a halt and cast us back on an unfamiliar reliance on small family networks. Life in less regularized outdoor spaces such as city parks flourished. So too did the virtual world, online. Not shutting down risked turning modernity's organizing nodes into centers of mass infection, panopticons into petri dishes. It was the potential of such hubs of public life to generate explosive growth in infections that made the idea of a trade-off between disease control and "the economy" not just intellectually fraught and politically and morally contentious, but also hopelessly unrealistic.

The economy is an abstraction, a real abstraction perhaps, but an abstraction, a set of ideas, concepts, and statistics that aggregate actual people and things, real networks of production and reproduction.[43] Normally numbers like GDP adequately capture that totality, but they create a delusive sense of separation. They make it seem meaningful to "trade off" GDP growth against other social imperatives. A virus exposes the illusion of imagining that there is a thing called the economy that is separate from society. It was through the bodies of workers, through the air circulating in workplaces, that the virus was rapidly multiplying. This is not to say that everything is equally connected. As we would find out, there are some more or less insulated circuits of goods and money that can continue functioning regardless of a pandemic, but to that extent they exposed the limits of the idea of a national economy. Global capitalism and business activity overlap only in part with the national economy. You might be able to get away with operating a small business, or even a large business if you could quarantine the staff, but it makes no sense to talk of maintaining "the American economy" or the "German economy" while separately fighting a highly infectious disease in schools, in public places, on buses and subways, and in people's homes.

If, as some Asian societies were able to do, you completely suppressed the disease across the socioeconomic system, the impact was short and sharp and the normal relationship of the economy, society, and politics was preserved. As in a victorious war, you could celebrate the recovery as a collective triumph. Whatever costs were incurred could be subsumed into a victory won at reasonable cost. If, as in Europe and the Americas, you lost control of the epidemic, the choices became starker. It was out of that loss of control and the exorbitant collective measures necessary to regain control that the antagonistic and contentious language of trade-offs arose. It was not impossible to claw your way back. You may, as many places in Europe and the Americas learned in the course of 2020, be able to resume much normal activity while keeping a lid on the disease. But those that succeeded in striking that balance did so not by trading the economy off against social and medical needs, but by recognizing the ramified connections that cut across domains and managing them as a whole. That could sound like a fantasy of social cohesion, or a nightmare of surveillance. It was often contentious. The deck was stacked against those with least resources to cope with protracted social distancing. Even more dramatic, however, as the Trump administration would demonstrate over the summer of 2020, were the consequences of abandoning the fight. Then, as America witnessed for a brief delirious few months, the entire relation-

ship between politics, society, and the economy could be thrown into
question.

In the end it came down to the medical system. Its capacity and resilience dictated what was a manageable and what was a terrifying level of disease. The ultimate fear was of hospital system overload. Hospital systems with more reserve capacity raised the survival threshold and the pace at which economic and social life could return to normal. Hospitals, however, are not outside the economy or society. By 2020, hospitals were no longer the giant organizational monoliths of the mid-twentieth century.[44] Since the 1980s they had been incorporated not just into the economy—they were always part of that—but into the market. They had become sites for experiments in modern management.[45] They were slimmed-down just-in-time operations, or at least they aspired to be, run like "normal" businesses according to criteria of efficiency. In the United States, many hospitals were commercial enterprises financed through the issuance of junk-rated debt. They maximized the throughput of patients and minimized the surplus capacity of beds. They stripped their stocks of essential equipment to minimal levels. Basics like masks and gloves were sourced from halfway around the world.

Given prevailing management doctrine, surplus capacity was viewed not as a responsible precaution but a regrettable drag on efficiency. This made sense if the caseload that you expected was stable and could be predicted. Like social life in general, the medical system was tuned to a particular pattern of morbidity. There were, of course, contingency plans and worst-case scenarios. The possibility of disaster was obvious. But there was no hospital system anywhere in the world that could absorb the caseload of a runaway pandemic. Organized irresponsibility ruled.

As bewildering as its impact was, the 2020 coronavirus crisis was an accident waiting to happen. Not only did our modern way of life supercharge the mutation of potentially dangerous viruses, we carry them around the world at the pace of jet aircraft. Experts understood the risks and made hypothetical plans as to how we might react. We, the population at large,

have high expectations of control and predictability. Our entire lives re-
volve around systems that are highly susceptible to mass contagion. Nevertheless, there was no willingness on the part of those who could have
afforded it to pay for genuine preparedness. There were teams of staffers
who had prepared paper plans for emergencies, but no one wanted to live
under the shadow that their hypotheticals might actually become real.
Who wanted to interrupt daily life to conduct Cold War–style "duck and
cover" drills? Meanwhile, democratic politics is both attenuated and polarized to the point that reaching political agreement on how to respond to a
pandemic crisis is hard even to imagine. It was a formula not for generating
solutions but for generating crises. With hindsight, the history of the last
century could be told as the narrative of a disaster foretold.

The analogue that was on everyone's minds in 2020 was the flu pandemic of 1918–19.[46] That affected hundreds of millions of people around
the world. Tens of millions died, a disaster vastly greater than our own. It
left deep scars across an entire generation. It stopped ordinary public life
in some cities for a matter of months, causing closures of businesses and
social distancing. But the remarkable thing from our vantage point is how
rapidly this appalling disaster was assimilated and how little it impacted
the political history of its moment. The negotiations at the Treaty of Ver-
sailles proceeded regardless of the epidemic. As dismayed as contemporar-
ies were, and as grief-stricken, they lived before the historic moment of the
epidemiologic transition. It was not unusual for people of any age to succumb
to infectious disease. TB, cholera, and plague were major killers worldwide.
Against the backdrop of a major war, a pandemic came as no surprise.

With hindsight, the Spanish flu was, however, a turning point in the
development of the mid-century public health regime of epidemic surveillance and flu vaccination, which is still with us today. Drawing on initiatives
in the 1920s and 1930s, a permanent system for identifying and monitoring influenza as it spread around the globe was established in the 1950s.
Those surveillance mechanisms allowed the Asian flu pandemic of 1957–58
and the Hong Kong flu of 1968–69 to be tracked in real time.[47] But they
were less lethal than Covid, let alone the Spanish flu, and there was no
generalized shutdown.

The next great test came in 1976, when a new strain of swine flu triggered an unprecedented effort by the Ford administration to inoculate a
large part of the American population in real time. It was a mixed success.
The virus proved much less dangerous than feared, but the vaccine had
serious side effects (a mishap that still haunts public perceptions of vaccination in the United States). The inoculation fiasco of 1976 set back the
confidence and self-belief of the public health bodies for years to come.[48]

It was in the 1990s under the banner of the fight against emerging
infectious diseases that public health entered the new age of globalization.
Worrying new strains of avian flu were making appearances in Hong Kong.
The Tokyo subway sarin attack of 1995 heightened awareness of new and
exotic types of terrorism. As befitted the unipolar hegemon of the time, it
was above all the United States that took the lead in defining a new agenda
of "global public health security."[49] The terrorist attack of 9/11 heightened
the level of alert. Successive U.S. administrations of both parties—Clinton,
George W. Bush, and Obama—all pumped resources into explorations of
pandemic risk.

After the millennium, a series of panics, real and imagined, came in
rapid sequence. SARS in 2003, the avian flu scare of 2005, and the swine
flu episode of 2008–9 all highlighted the possible threats. A consensus was
emerging among virologists that the lottery wheel of zoonotic mutation
was being spun at ever closer intervals. But judging the precise moment for
action was delicate as ever. The WHO's reaction to the swine flu epidemic
in 2009 was widely seen as premature and exaggerated. That made the organization cautious in confronting Ebola in 2014, a delay which earned it
much criticism.[50] Though Ebola remained confined to some of the poorest
parts of sub-Saharan Africa, the horrifying nature of the disease made it
into a driver of global vaccine development efforts.

Whereas African epidemics could be pigeonholed as problems of poverty and underdevelopment, China was in a different category—both integral
to globalization and in the front line of the battle with emerging infectious
diseases. Hong Kong had been repeatedly caught in the epidemic flow. Huge
flocks of poultry had been slaughtered to limit the risk of bird flu. The
SARS crisis of 2003, which originated in the Guangdong region of South-

ern China, infected 8,098 worldwide and killed 774. It was a defining event for the current generation of CCP leaders.[51] Drawing inspiration from America's Centers for Disease Control and Prevention (CDC), China built a health reporting system that it hoped would be immune to political pressure and ensure reliable reporting of regional outbreaks.[52] Given the vast scale of the Chinese state, that was always a pious hope. But China did not hide behind the Great Firewall. In the spirit of sharing expertise, the Chinese granted to the American CDC the exclusive right to embed officials inside the Chinese apparatus.

Meanwhile, China's neighbors had their own brushes with epidemic disaster. South Korea's government showed an alarming inability to contain the rapid spread of MERS in 2015.[53] The failure to handle the epidemic contributed to the electoral victory of a liberal government dedicated to modernizing governance and promoting the Korean biotech sector.[54] It would be the successor to the heavy industries that had powered South Korea's remarkable economic development.[55]

But despite the drumbeat of alarm, after the Ebola and then the Zika scares, global interest in pandemic disease flagged. In 2017, the emergence of a dangerous new strain of H7N9 avian flu across large parts of provincial China barely made the news.[56] For those preoccupied with the Anthropocene, what was "top of stack" was climate. And then there was the Trump factor.

With hindsight, it is hard to avoid focusing on the glaring missteps of the years before 2020. And in such postmortems, the administration of Donald Trump in the United States unavoidably takes center stage. As 2020 began, Trump's staff were hatching a budget that slashed funding for global disease control. Inside the American national security apparatus, the unit established under Obama to link disease control to national security policy was eviscerated. In the midst of the rising trade tensions with China, the United States unilaterally withdrew its observer from China's Center for Disease Control and Prevention. America was blinding itself to the coming storm. All of this was in marked contrast to the much stronger focus on global health security under previous Democratic and Republican administrations. It was consistent with the populism, nationalism, and

know-nothing posturing of Trump's administration. It reflected its preferences for dealing with China on an antagonistic basis. But much of it was
bravado, symbolic rather than real politics. Proposing to slash global health
budgets was one thing. Getting Congress to agree was quite another. One
could not easily undo an apparatus so deeply entrenched as the U.S. public
health bureaucracy. Rejecting the proposed cuts, Congress in 2019 restored
America's contribution to the global public health apparatus.[57] Pandemic
planning by the professional staffs of the American state apparatus continued. Normality was resilient in the face of the Trumpian assault, but that
should be no comfort.

Organized irresponsibility did not start in 2017. For decades we had
been hurtling into an ever-riskier future, spawning threats, increasing biological stress without adequately funding global public health institutions
to meet the predictable blowback. Dysfunction was not the Trumpian exception. It was the norm.[58] We were all preoccupied with preparing. Hardly
any of us were prepared.

Chapter 2

WUHAN, NOT CHERNOBYL

The virus we would come to know as SARS-CoV-2 began circulating in the eleven-million-strong city of Wuhan in Hubei province in late November 2019. China's virus reporting system ought to have been triggered. But the timing was terrible. The provincial CCP leadership had no desire to interrupt the normal flow of major political meetings and New Year's celebrations. Their main focus was on the buildup to the "two sessions" of the People's Political Consultative Conference and the National People's Congress in the Great Hall of the People in Beijing in March, the most important date in the ceremonial calendar of Chinese politics. The virus was an unwelcome distraction from the intense round of meetings and politicking. Wuhan is over a thousand kilometers (621 miles) from Beijing. Hubei province is itself the size of a large European country. There was no need to involve the center. Officials in Wuhan and Hubei did their best to suppress the inconvenient news about a new virus.

By the first days of January 2020, scientists in labs across China had wind that a new virus had emerged. Xi himself seems to have been informed on January 6.[1] Despite fears that human-to-human transmission was occurring at a dangerous rate, the center was slow to gauge the scale of the risk. It was preoccupied with its own busy January schedule. Xi's priorities were the campaign to instill Communist values in China's officialdom and the trade talks with America. By January 8, the head of China's

CDC admitted to his American counterpart that the disease was highly infectious, but Wuhan's local government refused to raise the alert.[2] Following the detection of the first case outside China, the National Health Commission convened a nationwide teleconference to alert provincial officials and convey "instructions" from Beijing. What those instructions were remains unclear. Though China's CDC was now on high alert, the public was not warned. Person-to-person infection had not yet been confirmed.[3] To overcome the roadblock, on January 18, China's National Health Commission persuaded Dr. Zhong Nanshan, a trusted party stalwart and hero of the fight against SARS, to visit Wuhan in person. What he found—rapid person-to-person infection, hospitals struggling to cope—set all the alarm bells ringing. The following day in the Zhongnanhai, the CCP's walled compound in Beijing, Zhong confronted Prime Minister Li Keqiang with the news. Xi was on tour in southwestern China, but on January 20 he remotely addressed a televised meeting organized by the State Council, calling for the virus to be taken "seriously." A few hours later Dr. Zhong confirmed publicly that there was human-to-human transmission. By that point the disease had already spread across China and to the wider world.

The failure to contain the virus in the winter of 2019–2020 came amid heightened tension between China and the West. Since 2017, Sino-American relations had lurched back and forth between trade war and trade truce. There was increasing alarm about the extent of Beijing's influence outside its borders and repression at home. For Beijing, the upsurge in popular protest in Hong Kong raised the question of how long it could tolerate the license granted to the city under the one country/two systems regime. Against this backdrop, China skeptics in the West eagerly seized on the coronavirus outbreak. It was precisely the kind of discrediting mishap they had long predicted would befall the CCP regime.

The analogy that was readily to hand was Chernobyl, the nuclear accident in 1986 that had done so much to discredit the Soviet regime.[4] As chance would have it, HBO had premiered a compelling docudrama about the Chernobyl incident in May 2019. As the coronavirus crisis escalated in late January, China's netizens availed themselves of movie review sites to draw the obvious analogy.[5] The liberal academic Xu Zhangrun, who had

publicly criticized Xi's personal rule and been disciplined, now published
an article denouncing the CCP's political system, claiming it was collapsing under the weight of its own "tyranny." A government of bureaucrats was
"floundering." Xi's turn toward one-man rule had set back the clock. "The
mess in Hubei is only the tip of the iceberg and it's the same with every
province," Xu opined.[6] It was only a matter of time, therefore, before the
Communist regime suffered its comeuppance.

Xu would pay for his audacity with dismissal and house arrest. But
worse than that, his prediction of comprehensive regime failure was re-
futed too. As for the West, mistaking Wuhan for Chernobyl would cost it
dearly. Wuhan was not a backwater deep behind the Iron Curtain. It was a
globalized megacity, which is why the outbreak was so dangerous. Come
the holidays, roughly half Wuhan's population left to visit family and
friends. That meant 5 million travelers spreading the infection by car, bullet train, and airplane not just to the rest of China but to the entire world.[7]
In January, 15,000 Chinese tourists left Wuhan's international airport for
Japan alone.[8] Within a few weeks, cases were reported in twenty-five countries, the first in Thailand.

Given the infectivity of SARS-CoV-2, this was an absolutely urgent
threat that brooked no delay. Beijing grasped that. The West did not. In
China, a public health failure on the scale of that which occurred in Italy, the
UK, or the United States would have cost millions of lives. If the political
management of the crisis had been as cack-handed in Beijing as it was in
Washington or in London, it might well have rocked Xi's iron grip on power.
But this is not what happened. Not only did China not suffer a Soviet-style
collapse, but it turned the tables on its foreign critics. In China, the first
country to face the disease, the threat was rapidly contained, freeing and
energizing Xi's regime for further action. It was in Europe, the United States,
Latin America, and India that the virus ran out of control. That basic difference set the frame for everything else that happened in 2020 and beyond.

The failure of disease reporting in Wuhan in January 2020 rattled Beijing.
Risk management was key to Xi's entire conception of power.[9] The case for

Xi's personal rule was based on the claim that China was entering an unprecedentedly serious period of challenges, one "not seen in a century," that could be mastered only with determined leadership from the "core" of the CCP.[10] Countering these threats required wide-ranging countermeasures, ranging from stamping out political opposition to taming the real estate boom. The memories of the near-miss financial crisis in 2015, when $1 trillion in reserves had fled the country, were still fresh. And the regime also remembered SARS. The 2003 epidemic had shaken Beijing. Several of Xi's entourage owed their rise to power to the cleanup within the party hierarchy that followed.[11] When the scale of the Wuhan outbreak did finally dawn on the CCP leadership, the cadres around Xi acted with ruthlessness and speed.

There is a tendency in the West to suggest that China's draconian measures were a familiar part of the CCP's repertoire. But that both mistakes Chinese realities and underestimates Beijing's boldness. The lockdown ordered in Wuhan had no precedent in recent Chinese history. In 2003, 4,000 Beijing residents who had been exposed to SARS had been kept in isolation and 300 college students were detained in a military camp for two weeks.[12] That was nothing like the closure of an entire city of 11 million people, let alone a province or a country.[13]

Beijing got no encouragement from the local government in Wuhan or Hubei province. As Zeng Guang, chief epidemiologist at China's Center for Disease Control and Prevention, remarked to the official *Global Times*: "[Local governments] take a political perspective and consider social stability, the economy and whether people could happily enjoy Lunar New Year."[14] Western experts too were skeptical about the possibility of shutting down an entire city. It would be impractical and would violate human rights.[15] Incongruously, they dug back in the historical record to argue that citywide quarantines had not worked in 1918–19. They also pointed out that in Liberia the use of cordons sanitaires to contain Ebola had ended in rioting.

Whatever the relevance of those examples to China in 2020, a total lockdown was not the first policy option presented to the Chinese leadership by Zhong and his team. It was a recommendation likely worked out by

Premier Li Keqiang and the State Council before being presented to Xi.[16] The radical decision reflects not only the regime's authoritarian proclivities and the mounting evidence of an epidemic out of control, but the fact that Beijing viewed the new coronavirus from the outset through the lens of SARS or MERS. Unlike in the West, there was never any question of conflating SARS-CoV-2 with flu. Letting the disease run through the population unchecked in an attempt to achieve "herd immunity" was not entertained as an option. For Beijing—preoccupied as it was with delivering "output legitimacy"—letting "nature take its course" was unthinkable.[17] To their detriment, European and American policymakers found it harder to detach themselves from the cold-blooded calculus of the flu paradigm.

On January 22, the Chinese leadership opted for a countrywide shutdown, and on the twenty-fifth, a publicly broadcast meeting of senior leadership set the giant state-party machine in motion. Following the Chinese New Year holiday, the vacation was extended until Sunday, February 2, and major economic hubs like the financial center in Shanghai declared that business would not resume until February 9, school classes not until February 17. By early February, fourteen provinces and cities that accounted for almost 70 percent of the population had shut down. The Chinese economy—the second largest in the world, the main engine of global growth—was being put on hold.

Some containment measures were high tech. In Shanghai, before leaving either the train station or the airport, travelers were required to sign up for a contact tracing app.[18] If you could not remember your own movements, a quick text to one of the cell phone providers would produce a list. Yunnan province installed QR codes in all public places so that people could scan themselves on entry.[19] In most of China, control worked through more hands-on methods led by neighborhood committees, backed up by the regime's "grid management" system of local party organizations. This had been a focus of recent efforts on the part of the CCP to consolidate its grip on China's sprawling new megacities.[20] In 2020, that investment in what was called "social administration innovation" paid dividends.

Zhejiang province, on China's southeastern seaboard, is where Xi had made his name as a provincial official. It had a population of nearly 60 million and enlisted 330,000 "grid workers." Hubei managed 170,000, Guangdong 177,000. Sichuan mobilized 308,000, and in the megacity of Chongqing, there were 118,000 grid workers monitoring every neighborhood. This was the equivalent in terms of density of coverage of a big city police force in the United States.[21] Working with the property management companies that service China's private apartment complexes, enrolling millions of volunteers from the ranks of the party, they turned each compound into a lockdown zone.[22]

The aim was to find infected people and quarantine them. As a helpful nudge, the authorities in Hangzhou banned pharmacies from selling pain-killers. This would prevent citizens from self-medicating and force them to seek hospital treatment. The coastal city of Wenzhou 900 kilometers (559 miles) to the southeast of Wuhan limited families to one shopping trip every two days by one family member. Freeways were closed. In Poyang County in Jiangxi, local officials resorted to the imaginative expedient of turning all traffic lights permanently to red.[23]

In the words of a European observer, "Every city has turned into a little Alamo."[24] In the week starting on February 3, daily passenger traffic on China's railway system was down some 75 percent.[25] Malls and fashionable shopping districts emptied. Starbucks shuttered half its stores. Ikea was closed across the country. For China's restaurant, tourism, and movie in-dustry, it meant losing the biggest days of spending in the entire year. A ban on New Year banquets is estimated to have cost China's restaurant indus-try $144 billion in a single week.[26]

Factories too were shut down, including the prestigious manufactur-ing plants of Western brand names. In Suzhou, where iPhone contractor Foxconn, Johnson & Johnson, and Samsung Electronics have concentrated their plants, migrant workers were asked not to return. Tesla shut its Shang-hai operation at the request of local authorities, as did GM, Toyota, and Volkswagen.[27] Nissan and the French car groups PSA and Renault an-nounced that they were evacuating their foreign staff. [28]

But the lockdown was not just a matter of big cities or prestigious global firms. A telephone poll by a research team based in Stanford found that every single rural village they contacted in China had shut itself off.

"It's like Europe in medieval times," said Jörg Wuttke, the president of the European Chamber of Commerce in China, "each city has its checks and crosschecks."[29] In the countryside, all the locals needed to do was to park a few trucks or oil drums across the roads. They would accost travelers seeking to pass through. A familiar dialect was enough to secure passage. Everyone else waited.

In Wuhan itself, the first full week of the shutdown was the worst period of chaos. A team of 40,000 construction workers toiled day and night to finish two emergency hospitals, the first of which, Huoshenshan (Fire God Mountain) Hospital, began operating on February 4. But with the caseload being haphazardly managed, severely sick patients were left to die in their homes. It was not until Sunday, February 2, that a new system for dividing and isolating four categories of patients was established. Crucially, this enabled confirmed and suspected cases to be rapidly isolated from their families, limiting transmission. No one knew it yet, but China had found a method to manage the crisis.

On February 3, rather than welcoming China back to work, Xi gave a detailed report to the Politburo on what was now proclaimed as China's "People's War" on the virus.[30] That may have been a stirring rallying cry, evoking memories of the Mao era, but the Shanghai stock market needed some convincing. When traders fired up their terminals on the first day of trading after the Chinese New Year, it was generally assumed that buying by the "national team"—a group of leading banks, insurers, and fund managers—would support the market.[31] But despite the People's Bank of China providing a massive $171 billion in credits to traders, the markets sold off. The Shanghai Stock Exchange lost 7.9 percent in a single day.[32] It was the worst day of trading since the crisis of August 2015.[33]

In Wuhan and Hubei, the situation was dire, and China's media did not disguise the fact. The medical containment centers were grim, more like warehouses than hospitals. Doctors struggled vainly against a wave of death.[34] Among the victims were doctors themselves. Dr. Li Wenliang had been among the first to warn of the disease, a step for which he was threatened with discipline by local authorities. By early February, Li was severely ill and sharing photos of himself struggling for oxygen on Weibo. His death on February 6 was a PR disaster. The hashtag "The Wuhan government owes Li Wenliang an apology" was viewed 180 million times before it was blocked by censors.[35]

Dismay at the regime's mishandling of the pandemic quickly spilled over into more general political demands. On Friday, February 7, an open letter by professors of Wuhan's well-regarded university called on the authorities to honor the freedom of expression guaranteed in China's constitution. Another letter addressed to China's National People's Congress by leading intellectuals started by declaring: "We assert, starting today, that no Chinese citizen should be threatened by any state apparatus or political group for his or her speech . . . The state must immediately cease censoring social media and deleting or blocking accounts."[36] Only weeks earlier, Xi's authority had seemed unquestionable. Now the censors were struggling to prevent web users from posting lyrics from "Do You Hear the People Sing?," *Les Misérables*'s theme tune, which had recently been adopted as an anthem of defiance by protesters in Hong Kong.

February 7 was the moment at which the authority of the CCP was most seriously challenged. But it was also the turning point in the government's response. The upsurge of protest was met with tough repression. Censorship went into overdrive. Social media posts were rapidly wiped. Local Wuhan reporters who dared to post critical video online disappeared. Xu Zhangrun was placed under house arrest and cut off from the outside world.[37]

The CCP's security apparatus is formidable, but the repression was as effective as it was because it was combined with success in controlling the epidemic. By the middle of February, as far as we can judge from the available data, the virus caseload across China was coming down fast. This meant that Beijing was fighting a major epidemic in one province, Hubei, with the resources of a nation of 1.4 billion. Led by the military, over 40,000 medical workers could be concentrated to focus first on the Wuhan hotspot and then on the rest of the province.[38]

Containing the spread was crucial to gaining this strategic flexibility. Beijing was a key point in that battle. During the SARS epidemic in 2003, the municipal authorities in the capital city had failed. By February 10, 2020, there were 337 confirmed Covid-19 cases in Beijing, with many more suspected. If ordinary life resumed after the holidays, officials feared that 600,000 residents and workers returning by train and 140,000 by air would cause a surge in new infections.[39] To forestall disaster, Beijing municipal authorities began a comprehensive washdown and instituted a "no outsiders" policy. To project a sense of calm, on Monday, February 10, Xi conducted a personal tour of the capital. The message was clear: outside Hubei, China was returning to normal.

By mid-February, from Beijing's point of view, the crisis had tipped from one pole to another. The problem was not that other provinces were failing like Hubei to control the disease, but rather that, driven by fear of another failure, local officials were overreacting. The shutdown had taken on a momentum of its own and was threatening to stall the growth motor of the Chinese economy. Major economic centers like Shanghai, Zhejiang, Jiangsu, and Guangdong were frozen by extended school closures and limits on the movement of migrant workers. Minor towns were requiring two-week quarantines for truck drivers who picked up cargoes in Covid-hit cities or had merely passed through them. Meanwhile, prominent global corporations like Foxconn and VW weighed the risks of restarting too early.[40] No one wanted to find themselves in the dock, accused of putting the national health at risk. In Shanghai, one of the great hubs of the world economy, the city authorities reported by February 10 that only 70 percent of local factories had registered any interest in restarting production, let alone received certification to do so. As the president of the American Chamber of Commerce in China remarked, employers "want to protect staff, but also nobody wants to get caught offsides when it comes to the labor law or the daily announcements from the government."[41]

What worried the center was no longer Hubei-style malfeasance and foot-dragging, but the centrifugal tendencies unleashed by overzealous local action. It was indicative that the General Office of the State Council saw fit to issue a notice strictly prohibiting "the arbitrary closure of high-speed

roads, the obstruction of major provincial highways, the forcible quaran-
tining of villages, the digging up of village roads, and obstructing the flow
of emergency vehicles."[42] But if Beijing wanted to get things moving again,
local party committees were not easy to convince. Clearly it was important
to restart the circulation of goods and people, but no one wanted to be
blamed for another Wuhan. Faced with Beijing's demands to stick to the
rules, local party officials took the line that "disease control should be free
from abstract, sometimes-pedantic debates about the rule of law." It was
easy for sticklers in Beijing to criticize local heavy-handedness. They wouldn't
end up carrying the can if the epidemic got out of control again. Yes, some
quarantine measures might be harsh, but miscarriages and abuses could be
corrected later. The priority was to act now and to act decisively. If Beijing
didn't like the obstruction this caused, it should come up with a "better
idea."[43]

The case for stringency was all the easier to make because the pain was
felt above all by outsiders. China's huge army of migrant workers, 291 million strong, made up a third of the total labor force of 775 million. In struggling to return to work, they faced "three gates": the "local exit gate," the
"transportation gate," and finally, the "quarantine gate" at the destination.[44]
For those with any association with Hubei, it was hopeless. In Beijing, families from Hubei faced eviction from rented accommodation. Local residents' committees began labeling apartments known to be inhabited by
people with ties to the afflicted province. Local activists offered rewards of
RMB 500 ($71) for information on anyone who might hail from or have had
contacts with Hubei. Unfortunately for the individuals in question, the ac-
cent of those from Hubei is unmistakable. Added to which every identity
card identifies a person's province of origin.[45] There were pronouncements
from the top forbidding discrimination, but they were ignored.

By mid-February, official figures confirmed that of the 290 to 300 million migrant workers who would normally be expected to return from the
holidays, only 80 million had made it back to their workplaces. Another
120 million were expected by the end of the month, leaving a third still out
of work.[46] The impact on economic activity was undeniable.[47] Mid-February
passenger traffic was down 85 percent from the previous year, and daily

coal consumption at six large power generation groups was down by 43 percent. As skies cleared over the major urban centers, China's CO_2 emissions crashed.[48]

This was the background behind Xi's comments on his inspection tour of Beijing on February 10 that the priority was to avoid "large layoffs" and for local government to respect the law.[49] State media took to quoting Xi on the need to "correct overreactions [to the epidemic] and avoid an oversimplified approach involving blanket closures or suspensions of business."[50] But even the State Planning Ministry recognized the need for flexibility and left it up to provinces and cities to resume work "at their own discretion based on the spread of the virus."[51] On February 17, the official news agency Xinhua announced that discussions were beginning about the postponement of the "two sessions."[52] A third of the national legislators were also local government officials, and they had their hands full.

There was no more conspicuous example of the dilemmas involved in managing the lockdown than Foxconn, the Taiwanese corporation responsible for assembling 40 percent of Apple's iPhones worldwide. At full capacity, its giant Zhengzhou plant in Henan province employed 200,000. Workers returning from outside the city had to be quarantined and Foxconn did not have enough dormitory space to house them.[53] A shutdown of Apple's main production line was not just a matter of domestic concern. On February 21 President Xi himself warned of the growing risk to China's status as a global supplier. In a hostile world, if China wanted to preserve its place as a contractor of choice, it had to demonstrate that it could restore production as soon as possible.[54]

To manage the risks, Foxconn began to implement the kind of regime that would soon spread across the entire world. Workers from high-risk provinces were required to self-quarantine for fourteen days. Those from moderate-risk regions had to prove a clean bill of health before returning to work. Henceforth, Foxconn would recruit primarily from Henan province, where the incidence of the virus had been slight.[55] In an effort to get the trucks rolling again, all tolls on highways throughout China were lifted.[56] But 90 percent of truck drivers in the port cities of Shanghai and Ningbo had still not returned to work.[57] So desperate were production centers like the coastal province of Zhejiang that they were laying on dedicated transport. Smiling lines of flag-waving workers were shown on TV trooping onto chartered bullet trains.

One month after the push for a general lockdown began, on Sunday, February 23, President Xi addressed the Chinese leadership.[58] Of all the teleconferences and Zoom meetings around the world in 2020, this was surely the most spectacular. No less than 170,000 cadres—representatives from every county government and every military regiment throughout the country—attended. All the data showed that the caseload was rapidly falling. It was time to shift gear. Xi, the *South China Morning Post* opined, was ringing the "alarm bell on China's economic growth." The country's social and economic system "can't be paused for long." With the virus suppressed, the emphasis was now on restoring production. Rather than reporting on new infections, officials were enjoined to report the rate of reopening. Xi's own power base, the province of Zhejiang, led the way. Some 90 percent of its large industrial firms had restarted, though at low capacity.[59]

As Xi intoned, the crisis was bound to deal a "big blow to China's economic and social development. However, at such a time it is even more important to view China's development in a comprehensive, dialectical, and long-term perspective, and to strengthen and firm up confidence." The emphasis now was on selectivity and discipline. About half of China's counties had no coronavirus cases. There, the priority should be "on forestalling imported cases and comprehensively restoring the order of production and life." For medium-risk regions, the priority should also be to promote "work and production resumption in an orderly manner based on local epidemic-control situation." High-risk regions should continue in lockdown.[60] Behind the boilerplate, the message was clear. The central leadership of the CCP was restoring control.

On Monday, February 24, as if on cue, the WHO hailed China's virus control efforts and declared that the moment of maximum danger had passed.[61] Responding to Xi's call, the factory hub of Guangdong lowered its public health emergency rating, and Shanxi, Gansu, Liaoning, Guizhou, and Yunnan did the same.[62] The provincial government enjoined local officials to "aid Foxconn Technology Group's Zhengzhou plant return to work." Workers from safe areas were hustled back to work. Health declaration forms were stamped, temperatures checked, and workers certified fit. In at least one case, a police escort accompanied the bus convoys direct to the factory gates. Meanwhile, Foxconn's rival Pegatron was offering RMB 10,000 bonuses to lure workers back to its Shanghai factory.

Not everyone was in a position to do that. Despite Xi's call to return to work, by the end of February, even in the most active provinces, only an estimated 30 percent of small and medium-sized businesses had reopened, as against 60 percent for large industrial corporations.[63] Despite the amount of attention lavished on the likes of Foxconn and the giant state-owned enterprises, small and medium-sized enterprises, almost all of which are privately owned, account for 99.8 percent of registered companies in China and employ almost 80 percent of workers. Together, this huge mass of small businesses contributes more than 60 percent of gross domestic product and more than half of all tax revenue.[64] They had been hard hit by the lockdown. Whereas industrial production revived quickly, urban mass consumption would lag all year. The banking system was directed to make loans on terms as generous as possible. Unfortunately, as Premier Li Keqiang acknowledged, the vast majority of smaller firms were not fully enrolled in the financial system. Only a fifth of China's giant population of small businesses had ever applied for and received a bank loan.[65] They were beyond the easy reach of central government stimulus. Their survival depended on the general economic recovery and the restoration of normal life, and that still hung in the balance.

The best general indicator of an economy's health is the rate of employment and unemployment. China's official unemployment statistics showed a tiny increase during the crisis from just 5.3 percent to 6 percent. But the unemployment insurance system covers only half of the urban workforce and a fifth of migrant workers. Despite the concerted effort to restart production, in March 2020, of the normal workforce of 174 million long-range migrants, only 129 million were at work.[66] That implied a loss of at least 45 million jobs. Allowing for migrant workers not counted in the official data, the number in March was probably closer to 80 million lost jobs. Even the National Bureau of Statistics was willing to admit that at the worst point in the crisis, the number of people idled in China's cities amounted to 18.3 percent. Combing carefully through the data, analysts at BNP Paribas concluded that as many as 132 million workers were either temporarily unemployed, displaced, or furloughed, which would amount to 30 percent of China's urban workforce.[67] The numbers are estimates, and Beijing did its best to suppress any in-depth discussion of the social crisis. What is clear is that the impact on the labor market was gigantic—far worse than the recession of 2008 or the SARS epidemic of 2003.[68] Up to that point, it was the worst labor market shock ever experienced by any economy in the world.

On February 25, two days after Xi had delivered his address to 170,000 loyalists, one of the most closely watched indices of business confidence, compiled by one of Beijing's leading business schools, delivered its verdict. On the index scale, a reading of 50 indicates the economy is in neutral. In January it stood at a modestly confident 56.2. By the end of February, it had plunged to 37.3, indicating a serious contraction. The data-gatherers were horrified: As Professor Li Wei remarked, "We were psychologically prepared for poor results . . . but the actual figures are worse than we had imagined."[69]

What China was experiencing was not a blast from the Cold War past, not a "Chernobyl moment," but a novel and unprecedented social and economic shock. Through their urgent and effective response, the regime and the people of China were suppressing the virus. But that success came at a huge cost. In the first half of 2020, China suffered its first serious setback to economic growth since the new era of economic transformation began. Nor was there any doubt about culpability. It was the appallingly short-sighted resistance of the Hubei party leadership that had allowed the virus to spread as far as it did. If SARS had discredited the CCP back in 2003, this was clearly far worse. Despite the successful suppression campaign in February, the coronavirus crisis of 2020 could easily have been a major liability for Xi's regime. Instead, it became an occasion for what has been aptly

termed "disaster nationalism," an opportunity to demonstrate collective resilience under the leadership of the party.[70]

That sense of community could be turned outward as well as inward.
In a globalized world, how one judged China's performance depended crit-
ically on how the rest of the world dealt with the coronavirus outbreak. If
control measures in Europe and the United States had been more effective
and only China had had to go through the full rigors of the shutdown, Xi's
authority might well have suffered a heavy blow. That is not what happened. The rest of the world failed, and when Western observers sought to
point the finger of blame at China, that served only to harden the sense of
embattled collectivity fostered by the CCP. China had in fact paid a heavy
price, but the success of the suppression efforts contained the overall bill
and allowed the regime rapidly to restore control. The entire episode could
be presented as an exercise in decisive leadership that put the people first
in terms of both public health and the economy. When on May 21–22,
2020, the two sessions finally convened in Beijing, the story that the regime
had to tell was one of heroic national recovery.[71] The failure of the West
handed the CCP a historic triumph.

Chapter 3

FEBRUARY: WASTING TIME

In late January, the news out of Wuhan sent a ripple of alarm around the world. Was this the pandemic nightmare that had long been predicted? For a brief moment, *Contagion*, the 2011 Hollywood shocker about a disease outbreak in China, surged into the top ten on iTunes movie rentals.[1] But for those outside China, the crisis still had an unreal quality. It was a long way away. Talk of "China's Chernobyl" exoticized the risk. The rigor of China's countermeasures was easily typecast as totalitarian. Surely, nothing like that could be imagined in the West. Even the spectacle of China conjuring hospitals out of nothing confirmed stereotypes about the Communist regime rather than being seen as a warning of things to come.

For a disastrous month, most of the rest of the world registered the events in China as something that had no immediate relevance to them.[2] It reflected a deep underestimation of the virus, a complacency about the ability to cope, and an unspoken sense that for all the talk of globalization, a Chinese problem was Chinese. Beijing may have had to adopt radical measures in response to the outbreak in Wuhan, a city 1,000 kilometers away. But the idea that containing a virus emanating from a city in central China might require immediate action in places as far away as London and New York seemed unimaginable. The year 2020 revealed that our ability to fly around the world vastly outpaced our understanding of what that interconnectedness entailed.

It was a historic failure. By early February, experts outside China knew enough to gauge the extent and urgency of the threat that the novel coronavirus posed.[3] What China was having to do to contain the spread of the virus should have been warning enough. In an ideal world, one could imagine a group of governments, such as the G20, with the United States and the EU in the lead, agreeing on an immediate coordinated and phased shutdown of air travel, combined with intensive sharing and production of test kits and other PPE. That was essentially what China had implemented at the scale of one country, a country of 1.4 billion people. To cover the most densely connected nodes in the global transport network, China's "People's War" against the virus would have needed to have been scaled up by a factor of two.

One needs only to spell out the fantasy to see how far from reality it was. No concerted leadership was forthcoming. Global institutions like the World Health Organization (WHO) and the International Monetary Fund (IMF) did sound the alarm, but neither the United States nor the EU threw their weight behind those warnings. Nor did China put itself in quarantine or constructively advocate for movement restrictions.[4] The WHO condoned that position, arguing against unnecessary travel bans.[5] On all sides February 2020 delivered a staggering demonstration of the collective inability of the global elite to grasp what it would actually mean to govern the deeply globalized and interconnected world they have created.

Among those who had immediate reason to take the virus seriously were those who manage global supply chains. At the time of the SARS crisis, China had accounted for only 4 percent of the world economy. In 2020, its world share was closer to 20 percent. For a manufacturing sector like automobiles, China was both the largest market and the largest production hub. In 2019, 80 percent of car production around the world involved Chinese parts.[6] As one carmaker noted: "Everyone sources from China." If there was a shutdown in China, no one could say, "I'm not affected." In February, Hyundai in South Korea was forced to stop production altogether. Both Nissan and Fiat Chrysler struggled to keep their factories running. Several European companies resorted to airlifting parts out of China. That came with risks. In Germany, the first cluster of Covid-19 cases was in Bavaria, at the auto parts supplier Webasto, after a visit by a colleague from a Chinese joint venture.[7]

In recent decades, sophisticated traders in global financial centers had learned to use satellite imagery to track the movement of commodities in real time.[8] Unlike oil tankers, coronavirus wasn't visible from space. But you could see the effects of the shutdown. By the middle of February, satellite imagery showed an unprecedented decline in air pollution across China. Usage data for satnav systems like TomTom showed a collapse in road traffic.[9] Data scraped from China's main search engine, Baidu, showed an alarming surge in keyword searches on terms like "layoffs," "unemployment," "shutdown," and "bankruptcy."[10]

But it was one thing to worry about the global impact of a crisis in China. It was quite another to worry about a Chinese crisis becoming global. Even leading figures in the pharmaceutical industry found it hard to make that leap. Dr. Albert Bourla, Pfizer's chief executive, who would soon be playing a starring role in the vaccine race, admitted later that when the virus first emerged, he "wasn't under the impression . . . that this would become a major global issue that would require a major intervention."[11] He was not alone. Though some Covid-19 vaccine makers launched their projects within days of the SARS-CoV-2 sequence being made public, CanSino CEO Yu Xuefeng also had reservations. He worried that Covid-19 would, like SARS, prove to be a "blip."[12] In the science community, it was the news of the extreme infectivity of SARS-CoV-2 and the alarming rate of hospitalization that changed the game. If you applied those numbers to standard epidemiological models, it was hard to avoid the conclusion that if left unchecked, this disease would infect hundreds of millions. Millions might die.

Vladimir Putin staged his first public remarks about the virus on January 29 shortly before Russia closed its land border with China.[13] In late January, several countries began to implement restrictions on travelers from China. On January 31, both Italy and the United States unilaterally halted the entry of non-nationals arriving from China, but this was contentious. Beijing immediately protested.

In Washington, D.C., the news of the "Wuhan virus" was seized on by

China hawks like Trump's trade advisor Peter Navarro, who had long been arguing for severing relations. On February 9, Navarro submitted a memo warning that "We face a significant probability of a serious pandemic coronavirus event in the US that may extend well into 2021."[14] By February 23 he was warning of a disaster that would claim the lives of millions.[15]

Navarro was devoutly convinced that the world was heading toward an epic confrontation of East and West. The idea of a virus deliberately "seeded" by China fitted his script.[16] But not everyone shared his dark vision. President Trump boasted of his nationalism and liked to talk tough on China, but what he liked even more was a deal. In February 2020, Trump was not going to let a virus get in the way of touting his Phase I trade agreement. He was only too happy to leave the epidemic to Beijing. "China has been working very hard to contain the Coronavirus," the president tweeted. "The United States greatly appreciates their efforts and transparency. It will all work out well. In particular, on behalf of the American People, I want to thank President Xi!"[17] Flouting advice by several of his team who called for a tougher stance, in February, Trump praised Xi's handling of the pandemic thirteen more times. And it didn't end with admiring rhetoric. On February 7, Secretary of State Mike Pompeo announced the shipment of eighteen tons of medical equipment from the United States to China. Several European countries also airlifted supplies to China. It was all too convenient to leave Covid-19 to the Chinese. Both Trump and the Europeans had plenty of other things to worry about at home.

As the crisis began, President Trump was dealing with the impeachment scandal. He was not acquitted by the Senate until February 5. After that ordeal, he treated himself to a victory lap of rallies with supporters across the red states. When public health advisors urged Trump to take the virus threat seriously, Treasury Secretary Steven Mnuchin and son-in-law Jared Kushner pushed back.[18] Their priority was not to disturb the financial markets with scaremongering virus stories. On February 10 the administration released a budget proposal that called for deep cuts to WHO and global health funding. Meanwhile, for commerce secretary Wilbur Ross, China's crisis was an opportunity to encourage manufacturers to return to America's safer shores.[19]

In Britain, Prime Minister Boris Johnson's administration was similarly distracted. On January 31, an evacuation flight brought eighty-three Britons home from Wuhan, and the first case in Britain, a Chinese visitor, was identified in York in the North of England.[20] But the headlines of the day were dominated by Brexit. On January 31, Britain left the EU. That evening a beaming prime minister delivered a fireside chat from 10 Downing Street promising the UK that this was the "moment when the dawn breaks and the curtain goes up on a new act in our great national drama." Recapturing "sovereignty" would unleash the "full potential of this brilliant country."[21] On February 3, speaking in Greenwich, the home of the Royal Naval College, Johnson pitted Britain and its commitment to free trade not only against the EU, but against pandemic panic. "When there is a risk that new diseases such as coronavirus will trigger a panic and a desire for market segregation that go beyond what is medically rational, to the point of doing real and unnecessary economic damage, then at that moment humanity needs some government, somewhere, that is willing . . . to make the case . . . for freedom of exchange. Some country ready to take off its Clark Kent spectacles and leap into the phone booth, and emerge with its cloak flowing as the supercharged champion of the right of the populations of the Earth to buy and sell freely among each other."[22] While Johnson dreamed of leaping from phone booths, the National Audit Office estimated that 27,500 British civil servants were spending their days trying to figure out how to actually implement Brexit.[23]

Health care had never been high on the list of subjects to be addressed by the EU. It was not until the SARS crisis of 2003 that the EU had equipped itself with a European Centre for Disease Prevention and Control (ECDC).[24] When it convened the ECDC's membership on February 13 to discuss the Covid-19 crisis, the focus was not on Europe itself, but on how Europe might help other people in coping with the epidemic.[25] The WHO's emergency chief Mike Ryan highlighted Africa as a potential trouble spot. If Covid gained a foothold there, there were only two labs for a continent with a population almost three times that of the EU. That same day, a sixty-nine-year-old man recently returned from Nepal died of pneumonia in a hospital in Valencia. It would take the authorities three weeks to identify him as Spain's first Covid-19 victim. The first officially confirmed European Covid-19 fatality came a day later, on February 14, in France. And yet it seemed that the situation was under control. Only forty Covid patients had been identified across Europe. China's success in containing its epidemic emboldened Germany's health minister Jens Spahn to describe it as a "regional outbreak."[26] For Europe to react with comprehensive citywide lockdowns would be quite out of proportion.

When the Munich Security Conference convened on February 15, there was plenty of navel-gazing, yet the theme was not the adequacy of public health systems but transatlantic divisions between the United States and Europe, over trade, NATO, and climate policy. Those who were warning about coronavirus, including the WHO boss Tedros Adhanom Ghebreyesus and Kristalina Georgieva of the IMF, struggled to make themselves heard. The main stage was given over to jousting between President Emmanuel Macron of France and U.S. Secretary of State Pompeo.[27]

In the third week of February the mood in the markets was increasingly polarized. On the one hand, as analysts digested the scale of the shock to the Chinese economy, there was intensifying demand for safe-haven bonds. The dollar rose. Commodity exporters to China felt the impact indirectly. By the end of February, Brazil's currency had depreciated by 10 percent since the start of the year. On the other hand, influential advisors like Goldman Sachs and BlackRock were counseling calm. If Covid was like SARS, swine flu, and Zika, it would pass quickly and the rebound would be strong. If some investors were rushing into bonds in search of safety, there was profit to be made in taking the other side of the trade.[28] Confidence in equities remained strong. As bad as the shutdown had been, the latest news out of China gave grounds for optimism. In the topsy-turvy world of twenty-first-century capitalism, Xi's epic teleconference on February 23 with the massed ranks of Communist Party apparatchiks was great news for Western stock markets. If the Chinese economy faltered, the regime could surely be counted on to deliver more stimulus.

Meanwhile, Europeans were looking forward to February holidays.

Hundreds of thousands flocked to the ski resorts in the Alps. There was a big football match in Northern Italy. And unfortunately for them, thousands of better-off Latin Americans were holidaying in Europe too. Silently, the infection was spreading.

Meeting in the comfortable winter climate in Riyadh, Saudi Arabia, on Saturday, February 22, the mood of the G20 finance ministers was not yet one of alarm.[29] U.S. Treasury Secretary Mnuchin and Fed chair Jerome Powell quoted private sector economists who were forecasting a rapid rebound in China. There were skeptics, the most notable being French finance minister Bruno Le Maire, who expressed serious concerns about the spread of the virus. Kristalina Georgieva, IMF managing director, repeated the warning she had made in Munich the week before. But what those warnings added up to was a downward revision of the IMF's growth forecasts for China from 6 to 5.6 percent. Bad news, but hardly a disaster.

That was about to change. With hindsight, we can see that it was in the third week of February that the global pandemic began in earnest. Starting on February 15, significant outbreaks were registered in South Korea, Iran, and Italy. The first death in Iran may have occurred on January 22, though it was not registered at the time.[30] The regime was too busy celebrating the forty-first anniversary of the return of Ayatollah Khomeini to Tehran and rigging local elections. By February 19, when Iran officially acknowledged the outbreak, fifty-two people had already died. Retrospective analysis suggests that by that point the virus was already circulating invisibly in France, Spain, London, New York City, and Latin America, notably in Ecuador.

On Thursday, February 20, the mayor of Daegu, South Korea's fourth biggest city, appealed to residents to stay at home. The Shincheonji Church of Jesus had been pinpointed as the epicenter of an outbreak. Likewise, the pilgrimage city of Qom in Iran called for its inhabitants to limit their movements. In Rome, the cabinet met on Saturday, February 22, in the offices of the national Civil Protection Agency. With Prime Minister Giuseppe Conte chairing the meeting, they resolved to place 50,000 people in eleven small municipalities in the Lodi region of Northern Italy under quarantine.[31] All public events were canceled, and police and military formed a cordon. A run began on supermarkets. The following day, the day that Xi hailed China's success in containing the outbreak, Milan wrapped up its fashion week with a catwalk show by Armani, livestreamed from behind closed doors.[32] What had previously been an exotic Chinese crisis was coming closer day by day.

On Monday, February 24, when the EU tried to stage-manage a press conference to celebrate the €129 million it was donating for African labs, the audience of journalists became impatient. Why were the Eurocrats talking about Africa and not South Korea or Iran, or, indeed, Italy? "The only people who are not sick are the Africans!" exclaimed one reporter. But the commission officials dug in. Covid wasn't a European story, they insisted. It was a "global story," a threat to developing countries with inadequate health systems. Only under insistent questioning would the commission admit that Covid might actually challenge Europe too.[33]

National governments were quicker to come to that conclusion. Or at least they were quicker to conclude that Italy had a problem. Switzerland and Austria announced they were tightening border controls. German health minister Jens Spahn acknowledged that the explosion of new cases in Italy made it increasingly impossible to trace the course of new infections in Germany. There had simply been too many vacationers. At London's Heathrow Airport, aircraft bound for Milan were turning around on the tarmac to off-load passengers who had got cold feet.[34]

As far as financial markets were concerned, it was on Monday, February 24, that Covid-19 ceased being principally an Asian story. The discrepancy between depressed bond yields and buoyant equity market valuations closed, to the downside. One market correspondent described the "odour of screeching brakes and hot tyres skidding to an abrupt stop."[35] Investors dumped Italian stocks. Shares in low-cost European airlines easyJet and Ryanair plummeted. When markets opened in New York later in the day, demand for the benchmark ten-year Treasury surged. It was a classic run to safety. The yield curve inverted—it was cheaper to borrow long term than short term. Investors were more worried about the immediate future than the long term, a classic foreboding of a recession.

For the first time, estimates began to circulate about the damage to be expected from an epidemic that was not confined to China but spread to the entire world. Even a back-of-the-envelope calculation suggested it could be huge.[36] The global tourism industry alone accounted for $9 trillion, across a vast array of countries.[37] In the last week of February, the FTSE All-World stock market index fell almost 13 percent. It was one of the worst weeks ever recorded in global stock markets. In the course of the disastrous dot-com crash of 2000, it had taken the Nasdaq two years to lose $4.6 trillion.[38] Twenty years later, markets sliced nearly $6 trillion off the value of global equities in a week.

The fall in share prices sent financial analysts frantically clawing through medical papers. How bad would it get? Who was to judge? After all, the gloom mongers who were crashing equity markets did not have medical degrees either.[39] Bankers made calls to epidemiologists. There was talk of the "McNamara fallacy," referring to the Vietnam-era methodology of judging success and failure by body count.[40]

It is a truism of globalese that risks do not respect borders. This was true in the banal sense that SARS-CoV-2 was a disease that could affect the vast majority of humanity. But as soon as the epidemic widened and gathered steam, stark differences in national responses became evident. The pandemic became an Olympics of national governance.

Japan's national government was not quick off the mark. Prime Minister Shinzo Abe had his mind focused on the Summer Olympics. Tokyo got lucky. Faced with a local outbreak, the governor of Hokkaido, acting without legal powers, ordered an immediate lockdown, containing the spread.[41]

It was South Korea that best illustrates what might have been possible with an early and decisive response. Koreans had painful memories of the MERS crisis in 2015, which claimed thirty-eight lives. Already on January 27, when Korea had only four confirmed coronavirus cases, the public health authorities convened an emergency meeting in a nondescript conference room in Seoul railway station. The government asked Korea's biotech firms to deliver not a cure or a vaccine, but a test.[42] With a test, they could track and trace the outbreak as it happened.

South Korea had no monopoly of testing technology. Germany, the UK, and the U.S. all had early starts. But due to its focus on influenza as a model for crisis management, the UK did not integrate testing into its Covid-19 response until weeks later. There was no point in testing for a disease that spread as fast as the flu. In the United States, the first set of CDC tests began to be shipped to a hundred key labs across the country on February 4. They turned out to be faulty.[43] It then took weeks to develop a new test. Meanwhile, the FDA refused to authorize alternatives. The regulators were concerned that the crisis might be exploited for profiteering. They did not want to unleash a "Wild West." But without an effective test, the American authorities were blind to the scale of the epidemic spreading on both coasts. Even in their worst-case scenarios they had never envisioned having to meet an epidemic without the capacity to test for it.[44]

For South Korea's biotech firms, the priority was not absolute reliability of the tests, but speed.[45] By February 4, the first test, by Kogene, was approved. A second was okayed on February 12. They were not foolproof, but they could be ramped up to scale. The significance of getting an early start was that from the moment that the epidemic hit with real force in mid-February, South Korea had the means to track it.

It was a race against time. From February 7 until the end of the month, South Korea's testing capacity surged from 3,000 to 20,000 tests per day. By the standards of the summer, those were small numbers. But they were sufficient to cover an epidemic in its early stages. And crucially the Koreans achieved a fast turnaround of results, within six to twenty-four hours. By February 20, anyone with symptoms was being tested regardless of travel history. All told, within seven weeks of January 27, South Korea tested well over 290,000 people and identified over 8,000 infections. The shutdown in Daegu cut movement in the city by 80 percent, and on February 23, schools across the country were closed. Students transitioned to remote learning on the world's best broadband network. The result was that South Korea achieved control of the epidemic at the same time as Beijing. The peak in infections came on February 29, days after that in China.

Had the rest of the world reacted to the challenge like South Korea, with rapid and intensive testing of the early outbreaks and selective social distancing measures, the history of 2020 might have looked very different. The West European country that came closest was Germany. Like South Korea, it had a large testing capacity. But given the huge circulation of disease around Europe by the end of February, there was little hope that a major epidemic could be avoided. Germany continued to track and trace. Elsewhere, the priority increasingly shifted to "flattening the curve," moderating the spread of the epidemic and protecting the medical services themselves.

In Italy, even that was a tall order. On February 25, realizing the scale of the epidemic in Northern Italy, Rome called on its European partners for help. But there was no concerted response. Denial died hard. The epicenter of the Italian pandemic in the northern regions of Lombardy prides itself on its work ethic. Milan does not shut down easily. On March 2 the famous duomo reopened for visitors.

Around Europe the attitude was increasingly one of *sauve qui peut*. On March 3, France moved to ban the export of the supply of personal protective equipment (PPE), triggering a European race to secure equipment. Germany declared that it would also restrict the export of PPE. With the two leading EU powers acting unilaterally, it was hard to coordinate a response. In Brussels, the EU leadership continued to be focused on other issues, notably the flare-up in the Syrian crisis. The last thing the EU needed was a repeat of the refugee crisis of 2015.[46] On March 3, Europe's top officials were in Greece and Bulgaria carrying out personal inspections of refugee camps. Their next stop was Ankara for talks with President Erdoğan. In Brussels by early March, the virus was circulating at speed.

Meanwhile, the American government was divided against itself. On February 25, San Francisco was the first American city to declare a state of emergency. That same day Dr. Nancy Messonnier, director of the CDC's National Center for Immunization and Respiratory Diseases, declared that a major outbreak in the United States was inevitable and might well lead to severe disruption of everyday life. She was immediately contradicted both by Alex Azar of the Department of Health and Human Services (HHS) and the president's economics guru and cheerleader Larry Kudlow, who opined: "We have contained this. I won't say airtight, but it's pretty close to airtight. . . . I don't think it's going to be an economic tragedy at all."[47]

The president himself took a determinedly bullish line. After the market sold off on Monday, February 24, his advice to investors was to "buy the dip." Two days later, frustrated with the gloomy messages coming out of the public health bureaucracy, he installed Vice President Mike Pence as head of the coronavirus task force. "We're going to be pretty soon at only five people," the president boasted. "That's a pretty good job we've done." As Stephen Moore, another of Trump's favorite economic advisors, remarked, the mood in the White House in early March was "borderline ecstatic . . . The economy was just steaming along, the stock market was firing on all cylinders and that jobs report was fantastic. It was almost too perfect."[48] All eyes were on the election on November 3. Son-in-law Jared Kushner was a vital gatekeeper. As far as he was concerned, anything that spooked the markets, whether it be testing too many people or placing bulk orders for ventilators, was something to be avoided.

When the leading financial officials of the G7 reconvened on March 3, there was a transatlantic divide. While Mark Carney in his last few days as governor of the Bank of England joined French finance minister Bruno Le Maire in expressing serious concern about the pandemic, Mnuchin and Kudlow for the Trump administration exuded bullish optimism.[49] Kudlow was talking up the wonders of Trump's formula of tax cuts and deregulation. He wanted America to lead, but not on the pandemic. Kudlow's priority was economic growth. His question was why "what we used to call the western alliance" was not "delivering the goods." More consequential was the position of the Fed. At the G7 meeting, Jerome Powell gave no indication of his next move, but, by the end of the day, he had approved an emergency cut to interest rates. The Fed had not seen fit to inform any of its partners. But it was now clear that the markets needed help and it was up to the Fed to make the first move. In so doing, it opened the space for other central banks to follow. The question was how far conventional monetary policy could really help. As Katie Martin of the *Financial Times* remarked: "Anyone who can clearly articulate how easier [central bank] policy can fix an economic pullback based on deaths, grounded flights, closed factories and ghost cities is very welcome to get in touch."[50] The new thing to get used to, in the words of one investor, was that "who is in charge here is the WHO, not the central banks."[51]

In a backhanded recognition of that fact, on Friday, March 6, Trump and his entourage visited the CDC to rally the troops. It was a vintage Trump performance. He sparred with the media, bragged about his high ratings on Fox and the recent stock market highs, and attacked the Democratic governor of Washington State, who was struggling to contain one of America's worst early outbreaks. Trump then went on to admit that he had not known how many people died every year of the flu. He was impressed. Perhaps to reassure the public, he called to mind his "super genius" uncle, who had been a professor at MIT. Trump suspected that he might have inherited his natural scientific ability. Turning to the actual crisis, he promised "four million testing kits available within a week." The tests were "beautiful." "Anybody that needs a test gets a test." In fact, America's entire test system was in disarray. But this did not stop Trump from declaring that South Korea was calling on America for help. "They have a lot of people that are infected; we don't. All I say is, 'Be calm.' Everyone is relying on us. The world is relying on us."[52] It was reminiscent not so much of Mikhail Gorbachev responding to Chernobyl as of Saddam Hussein in the face of Shock and Awe.

Trump's delusional state was no doubt special, but he was not alone. In Mexico, populist president AMLO took a no-less-blasé attitude. In 2009 he had campaigned against the swine fever lockdown under President Felipe Calderón.[53] Eleven years later he called on Mexicans to remain calm and remember that Covid was not as bad as the flu.[54] In Brazil, President Bolsonaro's approach was characteristically macho. It was a matter of toughing it out. In Tanzania, President John Magufuli promised that divine assistance would put paid to the disease.[55]

It is easy to mock such reactions, but the idea that scientific expertise would provide a solid guide to action was itself illusory.[56] On March 3, Downing Street convened a press conference at which Prime Minister Johnson appeared alongside his chief medical advisor Chris Whitty. The meeting would later become notorious for Johnson's boast that he had been touring hospitals and shaking hands. Within the month he would be fighting for his life in intensive care. But Whitty's performance is no less telling. On the one hand, he laid out the worst-case scenario, which "estimated 80% of people could become infected, and 1 percent of those could die." But rather than stressing the catastrophic implications of those numbers, Whitty chose to play them down, insisting that they were merely hypotheticals. It was that admission that opened the door for Johnson to dispense bromides about Britain's excellent health service and testing facilities.[57] Behind closed doors, British scientific advisors dismissed urgent talk of Chinese-style lockdowns. It was important not to go too early. There would be fatigue and noncompliance.

This was, as it turned out, precisely the wrong conclusion to draw from the Chinese experience. The lesson should have been that the sooner and more comprehensively you acted, the shorter the period of shutdown would have to be and the easier it would be to recover. Being willing to sacrifice normality was actually the best way to preserve normality. That profoundly counterintuitive leap was not easy to make. The promptness with which South Korea responded was truly the exception. Judged by the standards of any other crisis, the reaction of the governments of the world can hardly be found wanting. It took no more than a few weeks between recognizing the problem and taking radical action. That was fine for most situations. It was disastrously inadequate when dealing with a fast-moving pandemic.

In the first week of March, it became clear that the outbreak in Lombardy was beyond control.[58] Over the weekend of March 7–8, as rumors spread that Rome was about to order a general shutdown, hundreds of thousands of people made last-minute dashes across the country to ensure that they were confined in the right place. China's crisis had been easy for Westerners to exoticize. Italy was different. Millions of people had visited the country during the February vacation. If the epidemic was out of control in Italy, then it was running rampant across Europe and by extension the United States and Latin America. If Italy was shutting down, it was no longer inconceivable that they would have to as well.

Chapter 4

MARCH: GLOBAL LOCKDOWN

The common denominator of the global economy is energy. With an annual turnover of around 35 billion barrels, the oil market is larger than all the other commodity markets put together.[1] Its daily price fluctuations affect entire national economies. On the supply side, the two largest producers, Saudi Arabia, at the head of OPEC, and Russia, perform a delicate dance around each other, balancing the need for revenue against the risk of glutting the market. On the demand side, since the start of the millennium, China's surging economic growth has been the main driver. In February 2020 the shutdown in China rocked the market. The International Energy Agency warned of the first quarterly contraction in the demand for oil since the financial crisis of 2008.[2] The spread of the disease to Europe and Asia compounded the stress. Faced with falling demand, the Saudis wanted to stabilize prices by cutting production. Russia preferred a price war. That, they hoped, would throttle the upstart American producers of shale oil. On Friday, March 6, it became clear that they would not be able to agree.[3] Riyadh announced that it would be ramping up production to flood the market. That would help consumers, but the hurt inflicted on the high-cost producers would be devastating. Within five weeks, oil prices would not just fall. For a terrifying twenty-four-hour period, as surplus stocks of crude piled up in storage facilities across the United States, the price for futures contracts would plunge into negative territory.

For the wider economy, the chaos in the oil market sent a clear signal. There was a global recession ahead. As the news of the Saudi-Russian breakdown sank in, on the morning of March 9, first Asian and then European markets began selling off.[4] When Wall Street opened, it followed suit. After the turmoil of the last week of February, the people who manage the world's money were now facing the full force of the crisis to come.

President Trump had spent a pleasant weekend at his Florida resort, partying with his son and his son's girlfriend and hobnobbing with his soulmate President Jair Bolsonaro. Within days, two dozen of Bolsonaro's entourage would test positive. But on Monday, March 9, it was not the virus but the markets that were preoccupying Trump. The S&P 500 had been his good news story. Now it was in free fall. Fake news was to blame. As he furiously tweeted: "So last year 37,000 Americans died from the common Flu. It averages between 27,000 and 70,000 per year. Nothing is shut down, life & the economy go on. At this moment there are 546 confirmed cases of CoronaVirus, with 22 deaths. Think about that!"[5]

The World Health Organization did. Community transmission was now confirmed in Europe and some parts of Asia. The virus had been reported in 110 countries. On March 11, WHO officially declared a pandemic.[6]

What was to be done? South Korea had achieved suppression through mass testing and quarantine. But the viability of that strategy depended on catching and tracking the epidemic in its early stages. Most of Europe and the United States were well past that point. Their choices were now stark and getting more so by the day. If the virus was to be suppressed, it would involve massive social distancing and a total interruption of ordinary life. The timeline was now counted in days and hours.

The pandemic was above all a threat to cities. On March 9 in New York City, a group of eighteen academics and community leaders lobbied Mayor Bill de Blasio and his health commissioner, calling for them to consider closing schools and curtailing business hours.[7] In the city's health department, there was talk of a mutiny if action was not forthcoming.

By the second week of March, New York had become a global hub of infection. With New York's vast number of daily arrivals from Asia and Europe, this was predictable. To have prevented it would have required a comprehensive program of travel limitations, testing, and quarantine. That required a national policy decision. But the Trump administration, like other Western governments, proceeded in an ad hoc fashion. China vigorously protested the exclusion of its nationals. Facing a mounting clamor for action, on the evening of March 11, Trump went on television to announce that he was closing the United States to travelers from continental Europe.[8] He did not alert the European governments ahead of time. He did not make clear how returning American nationals would be treated. And he made a point of exempting the UK and Ireland. While crowds of desperate Americans gathered at Charles de Gaulle Airport, France's outspoken finance minister Bruno Le Maire denounced Trump's actions as an "aberration."[9] "There is no longer any coordination between Europe and the USA." Le Maire went on to draw wider conclusions: "Europe must defend itself alone, protect itself alone, and be able to confront things alone, to come together as a sovereign bloc to defend its economic interests because nobody—including the U.S. evidently—will help us."[10] Corona was becoming a polycrisis.

Though the UK had been exempted from Trump's travel ban, there was little cause for glee there. On March 12, Prime Minister Johnson adopted an unfamiliar tone of seriousness. Gone was the braggadocio about superheroes and handshakes. "I must level with you, level with the British public—more families, many more families are going to lose loved ones before their time."[11] Johnson asked Britons to prepare themselves for tough measures that might be necessary "at some point in the next few weeks." But what he did *not* do was to order a shutdown. Inside the British government, a battle was waging about the appropriate response. After all, if the virus was highly infectious and there was no vaccine, then in due course everyone would get sick. In the vast majority of cases the symptoms were mild. Did it not make sense to allow the virus to pass through the population while protecting the most vulnerable?[12] Rather than complete suppression, should the aim be "herd immunity"?

Others simply continued business as usual. In Spain on Sunday, March 8, the government did not think to halt the giant march to celebrate International Women's Day.[13] The following week, the British authorities allowed 3,000 Spanish fans of Atlético Madrid to travel to Anfield to watch their team play Liverpool in a Champions League match.[14] It took courage to do as the Irish government did on March 9 and cancel St. Patrick's Day and begin the process of shutting down pubs.[15] In Berlin, meanwhile, Angela Merkel's government busied itself with coordinating measures across sixteen state governments and 400 regional health offices. On March 12, French president Emmanuel Macron announced school closures and banned gatherings of more than 1,000 people.

Though the response to Covid was triggered in an ad hoc fashion, country by country, city by city, one organization and business at a time, what began to build, following the market panic of March 9 and the WHO announcement on March 11, was global momentum. Individual, local shutdown decisions were beginning to cumulate into a general expectation of government-mandated lockdowns. As one group of behavioral scientists advised the UK government: "trust will be lost in sections of the public if measures witnessed in other countries are not adopted in the UK." Any deviation from global norms would need to be "well explained."[16] Individuals and organizations were no longer waiting for instructions. After the Swiss, Italian, Spanish, and French soccer leagues shut down, so too did the English Premier League, the highest-profile soccer league. The banner headline of the *Daily Mirror* tabloid on March 13 summed up the question being posed not just in the UK: "Is It Enough?"[17] That same day, President Trump was forced to declare a national emergency.

Decision makers in every large organization and institution around the world were forced to act. On March 13, Mexico's giant UNAM university complex announced that it was shifting its 350,000 students to online learning. The same day, Los Angeles closed its public schools. In a school district where over a million children from low-income households rely on school for free meals, this was not an easy decision.[18] On March 14, discussions began in California that would lead to a shutdown in San Francisco on March 16 and statewide closures on March 19. In Russia, the Ministry of Education was on the same timeline. It asked schools to begin preparing distance learning on March 14 and ordered school closures from March 18. Meanwhile, in New York, Mayor de Blasio, who had been slow to accept the brutal logic of the pandemic, was now urging Andrew Cuomo, the governor of New York State, to act.[19] It would not be until March 20 that he instructed New Yorkers to stay at home.

France began with closures of schools on March 12 and of bars and restaurants on March 14, and a full lockdown was declared on March 16.[20] That evening in a televised address watched by a record 35 million French citizens, President Macron called for a "general mobilization." Six times he hammered home the phrase *nous sommes en guerre*—we are at war.[21] Apparently, the inspiration was the orations of the great World War I leader Georges Clemenceau. A hundred thousand police who had previously been involved in the campaign to contain suicide bombers and the Gilets Jaunes protesters were redeployed to impose the new rules. Permits were required to leave one's home. Those without permits would be fined. The measures applied not just to mainland France, but to all its overseas territories including those as far away as the Caribbean.

Closures were by no means limited to the more advanced economies. The vulnerability of health systems in middle-income and low-income countries was greater, and their exposure through the flow of migrant workers, every bit as bad. In the Philippines, President Duterte announced a partial lockdown for the Manila region on March 12, to come into effect on March 15.[22] Amid scenes of chaos, it was extended the next day to the entire Luzon island complex, with a population of 57 million people. Indonesia, the fourth largest country in the world, adopted national rules on social distancing on March 15; school closures began over the following weeks.[23] Over the weekend of March 14–15, Pakistan, with a school-age population of over 50 million young people, announced school closures. Despite fears of an outbreak triggered by pilgrims returning from Iran, Pakistan's prime minister Imran Khan refused to order a national lockdown, but regional governors imposed such stringent limitations that the cities of Lahore and Karachi were in danger of running out of food.[24] Egypt closed its schools and universities on March 15. It shut down air travel on

March 19 and suspended mosque services on March 21.[25] In mid-March, Ethiopia suspended regular schooling.[26]

As country after country followed the global trend, the shutdown became what French president Macron would call a "profound anthropological shock."[27] It certainly felt that way in households around the globe. By mid-April the UN reported that close to 1.6 billion young people were furloughed from classroom education.[28]

It was not the children who were principally at risk, or even their teachers. As Italy's experience had revealed, the critical issue was the concentration of infections among the more vulnerable older population and the pressure that those cases would impose on health care systems—in particular, intensive care units. The critical variable was R-naught (R_0), the reproduction number, which described how rapidly the disease was spreading. If it rose significantly above 1, it produced a runaway epidemic, which no health care system could realistically contain. Differences in ICU capacity would be swamped by the exponential growth in the disease.

When the epidemiological models were updated with the latest numbers from Italy, the results were ominous. Particularly devastating were the results published by an epidemiological group of Imperial College London on March 16. An unmitigated epidemic, the team predicted, would exceed the UK's ICU capacity by a factor of 30 or more. Overload of the hospital system on that scale would result in the death of 510,000 people in the UK and 2.2 million in the United States. Even an effective mitigation policy that resulted in half that number of deaths would lead to the collapse of both the UK and the U.S. health care systems. Though it was late in the day, the only option was to aim for full-scale suppression, to reduce the caseload as far as possible. To that end, they recommended "social distancing of the entire population, case isolation, household quarantine, and school and university closure" for a period of at least five months. They made that recommendation despite the fact that it "is not at all certain that suppression will succeed long term; no public health intervention with such disruptive effects on society has been previously attempted for such a long duration of time. How populations and societies will respond remains unclear."[29]

Faced with such alarming alternatives, the only country to opt out of the general push toward ever more draconian shutdown was Sweden, the only country with strict limits on ministerial-political government.[30] Public health management there is reserved for a specialized agency that issues recommendations to the government. Sweden's Public Health Agency, the Folkhälsomyndigheten, recommended some restrictions on travel, social distancing by the elderly, and the closure only of middle and high schools. But no general lockdown and no mask mandate. There is nothing to suggest that it took the decision principally for economic reasons. It just didn't see the public health logic. The critical question was whether Sweden's medical system would stand up to the load imposed on it. No one else was willing to take the gamble.

The Imperial College report was principally directed at the UK and the United States, and it had its intended effect. In Downing Street, the report shifted reluctant decision makers toward a full shutdown.[31] The mantra became "Protect the NHS." This was taken so far that sick and vulnerable patients were off-loaded from overstretched hospitals into ill-equipped care homes, where the death rate then surged.[32] On the other side of the Atlantic, the same Imperial College report seems to have effected a mood change in the White House. As Edward Luce of the *Financial Times* put it, "something snapped in Trump's mind. Citing a call with one of his sons, Trump said on March 16: 'It's bad. It's bad . . . They think August [before the disease peaks]. Could be July. Could be longer than that.'"[33] That day the White House for the first time issued national social distancing guidelines and recommended that Americans should not gather in groups larger than ten persons. The new slogan from the White House was "15 Days to Slow the Spread."[34]

Pressure to shut down was now coming from all sides.[35] On the morning of March 16, workers at the Mercedes-Benz factory in Vitoria in Basque Country went on strike to force the plant to close. Tests had confirmed one positive case. Twenty-three workers were in quarantine. Across Spain, Nissan, Volkswagen SEAT, Renault, and Michelin had already closed their factories. In Italy too, workers at Fiat Chrysler plants had launched wildcat strikes to insist that their employers follow a responsible public health policy. Under pressure from Confindustria, the powerful national business association, the Italian government had recommended closure for "nonessential" plants but left it up to firms to regulate themselves. This triggered an indignant response from labor unions. "Factory workers are not citizens for 24 hours minus eight. It is not tolerable that they see their everyday life protected and guaranteed by many rules, but once they have passed the factory gates they are in a no-man's-land," declared Francesca Re David of the metalworkers union, FIOM-CGIL.[36]

On the other side of the Atlantic, on March 18, under pressure from the United Auto Workers, the big three Detroit car producers—GM, Ford, and Fiat Chrysler—agreed a more or less complete nationwide shutdown. The one holdout, predictably enough, was Tesla. Whereas in China, Elon Musk had complied with official instructions, in California he decided to make a stand. He announced that concern about Covid was exaggerated. "My frank opinion remains that the harm from the coronavirus panic far exceeds that of the virus itself," he told his staff.[37] A day later, he too folded.

It was typical of Musk's belligerent egotism that he should have turned the question of the shutdown into a matter of his personal judgment. In fact, the official shutdown was ratifying decisions not just on the part of the workforce but on the part of consumers as well. Shoppers were no longer buying, not cars or anything else for which they normally left their homes. By mid-March, the fashion chain Primark with stores across Europe had announced sweeping shutdowns.[38] So too did Sweden's H&M, Nike, Under Armour, Lululemon, and fashion groups Urban Outfitters and Abercrombie & Fitch. Neither their staff nor their customers wanted to be anywhere near the stores. The collapse in demand spread down the supply chain to garment factories in Bangladesh, India, Sri Lanka, Vietnam, and China.[39] Without workers, without suppliers, without markets, with unsold merchandise piling up in stock, shutting down was not a matter of overprotective public health policy—it was the only thing that made business sense.

Government-mandated lockdowns served to generalize and support private decisions. This happened at national, regional, and city level. In Brazil, the governor of Rio de Janeiro, who himself tested positive, declared a state of emergency on March 18, shutting the famous Christ the Redeemer statue and emptying the beaches.[40] He did not want "the blood of thousands of people on his hands." Mandating closures was one thing. Enforcing compliance was something else. In that regard the governor got help from an unexpected corner. Comando Vermelho, or Red Command, the notorious gang that controls Rio's City of God favela, came out in favor of the lockdown, threatening anyone violating the curfew with severe punishment.[41] Meanwhile, numerous indigenous communities in Amazonia, aware of their historic susceptibility to diseases brought in by outsiders, blocked roads and withdrew deeper into the forest.

On March 18, at the White House, President Trump had a new message. The relentlessly boastful tone was the same, but gone was the flippancy of February. America was at war. "To this day, nobody has seen anything like what they were able to do during World War II," Trump told reporters. "And now it's our time. We must sacrifice together because we are all in this together and we'll come through together." In a show of force, he invoked a Cold War–era law—the Defense Production Act—granting him broad authority to direct manufacturers to make the equipment needed in a crisis. But he said he would resort to the law only in a "worst-case scenario."[42]

If the predictions for the UK and the U.S. were bad, in India they were apocalyptic. By the third week of March, fewer than 600 cases had been confirmed by India's limited testing capacity. But according to the models, if no countermeasures were adopted, "300 million to 500 million Indians could be infected by the end of July and 30 million to 50 million could have severe disease."[43] India had a huge population of poor city dwellers living in crowded conditions with poor sanitation. It had just 0.7 hospital beds per 1,000 persons, as against 2.9 in the United States and 3.4 in Italy. For a population of 1.3 billion, there were only 50,000 ventilators.[44]

India had shut its borders early. The case count was still low. But no one trusted that the testing was adequate. The question was: when would Delhi act? Prime Minister Narendra Modi was nothing if not unpredictable. When it was announced that he intended to address the nation at eight p.m. on March 19, a ripple of anxiety swept the country. The last time he had made an eight p.m. speech, in 2016, he had, at a stroke, taken 86 percent of all currency notes out of circulation and tumbled the economy into a steep downturn. On March 19, 2020, Modi was more sober. He asked Indians to observe a one-day "people's curfew"—Janata Curfew—on Sunday, March 22, to be followed by a national round of applause for those working in frontline services—doctors, nurses, security personnel.[45] On the appointed day, Indians in their hundreds of millions followed the call and remained indoors. Then, in the evening, they poured into the streets to celebrate. Nationalist cheerleaders hailed Modi's "masterstroke." On social media, enthusiasts for "energy medicine" promised that the virus would be "vaporized by the reverberations of mass clapping."[46]

The following day, the UK finally announced a general lockdown, as did Cuba, Nigeria, and Zimbabwe. Bowing to the inevitable, Tokyo postponed the Olympics. On March 24, with every state and union territory in India having announced closures and lockdowns, Modi made another eight p.m. TV appearance, and this time he delivered the much-feared surprise. India was indeed shutting down.[47] Not one city or a single province, but the entire country, and it was doing so with three hours' warning. Nigh on 1.4 billion people suddenly faced the prospect of being confined to their homes, many in makeshift circumstances with no means of support.

India was followed by Bangladesh on March 26 and by South Africa on March 27. The entire world was now shut down. It was like nothing ever before experienced. Piece by piece, public life across the planet had stopped. The International Labour Organization estimated that as of early April 2020, 81 percent of the world's workforce were under one or other type of restriction.[48]

It was staggering and, for many, impossible to accept. Around the world, opposition expressed itself in national idiolects. In France and Italy, the radical left railed against the normalization of the "state of exception" and the spectacular accretion of power it conferred on the government.[49] Perversely, Prime Minister Boris Johnson agreed: "We're taking away the ancient, inalienable right of free-born people of the United Kingdom to go to the pub. And I can understand how people feel about that . . . I know how difficult this is, how it seems to go against the freedom-loving instincts of the British people."[50]

In Brazil, President Bolsonaro, a skeptic from the start, continued to rant against lockdown measures. His entourage indulged themselves in outbursts of Sinophobia, attacking the "Communavirus" and mocking Chinese accents.[51] Bypassing Brazil's health ministry, in the last week of March, the presidential office launched an all-out attack on regional shutdown measures.[52] In the streets, Bolsonaro's supporters in raucous caravans campaigned for a reopening.[53] Only a judicial intervention stopped the president from throwing his full weight behind a publicity campaign under the slogan #Brazilcannotstop. "For the neighborhood salesmen, for the shop owners in city centers, for domestic employees, for millions of Brazilians, Brazil cannot stop," the ad said. Would there be casualties? Yes. As Bolsonaro remarked with a shrug: "Sorry, some will die."

On the familiar left-right political spectrum, President AMLO of Mexico is the antithesis of Bolsonaro, but even after the global pandemic was officially declared, he showed a similar disregard for the disease. Early cases were largely imported by wealthy Mexicans holidaying in America. This gave succor to the idea that the Mexican masses enjoyed immunity.[54] AMLO urged audiences across the country not to be disturbed by exaggerated media reports.[55] He accused conservatives of delighting in the spread of the epidemic and exaggerating failures of policy so as to destabilize his government.[56] While establishment media spluttered with indignation, AMLO himself flouted scientific advice, refusing to wear a mask or to comply with social distancing. As late as March 29 he traveled to Sinaloa, the stomping ground of the notorious Guzmán ganglords, where he was filmed greeting the mother of "El Chapo" while surrounded by a tightly packed group of backslapping local officials and clan henchmen.[57]

Across the border in the United States, a broad swath of Republican opinion agreed with him. Inside reports from the White House confirmed that Trump was "inundated with calls from business leaders, wealthy supporters and conservative allies urging him to get Americans back to work and stave off further calamity, even if doing so carries health risks."[58] On Monday, March 23, less than a week after he had struck the pose of a wartime president, Trump said at a press conference: "Our country wasn't built to be shut down." The next day he followed up with the familiar line that "this cure is worse than the problem." Adding, for good measure, "in my opinion, more people are going to die if we allow this to continue." To the horror of his medical advisor, he announced that he wanted to see America back at work by Easter, April 12. Once again Trump was returning to the flu analogy. As he remarked: "We lose thousands and thousands of people a year to the flu, we don't turn the country off every year."[59] Since the epidemic in the United States was largely confined to the Democratic states of the eastern seaboard, Trump, like Xi a month before, advocated a progressive relaxation of controls, county by county. The difference was that America at that point did not have control of the virus anywhere in the country; furthermore there was no means of controlling the movement of people or of testing for the incidence of the disease.

Johnson, Bolsonaro, AMLO, and Trump each dressed their opposition to lockdowns in their particular political idiom. But on its face, their attitude was not difficult to understand. After all, the economic impact of the lockdowns was disastrous. China and South Korea made it look easy. After achieving effective suppression, they were on the road back to normality. By March, those were not the options available in Europe, the United States, or Latin America. Demanding a rapid return to economic normalcy now meant accepting the risk of a mass death.

In the last week of March, America's leading public health experts mounted an urgent campaign to maintain the lockdown. Almost a thousand people were dying every day in New York City, so Trump's talk of easing the lockdown was dangerously premature. America lacked the test and tracing capacity that would make it safe to reopen less affected areas. In debates at the White House, Deborah Birx and Anthony S. Fauci led the team defending the shutdown. Their main weapons were the predictive models that showed that without an attempt at suppression, between 1.6 million and 2.2 million Americans might die. A continued lockdown could bring that figure down to between 100,000 and 240,000 fatalities.[60] These were hypotheticals, but they were backed by the best available science, and the drama of their predictions could not be denied.

As Fauci later described their confrontation with President Trump: "Dr. Debbie Birx and I went into the Oval Office and leaned over the desk and said, 'Here are the data, take a look.' . . . We showed him the data. He looked at the data. He got it right away." The data were impressive, but so too were the TV images of corpses in bags being carried out of Elmhurst Hospital in Queens, New York, the president's childhood home. "This is essentially in my community, in Queens, Queens, New York," Trump said. "I've seen things that I've never seen before."[61] As Fauci remembered it, the president just shook his head and conceded, "I guess we got to do it."

Queens was at the epicenter of the crisis in the United States. It was one of the worst points of infection in the world. Trump could have waved it aside as an exception. Instead, moved by the TV images and imagining, by way of the data, a similar disaster spreading to the rest of the country, Trump abandoned his tough talk. On March 29, he announced the extension of the lockdown through April. "I want every American to be prepared for the hard days that lie ahead," he declared. The virus was a "great national trial unlike any we have ever faced before." To minimize the number of people infected would require the "full absolute measure of our collective strength, love and devotion. . . . It's a matter of life and death, frankly . . . It's a matter of life and death."[62] Try as one might—and Trump would explore every option—in the spring of 2020 there was no escaping the force of the coronavirus shock.

Part II

A GLOBAL CRISIS
LIKE NO OTHER

Chapter 5

FREE FALL

The decisions taken by the Italian national government in Rome over the weekend of March 7–8 set in motion an avalanche of decision-making by national governments around the world. That was unprecedented. Even more so was the adjustment in the way of life of literally billions of people as they responded to the virus, or rather our media-filtered understanding of it. The dramas in hospitals captured on smartphone cameras, the dark projections conjured by doctors, scientists, and epidemiologists were the driving force. As the world's media relayed the news, first from China and then from Europe, the United States, and Latin America, it sparked a dramatic, multifaceted response. Organizations of all kinds, businesses, consumers, families, schools, workers, billions of individuals all over the world began reacting. This didn't take place all at once. Sometimes governments, whether at the national or local level, were ahead of the game. Often they were not. Quite often society—families, businesses, organizations—moved to defend itself in the face of government inaction. The point is that it was, everywhere, a complex and collective movement. Even when governments did take the initiative, the efficacy of the measures put in place depended in large part on the active compliance of citizens, businesses, and organizations, for whom government instructions served as a means to coordinate and rationalize their own responses.

We can read this self-protective behavior in the economic data. In

early March, weeks before the British government finally declared a national lockdown, household discretionary spending plunged, from £300
per week to £180.[1] The same sudden lurch can be seen in the United States.
There it was the stock market crash of March 9 that seems to have conveyed
the seriousness of the crisis even to the skeptics. The result was that the
consumer-led shutdown long preceded government-ordered lockdowns.
This was not universally the case. It depended on how sanguine the population was and how rapidly the government acted. In Spain, a full lockdown
was announced on March 14. On that same day, credit card spending
plunged.[2] The Indian lockdown ten days later was similarly abrupt.

Applying econometric techniques to cell phone data, the International
Monetary Fund (IMF) has compiled estimates of what share of the reduction in mobility—a measure of the degree of shutdown—can be accounted
for by government orders as opposed to voluntary social distancing. Its
conclusions are clear. For rich countries, self-activated social distancing
far outweighed government orders. Of the 19 percent reduction in mobility
that occurred in the ninety days after the first recorded infection, only just
over a third could be explained by relative lockdown stringency. The rest
was due to voluntary social distancing.[3]

To describe the reaction to the coronavirus as a moment of collective
agency, to call it a "shutdown" rather than a "lockdown," is not to deny the
costs or the restrictions involved. To say that governmental authority was
complementary to private action is not to say that its application was harmonious or that it lacked a repressive element. The costs were all too real.
So was the political conflict that followed.

In analyzing a shock, economists like to disentangle changes in supply
from changes in demand.[4] The distinction matters because different causes
require different remedies. If production, employment, and income contract because of a supply shock, then what is required to restore economic
activity is an adjustment in the way we produce, deliver, and consume goods
and services. This is what economists tend to call a "real" adjustment. If the
problem is inadequate demand, then the system of production and distri-

bution can remain as it is. What we need to do is to stimulate more spending by loosening budget constraints, for instance, through lower taxes, government spending, or easier credit.

The immediate impact of the coronavirus was to deliver a supply shock. Big negative supply shocks are rare. One example would be the shutdown of the Gulf Coast oil refinery complex in the face of a hurricane sweeping out of the Atlantic.[5] More common are positive shocks such as technological breakthroughs that enable us to do new things more cheaply. The pandemic was like technical progress in reverse. Take airline travel as an example. The problem in 2020 was not that we had become any less good at operating aircraft. What had become more difficult was operating safe flights. A seat in a crowded economy class cabin now came with the added risk of Covid. How great that risk was, was much debated, but there were simple ways to minimize it.[6] If you limited each plane to one family group and provided them with cocooned VIP transit through the airport, they could still travel safely. In other words, it was still safe to travel, if you did so as the wealthy do, wafting through the airport on the way to your private jet. Private jet travel did in fact continue throughout 2020 with relatively little interruption. It was just as exorbitantly expensive as ever. Similarly, the chartering of private yachts, villas, and islands held up well.[7] By contrast, if you wanted to ensure safety on a commercial flight, you had to buy not one but all the tickets on the plane and make sure the crew was tested. It was prohibitively expensive. Nor could you get around the problem by issuing stimulus vouchers for free private flights, to be paid from government coffers. If you flew only one family group at a time, there were simply not enough planes to maintain anything like the previous level of mobility. There would be decade-long waiting lists. This is the definition of a supply shock. No stimulus checks or additional air miles can address it.

The impact on the airline industry was savage. By April 2020, London Heathrow Airport's throughput of passengers had fallen 97 percent, to levels last seen in the 1950s. Worldwide, traffic fell 94 percent. Estimates in the summer of 2020 put the industry's expected losses for 2020 at $84.3 billion worldwide.[8] Ten million jobs were directly at risk.[9]

An epidemic was an unusual supply shock because it acted not through the economic variables that we normally focus on—technologies, or endowments with income or wealth. Instead, it acted on our bodies. It exposed the individual and collective body of humanity as the common denominator of social and economic life.[10] Through our bodies, it affected us comprehensively, entangling the worlds of work and family life, production and reproduction.

If children went to school, they were at risk of becoming carriers of the disease. If children stayed at home, that disrupted the childcare arrangements of hundreds of millions of working families. As is evident, for instance, from the differential publication rates of male and female academics during the crisis, the extra burden of care was shouldered overwhelmingly by women.[11] If families relied on intergenerational networks or communities to support their children, if the spaces of home and work were blurred, if home was a relative category—in informal shantytowns, slums, and townships with shared water supply, bathrooms, kitchens, or washing facilities—the dilemmas were even more acute.

In a labor market hierarchy that, in any case, rewards abstract, disembodied labor, the coronavirus crisis massively compounded existing inequalities. If you had the capacity to extract yourself, you were okay. You could work remotely. You could shop remotely. You could travel in your mind to remote destinations. You could even enjoy remote intimacies of various kinds. While sex work was banned and licensed prostitutes in countries like Germany and the Netherlands claimed furlough support, in one surreal moment the City of New York recommended to its denizens that they limit themselves to masturbation for the duration of the pandemic.[12] As wags had it, suitably stimulating material was provided by the manly performance of Governor Cuomo at his daily televised crisis briefings.

All of this abstraction was easier if you had a comfortable place to which to retreat with a good internet connection and an efficient, well-stocked delivery service. Worldwide, when the crisis hit, there were more than 1.1 billion households and businesses lucky enough to have a fixed broadband connection, more than twice the number in 2010.[13] Thanks to this infrastructure, which barely existed twenty years earlier, much Western office work could continue virtually without interruption. These amenities, however, were not universal, even in rich countries. In the UK, the crisis exposed the fact that 9 percent of children did not have a computer, laptop, or tablet at home.[14] According to UNICEF, more than two-thirds of children worldwide were without access to home internet connections—830 million young people.[15]

In India, the IT and outsourcing industry struggled to adjust. Employees often lacked home internet connections, and tight security rules demanded by Western clients limited remote working. High-end software developers set up secure connections for their staff. The business process outsourcing (BPO) industry with its 1.3 million workers resorted to arguing that their operations belonged to the essential financial service industry and were thus exempt from the lockdown.[16] Western clients, facing an avalanche of complaints about long wait times, were only too happy to endorse the claim.

The possibility of leapfrogging into a new mode of remote living depended not just on technology and infrastructure, but also on hands-on manual labor. The social hierarchy made itself glaringly apparent. Whereas 75 percent of employees earning $200,000 or more in the United States were able to telework, for those earning less than $25,000, the share was as little as 11 percent. Amazon's deliveries became a de facto public service. To meet demand, between January and October 2020, Amazon added 427,300 employees. At the peak of the crisis, it was hiring at the rate of 2,800 new workers per day. By the end of the year, its global workforce would reach 1.2 million, twice what it had been a year earlier. The parcel delivery services of FedEx, UPS, and DHL all struggled to keep up with the huge surge in demand. Safety requirements were stretched to the limit and beyond.[17]

The threat of contagion ramified across the media and services industries. Next to a crowded airplane, a movie theater is a well-nigh ideal place to catch corona.[18] In 2020, China had been on track to overtake the United States as the largest box office worldwide. Instead, on January 23, it shut all 72,000 of its screens. On February 16, MGM announced that it was canceling the premiere in China of the new James Bond movie, *No Time to Die*, a film still unseen a year later. The title turned out to be all too apt. It was the first of many. Between April and June, not a single Hollywood film had a release. In India, a million people depend for their living on Bollywood. In a normal year they turn out 1,800 films per annum in the twenty-eight major languages of the subcontinent. All production and releases stopped in mid-March. A relief fund was set up to support the paparazzi, whose snaps of stars on the way to the gym or the airport normally feed the Bollywood publicity machine. When production resumed, older actors stayed at home and there were none of the crowd scenes and lingering romantic sequences for which Indian cinema is famous. When China attempted a token reopening on March 22, no one came. A week later the screens shut for a second time. In the words of Chairman Xi: "If you want to see movies, just go watch them online!"[19]

It is tempting to think of shopping; travel; visits to hairdressers, dentists, and doctors; and attendance at gyms or cinemas as ephemeral parts of the economy. Normally, it is construction and manufacturing that dominate the narrative of the business cycle. We track variables like South Korean chip exports or orders for giant American big-rig trucks. Dramatic as their fluctuations may be, such highly cyclical industrial sectors make up a small part of most modern economies. The service sector is far larger, both in terms of employment and value added. In the spring of 2020, the largest single contributor to the precipitous fall in U.S. gross domestic product (GDP) was the closure of the offices of doctors and dentists. More Americans lost jobs in health care and social assistance alone than in all of manufacturing.[20]

Everyday commerce in every city in the world was affected. For the shopkeepers, street vendors, and bus touts who crowd the streets of Lagos, Nigeria's 20-million-strong commercial capital, April 2020 was a "month of hunger."[21] Cash was so short even improvised 26-cent face masks were out of reach.[22] In the vacuum created by the lockdown, panicky rumors spread. Gangs led by the notorious "One Million Boys" distributed menacing flyers announcing that they would soon begin organized looting. Neighborhoods formed vigilantes to protect themselves against attacks, which for the most part never came.[23]

For anyone who ventured out, it was the emptiness that was impressive. Shopping malls that for a long time had in any event been living on the edge of commercial extinction tottered precariously. In the United States, a clutch of historic retailers declared bankruptcy.[24] JCPenney announced it would close 242 stores. Neiman Marcus, J.Crew, and Brooks Brothers all filed for bankruptcy protection. Brooks Brothers had been a staple of American business attire since 1818. In a world of Zoom meetings, there was not much call for suits.[25] In Germany, department store chain Galeria Karstadt Kaufhof announced a wave of closures, with thousands of job losses. Tati, the emblematic discount retailer in the Barbès neighborhood of northern Paris, a pillar of affordable retailing since the 1940s, closed down in July.[26] Gibert Jeune, one of the legendary bookshops of Paris, began closure negotiations with its unionized workforce.[27] In Britain, Laura Ashley, a fashion chain synonymous with the eighties chic of Princess Diana, tumbled into administration.[28] Among those that went under were the department store Debenhams and fast fashion pioneer Topshop, putting 25,000 jobs at risk.[29] Clothing and sandwich stalwart Marks & Spencer survived, but its debt was downgraded to junk and 8,000 workers lost their jobs.

Because it was a crisis of the service sector, the coronavirus recession was gendered in its impact. It was a "shecession."[30] This was bitterly ironic. The second half of 2019 was the first time outside a major recession in which women outnumbered men in paid employment in the United States.[31] A year later, 2020 was the first recession in which women's job losses and unemployment outnumbered men's.[32] As the mainstays of manual service labor, Latina women suffered most. Their unemployment rate soared above 20 percent. In Europe too, women workers in the bottom quintile of the income distribution suffered the largest loss of employment.[33] Mass closure of childcare facilities compounded the difficulties facing parents, and the brunt was borne by women. By the end of the summer, over a million working women had dropped out of paid employment in the United States to care for family members.[34]

If the first-order effect of the pandemic was to reduce our ability to safely supply goods and that put the livelihoods of hundreds of millions of people in jeopardy, the second-order effect came from the demand side. Insecurity slashed consumption and investment. Collapsing demand bred further unemployment. The idiosyncratic Covid shock thus morphed into a more familiar demand-driven recession that radiated out in every direction all over the world.

Return once more to the tourism and travel sector. If Western tourists would no longer fly, the entire global tourism industry was at risk. The World Travel and Tourism Council warned that 75 million jobs were on the line. Lost revenue might run to US$2.1 trillion.[35] Those numbers are more plausible when one considers that travel and tourism together are reckoned to account directly for 3.3 percent of global GDP.[36] Even a niche sector such as wildlife tourism in 2018 had generated US$120 billion in value added, supporting 9.1 million jobs directly across the world.[37]

In the spring of 2020, the Thai city of Lopburi found itself overrun by packs of monkeys. Normally fed by tourists, they were now fighting one another for whatever food they might find.[38] There was concern over the welfare of 3,000 elephants held in captivity in Thailand.[39] In East Africa and South Africa, the safari business had been booming, bringing in $12.4 billion per annum. The year had started well. In February the parks, lodges, and open-topped Land Cruisers were full up. Then suddenly in March the cancellations started. By April, business had stopped dead. Without guides and visitors, the parks were abandoned, prey to poachers. To prevent the worst, three major game parks in South Africa dehorned their populations of rhinos as a preventative measure, "hoping that it would make them less attractive targets for poachers." Meanwhile, tourism minister Mmamoloko Kubayi-Ngubane warned the South African parliament that up to 600,000 jobs were at risk in tourism alone.[40] Overall, in South Africa, Africa's second largest economy, employment declined by about 18 percent between February and April. Every third income earner in February was without an income in April, with job losses concentrated above all among women and manual laborers.[41]

The garment factories of Sri Lanka, Vietnam, India, and Bangladesh first felt the effect of the pandemic in February through their Chinese supply chains. There was no cloth or thread from the Chinese mills. Then, in

March, orders worth billions were canceled by Western brands, often invoking force majeure and refusing to pay for material and wage costs already incurred.[42] Garment exports from Bangladesh plummeted 85 percent.[43] And then the fear of Covid contagion spread to South Asia itself. It was a triple impact: disruption of supply chain, collapse in demand, and a threat to the workforce and their families. By early April, at least 1 million garment workers were either unemployed or furloughed in Bangladesh alone, a quarter of the garment workforce in that country, 80 percent of them women.[44] As both work at home and remittances from abroad dried up, the poverty rate was predicted to surge to 40 percent.[45] In Pakistan, garment workers were locked out, often without warning. It took protests in the face of menacing armed guards to extract the wages owed to them.[46] Behind them stood an even larger army of home-based workers, who did not appear on the books of any employer or national social insurance system but were left destitute by the sudden shutdown. In Pakistan alone, there were thought to be 12 million homeworkers working twelve-hour days for less than 40 cents per hour, all of whose livelihoods were in jeopardy.[47]

In normal times the relatively steady cash income of garment workers enabled them to take advantage of microloans to finance, for instance, the construction of a house in their home village. In Cambodia the garment workforce held about a fifth of all such loans, owing a total of several billion dollars.[48] This added hugely to the terror of unemployment, since failure to pay the loan would make the collateral forfeit, and in the worst-case scenario, the family home would be lost. To make matters worse, as they struggled to find alternative sources of income, unemployed garment workers found themselves competing with hundreds of thousands of migrant workers streaming home from neighboring Thailand.

As huge workforces were idled and quarantined, around the world Covid became a crash test of labor market institutions.

In global comparison, Europe's welfare states are uniquely generous. Covid put them to a new test. The most important innovation was the widespread adoption of short-time working. This was a system that had been used successfully by Germany to cushion the impact of the 2008 crisis.[49] Workers continued in employment, with public funds helping to pay all or part of their salary. When the shutdown was at its most intense in May 2020, about one-third of employees in Austria, France, and the Netherlands and one-fifth in Germany, Spain, and Ireland were on short-time working schemes.[50] These schemes provided a large public subsidy to employers, especially those who might otherwise have retained workers at their own expense. It was a price worth paying. In Europe they were the principal means through which the social crisis was contained.

The short-time working systems were originally conceived for classic industrial work. In the course of 2020, they were expanded to include the self-employed, workers in the "gig economy," and even stigmatized groups such as sex workers.[51] The programs were innovative and solidaristic, but no more than other forms of welfare provisions did they erase social inequality. Contract workers hired by agencies found themselves in limbo, housed in cramped quarters, without either jobs or welfare support. At the very bottom were the migrant workers shipped in, as usual, to the wealthier countries of Europe, but now in even more humiliating circumstances and more or less regardless of health regulations.[52] The fact that rural Romanians and Bulgarians were desperate enough to take such work highlighted the huge disparity in life chances across the EU. In a bizarre twist of fate, by April 2020 the last Europeans to still be on the move were low-paid East European migrant workers.[53]

If Europe's welfare states adapted to contain the worst impact of the crisis, large developing economies struggled with far more basic problems.

Of India's workforce of 471 million, only 19 percent are covered by social security, two-thirds have no formal employment contract, and at least 100 million are migrant workers, moving back and forth between the countryside and the city, making do with informal and improvised housing or simply sleeping on the street.[54] Indian prime minister Modi's sudden lockdown triggered a flight from the cities to the villages of perhaps as many as 20 million people—what has been described as "lockdown and scatter."[55] En route, perhaps half of the migrants found themselves stranded by tight state-level restrictions, living in improvised camps.[56] There has been nothing like it since the violent partition of India and Pakistan in 1947. Indian unemployment during the lockdown can only be estimated, but the scale was clearly staggering. The best available data suggest that there were 122 million fewer people employed in April 2020 than a year earlier. Some went back to farm labor in their home villages, but in the week ending May 3, 2020, the unemployment rate probably exceeded 27 percent.[57] India's lockdown rivals that of China in February as the biggest shock ever suffered by any labor market in history.

If India was at one end of the spectrum of labor market organization and Europe at the other, the United States fell uncomfortably in between. The U.S. has formal labor markets and regular unemployment statistics, but there are none of the administrative systems and legal protections in place that would allow for a European-style short-time working system. America does not have a national system of unemployment insurance. The most that could be put in place during the New Deal of the 1930s was a patchwork of state-level systems. Benefits are low and expire in most states after twenty-six weeks. Southern states like Florida and North Carolina offer no more than twelve weeks of cover.[58] This creaky and punitive system is designed more or less explicitly to deter applicants and to reject many who do apply. By March 2020, it was groaning under a weight it had never before experienced. Despite the health risks, tens of thousands queued up to sign on in person, or in New York City, to withdraw benefit cash from a limited number of ATMs.[59]

Every Thursday morning, the U.S. Department of Labor releases a weekly compilation of data on the number of people newly applying for unemployment benefits. The national numbers are compiled from state-level claims. In the third week of March 2020, it was clear that a catastrophe was in the making. Stories had been circulating about the extraordinary surge in applications received by state offices. Several online registration systems had become overloaded and simply stopped working. The Trump administration tried to embargo the alarming news.[60] And then on March 26 at 8:30 a.m., the release hit the wires. In the preceding week, 3.3 million Americans had signed on for unemployment insurance benefits. This was completely unprecedented. In a normal week, previously, 200,000 to

300,000 might apply for benefits. Following the financial crisis of 2008, the worst week had been in March 2009, with a total of 665,000.[61] The number for March 26 was five times worse. A graph stretching back over half a century turned upward in a vertical spike. The following week the number leaped even higher, to a staggering 6.648 million. In April the economic crisis facing America took on an apocalyptic quality. In a matter of three months, more than a quarter of those under the age of twenty-five lost their jobs.[62] James Bullard, the normally stoical president of the St. Louis Federal Reserve, warned that if lockdowns were taken as far as might be necessary, the national unemployment rate could reach 30 percent—greater than during the Great Depression of the 1930s.[63]

With production and consumption contracting around the world, the outlook for trade looked disastrous. On April 8, ahead of the spring meetings of the International Monetary Fund (IMF) and the World Bank, the World Trade Organization (WTO) predicted that international trade in 2020 would contract by between 12 and 30 percent. The margin of error was indicative of the profound uncertainty brought on by the pandemic.[64]

The industry that felt the impact most directly was shipping. When measured by weight, over 90 percent of world trade is carried by sea. Some 60,000 cargo ships move the world's goods. Bulk carriers move oil, coal, grains, and iron ore. Container ships convey higher value cargo; 1.2 million seafarers crew the cargo vessels.[65] Another 600,000 men and women staff the cruise ships that carry tourists around the world. The main sources of labor are India, Indonesia, China, and the Philippines. Every week, a complex schedule of crew stops and exchanges shuffles 50,000 crew members on and off the ships at hubs such as Dubai, Hong Kong, and Singapore.

The 2020 shutdown convulsed the industry. Freight trips were canceled. Containers piled up in port. Pandemic regulations allowed the cargo to be off-loaded, but crews were not cleared to disembark. The Philippines, as the home of hundreds of thousands of seafarers, offered itself as a quarantine entrepôt. By the third week of May, a fleet of twenty-one giant cruise ships had gathered in Manila Bay in the hope of disembarking the crews.

However, administrative holdups and the cancellation of all flights out of Manila left tens of thousands stranded on board, often without communications to the outside word.[66] All told, by the end of June, perhaps as many as 400,000 mariners were confined offshore in a giant floating quarantine.[67] By the end of the year there was still no resolution, and those trapped on board were still numbered in the hundreds of thousands.[68] They were not so much locked down as locked in, facing a seemingly endless confinement in their places of work.

The supply shock fed a demand shock, which pulled down sales, income, and employment and induced a further contraction in consumption and investment. Never before had this vicious circle operated so comprehensively, on such a scale and at such a pace, as it did in the spring of 2020. Never before had the connections that tie the world's economy together as a functional whole been so suddenly stressed or put in question.

Using real-time data on social distancing and lockdown measures, we can estimate the biggest aggregate of all, global GDP, on a daily basis. The result is a picture of extraordinary drama. For 2019, global GDP stood at something like $87.55 trillion. Over the course of a mediocre year, it had grown by 3.2 percent. In 2009, the worst year in recent record, global GDP had contracted by 1.67 percent. In February 2020, as a result of China's shutdown, this huge flow of production contracted by 6 percent. And then in March it went off a cliff. Global GDP reached its nadir on or around Good Friday, April 10, 20 percent down from where it had been at the beginning of the year.[69] Never before in history had economic activity contracted this fast and this comprehensively across the world. It was a more sudden and precipitous contraction even than during the Great Depression of the 1930s.

This unprecedented recession did more than just dislocate production and wipe out jobs; it also shook the system of credit. Businesses, governments, and households rely on loans. On the other side of the balance sheet, those loans appear as assets of other businesses, governments, and households. Power and inequality, risk and return are encoded into who

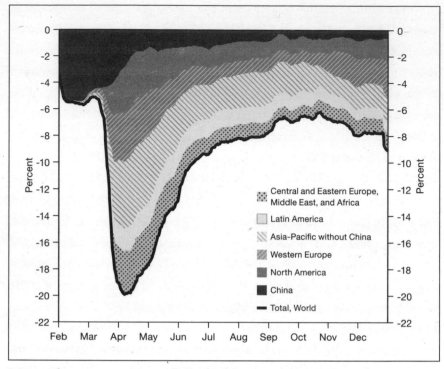

Impact of virus restrictions on global GDP estimated from Goldman Sachs effective lockdown index, 7dma

Goldman Sachs Global Investment Research, via Dailyshot.com.

owes what to whom and on what terms. The massive and fragile edifice is conditioned on expectations about the future. When those expectations shift as radically as they did in March and April 2020, the whole building may collapse.

The run to safety began in global financial markets in February. On March 9, it became something more like a panic. Weeks ahead of government-mandated lockdowns in most of Europe or in the United States, global financial markets were in flight mode. There is no better example of the way in which news of the coronavirus induced a private search for safety—a shutdown. The financial run for safety happened very fast. It made sense individually. But when implemented simultaneously by the men and women who manage tens of trillions of dollars worldwide, it threatened total systemic collapse and forced massive intervention by the state.

The headline-grabbing element of the crisis was the sudden plunge in share prices. In societies like the United States, where the upper middle class is intensely interested in their private retirement portfolios, this unleashed a wave of fear. A deeper level of anxiety concerned the mountain of debts in the emerging markets and the liabilities on the balance sheets of big corporations. By mid-March, with Europe reeling under the impact of the disease, the euro area sovereign debt market was coming under stress. All this was bad, but the truly terrifying shock of March 2020 was the seismic tremor that ran through the market for U.S. Treasuries, American government debt.

A stock market collapse would have been bad for wealth and for raising new corporate capital. A credit collapse would have been debilitating for business. A eurozone sovereign debt crisis would have hobbled the ability of the governments of Italy, Spain, and France to respond to the epidemic. An inversion of the U.S. Treasury market, however, was a problem of a different order. Its implications went further even than the North Atlantic banking crisis of 2008. American government debts are the safe assets on which the entire structure of private finance rests. They are the foundation of America's financial might and thus of the world order as we know it.

Chapter 6

"WHATEVER IT TAKES," AGAIN

O n Thursday, March 12, the news from the financial markets was grim. America's stock markets suffered losses worse than anything in 2008. Only "Black Monday" in October 1987 and the darkest days of 1929 were worse.[1] That was bad, but for insiders, the stock market was not the real worry. A "correction" was in order. The world was heading into shutdown. It was to be expected that share prices would fall. The function of shares as risk-bearing capital is to act as a shock absorber in hard times. Far more worrying than equity markets was what was happening in the market for bonds, and above all, U.S. Treasuries—the safe assets that promise a counterbalance to volatile equities.

In times of uncertainty and recession, as investors lose confidence, they tend to shift from shares, whose prices fluctuate with business fortunes, to government debt that can be sold at a steady price or can be used as collateral for borrowing on good terms. At the top of the pyramid of safe assets are dollar-denominated U.S. Treasuries.[2] Their status as the ultimate safe asset is not due to the strength of the dollar, which has progressively depreciated for half a century. Nor does it stem from the fact that U.S. fiscal policy has the highest reputation for probity. U.S. Treasuries are the ultimate safe asset because the market is gigantic. At the start of 2020, there was almost $17 trillion in U.S. government IOUs in public circulation. These are backed by the most powerful state with the biggest tax base, and they trade in the deepest and most sophisticated debt market.[3] You buy U.S. Treasury securities because the market is so big that in an emergency you can sell them without your sale affecting the price. There will always be someone who wants to buy your Treasuries. And there will always be important bills you can settle in dollars. When we say that the U.S. dollar is the reserve currency of the world, what we are talking about are not America's nondescript green banknotes. What we are talking about is the wealth stored in interest-bearing U.S. Treasuries.

A common chain of events in a recession is, therefore, for the price of equities to fall and the price of Treasuries to rise. When the price you pay for a Treasury rises, their yields—the annual interest coupon payment divided by the price you paid to own the bond—fall. And in response to the first impact of the virus, in February 2020, that is what had happened. Shares fell. Bond prices rose and yields came down. Falling yields lower interest rates, make it easier for firms to borrow, and should in due course stimulate new investment. The financial markets were helping the economy to adjust. But then, gathering force from Monday, March 9, something more alarming began to happen. The run for safety turned into a panic-stricken dash for cash.[4] Investors sold *everything*—not just shares, but Treasuries too. That was very bad news for the economy, because it sent interest rates up—the opposite of what business needed. Even more disturbing than the perverse movement of bond prices and yields was the fact that the biggest financial market in the world was, in the words of one market participant, "just not functioning."[5] The trillion-dollar Treasury market, which is the foundation of all other financial trades, was lurching up and down in stomach-churning spasms. On the terminal screens, prices danced erratically. Or, even worse, there were no prices at all. In the one market where you could always be sure to find a buyer, there were suddenly none. On March 13, J.P. Morgan reported that rather than a normal market depth of hundreds of millions of dollars in U.S. Treasuries, it was possible to trade no more than $12 million without noticeably moving the price.[6] That was less than one-tenth of normal market liquidity. This was a state of financial panic, which if it had been allowed to develop, would have been more destabilizing even than the failure of Lehman Brothers in September 2008.

In 2008 it had been mortgage-backed securities that almost brought the house down.[7] The risks were concentrated on bank balance sheets on both sides of the Atlantic. A downturn in real estate, which triggered mortgage defaults, turned into a banking crisis. The prospect of bank failures forced interventions by central banks and treasuries in the form of asset purchases, to prop up markets for mortgage-backed securities, a desperate effort to supply liquidity to the ailing banks, and bailouts in the strict sense of the word, in the form of government stakes in the weakest banks.

In 2020, real estate was solid. Indeed, in many locations in 2020, house prices went up.[8] People wanted to move to the suburbs. The market for

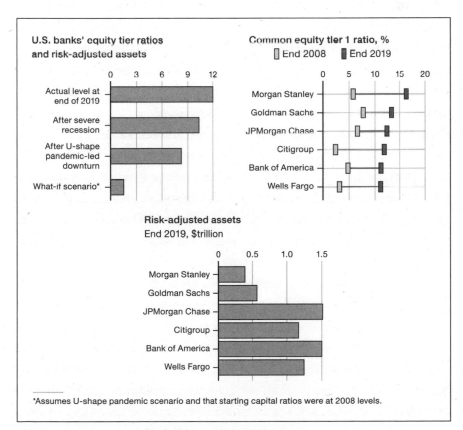

U.S. banks' equity tier ratios and risk-adjusted assets

https://www.economist.com/finance-and-economics/2020/07/02/how-resilient-are-the-banks

home improvements boomed. Banks, on the other hand, would face losses on their loan books. Low interest rates would be bad for their profit margins on lending. So their shares sold off hard. The setback to the banks was so severe that it caused a ripple of anxiety among the regulators.[9] If the banks had been as weak in 2020 as they had been in 2008, the situation might well have been catastrophic.

How catastrophic a coronavirus banking crisis might have been can be gauged by applying, hypothetically, the losses expected in the spring of 2020 to the balance sheets of the major U.S. banks as they were in 2008 at the time of the mortgage crisis. The result is horrifying. If the banks had been as weak in 2020 as they were in 2008, core loss-absorbing capital across the entire system would have been slashed to a low of 1.5 percent of assets, less than a sixth of what is considered safe. Several of America's biggest banks would have failed, requiring gigantic and politically toxic bailouts.[10] Mercifully, thanks to tough new regulations and the banks' own efforts at self-preservation, their balance sheets on both sides of the Atlantic were far stronger in 2020 than in 2008. To ensure that they stayed that way, bank regulators around the world in March 2020 barred banks from paying out dividends or engaging in stock buybacks for the foreseeable future.[11]

The relative solidity of bank balance sheets was little comfort, however, if the risk had migrated elsewhere. Financial capitalism continuously expands and evolves. After 2008, regulators and financial analysts were preoccupied with new types of risk building up on the balance sheets of asset managers and in funds that specialized in repacking high-risk corporate debt, loans, and mortgages on commercial real estate.[12] There was also concern about the stability of corporate borrowers in emerging markets around the world who had issued debt denominated in dollars.[13] All of these were instances of what is known as market-based finance: financial relationships that are not based on the balance sheets of banks, but are mediated through markets in which loans and bonds, and the derivatives built on them, are bought, sold, rebought, and resold. The main hub of market-based finance is the so-called repo market (repo is short for repurchase), where bonds can be traded temporarily for cash with a commitment to repurchase within a short period of time.[14] Every day, trillions of dollars in long-term bonds are refinanced in the repo market on a daily and monthly basis. By continuously selling and repurchasing bonds, large port-folios can be held on the basis of small amounts of capital. It was these market-based financial arrangements that were the line of continuity con-necting the mortgage crisis of 2008 to the bond market turmoil of 2020.

In 2008, it wasn't bad mortgages per se, let alone the retail banking business of goliaths like Citigroup or Deutsche Bank, that drove the crisis. The danger arose from the fact that those banks had outgrown their de-posit funding base and instead funded their holdings of mortgage-backed securities by continuously buying and selling them into the repo markets. Lehman was a case in point. What brought it to its knees in September 2008 was not large losses on mortgages. What brought Lehman down and threatened all the other banks was the fact that it lost access to the repo markets in which it had previously funded its giant balance sheet of mortgage-backed securities.[15] The collective withdrawal of confidence on the part of its repo market counterparties was the equivalent of an instant bank run on the scale of hundreds of billions of dollars.

Mortgage-backed securities had been put up for repo to such a large extent because they had been rated as AAA. In other words, they had been packaged to appear as safe assets. Most were in fact quite safe, but in a super-fast-moving market, all you needed was a whisper of doubt to shut off repo funding completely, for mortgage-backed securities or any other type of private debt. If such a market-based system of finance was to con-tinue to function and expand, what it really needed were unquestionably safe assets, and the safest of all were American Treasuries.

Between 2008 and 2019, thanks to the financial crisis of 2008 and Donald Trump's tax cuts, the stock of U.S. government bonds surged, and this supply was met with ready demand.[16] With the Fed's encouragement, interest rates did edge up a bit between 2016 and 2019, but they remained historically low. Because Treasuries were the ideal raw material for fast-moving and complex financial markets, there was no shortage of demand for them. Mutual funds absorbed them as an interest-bearing liquidity re-serve. Hedge funds built elaborate strategies to profit from tiny deviations in their price. Banks held them to meet the liquidity buffer requirements of the new Basel III regulations. From 2014 onward, foreign investors were no longer big buyers in net terms, but they already had huge holdings of U.S. Treasuries and they rolled those over uncomplainingly. If you were the foreign exchange reserve manager of a big emerging market central bank, you held Treasuries against the currency risk that business borrowers in your jurisdiction had incurred by borrowing in dollars. Everyone held them on the assumption that they could be sold or repoed in markets of limitless liquidity. Crucially, you assumed that you could liquidate your holdings without affecting their price. If that was not true, then all other bets were off too. That's what made the events in the U.S. Treasury market beginning on March 9 so terrifying.

It turned out that even in the Treasury market, at least as it was constructed in March 2020, not everyone could sell at once. And that risked unleashing a fire sale of everything else too. In March 2020 the run extended to every class of assets in the financial system. It was no longer a run into safer investments, but a general dash for cash. And the cash that everyone wanted was dollars. It was a run out of assets into dollars.[17]

The demand for dollars is important to emphasize because according to the best available data, two-thirds of the Treasury sales in March 2020, to the tune of $400 billion, were by foreign holders of U.S. assets.[18]

A Chinese sell-off of Treasuries had long been a nightmare of American strategists. Huge sales by China would drive prices down, push interest rates up, and send the dollar plunging. That was the great fear in 2008. It did not transpire. China continued to increase its holdings of Treasuries through 2013. In 2020, emerging markets did sell and it did disturb the Treasury market, but this too was not the much-feared "bear raid." Rather than falling, the dollar was rising. Indeed, that was the problem. Emerging market reserve managers were selling Treasuries to supply dollars to borrowers in their jurisdictions who were having a hard time rolling over funding. Due to the global extension of the dollar system, much of the world is effectively part of the U.S. financial system. The EM reserve managers were not looking for the exit. Like everyone else they were hunkering down, winding down exposed positions and reallocating dollar portfolios.

The rest of the Treasury sales in March 2020 came from inside the U.S. financial system itself. The two key actors were mutual funds and hedge funds. Their sales on top of those by EM reserve managers were a stark demonstration of how the fragility of the market-based financial system could unsettle not just banks and the market for mortgage-backed securities, but even the mighty Treasury market.

As mutual fund managers faced massive withdrawals, they needed cash urgently and had to choose which assets to sell first. They would no doubt have preferred to sell the riskiest assets on their books, like shares and corporate bonds. In a normal market, that would have been the best strategy. In March 2020 they could be disposed of only at a large loss. So, instead, fund managers sold their most liquid and safe assets, government bonds. As a result, uncertainty in equity and corporate debt markets spread to the Treasury market. As selling pressure built up, it unraveled the conventional assumption that as shares go down, bonds go up, and vice versa. Rather than balancing out, the prices of shares and bonds were collapsing together.

As familiar correlations broke down, trading became increasingly chaotic. The work-from-home arrangements adopted by Wall Street and the City of London added to the panic. Traders hunched over improvised home workstations—known in the new slang of March 2020 as "'rona rigs"—screamed with frustration as their sluggish home wi-fi systems dragged behind the movement of the markets. As one fund manager remarked, "The average trader on Wall Street is inexperienced, can't take risk, and now can't communicate with colleagues properly . . . They're isolated at home in their sweatpants . . . Psychologically it's a bad situation."[19] Bad as the situation was for the traders, it was the computerized algorithms that were doing much of the damage. In one of the most sophisticated markets in the world, 75 percent of the market-making in U.S. Treasuries is done by algorithmic trading. As volatility surged and risk increased, the algorithms automatically reduced the size of the positions they would take. At the same time, they hiked the spread between prices at which they would buy and sell bonds. This was programmed into the algorithms because it was a sensible reaction to a turbulent market that had taken a turn to the down-side. It was destabilizing because it applied a squeeze to another key node in the fragile system of market-based finance: the hedge funds.

The sudden downward movement in bond prices and the surge in the bid-ask spread was bad news for hedge funds that trade on the tiny differ-ences between the price of Treasuries and futures secured on them. Hedge funds are relatively small actors relative to giant banks or asset managers like BlackRock, but they had assumed an outsize role in Treasury markets thanks to leveraged strategies based on the repo market. To multiply their profits, they refinanced their stockpiles of Treasuries in the repo market, swapping the Treasuries for cash with which to buy more Treasuries. Each of those swaps was backed by a bare minimum of capital. As it became apparent that their trades were loss making, the hedge funds faced margin calls, requiring them to post more capital. March 2020 was not a moment to find new investors. So they were forced to unwind their positions, sud-denly off-loading over $100 billion of Treasuries into a market already un-settled by sales by emerging market reserve managers and mutual funds.

With a lot of desperate sellers, there should have been profits to be made on the buy side. If you picked up Treasuries at fire-sale prices and warehoused them until the markets stabilized, you could sell them later at something closer to normal prices. Normally, that role would have fallen to big banks as market makers, and above all JPMorgan Chase, which domi-nated the repo market. In 2020, however, the banks were already satiated with Treasuries. The huge budget deficits run up by the Trump adminis-tration since 2017 had swamped the U.S. financial markets with bonds. That had already led to a major malfunction of the repo markets in the autumn of 2019, when there had been wild swings in prices and the Fed had had to step in. In 2020 the big banks wanted no more. Off-loading a large package of bonds to one of the big broker-dealers, a transaction that would once have taken minutes, now took hours and had to be signed off at the most senior levels. The banks, with JPMorgan in the lead, argued that things might have been easier if only they had not been saddled with so many regulations since 2008. Those regulations may have made a differ-ence at the margin, but in truth, the disturbances in the Treasury market in

March 2020 were so large that no conceivable expansion in bank balance sheet capacity could have absorbed them.[20] One of the few consolations of 2020 was that no big banks were immediately in harm's way.

But something needed to be done. The prospect of escalating dysfunction in the Treasury market collapse was horrifying. A "safe" asset that could no longer be easily sold, or could be sold only at a fluctuating discount, was no longer a safe asset. It ought to have been unthinkable to even ask that question about U.S. Treasuries. And if the implosion of the financial system was not bad enough, Bank of America strategist Mark Cabana spelled out the wider implications. As he warned in mid-March, if the Treasury market stopped functioning, it was "a national security issue." It would "limit the ability of the US government to respond to the coronavirus." That was ominous, but for Cabana too the biggest risk was in the financial markets. "If the US Treasury market experiences large-scale illiquidity it will be difficult for other markets to price effectively and could lead to large-scale position liquidations elsewhere."[21] If you could not be sure of being able to convert your piggy bank of safe Treasuries into cash, it was not safe to hold the rest of your portfolio either, and if that was true for the United States, it was also true for the rest of the world. Beginning on March 12, the European Central Bank (ECB) registered outflows from all kinds of euro area funds on a scale not seen since September 2008.[22] Funds that had slimmed down their liquidity buffers to a bare minimum found themselves caught short and resorting to desperate measures like gating outflows. The fear of not being able to exit helped to spread the panic.

In a general run like that which had set in in March 2020, only one thing will restore confidence—limitless cash. And in the world's dollar-centered financial system, only one actor can provide that: the U.S. Federal Reserve. It would need to act not just as a lender of last resort, but as a market maker.[23]

The Fed's first reaction to the coronavirus crisis on March 3 was to cut rates, the conventional way to support markets. In the second week of March 2020, it became clear that this was not a conventional crisis. Stock markets were suffering historic losses. The Treasury market was in chaos. The only thing that anyone wanted was cash, and what they wanted above all was the U.S. currency. As the dollar surged, it transmitted the financial pressure to the entire world. Anyone who had debts outstanding in dollars, and that meant virtually every major corporation in the world along with many governments, was under pressure.

President Trump was not one for the finer points of hedge fund strategy or the details of the Treasury market, but he followed the S&P 500 obsessively, and on Monday, March 9, he was incandescent. Why were the "boneheads" at the Fed not reacting to the collapse in the market? Trump summoned Treasury Secretary Steve Mnuchin, whom he blamed for his choice of Jerome Powell as Fed chair, and demanded that the treasury secretary push the Fed into action.[24] On Tuesday, unable to contain his rage, he tweeted: "Our pathetic, slow moving Federal Reserve, headed by Jay Powell, who raised rates too fast and lowered too late, should get our Fed Rate down to the levels of our competitor nations. They now have as much as a two point advantage, with even bigger currency help. Also, stimulate!"[25] So alarming was Trump's tone that his staff were afraid that he might try to sack Powell midcrisis. Nothing could be worse for market confidence.

On the evening of March 11, the president dropped his bombshell, abruptly announcing the closure of America's borders to European travelers. As Philipp Hildebrand, the former governor of the Swiss National Bank and now vice chairman at giant fund manager BlackRock, remarked rather primly: "This is one of the concerns that sort of sits in an overarching way over the whole system right now: Where is the leadership? Where is the U.S. leadership, which was one of the defining features of the crisis in 2008?"[26] The answer would come not from the White House, but from the Fed.

Jay Powell was an unlikely hero. It is not that he did not look the part. According to legend, Powell was picked by Trump to replace Janet Yellen because Trump thought Yellen at five-three was too short to be America's central banker and Powell cut a more imposing figure.[27] He was also wealthy, which Trump liked. What Powell lacked were the impressive academic credentials of either Yellen or Ben Bernanke. In this sense he was a Fed chair for an era no longer in love with expertise. What Powell did have was plenty of experience in business, as a corporate lawyer. He also knew the importance of politics. Powell was nominated to the Fed board in 2011 as a bipartisan candidate after he helped to convince Tea Party diehards in Congress that refusing to authorize new borrowing and forcing the federal government to live hand to mouth from tax revenue would be disastrous.[28] Powell was not just a smooth operator. He was also a man with a philanthropic conscience. He favored a tight labor market as the best way to address inequality and inherited a Fed organization that under both Bernanke and Yellen had recognized that it could not ignore America's stark social disparities.[29] Powell was supported in key operational positions by a Fed team staffed with veterans of 2008. Lorie Logan had been in the front line of the first generation of quantitative easing (QE) at the New York Fed. She knew how to do asset purchases. In December 2019, Logan took overall charge of the Fed's portfolio.[30] At the policymaking level, Powell was supported by an activist generation, of which Lael Brainard, formerly of the Obama Treasury, was the leading exponent.[31] As Fed chair, Powell would suffer fewer dissenting votes than any of his recent predecessors.[32]

The Fed was a competent, high-functioning piece of the U.S. state apparatus. As such, it had unsurprisingly attracted Trump's ire in the years prior to 2020. What was surprising was that in 2020 it became once again the driver of an expansive interventionist program of stabilization. It will be years before we have an inside view based on documentary evidence. For now, the simplest interpretation is that a team of veterans, conditioned by the experience of 2008, under undogmatic but broad-minded leadership, equipped with an acute political antenna, responded to a crisis of confidence that was threatening to become existential in the way that such a crisis demands: with maximum force. The fact that it was not accompanied by more drama was part of the confidence-building exercise. This should not lead us to underestimate the scale of what was done.

The first direct intervention in the market was led by the New York Fed, which is closest to the action on Wall Street. Its immediate aim was to restore depth to the Treasury market by making it as cheap as possible for dealers to fund their portfolios. On March 9, the New York Fed made available $150 billion in overnight repo funding. On March 11, it announced an increase to $175 billion, as well as a further $95 billion in two-week and one-month repo. On March 12, the Fed began to offer one-month and three-month repo in $500 billion batches. The fact that the Fed was responding on a daily basis to the market's mounting liquidity needs helped to calm nerves. "This is all very welcome if overdue," opined Krishna Guha, head of the global policy and central bank strategy team at Evercore ISI, but, he added, "we are not sure that it will prove to be enough."[33] As a repo lender, the Fed was propping up the Treasury market by helping others to buy. The question was when it would step in itself.

By the end of the week, uncertainty was spreading around the world. Euro area bond markets were unsettled by mixed messages from the European Central Bank. Big emerging markets—including G20 members Brazil, Mexico, and Indonesia—were under pressure from the soaring dollar. On Sunday, March 15, Powell made his next dramatic move. He called an unscheduled press conference and announced that with immediate effect the Fed was cutting interest rates to zero—something that it had done just once before, at the height of the crisis in 2008. To stabilize the market, it would be buying at least $500 billion in Treasuries and $200 billion in mortgage-backed securities, and it would start big.[34] By Tuesday, $80 billion would be off the hands of the broker-dealers, more in forty-eight hours than Ben Bernanke's Fed had bought in a typical month. And to satisfy the global craving for dollars, the Fed would be easing the terms on the so-called liquidity swap lines—deals under which the Fed swaps dollars for sterling, euros, Swiss francs, and yen in potentially unlimited amounts. In effect, the Fed was assuming the role of a central bank to the world, dispensing dollars to every part of the credit system that was tight. In 2008 the swap lines had thrown a lifeline to Europe's ailing banks. Now it was above all the Asian financial institutions that needed support.[35] If they could get dollar funding from the Bank of Japan or the South Korean central bank, that would reduce the need to sell Treasuries.

Activating these elements of what is known as the global financial safety net does not require a dramatic stage-managed meeting of heads of government, at the G20 or somewhere like it. It can be done through relatively informal conference calls between a group of central bankers and their senior staff. It is a community as cosmopolitan as that in a scientific discipline, but smaller and even more close-knit. It has outliers in national treasuries, at the IMF and the BIS, and in many of the largest banks and asset managers. The ecosystem is completed by academic commentators and influential journalists who translate and amplify the common sense of this functional elite group. Within this community, there was no doubt by March 2020 that it was essential for the Fed to step in as a global lender of last resort, as it had done in 2008.[36] This was in the interest of financial stability both in the United States and in the world at large. It was also a moment of truth as far as the Trump presidency was concerned. When he took office in 2017, many in the international finance community had feared that his administration would undercut the Fed's role as the de facto central bank to the world. It seemed too enlightened to be compatible with his agenda of "America first." If not Trump himself, then the flat-earth brigade in the congressional ranks of the GOP would shackle the Fed. A culture clash seemed predestined. But no such thing happened. After Powell's performance on March 15, the president was full of praise for the Fed.[37] Trump was all in favor of Fed intervention, no questions asked. The problem, it turned out, was not Trump. The problem was the markets.

On the night of March 15, as Powell finished his press conference, the futures market that anticipates the opening of the equity market on Wall Street on Monday morning sold off to the point that the circuit breakers, which are supposed to prevent the market from going into free fall, kicked in and further trading was automatically halted.[38] When trading started on Monday morning, the fall was vertiginous. Once again, the circuit breakers were activated. The VIX, a measure of market volatility also known as the "fear index," surged to levels last seen in the dark days of November 2008. The panic in the markets was now feeding on itself. If the Fed's magic no longer worked, then what would? This was a question for the entire world.

The Bank of England had watched the chaos of the previous week with a degree of detachment. Governor Andrew Bailey had just taken over from Mark Carney. The liquidity squeeze had been in dollars, not sterling. Perhaps the Fed's actions would do the trick. On Monday the sixteenth, it became clear that this was dangerously complacent.[39]

The foreign exchange market, where currencies are traded, is the biggest market in the world. Despite Britain's faded status as a financial power, the place where most transactions are booked is the City of London. In 2019, on an average day, turnover ran to $6.6 trillion. In the week starting Monday, March 16, London was in turmoil. Boris Johnson's laissez-faire coronavirus strategy was in tatters. The report from the Imperial College team made it clear beyond doubt that there needed to be an immediate shutdown. Would Downing Street bite the bullet? No major Western metropolis had yet gone into full shutdown—not London, not New York. On Wednesday, March 18, on the terminals in the banking towers of Canary Wharf there was only one trade: Sell every currency in the world. Buy dollars.[40]

The bluest of blue-chip companies like Apple were facing stiff premiums to borrow even for as little as three months ahead.[41] Hedge funds were placing multibillion-dollar bets on a protracted recession in Europe.[42] Even gold, a classic safe haven, was selling off.[43] And as the dash for cash reached its peak, the yields for U.S. Treasuries surged more sharply than they had since the days of Paul Volcker in 1982.[44]

"[It] was mind-boggling," said Bob Michele, chief investment officer at J.P. Morgan Asset Management. "I have been doing this now for almost 40 years, and this is the strangest market I have ever seen." Andrew Wilson, chairman of global fixed income at Goldman Sachs Asset Management, commented: "Our primary responsibility is generating the liquidity our clients want. All of us are having to sell the things we can, rather than the things we would want to sell . . . That's why this ripples right across everything."[45] Rick Rieder, BlackRock's chief investment officer, agreed. The only hedge he wanted in his portfolio was cash. If J.P. Morgan, Goldman Sachs, and BlackRock were all selling, it took a brave person to be a buyer.

In an effort to reassure markets, on Wednesday, March 18, the Bank of England organized a press conference.[46] As Bailey was speaking, sterling plunged by 5 percent to its lowest level against the dollar since 1985. Meanwhile, the market for UK government bonds—the oldest major asset market in the world—was experiencing unprecedented turmoil. For a ten-year gilt, the yield surged between March 9 and March 18 from a low of 0.098 percent to a high of 0.79 percent. Those were low rates, of course, but it was the scale of the movement that mattered. It was an eightfold increase in yield in a matter of days. Furthermore, unusual discrepancies were emerging between the prices for gilts of different duration, signaling a failure of dealers to adjust demand and supply. The Bank of England's market team, operating remotely from terminals on kitchen tables and attic bedrooms, reported "critical market stress." The government debt markets were in "free fall." As Bailey later confirmed, "We basically had a pretty near meltdown of some of the core financial markets." If it had been allowed to continue, "the government would have struggled to fund itself."[47]

After ten days of turmoil, as financial markets in the UK, Europe, and the United States rocked, central banks began a new round of initiatives. In London, an emergency meeting of the Bank of England Monetary Policy Committee on March 19 announced that the bank would be buying £200 billion in gilts.[48] Unlike in 2008, it would not be doing so on a prearranged schedule. As Bailey explained: "We will act in the markets promptly and rapidly as we see appropriate." This was no moment for timetables. The central bank was, by its own admission, flying by the seat of its pants.[49] The previous night, late on March 18, the ECB had announced a major bond-buying program that set the stage for a turnaround in Europe.

Meanwhile, in America's complex credit system, the Fed was tackling one crisis at a time. On March 17, it announced support for the markets that lend to businesses to cover payroll and other short-term expenses. On March 18, it widened its support to include the mutual funds, in which better-off Americans like to keep their savings. On March 19, the Fed widened the network of liquidity swap lines to cover fourteen major economies, including Mexico, Brazil, and South Korea. The next day the provision of dollars to the European Central Bank and the Bank of Japan was speeded up. Whether or not you were a recipient of a swap line, the Fed's action set the tone. The Fed even opened a new facility that would allow foreign central banks to repo U.S. Treasuries. Anything to avoid their having to actually sell them.

With the Fed signaling that it would provide dollars in abundance, the appreciation of the dollar eased and the door was opened for other central banks to act. The Bank of Japan bought bonds. The Reserve Bank of Australia slashed rates. Emerging market central banks that had previously to worry about the strength of the dollar relative to their local currencies were now free to act as well.[50] By the end of the third week of March, thirty-nine central banks from Mongolia to Trinidad had lowered interest rates, eased banking regulations, and set up special lending facilities.[51]

Would it be enough? Powell had activated all the basic elements of the 2008 repertoire—interest rate cuts, quantitative easing, support for money markets, swap lines. These familiar tools had worked to calm the acute stress in Treasury markets. As demand recovered, yields came down, but it was not enough to calm stock markets or the corporate debt market. So long as instability continued there, the ripples would reverberate throughout the entire system.

The basic problem was that central banks could shift credit supply and interest rates, but unlike in the banking crisis of 2008, they could not reach the source of the crisis itself, the coronavirus and the lockdown. The markets were waiting for news from Washington, but not from the Fed, from Congress. How much would America's politicians mobilize in support of incomes, spending, and the medical response? The news on Sunday, March 22, was not good. Democrats and Republicans were at loggerheads. As trading began in Asia on the morning of Monday, March 23, the futures market crashed, and the plunge continued when Wall Street opened. At the low point of the trading day on Monday, March 23, the S&P 500 and the Dow Jones had lost about 30 percent of their value. Around the world, equity markets had inflicted losses of $26 trillion on the fortunate few who own large portfolios of shares and on the collective pools of savings held by pension and insurance funds. If it wanted to stop the slide, the Fed would have to make another move.

At eight a.m. on March 23, ninety minutes before markets opened, Jerome Powell met his "whatever it takes" moment. "Aggressive efforts must be taken across the public and private sectors to limit the losses to jobs and incomes and to promote a swift recovery once the disruptions abate," he declared. By the middle of April, the Fed would go on to establish a total of nine separate facilities to backstop the private credit market. They went by a scrambled assortment of acronyms, but their purpose was to extend a huge overdraft facility to an economy whose revenues were shrinking, workers were furloughed, and markets were cracking "under a stampede of sellers."[52] As with any bank overdraft, the Fed's money did not need to be drawn. It was the fact that it was there that provided essential reassurance.

Powell's approach to stabilization was three pronged.

In its role as lender of last resort, on March 23 the Fed revived the Term Asset-Backed Securities Loan Facility, or TALF—one of the stalwarts of the 2008 crisis—to backstop auto, credit card, small-business, and student loans. This was on top of the facilities it had already opened for issuers of commercial paper, money market mutual funds, and primary dealers in Treasury securities. These loans were largely internal to the financial system and involved the Fed in minimal lending risk. They fulfilled the classic function of central banks—to provide liquidity in emergencies against good collateral. But by March 23, it was clear that the Fed needed to do more.

In a second, more radical step, Powell announced the establishment of two facilities to support credit to large employers. The Fed was no longer just backstopping lending by others. It would offer to provide the credit itself. The Primary Market Corporate Credit Facility (PMCCF) was intended to buy debt or loans directly from corporations. The Secondary Market Corporate Credit Facility (SMCCF) would buy corporate debt off the books of other investors, including the sort of exchange-traded funds that specialize in high-risk, high-yield debt. The volume proposed for the two facilities was $750 billion. By buying corporate bonds, the Fed would take a far larger risk of loss than it did in conventional lender-of-last-resort operations. To cover the worst-case contingency, it invoked an emergency under article 13(3) of the Federal Reserve Act. This meant that losses, if they arose, could be met out of $30 billion in equity provided by the U.S. Treasury Exchange Stabilization Fund, a relic of the 1930s that served as a convenient source of capital for emergency interventions.

The Fed has always steered clear of this kind of direct lending to businesses. If you bought the debt of individual firms, you were picking favorites. If you bought a cross section of corporate debt, you ended up holding many poor-quality loans. The higher-risk end of the corporate debt market, so-called high-yield or junk bonds, was where private equity firms made winnings before which the bonuses of Wall Street bankers paled into insignificance. For political and legal reasons, if nothing else, the Fed preferred not to be in the business of backstopping the most speculative end of the financial system.

In refusing to buy corporate debt, the Fed was unusual among major central banks. Both the Bank of England and the European Central Bank bought corporate debt. In Europe in March 2020, large corporates like VW were unabashed in their lobbying for support from the ECB.[53] The Bank of Japan went even further. It bought shares, taking the risk of equity ownership. Between 2010 and the end of 2020, it built a $434 billion holding in the Japanese equity market.[54] That was impressive, but America is the world's benchmark capital market. And none of the other central banks had ever done anything on the scale that Powell was now contemplating.

What the Fed really needed from Congress was political cover for its adventurous policy. The unspoken premise of the Fed's announcement was that a new partnership would be forthcoming with the Treasury and Congress. Ideally, the Fed would have made its grand announcement on the morning of Monday, March 23, in conjunction with a congressional stimulus package. That would have to wait until later in the week. In the meantime, anticipating the priorities of Congress, the Federal Reserve declared that it would flank its lending programs for big business with a Main Street Lending Program to support lending to small and medium-sized businesses.

Finally, as the third key prong of its support operation, the Fed threw its full weight behind the markets for public debt.

Municipalities were in the front line of the corona fight, managing the pandemic response and paying for extra precautions, while facing plunging tax revenues. On March 23, the Fed announced changes to both the

Money Market Mutual Fund Liquidity Facility (MMLF) and the Commercial Paper Funding Facility (CPFF) that promised to ease the flow of credit to municipalities. On April 9, this would develop into the Municipal Liquidity Facility, under which the Fed notionally earmarked $500 billion to support short-term notes issued by large cities and counties and states.

All these facilities were confidence-building measures for the financial system as a whole. Indirectly, they served to relieve pressure on the Treasury market. The Fed did not stop there. The most direct way to support the market for Treasuries was for the Fed to buy them. By the weekend of March 20–21, the Fed's Open Market Committee had already announced $500 billion of Treasury purchases and $200 billion of mortgage-backed securities. Powell now lifted even that ceiling. On the morning of March 23, the Federal Open Market Committee (FOMC) declared simply that it would "purchase Treasury securities and agency mortgage-backed securities in the amounts needed to support smooth market functioning and effective transmission of monetary policy to broader financial conditions and the economy."[55] Over the week that followed, the Fed bought an astonishing total of $375 billion in Treasury securities and $250 billion in mortgage securities. At the high point of the program, the Fed was buying bonds at the rate of a million dollars per second. In a matter of weeks, it bought 5 percent of the $20 trillion market.[56]

The effect of these interventions on the market was extraordinary. March 23 was the turning point. Once investors knew the lender and market maker of last resort was in place, confidence returned, credit flowed, and financial markets, particularly in the United States, began an astonishing recovery. By mid-August the S&P 500 had fully recovered its losses since February and had begun an ascent into record territory. It restored wealth to that small minority who had a substantial direct stake in the financial markets. It helped to revive corporate fortunes more generally and thus revive the economy. If the financial markets had suffered a heart attack in March 2020, most of the world would have suffered, but the benefits of the recovery were distributed unequally. Worldwide, the wealth of billionaires rose by $1.9 trillion in 2020, with $560 billion of that benefiting

America's wealthiest people.[57] Among the surreal and jarring juxtapositions of 2020, the disconnect between high finance and the day-to-day struggles of billions of people around the world stood out.

In the years since the dot-com bust of 2000–2001, central bankers had moved from being ringmasters to ever more frantic jugglers of liquidity. It was Mario Draghi who in 2012 gave the era its mantra: "whatever it takes." Central banks dropped interest rates to zero. They engineered the rescue of ailing banks. They provided cheap credit to satisfy liquidity needs on an enormous scale. They purchased assets to stabilize financial markets. Nevertheless, for all the radicalism of these interventions, there was a sense that they could not go on forever. There must come a point where balance sheets were unwound and interest rates returned to something more like normal. When Jay Powell, Andrew Bailey at the Bank of England, and Christine Lagarde at the ECB were chosen to head their respective central banks, there was a sense that they belonged to a postheroic generation. After the radical interventions of the period between 2008 and 2015, their primary task was to restore order. Their goal was normalization.

The jitters in the world economy in 2019 had already put the prospect of normalization in question. The year 2020 overturned it completely. Not only did the central banks act on an unprecedented scale, but they did so with an alacrity that betrayed the increasing disinhibition of the preceding decades. In 2008 there had still been a note of hesitancy about central bank interventions. In 2020, that was gone. The full implications of the opening of the monetary floodgates would become clear over the weeks that followed, as fiscal policy caught up. This was emergency action of the most radical kind. But what now was normality?

Chapter 7

ECONOMY ON LIFE SUPPORT

J ust before midnight on Wednesday, March 25, 2020, the U.S. Senate voted unanimously to approve the Coronavirus Aid, Relief, and Economic Security Act, also known as the CARES Act. It had taken two weeks of negotiation, but America's divided polity had agreed on an omnibus bill of extra spending, tax cuts, and funding allocations, amounting to $2.2 trillion, or 10 percent of the U.S. gross domestic product (GDP).[1] It was the largest slug of fiscal support ever delivered to an economy—anywhere, ever.

In the spring of 2020, the Americans went bigger than anyone else, but they were not alone. In April the International Monetary Fund estimated that the total fiscal effort worldwide in all forms already came to $8 trillion. In May it revised that to $9 trillion and in October to a staggering $12 trillion. By January 2021 the total had reached $14 trillion.[2] That was vastly larger than the stimulus following the 2008 banking crisis. The scale of this spending and tax relief in 2020 was crucial in mitigating the social disaster that might otherwise have resulted from the shutdowns. Indeed, it was of such a scale that it warranted talk of war economies and a new social contract. As government budgets surged and central banks undertook supportive interventions, it seemed that monetary and fiscal policy were being stitched together as not since World War II.[3] The central banks had done their job in March in stabilizing Treasury markets. Now it was time for fiscal policy to take over.[4] It was the public health authorities and elected governments who were allocating resources, setting priorities addressing the social and economic legacy of the crisis.

Such comparisons with the mid-century heyday of Keynesianism no doubt help to capture the drama of the moment. They express the wish of many, on the left as well as the right, to return to that moment when the national economy was first constituted as an integrated and governable entity. As the interconnected implosion of demand and supply demonstrated, macroeconomic connections are very real. But as a frame for reading the crisis response in 2020, this retrofitting risks anachronism. The fiscal-monetary synthesis of 2020 was a synthesis for the twenty-first century.[5] While it overturned the nostrums of neoliberalism, notably with regard to the scale of government interventions, it was framed by neoliberalism's legacies, in the form of hyperglobalization, fragile and attenuated welfare states, profound social and economic inequality, and the overweening size and influence of private finance.

The fiscal response to coronavirus was a striking expression of combined and uneven development. On the one hand, since virtually every country in the world joined the collective move to shut down, practically every country in the world engaged in crisis spending too. On the other hand, the amounts that they were able to mobilize varied hugely. According to the International Monetary Fund, by October 2020 the average advanced economy managed a discretionary fiscal effort of almost 8.5 percent of GDP. The average for middle-income emerging market countries was just shy of 4 percent. Low-income countries generally mobilized less than 2 percent of GDP for coronavirus measures.[6]

Within each broad class, there was a range. Impoverished Haiti launched a stimulus program amounting to an impressive 4 percent of GDP.[7] On April 21, South Africa's government launched a substantial $29.9 billion package focused on health care spending, financial relief to municipalities, and a system of social grants for the least well off. It came to almost 10 percent of national income. On the other hand, Nigeria, battered by the collapse in oil prices, managed barely 1.5 percent of GDP in tax cuts

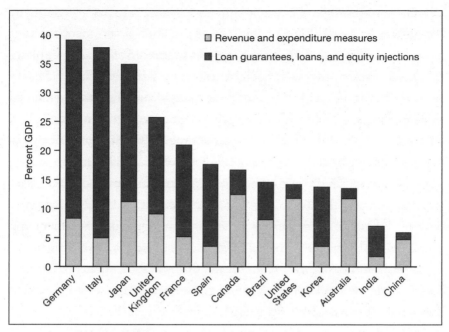

G20 fiscal effort in the first phase of the Covid-19 crisis
Deutsche Bank research, IMF data as of September 11 2020.

and spending. This included a 50 billion naira (US$128 million) relief pro-
gram, which paid 20,000 naira (US$52) to 3.6 million of the most vulnerable
households.[8] That was a drop in the bucket in a country where 87 million
people live on less than $1.90 per day, the largest number of extremely poor
people in the world.[9] Among the big emerging markets, in 2020 India and
Mexico stood out for the low level of fiscal stimulus. Brazil's crisis response,
by contrast, bore comparison with that in the richest countries in the world.

Europe was one of the surprises of 2020. After the eurozone crisis, the
EU had been the poster child for austerity. That had left an acrimonious
legacy, particularly in France and Southern Europe.[10] In 2020, hit hard by
coronavirus, governments of every political stripe across Europe opened
the taps. The numbers are flattered by heavy reliance on loan guarantees.
These did not involve immediate spending, but a promise to cover losses
on loans to firms. In the UK, guarantees came to around 15 percent of
GDP. In Germany, in 2020 they totaled more than 30 percent.[11] For all
these provisos, however, the shift in position was remarkable.

Given the balance of power within the EU, it was crucial that Germany led the way. In Angela Merkel's final Grand Coalition government, the conservative war horse Wolfgang Schäuble was replaced as finance minister by Olaf Scholz, a pragmatic Social Democrat.[12] Already in late February he came out in favor of suspending Germany's constitutionally enforced budget balance, so as to enable Germany's regional governments to respond to the crisis.[13] On March 25, at the same time as the American Congress voted its historic package, the Bundestag approved a 123 billion euro supplementary budget, which together with loan guarantees provided a 750 billion euro backstop to the German economy.[14] This was followed in June by a second 130 billion euro package aimed at pushing public investment and unburdening the budgets of local government, freeing up resources to improve local infrastructure.[15] Not only did this provide stimulus to Europe's largest economy, but Berlin was giving a green light to the rest of Europe to follow suit. When Brussels suspended the budget rules that constrained the deficits of all the euro area members, Berlin raised no objections.

The virus silenced moral hazard arguments against subsidies and welfare spending. No business or government could reasonably be blamed for bringing the pandemic on itself. When the Dutch finance minister demanded to know why the balance sheets of some European governments were not stronger ahead of the outbreak, his remarks were dismissed as repugnant by Portugal's prime minister, António Costa.[16] Covid was not a normal economic event for which it was reasonable to make long-term budgetary preparations. The argumentative boot was now on the other foot. If Italy and Spain were particularly vulnerable to the pandemic, it was because a decade of austerity had undermined their public health systems. Angela Merkel's health minister, the ambitious Jens Spahn, found himself embarrassed by his pre-crisis advocacy of cuts to "excess" hospital capacity. In 2020 that capacity stood Germany in good stead.[17] By the summer, the argument that the pandemic was a historically novel challenge would legitimize the EU in making a leap into a new system of collective financing.

If Europe was more activist in 2020 than in 2008, the reverse was true for China. In 2008, China had launched what in relative terms had been a huge stimulus. In 2020, with the epidemic under control and an eye to the overinvestment and over-borrowing of the past, Beijing was more restrained. The fiscal package announced at the "two sessions" in May 2020 amounted to RMB 3.6 trillion (c. $550 billion), slightly less than the RMB 4 trillion introduced after the 2008 financial crisis in what was a much larger economy. By the end of 2020, the total fiscal effort was estimated at 5.4 percent of GDP, of which 2.6 percent was support for investment, particularly at the local level. Unlike in the West, direct transfers to households played virtually no role in China's recovery. As in 2008 the largest stimulus came not through budgeted fiscal expenditure but through the so-called policy banks. In the month of March alone, their lending, as measured by what the Chinese call total social financing, hit a record RMB 5.15 trillion.[18]

Amid the drama of the corona shutdowns, the most common image invoked to justify the surge in spending was that of the war economy. Xi, Macron, Modi, and Trump all spoke of war. "We are a nation at war with invisible forces. The situation we are now facing is unprecedented in history," Prime Minister Muhyiddin Yassin of Malaysia said in a televised address.[19] Prime Minister Conte of Italy invoked Churchill's "darkest hour."[20] In the financial media, there were earnest discussions about how to commandeer factories to make PPE and ventilators.[21]

As tempting as the war analogy might be, it was not apt for the situation of 2020. The problem was not how to mobilize armies. The challenge was to demobilize the economy and keep people at home. Even within the health care system, non-emergency care and procedures were put on hold. What was needed was not stimulus or mobilization, but life support.

It is this particular quality of the emergency that helps to explain the huge scale of the American program. The CARES Act had to be so big because America's social fabric is built on work and employment. Its welfare system by contrast is fragile, worn thin by years of attacks on the public sector.

As the journalist Eric Levitz forcefully put it:

Steady GDP growth is the duct tape holding together this jerry-rigged social order in which low-income Americans have little to no emergency savings, many basic welfare benefits are contingent on employment, and the threadbare safety net is patchy by design. This top-heavy, gold-plated jalopy of a political economy can pass as road safe in fair weather; try to ride it through a once-in-a-century epidemiological storm and it starts to break apart.[22]

A society with a patchy and minimalist system of unemployment insurance, in which millions live paycheck to paycheck without the protection of paid sick leave, in which tens of millions of children rely on schools for food, cannot easily shut down. If it does, people need help immediately.[23]

In March and April, as the labor market imploded, the mood across much of America was one of barely repressed panic. Given the character of the Trump administration and the extreme polarization of American politics, an appropriate government response could not be taken for granted. In 2009, congressional Republicans had voted almost to a man and woman against the crisis measures of the Obama administration. In 2020, the political stars aligned very differently. The election was still ahead. The Republicans had their own man in the White House. If they wanted to pass a stimulus bill, they would need to come to terms with the Democrats. This did not stop conservative gadflies like Lindsey Graham from trying to derail the coronavirus stimulus over the $600-per-week supplement to unemployment benefits, which he considered excessive. In the summer, Graham's arguments would gain traction. In March, he was overridden. The political logic of the moment was additive rather than subtractive. In 2009, Obama's political managers insisted that they could not go as high as $1 trillion for fear of causing "sticker shock."[24] In March 2020, the initial headline was $2.2 trillion. The final appropriation under the so-called CARES Act would come to $2.7 trillion, nigh on three times the Obama stimulus of 2009. At its peak, in the week ending May 1, the federal government was pumping $200 billion per week into the economy. The rate of emergency spending did not fall below $50 billion per week until the third week of May.[25]

If the worst predictions of March and April did not come to pass, it was in part because of the scale of these interventions. The fiscal packages of 2020 were not stimulus in the conventional sense. Given the supply constraints due to the shutdown, they could not generate the multiplier effect one would normally hope for. What they did do was to provide income security and maintain demand in those areas of the economy that were still functioning.

Thanks to new micro data sets we can trace on a day-by-day basis the impact of the coronavirus crisis support on saving and spending.[26] The most important effect was simply that household disposable income was propped up. This gave hard-pressed families the confidence that they could pay bills and make rent, at least for a few months ahead. Credit card bills were paid off. In the United States, those on lower incomes stashed their CARES checks and repaid debts in anticipation of tough times to come. Higher income households were stuck with the money, unable to splurge on holidays and dining out. Even with a stimulus check in hand, no one was keen to go out to eat or to the beauty parlor or the dry cleaner. In April, the savings rate in the United States shot up from an average of 8 percent in 2019 to 32.2 percent, the highest figure ever recorded.[27] In Europe, savings rates rose too, from 13.1 percent in 2019 to 24.6 percent in the second quarter of 2020.[28] Insofar as CARES Act stimulus funds were spent, they tended to go on big-ticket household goods, benefiting large online retailers and far-flung supply chains rather than the local economy. As a result, the benefit of the U.S. stimulus did not remain confined to America. After falling sharply between February and May, from June, American imports rebounded strongly. For all Donald Trump's economic nationalism, in 2020 America did its bit for global demand.

Given the scale of the fiscal interventions in 2020, if the political will had been there, it would not have been unreasonable to talk about a new or at least a renewed social contract.[29] There were elements in the giant flow of money that were undoubtedly novel. The short-time working model originally pioneered in Germany and Denmark proved viable in countries like the UK, Spain, and Italy. It placed an unprecedented emphasis on maintaining employment relationships. Extending that privilege to "nonstandard" jobs was a significant extension of the welfare system, even if it was incomplete and underwrote highly unequal employment relations. Across the OECD as a whole, job retention schemes of various kinds supported 50 million jobs, ten times more than during the global financial crisis of 2008–2009.[30] Japan, Canada, and Australia set up new schemes. In New Zealand, applications for inclusion in the job retention scheme extended to fully two-thirds of the entire workforce.

Though the U.S. CARES Act was a short-lived emergency improvisation, constrained by the limitations of U.S. public administration, it had in its own way even more dramatic implications. Though it did not build new structures or solidify America's fragile labor market institutions, the sheer scale of spending was head-turning.[31] A major contributor to the extreme income inequality that distinguishes the United States from other rich countries is its ungenerous welfare system. In 2020, for a brief moment, that changed.

Thanks to the combination of stimulus checks and enhanced unem-

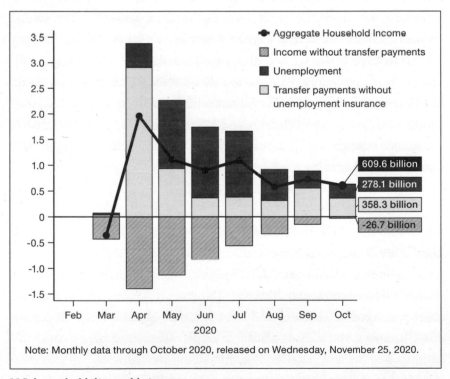

U.S. household disposable income

Based on Mizuho Securities, BEA

ployment benefits, many millions of Americans who lost their jobs saw
their incomes increase. Even as unemployment soared, Americans' disposable income went up.[32] It is hardly an exaggeration to say that the CARES
Act was America's first experiment since the 1960s with welfare on a
scale befitting a rich country. This would horrify conservatives. They com-
plained about the loss of incentive to work. That pertained above all to the
supplement to unemployment insurance benefits. The CARES Act stimulus checks, on the other hand, could easily have been cause for celebration
in the conservative camp. Not only was their president's name on the
checks. This was not the welfare state of old. Handed out to everyone below
a certain income level, this was "welfare without the welfare state"—cash
support, free of any intrusive, prescriptive, bureaucratic, paternalistic state
apparatus.[33] It was the kind of welfare that Milton Friedman might have supported, a stepping-stone toward a universal basic income as advocated by
figures like Democratic Party candidate Andrew Yang. There were all sorts
of things you could do with your stimulus check. You were free to choose.

Despite these innovative elements, there was, however, no disguising
the fact that the basic logic of the fiscal interventions in 2020 was conservative. Virtually none of the politicians who voted for the huge spending
had started the year planning to change society. When one thinks of fiscal
policy, it is tempting to associate it with redistribution and transformative
social engineering. In general, the net effect of tax and welfare systems in
all countries is to reduce inequality at least to some degree. However, welfare can also serve a conservative function. Indeed, the historic purpose of
the welfare state as it emerged in Bismarckian Germany in the 1880s was
precisely that—to preserve the social status hierarchy across the vicissi-
tudes of sickness, old age, and, eventually, unemployment.[34] That was the
principal logic of spending in 2020. The crisis affected the entire economy.
No one was to blame. Everyone should be made whole. So the range of
potential claimants on state support exploded. The EU suspended its normally strict rules on state aid.[35] Organizations like the OECD struggled to
keep track of the helter-skelter of tax breaks, loans, and subsidies.[36]

Small businesses were favorite beneficiaries of subsidies, tax breaks,
and loans. In Canada, state guarantees were provided for all small-business

loans, but also 80 percent guarantees for bank loans up to CAD 6.25 million for more substantial firms. South Korea provided tax reductions for small firms operating in areas hard-hit by the pandemic. VAT payments were slashed. Other taxes were deferred. Norway handed out subsidies to firms in all sectors other than energy, finance, and utility industries, to cover operating costs. In the United States, of the $2.7 trillion appropriated by Congress under the CARES Act, only $610 billion, less than a third, was used to provide unemployment and stimulus payments to households. $525 billion was set aside to support big businesses of all kinds, while $185 billion was set aside for health providers. A quota of $600 billion was reserved for small-business support.

At $669 billion, the Paycheck Protection Program (PPP) was the largest element in the CARES Act. Providing forgivable loans to businesses with 500 or fewer employees that retained their workers during the crisis, it was the closest thing America could manage to a European-style furlough scheme. The evidence suggests that the firms that applied for the forgivable loans were the ones who knew that they were not going to let workers go. It was therefore tantamount to a free grant. All told, the PPP may have supported 2.4 million jobs at the cost of $224,000 per job.[37] Those who defended the scheme did so explicitly on the grounds that it was as much a support for business owners as it was for their workers.[38]

In this welter of subsidies, there was little strategic rationale. There were calls for activist green policy, but these did not acquire real traction until the summer, when the first wave of the pandemic had passed.[39] In the meantime, hundreds of billions were sluiced into the airlines and fossil fuel industries. In the United States, $61 billion was allocated to support the aviation industry and its workforce.[40] Across the OECD, by August 2020 government support of the airline industry ran to $160 billion, of which a quarter was to pay wage bills and the rest took the form of direct subsidies, equity stakes, or loans.[41]

Meanwhile, tucked out of sight in the massive stimulus legislation were small but significant acts of lobbying that yielded outsize returns. In 2017 the Trump presidency and the GOP had enacted a huge tax cut that primarily benefited higher income earners. To get a congressional majority, they had been forced to accept technical restrictions that limited, for instance, the deductions available to the largest firms on the interest they pay on debt, or the extent to which business losses could be set against capital gains on stock portfolios. In the 2020 CARES Act, those limitations were lifted. The benefit, for America's rich, for private equity firms, for households earning over $500,000 per annum, and for firms with turnover of more than $25 million per annum, ran to $174 billion.[42]

If tax cuts and subsidies provided easy benefits, the spending programs triggered by the Covid emergency also offered rich opportunities for profiteering. Totally ineffective track-and-trace systems became notorious boondoggles.[43] In the UK, a "VIP lane" directed well-connected businesses to the front of the queue when it came to crisis contracts. A *New York Times* investigation found that of 1,200 contracts with a value of nearly £16 billion ($22 billion) issued by the UK government, half went to firms run by cronies of the Conservative Party or those with inadequate qualifications or with what was politely deemed "a history of controversy." Smaller firms did not get a shot.[44]

For all the talk of a new social contract and the scale of the spending, coronavirus fiscal policy was as much a reflection of preexisting interests and inequalities as any other area of government action. If the United States did not have an adequate unemployment insurance system, that was not, after all, by accident. If informal migrant workers fell outside the benefits of furlough systems, that was no surprise. Every detail of the trillion-dollar programs reveals the mark of inequality, but as revealing as such forensic investigation is, to fully grasp the political economy of the crisis response we need to take a step back and ask how the fiscal response was paid for. How did fiscal and monetary policy, treasuries, and central banks cooperate to enable the programs to go ahead?

As spending surged and tax revenues collapsed, governments around the world issued a huge volume of debt. Between January and May 2020, the OECD estimated that total debt issuance by advanced economy governments came to $11 trillion. By the end of the year, the total would reach $18 trillion. Of the huge surge in debt in the first five months of the year, some 67.5 percent was accounted for by the United States and 10 percent by Japan; the rest was divided among the Europeans.[45]

It was the most spectacular surge in debt ever recorded in peacetime. In conventional preconceptions, a flood of public debt on this scale presented a giant challenge to the balance between private saving and private investment. Government borrowing would suck scarce savings out of the economy, driving up interest rates, thus crowding out private investment. This was the economic complement to the naive conservative vision of the welfare state as being for poor people and the government as being a racket run by civil servants at the expense of the rest of society. What fiscal policy gave, the financial squeeze would take away.

If this logic held water, 2020 should have witnessed gigantic crowding out. In fact it was the reverse. A huge surge in debt coincided with a historic collapse in interest rates for both public and private borrowers. Across the OECD in 2020, almost 80 percent of government bonds were issued at less than 1 percent yield. Twenty percent were issued at negative rates, more than 50 percent in the euro area and 60 percent in Japan.[46] Even as deficits exploded, the share of government spending allocated to debt service fell. Despite being exceptionally heavy borrowers, Canada, the United States,

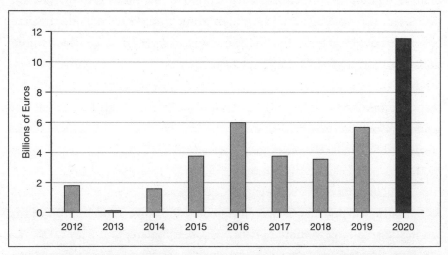

German federal government revenue from selling bonds at negative interest rates (in billion euros)

and the UK all saw their borrowing costs plunge. Over the course of the first half of 2020, the German government, which issues debt at negative rates, looked forward to being paid 12 billion euros to hold the money of anxious investors.[47] Private rates fell too. The yields on investment-grade corporate bonds in the United States plunged to lows not seen since the 1950s.[48]

While 2020 may have been extreme, the fact that interest rates fell as debt surged wasn't in fact a new trend. Over recent decades, even as public debt was on a secular upgrade, interest rates had been moving in the opposite direction. This was one of the phenomena that moved Larry Summers in 2013 to suggest that we were living in an age of secular stagnation.[49] True to the basic supply-and-demand framework, Summers argued that if the price of funds, the interest rate, was falling, it must be due to an imbalance. There was either too much saving or too little investment. Either way, it was a good moment for government investment to take up the slack. There was little reason to worry about debt levels. As Olivier Blanchard, the former chief economist of the International Monetary Fund, pointed out, so long as interest rates remained below the growth rate, any debt burden was sustainable.[50]

In the spring of 2020, Summers and Blanchard added their weight in support of active fiscal policy and against debt panic.[51] That was helpful, but if one was trying to explain the remarkable collapse in rates in 2020, long-run supply-and-demand explanations had their limits. The crucial thing to focus on was not secular trends but the immediate effect of the crisis on the flow of funds within the economy. As spending collapsed and the stimulus income flooded in, banks were flush with deposits. So too were investment vehicles like mutual funds. Companies were hoarding cash, drawing down credit lines from their bank connections but not spending the proceeds on investments or expanding production. These deposits had to be placed somewhere. Once the central banks had stabilized the markets in March, money market mutual funds were a safe haven of choice. By July, their assets under management had surged to $4.7 trillion. They bought the lion's share of the $2.2 trillion in short-term bills issued by the U.S. Treasury in the first half of 2020 to fund its deficits.[52]

At the same time, at the long end of the bond market, it was the central banks that did the work. The huge wave of central bank debt purchases unleashed in March stabilized the market. It drove government bond prices up and pushed the yield, the effective interest rate, down. In the final days of March, the Federal Reserve was buying Treasury bonds and mortgage-backed securities at the rate of roughly $90 billion per day. The European Central Bank, the Bank of Japan, and the Bank of England were all in the market. Their combined purchases were more than two and a half times larger than in any year after the 2008 crisis. All in all, the central banks of the OECD made purchases equivalent to more than half the net issuance of new debt in 2020.

So the most succinct answer to the question of how epic government deficits could be financed without driving up interest rates was that one branch of government, the central bank, was buying the debt issued by another branch of government, the Treasury.

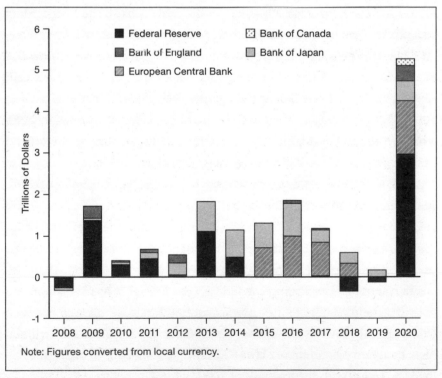

Central banks go on a bond-buying spree to support government responses to the pandemic.

Data compiled by Bloomberg, https://www.bloomberg.com/graphics/2021-coronavirus-global-debt

The central banks didn't, on the whole, buy the newly issued debt directly. They bought bonds held by banks and investment funds. What the central bank gave in exchange was "cash," which in an age of electronic banking meant digital entries of reserve deposits at the central bank. To make sure these funds stayed put, the central banks paid interest on the reserves. It was a roundabout mechanism, but the net effect was that in 2020 the central banks on both sides of the Atlantic were monetizing the government debt on a gigantic scale. Indeed, in the case of the UK, there was an embarrassingly close one-to-one correlation between the government borrowing requirement and the Bank of England's additional debt purchases.[53]

The constellation of low interest rates, large government deficits, and bond buying by the central bank had first emerged in Japan in the 1990s. It went hand in hand with a downward trend in price increases that ultimately resulted in deflation. After 2008, it had become common to the euro area and the United States as well—though in the U.S. the deflationary tendency was less pronounced. The central bank policy of government bond buying became known as quantitative easing (QE).

It was a disorienting scene, because while the central banks remained the key actor in the drama, they were doing precisely those things the prohibition of which was central to founding central bank independence in the 1970s and 1980s. In the era of the market revolution, the mandate of the central banks had been to fight inflation. In that struggle, it was taken as axiomatic that central bankers must refuse to monetize government deficits. Indeed, that prohibition was written into the founding statutes of the ECB. Nevertheless, from 2015 the ECB, like its sister institutions around the world, had bought bonds on a huge scale. That triggered a legal challenge that reached its culmination in the German constitutional court in May 2020. What it did not trigger was inflation. It took more than book entries on the central bank balance sheet to revive a general upward movement in prices and wages.

The shift from a world in which central bank independence was founded on *not* buying government debt to one in which central banks around the world warehoused trillions of dollars in debt was bewildering. And it was all the more so because it happened tacitly, without frank acknowledgment of the transformation. As Paul McCulley, the former chief economist at the giant bond house PIMCO, put it, "We've had a merger of monetary and fiscal policy. We've broken down the church-and-state separation between the two . . . We haven't had a declaration to that effect. But it would be surprising if you had a declaration—you just do it."[54]

If this was a revolution, what kind of revolution was it and whose interests did it serve? "Just doing it" left these questions up for grabs. Central banks found themselves at the center of increasingly feverish speculation about their actual and possible role.

One obvious interpretation was that the monetization of giant stimulus spending was the belated and long overdue triumph of radical Keynesianism, a return to the logic of so-called functional finance first spelled out in World War II.[55] The zealous new school of Modern Monetary Theory rode to prominence on the coattails of Bernie Sanders and his revival of the American left.[56] In the UK, there was talk in the circles around Jeremy Corbyn's Labour Party of "People's QE" and radical experiments with helicopter money.[57] If government spending, whether on welfare or tax cuts, was funded by issuing debt that was ultimately purchased by the central bank, why not cut out the financial sector and simply equip every citizen with a central bank account? Then you could airdrop money to those accounts in a combined and direct fiscal-monetary intervention. As Ben Bernanke would admit in retirement, the main problem with such a policy was "not its economic logic but its political legitimacy."[58] The risk was that the central bank's money printing power would be abused. For that too there was a solution. In 2019, a committee based at the giant fund manager BlackRock involving Stanley Fischer, one of the most eminent central bankers of his generation, recommended that rather than making central bankers into facilitators of fiscal policy decided by politicians, the independent central bankers should be equipped with a standing fiscal capacity of their own.[59] In times of crisis, the central bank would act as a fiscal authority in its own right.

One might perhaps have expected the markets to be ruffled by this kind of speculative thinking about monetary and fiscal policy. Money managers, however, are not sentimental.[60] Government debt is the rocket fuel of market finance. If managing the huge quantities of Treasury debt required close cooperation between central banks and treasuries, so be it. The money supply might be inflating according to some statistical measures, but no one could take the risk of inflation seriously. Not since the 1980s had there been a real threat from trade union power, strikes, and wage-price spirals. There were some Cassandras who warned that demographic factors would ultimately tilt the balance away from capital and back to labor, but that was a distant prospect.[61] For now, 2020 was the continuation in extreme form of the "new normal" of the last ten years. When the *Financial Times* polled influential bond market actors in London at the end of 2020 about how they interpreted central bank action since the beginning of the coronavirus crisis, the overwhelming majority were convinced that the principal role of the Bank of England had been to do "fiscal QE."—that is, to absorb and monetize government debt.[62]

Revolutions are open-ended moments. Part of what defines them as such is that protagonists disagree about their interpretation, and this was certainly true for central bank policy in the twenty-first century. The scale of the monetization could not be denied. Nor could the fact of low interest rates and low inflation, or indeed the fact that heretical doctrines had gained a strong grip on the mind of the market itself. That made it all the more striking that the one group that refused the "fiscal QE" interpretation of central bank policy were the central bankers who were supposedly delivering it.

The central banks did not deny that there had been a sea change. They had abandoned their role of enforcers of fiscal austerity, a role that both the ECB and the Bank of England had still performed in the aftermath of the Lehman crisis. In 2020, central bankers had loudly applauded government spending in response to the coronavirus crisis. They bought the debt in huge quantities, but, they insisted, this had nothing to do with funding the government. So-called fiscal dominance, they would not concede.[63] Even in 2020 that still smacked of Rudi Dornbusch's dreaded "democratic money." The logic the central bankers preferred to subordinate themselves to was that of the financial system.

The huge surge in central bank bond buying may have begun in March
in response to the turmoil in sovereign debt markets, but the aim, the central bankers insisted, was not to ease government funding. The aim was to
stabilize repo markets and the mountain of private debt that was piled on
them.[64] In practice that actually meant siphoning off Treasuries for which
there was no buyer. Whether that became de facto funding of the government depended on how long the central banks held the bonds for. Were
central banks active market makers, or, in practice, more like warehouses?

The defensive answer from the central banks was that they would off-
load the bonds as soon as they could do so without disturbing the market
and driving up interest rates. At that point, the market maker argument
converged with the second basic justification for their actions—the original argument for QE. They were buying debt to massage the interest rate,
and they were entitled to do that because their basic task was to ensure
price stability, which in 2020 meant that the economy must be prevented
from sliding into deflation. Avoiding deflation meant stimulating demand
by all means. For the central bank, that meant holding interest rates down.
Once again it came down to financial markets. As far as anyone could figure out, QE worked by driving government bond prices up and yields
down.[65] Lower interest rates helped to encourage borrowing for investment and consumption. Lower yields also prompted asset managers to re-
allocate funds from Treasury markets, where prices were driven up by
central bank buying, to riskier assets, like equity and corporate bonds. This
boosted corporate borrowing and the stock market. It increased financial
net worth and boosted demand.

The supportive cooperation between central banks and treasuries in
the common struggle against the coronavirus was thus, the central bankers adamantly insisted, no more than an incidental side effect of their frantic and clumsy efforts to manage the economy by way of financial markets.[66]
Despite the relentless accumulation of government debt on their balance
sheets, the central bankers insisted that this had nothing to do with financing public spending. Their priorities were to manage interest rates and ensure financial stability, which in practice meant underwriting the high-risk
investment strategies of hedge funds and other similar investment vehi-

cles. Rather remarkably, they insisted that tending to financial markets was a more legitimate social mission than openly acknowledging the highly functional, indeed essential role they played in backstopping the government budget at a time of crisis.

Even in its heyday, Keynesianism had been an incomplete revolution at best.[67] In 2020, the scale of the crisis-fighting raised the intensity of the cognitive dissonance to a new level. In the heat of the moment, the difference of interpretation mattered little in practical terms. It became consequential only if one looked to the future, when the economy did begin to recover, prices nudged up, and yields rose along with them. How would the divergent expectations of the markets and the central bank play out then?[68] If the bond markets believed that the central bank was there to monetize the government deficit, but as prices picked up, the central bank actually withdrew support—as would be indicated by a mandate of price stability, not support of government funding—would interest rates surge? Were these the makings of a shock to come?

History suggested that there was reason to worry. In the summer of 2013 Ben Bernanke had rocked bond markets by merely suggesting that the Fed might be thinking about reducing the scale of its third wave of QE.[69] In a humiliating climbdown, the Fed had been forced to retreat, but not before the "taper tantrum" had reverberated around the world. The Fed did not finally raise interest rates until December 2015, on Janet Yellen's watch. Jay Powell as her successor had continued the long haul back to normality but had fallen short of the promised land. In 2019, faced with new turmoil in markets and a slumping world economy, Powell had abandoned the attempt to raise real interest rates substantially into positive territory. In 2020, as central bank asset purchases and balance sheets exploded, normality was ever further out of reach. All the greater, at some point in the future, was the possibility of a giant taper tantrum.[70]

What on its face looked like a powerful synthesis of fiscal and monetary policy working in harmonious coordination to help fund a generous new social contract revealed itself on closer inspection to be a confused and ill-shapen monster, a policy regime somewhere on the spectrum between Frankenstein and Jekyll and Hyde.

On the one side, there were the dramatic fiscal programs. Governments around the world spent trillions to support the labor market and business. Tens of millions of people in the most precarious positions were dependent on these payments. A peculiarity of 2020 was that the aim was not stimulus, but life support, paying people not to work or produce. Since this was an exceptional crisis, political agreement to giant stimulus was bought by distributing largesse far and wide. A lot of money was handed out simply as cash—welfare without the welfare state.

To fund this scattershot spending, unprecedented quantities of debt were issued. Normally, that debt would be rated as a safe asset. In March the central banks found themselves facing a meltdown in the safest asset markets that threatened the entire system of market-based finance. Stepping into the breach, the central banks absorbed unprecedented quantities of government debt to restore the safety of the safe asset—that is, U.S. Treasuries, UK gilts, and euro area bonds. In the process they monetized the debt. The cash that the central banks paid out to buy the debt ended up in reserve deposit accounts in the name of private banks. To ensure that they kept it there, they were paid interest. Within the consolidated balance sheet of the public sector, rather than the Treasury paying bondholders, it paid interest to the central bank, which paid interest to the banks. The financial markets were pacified. The market-based financial actors—offshore dollar borrowers, hedge funds, open-ended mutual funds, et al.—were saved from disaster. Interest rates were driven to rock bottom. Following the logic of QE, this caused a redirection of funds into equities and corporate debt. Financial markets took off from their lows in March 2020 and did not look back. The affluent 10 percent in advanced societies who hold the most financial wealth received a stimulus that dwarfed anything openly declared in the public accounts.

Not only did QE shift private funds toward corporate bonds and equities, March had also seen a lurching shift, led by the Fed, toward direct central bank support for private credit. That was the role of the facilities set up between late March and early April to make or buy loans to business. It was those facilities combined with the CARES Act that completed the incestuous tie-up between monetary and fiscal policy.

When a central bank buys government debt, it takes no risk of loss on the principal. As a public sector institution, it owes the debt to itself. When a central bank buys a private debt, it is exposed to losses due to business failure. Governments routinely take such risks when they take on guarantees for loans. When a central bank does so, it enters a gray area. It is not like a private bank. A central bank cannot fail.[71] So far as local currency operations are concerned, it could in principle absorb huge losses and operate with no capital or even negative capital. The risk in absorbing losses is political and legal, not financial.[72] Given parliamentary prerogatives over the budget, no central bank wants to be accused of abusing its independence by putting taxpayer funds at risk—"spending money"—without explicit approval from the legislature. So in an artificial, but nevertheless potent-looking gesture, the CARES Act explicitly authorized the Fed to act as a publicly backed emergency lender.

Of the $2.3 trillion in funding originally approved under the CARES Act, $454 billion was reserved as a congressionally approved loss-absorbing fund for the Fed. The precise types of loan were left unspecified. So too were the terms under which the Fed would lend. It might choose to impose conditions, but at Treasury Secretary Steven Mnuchin's insistence, there was no general requirement to do so. It was simply a giant commitment to provide support to any part of the private credit system that needed it. How giant was determined by the degree of leverage. Again, to talk in terms of leverage was, as far as the Fed was concerned, an exercise in artificiality. It was, after all, literally the last bank in the world that could run out of cash. Leverage here had the significance of suggesting that taxpayer money lent by way of the Fed was more potent. Taxpayers were, Treasury Secretary Mnuchin was keen to emphasize, getting "more bang for their buck."[73] The ratio that was commonly bandied about was 10 to 1. Backed by the CARES Act, the Fed was now "equipped" to make at least $4.5 trillion in loans.

By buying Treasuries, the Fed had stabilized the financial system, while incidentally providing a monetary backstop for public debt. Now Congress was giving its blessing to this lopsided marriage. It gave the Fed

the explicit political authorization to spawn a congressionally backed lending operation on a scale 50 percent larger than the balance sheet of JP
Morgan. From a technical-financial point of view, the $454 billion appro-
priation was a shell game—the Fed was recasting its unlimited firepower
in the form of an imposing but "ordinary" bank. But confidence was all. The
Fed didn't actually need to buy debt. Others did the buying for it.

Together with the massive downward pressure that it was exercising on
Treasury yields, the Fed's promise that it would if necessary back the private bond market unleashed a tidal wave of money into corporate bonds.
Far from suffering a credit crunch, corporate borrowers embarked on a
historic binge of bond issuance.

In the second quarter of 2020, as American society reeled under the
effects of the shutdown and the sharpest recession on record, corporate
America made its own record. It issued $873 billion in bonds in a single
quarter.[74] As the stock market recovered, initial public offerings of shares
bounced back too. By the end of the year, total corporate bond issuance in
the United States had hit $2.5 trillion.[75] Worldwide, in bonds and share is-
sues, corporations raised $3.6 trillion.[76] Despite the prevailing uncertainty
and the immense volume of issuance, American investment-grade bonds
attracted a yield of as little as 2.6 percent, down from 2.8 percent in 2019.
With such easy funding available, only the weakest corporations needed
actually to avail themselves of the CARES Act.

In late March, troubled aircraft maker Boeing found itself locked out
of the capital market and lobbying hard for up to $60 billion in aid for itself
and its suppliers, who were in even worse shape. The final draft of CARES
included $17 billion for firms critical to America's national security, but
that money came with conditions.[77] Publicly traded companies that took
the national security funds were expected to give stock or stock warrants
to the government as security. They also had to accept restrictions on stock
buybacks, executive compensation, and layoffs.[78] Boeing had lobbied hard
for support, but it did not like the conditions. Instead, it turned to the bond
market. Boeing had hoped to raise $15 billion, but found itself with buyers

for $70 billion. The yields on offer were attractive and CARES had signaled to investors that Boeing had an implicit guarantee of survival. With that in place, it was able to raise $25 billion and still retain its somewhat implausible investment grade.[79] Then Boeing announced a wave of job cuts that by the end of the year had slashed the corporate payroll from 161,000 to 130,000.[80]

At the end of the year, of the $17 billion in CARES Act defense industry funding, only $736 million had been taken up. The only firms that applied were small and of marginal relevance to U.S. national security. The fact that they were willing to go through the paperwork and accept the restrictions of the government money was a sign of their desperation. The rate of interest of 5.5 percent was unattractive for any larger borrowers. In total, of its initial commitment to buy $750 billion in corporate bonds, by August the Fed had actually purchased only $12 billion.[81]

The dog-eat-dog logic of the bond market binge was clear from the start. The first big issue of bonds that fired the starting gun for higher risk bond issuers in April was, of all firms, Carnival Cruise Line.[82] Though Carnival's business was frozen and its giant liners were riding at anchor, though the *Diamond Princess* had suffered seven hundred cases of coronavirus and fourteen people had died, when the cruise business resumed, only the biggest firms would survive. This was the perfect moment, therefore, to invest in Carnival's future market dominance. On April 1, it raised $6.25 billion in bonds and equity. The rate of return was a handsome 12 percent.

Though the stock market indices surged from March 23, 2020, this was not a broad-based recovery. It was brutally selective. The boom was led by a small group of superstar firms, above all in the tech sector.[83] In light of the coronavirus crisis, their future seemed assured. We clearly could not live without them. By the end of the year, the most favored firms, like Amazon, could issue bonds at yields as low as 1.5 percent. At the same time, a large part of the "old" economy was in deep trouble. Bankruptcies spread particularly across the retail sector, a huge employer of low-wage workers, mainly women. Malls and department stores did not attract a national security rating. Inequality was not just a matter of inequality between those who owned wealth and those who did not, or between management and workers. It was also decided by which firms happened to prosper under the strange circumstances of 2020 and which did not, who attracted support and on what terms. If you were a contract worker in a meat-packing plant, a manager at Amazon, a West Texas rig oil worker, or a cosmetics salesperson in a failing suburban mall, your fortunes in 2020 were wildly different.

It was the discriminatory, uneven nature of the coronavirus crisis that unleashed a frenzy of stock market trading led by retail day traders. Deprived of the pleasures of sports betting, it was above all young men who in the spring of 2020 took to the share trading platform Robinhood to try their luck picking winners on the stock market.[84] Real-time account data strongly suggest that a significant fraction of America's stimulus checks found their way into the stock market.[85] In the week following the issue of the checks, people who received them noticeably increased their activity in buying and selling stocks. In the case of those earning between $35,000 and $75,000, stock trading increased by 90 percent. For those between $100,000 and $150,000 the bump was over 80 percent. Those who really wanted to make a killing added leverage. By September, 43 percent of one sample of retail investors reported that they were using stock options or margin trades to increase the size of their bets.[86] While risky, it was an entirely rational response to the lopsided nature of the recovery. The punters on Robinhood were not waiting for radical activists to win their argument for "People's QE" and citizens' accounts at the central bank. If the Fed's largesse was underpinning both the issuance of stimulus checks and a boom in the stock market, why wait for politics to connect the dots? Why not place whatever chips you could scrape together in the game where the real money was being made?

Chapter 8

THE TOOLKIT

The scale of fiscal and monetary policy deployed by governments in rich countries to counter the effect of the shutdowns was impressive. The resources of the rest of the world were far more limited. How would they cope?

The storm that hit the emerging markets and low-income economies in the early months of 2020 was fast moving and massive. According to economists at the Institute of International Finance, the organization which represents global high finance, between mid-January and mid-May 2020, equity and bond markets in twenty-one large emerging economies suffered a cross-border outflow of $103 billion. That was more than four times worse than the outflow after the start of the global financial crisis in September 2008.[1] For stressed borrowers in sub-Saharan Africa, the financial markets were effectively closed from February and the damage was not limited to them. Far stronger economies were hit hard as well.

With an annual economic output of over $3 trillion in purchasing power parity, Brazil is a giant among the emerging markets. Dwarfing the rest of Latin America, it ranks alongside Indonesia and Russia, behind only China and India. In the spring of 2020, Brazil faced a financial storm. In a matter of months, it saw the value of its currency plunge by 25 percent, delivering a huge hit to anyone buying imported goods or servicing debts denominated in dollars. The stock market in São Paulo lost half its value by late

March. The cost of taking out insurance against default on five-year sovereign debt surged from a low of 100 basis points in mid-February to 374 basis points a month later, hiking borrowing costs.[2] The collapse in raw material prices exerted painful pressure. Giant Brazilian firms with huge financial resources like oil group Petrobras and mining company Vale saw their long-dated foreign currency bonds lose 30 to 40 cents on the dollar. Normally, this would have been enough to put them in distressed debt territory. "It happened so quickly," said one bond analyst. "People weren't thinking about recovery value; this was priced to panic."[3]

How would the emerging markets weather the storm? Would a financial crisis cripple their ability to respond to coronavirus? Would the advanced economies and the international financial institutions, in which the Americans and Europeans have a controlling voice, offer assistance, or would they compound the pressure? The coronavirus crisis was a major test of the economic regime not just of the advanced economies, but of the entire world.

The capital flight of 2020 may have been exceptionally severe, but it was far from being the first financial storm to hit the developing world. Since the 1990s the growth of the so-called emerging markets had been the success story of the world economy. From a low base, considerable prosperity for enormous numbers of people had spread around the world, but this growth was uneven and unstable. It was punctuated by crises—in 1997 in East Asia, in 1998 in Russia, and in 2001 in Argentina and Turkey. Buoyed by China's growth, the emerging markets came through the global financial crisis of 2008 relatively well. However, all it took in 2013 was the suggestion that the Federal Reserve might be about to raise rates to unleash the "taper tantrum," sending money sloshing back to the United States. The following year, the bottom fell out of commodity markets. Nigeria and Angola, sub-Saharan Africa's largest oil exporters, saw their per capita income retreat. Venezuela spiraled down the drain. Brazil plunged into a severe recession. Political problems were never far away. Thailand was shaken by a coup in 2014. Under the misrule of Jacob Zuma, economic growth in

South Africa flatlined. Unemployment in the townships hovered around 25 percent. Even a growth engine like China was not immune to setbacks. In 2015 Shanghai's stock market crashed, the yuan slid, and $1 trillion in foreign reserves fled China. Beijing managed to countersteer, but China's slowdown added to the pressure on commodity prices.

Despite these setbacks, in a world in which interest rates were at rock bottom, emerging market borrowers continued to find willing lenders. They were one of the most promising frontiers of financial development. By 2019 the external debts of middle-income countries, the emerging markets in the true sense, came to $7.69 trillion, of which $484 billion was in the form of long-term bonds held by private investors, $2 trillion was long-term debts owed to banks, and $2.1 trillion was short-term borrowing. Even the highest risk low-income countries saw their hard currency debt triple over the five years to 2019 to more than $200 billion.[4] Increasingly, the low- and middle-income economies joined the system of market-based finance, under the terms of what Daniela Gabor has called the "Wall Street consensus," as distinct from the Washington consensus of the 1990s. In this new world of global finance, institutions like the IMF and the World Bank acted as auxiliaries not just to big banks, but also to asset managers and the operators of bond and derivative markets.[5] Membership in this network was alluring, offering vast amounts of credit on seemingly easy terms. The question was how stable it was and who, when the going got rough, would bear the risk.

Critics of globalization warned that these debts hung over the developing world like the sword of Damocles. In opening themselves up to international finance, they had placed themselves at the mercy of the global credit cycle.[6] If credit conditions tightened and the dollar strengthened, they could face a sudden stop in external funding. They would then be forced to make excruciating spending cuts that would cause huge pain to hundreds of millions of vulnerable people and put both their future economic growth and their political stability in jeopardy. At the end of 2019, almost half of the lowest-income countries in the world were already in debt distress.[7]

Decades of experience showed the peril, but rather than simply accepting their fate, the emerging markets learned.[8] From the 1990s, they developed a repertoire of policies with which to manage the risks arising from the global financial system. The toolkit was a compromise between key elements of the free-market Washington consensus and more interventionist policies.[9] Hedging the risks of global integration was not without cost. Nor did the new policy toolkit offer a guarantee of complete autonomy. The emerging markets had not discovered a magic formula for "taking back control." Nor was that the point. They had found ways to make the risks of globalization more manageable, and that, frankly, suited everyone.[10] Vulture funds might prey on distressed debtors. Disaster capitalism was real. But it was a niche business. What the biggest banks and fund managers wanted to see was emerging market central banks and treasuries developed into solid buttresses of the dollar-based Wall Street system.

One key move was to minimize sovereign borrowing in foreign currency. As far as possible, from the early 2000s, governments in emerging markets did as advanced economy governments did: they borrowed, whether from their own citizens or foreign lenders, in their own currency. Crucially, that enabled their national central banks to retain ultimate control over repayment. As a last resort they could simply print checks. Doing so risked inflation and a collapse in the external value of the currency, but what was taken off the table was an outright inability to pay. Argentina, which was forced back into default in 2020, was unusual. There, 80 percent of government debt was in foreign currency, an expression of distrust on the part of both domestic and foreign investors. For Indonesia, the share of local currency borrowing was over 70 percent. In Thailand, it was close to 100 percent. One might think that such loans would make unattractive investments for foreign investors, but in a world of very low interest rates, there were plenty of takers.[11] With a local currency sovereign bond market in place, you could start on the adventure of market-based finance, complete with securitization, derivatives, and repo markets.[12] In Peru, South Africa, and Indonesia ahead of the crisis, 40 percent of local currency government debt was held by foreign investors.[13] This did not eliminate the risk of a financial panic. Indeed, with larger and complicated debt markets came the risk of bigger panics. As in an advanced economy, the central bank might then have to step in to stabilize the market. Foreign lenders, on the other hand, bore the risks resulting from fluctuating bond prices and exchange rates.

A second crucial lesson was not to lessen the currency risk for foreign lenders by attempting to peg exchange rates. Fixing the exchange rate against the dollar or the euro offered a mirage of stability. In good times, it would attract excessive inflows of foreign capital. In bad times, money would run, and in that event, it was both futile and expensive to try to maintain a dollar peg. The amount of hot money that would be mobilized by both foreign and local investors was simply too great. Better to let them exit and pay the price in losses as the local currency depreciated. If investors needed to hedge their risks, there were always the derivatives markets.

Big devaluations were painful. They inflicted heavy losses on importers, who had to pay more for their goods, and on those who were unfortunate or unwise enough to have borrowed in dollars. A sudden devaluation, if it gathered momentum, might overshoot. Then the national authorities would have no alternative but to hike interest rates, amplifying the pain. To moderate these risks, what was warranted was not a rigid defense of a particular currency peg, but intervention to moderate the pace of exchange rate movements. For this the authorities needed ample foreign exchange reserves. From the beginning of the millennium, China's reserves rose to a peak in 2014 of $4 trillion. No one could match that, but Thailand, Indonesia, Russia, and Brazil all accumulated large foreign exchange reserves too. All told, by early 2020 the reserves of the major emerging markets other than China amounted to $2.6 trillion.[14]

Where national reserves were not enough, it helped to establish regional networks, which allowed countries to pool reserves and support one another in their efforts to manage capital flows. Asia led the world in this respect with its Chiang Mai network.[15] By contrast, both Latin America and sub-Saharan Africa lacked a strong regional financial network. In an emergency they would have to rely on the International Monetary Fund or on assistance from friendly central banks in the form of liquidity swap lines. The inner core of the liquidity swap network were the dollar swap lines established by the Federal Reserve since 2007. Those were reserved for only the most privileged of the EM, Mexico and Brazil being the two candidates chosen both in 2008 and 2020. Beyond the Fed network, since 2008 several other central banks had established liquidity lines, notably the Bank of Japan and the People's Bank of China.[16]

To talk about financial flows in the abstract obscured the fact that they were largely driven by a cluster of big businesses and financial firms and a handful of extremely wealthy individuals. The Lehman Brothers bankruptcy in September 2008 demonstrated the systemic damage that could be done by a single bank failure. In the aftermath, firm-by-firm regulation of systemically important financial institutions—so-called macroprudential regulation—was widely adopted. In emerging markets, that meant checking the foreign exchange exposure of banks and other corporations large enough by themselves to upset the national economy.[17] This kind of regulation was intrusive and apt to provoke opposition from the business lobby, but it was essential to securing financial stability.

Finally, if all else failed, capital controls were no longer taboo.[18] Between the 1970s and the 1990s the push to liberalize the movement of capital across borders had been the great crusade of neoliberalism. But in a world in which the Fed, the European Central Bank, and the Bank of Japan were engaged in wholesale manipulation of their bond markets, sending trillions of dollars sloshing around the world in search of yield, even agencies such as the IMF and the BIS acknowledged that the emerging markets were within their rights to ward off the inflow of capital and where necessary to slow the outflow. After all, no one could pretend that the capital flows in the 2010s, pushed by central bank policy in the West and pulled by the roaring development of China's state capitalism, were responding to what used to be known as market forces. If the advanced economies were undergoing a silent revolution in fiscal and monetary policy, if the Fed, the ECB, and the Bank of Japan were increasingly in charge of bond markets, then this had implications for the emerging markets too.

As the BIS remarked in its 2019 annual report, in managing the risks of financial globalization, practice had moved ahead of theory. After more than twenty-five years, the more sophisticated emerging markets were experienced in handling the volatility of global capital flows.[19] Though it lacked a slogan like "the Washington consensus," a new toolkit had emerged. And the international financial institutions, notably the International Monetary Fund, were learning too. Though it continued to run national programs with tough conditionality, the IMF preferred to see itself as a cooperative and self-reflexive partner in what was dubbed the Global Financial Safety Net.[20] Its principal role, at least according to its new self-understanding, was not to discipline rogue sovereigns, but to help developing countries acquire the capacities they needed to maneuver successfully in the world of market-based finance. That this helped to extend the reach of bond merchants, financial advisors, and asset managers hardly needed saying. Financial globalization was a given.

The question in 2020 was how the Wall Street consensus and the new toolkit of the EM would stand up under severe stress. Would emerging market borrowers be able to retain access to the dollar-based financial system, and at what price? Would they be able to prioritize the needs of their national economies, or would they, as so often, be forced to raise interest rates and cut spending to stanch outflows of capital?

In early April, ahead of the spring meetings of the IMF and the World Bank, there was a real sense of terror. Commodity prices were plunging. Oil and gas exporters like Algeria, Angola, and Ecuador were under huge pressure. The outlook for tourism and remittance revenue was bleak. Lockdowns were put into effect around sub-Saharan Africa and Latin America, but at the price of an alarming surge in poverty. The FAO warned of a food price surge and forecast that the Covid-19 pandemic would add between 83 and 132 million people to the total number of undernourished in the world.[21] The IMF announced that 102 members had applied for help.[22] That amounted to more than half the members of the UN General Assembly.

On March 26 the G20 governments had committed to "do whatever it takes and to use all available policy tools to minimize the economic and social damage from the pandemic, restore global growth, maintain market stability, and strengthen resilience."[23] But what did that mean? The IMF promised to commit its full lending capacities of $1 trillion.[24] Would that be enough? To meet the crisis, a coalition of African and European heads of government called for a collective emergency effort, including a new allocation of the IMF's synthetic currency, known as SDRs.[25] Held in accounts at the IMF, SDRs are the closest thing we have to a world currency. Expanding SDR issuance would give poor countries an instant infusion of "synthetic" IMF reserves that they could use as collateral for dollar borrowing. The question was whether the other stakeholders in the IMF would agree.

On the board of the IMF, the United States holds a controlling minority. The advent of the Trump administration had raised fears about its nationalist belligerence. And this was well merited as far as international trade was concerned. By 2020, U.S. obstruction had effectively paralyzed the World Trade Organization. Over the summer Washington would also begin a campaign against the World Health Organization. As far as international finance was concerned, the Trump administration had shown itself more cooperative. The White House raised no objection to the Fed's swap lines. At the end of March, at the urging of the U.S. Treasury, Congress approved a renewal of the IMF's New Arrangements to Borrow, a funding facility essential to maintaining the IMF's immediate firepower.[26] But when the African-European SDR proposal was tabled in April, the Trump administration drew the line. The sticking point was that a general issuance of SDRs would put new money in the pockets of Venezuela and Iran. Not only was that unacceptable to the Trump administration on political grounds, but it risked stirring up opposition from hawkish senators on Capitol Hill, notably Ted Cruz, an inveterate opponent of liberal internationalism of all kinds.

The Trump administration raised no objections, however, to a proposal backed by the G20 to introduce a moratorium on loan repayments for bilateral government-to-government loans owed by seventy-three of the poorest countries. Significantly, the so-called Debt Service Suspension Initiative (DSSI) was joined by China. This was crucial because China was for many borrowers by far the most important source of bilateral funding. Multilateral lenders like the IMF and the World Bank were not party to the DSSI, but they promised to step up their concessionary lending.[27]

If all eligible countries took advantage of the scheme, the deferral of

debt service would offer $12 billion in relief to some of the poorest econo-
mies in the world. That would free up funds for vital imports of PPE. But as
that modest figure suggests, in economic terms they were minnows. By one
calculation, the relief granted by DSSI in April amounted to 1.66 percent
of all the debt service owed by low-income and middle-income countries,
and this excluded China, Mexico, and Russia.[28] The DSSI applied only to
the poorest countries in the world. The debts of the large emerging markets
were an order of magnitude larger. According to Kristalina Georgieva, the
IMF managing director, the financing need of the world's emerging and
low-income countries might run to as much as $2.5 trillion.[29] Help for the
poorest was a moral imperative. But as far as global financial stability was
concerned, what mattered were the middle-income countries.[30]

　　To meet the crisis, the IMF rapidly expanded its lending. Never before
had it vetted so many programs. By the end of July, the fund had approved
credit to eighty-four countries to the amount of $88.1 billion.[31] The pattern
of the lending was striking. Only $8.3 billion was concessional lending,
which went to twenty-five countries mainly in Africa already classified as
being in debt distress. How they would emerge from the crisis remained
highly uncertain. Alarmingly the lending tended to be based on the assumption that they would recover rapidly, enabling budget consolidation as
early as 2021.[32] As far as the bulk of the IMF's lending was concerned, $79.8
billion or 90 percent of it took the form of non-concessional loan approvals.
That went in the main not to low-income but to middle-income borrowers.
The vast majority was not actually drawn. It was not so much a desperate
last resort as a precautionary backstop. Gaining approval for an IMF credit
line served as a way of bolstering available reserves and signaling credit-
worthiness to other potential lenders.

　　For the most stressed emerging market borrowers, on the other hand,
any help came too late. As the year began, Argentina, Lebanon, and Ecuador were at the top of the list of troubled debtors. By the summer, all three
had defaulted. Argentina had been struggling for years. In 2018, its record
$56 billion in IMF loans had not been enough to stabilize its situation. Leba-
non, torn by internal strife and caught in the force field of regional geopolitics, had long been on the endangered list. Ecuador was on the brink of

crisis as 2020 began and was hit hard by the sudden drop in oil prices. In each case, the default brought an abrupt stop to new credit and protracted legal wrangles with creditors. They raised fears of a wider wave of debt crises, but those turned out to be unfounded.

The surprising thing about the majority of the major emerging markets in 2020 proved to be their financial resilience. When faced with the sudden stop of the spring of 2020, the new toolkit for managing financial stress worked. As government borrowing surged to fund crisis spending and as the confidence of foreign investors wobbled, domestic central banks stepped in to buy the bonds they were selling. In March and April, the central banks of Korea, Colombia, Chile, South Africa, Poland, Romania, Hungary, Croatia, the Philippines, Mexico, Thailand, Turkey, India, and Indonesia all announced bond purchase programs.[33] Compared to the mammoth asset purchases of the Fed or the ECB, the scale was tiny, but for the central banks of countries classified as emerging markets to be engaging in such interventions at all would once have been thought a contradiction in terms. It would have provoked panicky talk about hyperinflation and a run on the relevant currency. In the coronavirus crisis, against the backdrop of gigantic interventions in the advanced economies, markets took the activism of the EM authorities in their stride.[34] The goalposts had shifted.

The world economy was in disarray. Huge cities were being shut down. The dollar was surging. But with substantial foreign exchange reserves at their disposal, once the acute pressures in global bond markets had been allayed in March 2020, emerging markets had no immediate cause for panic. The major EM could let their currencies slide, confident in their ability both to access dollars if they needed them and to slow the devaluation if it became disorderly. The Bank of Indonesia intervened heavily to slow the depreciation of the rupiah and to absorb whatever domestic government bonds were sold by investors.[35] Brazil's central bank was one of the most sophisticated managers of currency markets. By April it had spent $23 billion to prop up the real. That was a lot, but it amounted to no more than 6 percent of Brazil's enormous reserves.[36] Chile, Colombia, India,

Mexico, Russia, and Turkey all conducted operations to slow the rate of depreciation.

If they'd had to continue these interventions over many months, even the most robust emerging markets might have been in trouble. They would have needed to raise interest rates in an effort to reverse or at least slow the outflow of foreign funds. But the Fed's remarkable loosening of monetary policy changed the weather in the currency markets. Only a select few—Brazil, Mexico, and South Korea—could access dollars by way of the Fed's swap lines. Rumor had it that Indonesia, as a G20 member in good standing, had applied to the Fed for a swap line, to complement those it already had in place with the People's Bank of China and the Bank of Japan. It was denied but was offered instead a $60 billion repo facility with the New York Fed.[37] This made little difference. What mattered was the huge wave of liquidity that the Fed unleashed. With American interest rates plunging toward zero, the dollar reversed, the emerging market currencies rallied, and with them also the returns on offer for foreign investors.

Against this backdrop, the financial strangulation of the emerging markets that many had feared never materialized. Rather than raising rates to counter the loss of confidence, emerging market central banks followed their advanced economy counterparts in cutting them. By April, international capital markets were reopening too. The drive to raise funds was led by rich OPEC members who needed to offset the loss of oil and gas revenues. But Indonesia, and eventually Egypt, Honduras, and Panama, took advantage as well. The price of credit default swaps—insurance against default—on EM debt plunged—in the case of Indonesia from 290 to less than 100 basis points.[38] The average yield on emerging market dollar-denominated debt, which had spiked as high as 8 percent, fell back to where it started before the crisis at 4.5 percent. That was far more than advanced economies were paying, but it meant that the pain was tolerable. By the summer, in one of the more improbable comebacks imaginable, the junk bonds issued by distressed African sovereigns had become flavor of the month for more adventurous investors.[39]

In 2020 the emerging markets demonstrated their ability to ride out even a very severe capital flight. But coronavirus was not like other crises.

Cushioning the financial blows was one thing; managing the impact of the crisis on the real economy was quite another.

South Africa in the spring of 2020 was a case in point. Its public finances had long been under scrutiny, and on March 27, Moody's, the last of the major ratings agencies, downgraded its debt to junk status.[40] The rand sold off hard. Nevertheless, the South African central bank proceeded to cut interest rates to support the domestic economy. Rather than panicking, investors both at home and abroad continued to buy and hold South Africa's debt. Overcoming a taboo that had prevailed since the end of apartheid, the ANC government approached the IMF for a concessional loan of $4.3 billion, which was promptly granted.[41] Whatever financial medicine South Africa would be required to take would come later. For now, the problem was not finance, but the devastating impact on South Africa's already fragile economy of the drastic measures taken to counter the spread of the virus. Given its large urban population and the prevalence of HIV/AIDS, South Africa was one of the countries with the most reason to fear the pandemic. Under the impact of an exceptionally severe lockdown, the South African economy was hurled into an 8 percent contraction in 2020.[42] Unemployment rose to over 30 percent.

What made 2020 unique was that the financial shock was secondary to the real economic dislocation caused by the epidemic. In an inversion of the normal pattern during a financial crisis, developing country foreign exchange reserves increased in 2020. Why? Because the lockdowns repressed consumption. Imports plunged and the trade balance improved. The question was whether societies could withstand such a crash landing.[43] This far-reaching test was one that the United States and Europe were struggling to meet. Among the emerging markets in the first half of 2020, Latin America would face the toughest trial. By the early summer, along with the United States, it would become the epicenter of the global pandemic.

After the horror in Wuhan in February and the terrible scenes from Bergamo in March, perhaps the most lurid images of the epidemic in early April came from the Ecuadorian port city of Guayaquil. On one day, April 4, in the city and its surrounding province, 778 people died of Covid. Mortuaries were stacked high and ambulances overloaded. Bodies were left out on the street in body bags and improvised coffins. Vultures circled overhead.[44]

Guayaquil was the victim of horribly bad luck. Whereas Quito, the Ecuadorian capital situated in the foothills of the Andes just to the north of the equator, takes its summer holidays like the United States in July and August, the coastal city of Guayaquil just south of the equator takes a long "summer" holiday starting in early February. This meant that prosperous Guayaquileños were flying to Europe as the epidemic ran riot. At the same time, Ecuadorian expats flew home to enjoy their hometown's famous carnival.[45] Between February 1 and 14, according to Ecuadorian media, some 20,000 people arrived from Europe and North America. Patient zero was a seventy-one-year-old who landed in Guayaquil from Madrid in mid-February. By early March, she and two of her siblings were dead.

But for all the bad luck, the crisis in Guayaquil revealed far deeper problems not just in Ecuador, but in Latin America at large.[46] The fragility of public services in Guayaquil, a city deeply divided along lines of class and race, was symbolic of a continent-wide malaise that long predated the Covid crisis.

Thanks to economic growth driven in large part by commodity exports, the standard of living in Latin America had made considerable progress since the 1990s, and that extended to the health care system. Public and private health spending was running at 8.5 percent of GDP across the region, enough to fund basic access for all. Latin America also had ample experience of dealing with infectious epidemics—cholera in 1991, swine flu in 2009, and Zika virus in 2016. There were armies of world-class doctors and health care technocrats. The Pan American Health Organization, which dates to 1902, is the oldest international health body in the world.[47] The Oswaldo Cruz Foundation in Brazil has a standing similar to the Rockefeller or Ford Foundations in the United States or the Wellcome Trust in the United Kingdom. But a huge gulf separated expensive urban hospitals for those who could pay from cash-starved and decaying public health services.

Latin America is the most unequal continent in the world. While big

businesses thrived, 54 percent of the workforce is in the informal sector—
140 million workers all told, a figure comparable to the migrant labor forces
of India or China.[48] Crowded in giant, sprawling informal suburbs that
dominate the urban landscape of Latin America, they were easy prey for
the virus.

Ecuador was among the most vulnerable. Under President Rafael Cor-
rea, it had gone on a public spending spree recycling the profits of the oil
boom. When the bottom fell out of oil prices in 2014, Ecuador found itself
facing huge deficits. In February 2019, it obtained a $10.2 billion loan pack-
age from a group of multilateral lenders led by the IMF. But to unlock this
funding, the government was required to push through painful spending
cuts. By October 2019, the plan to abolish fuel subsidies was halted by
enormous popular protests. In 2020, Ecuador owed $4.1 billion in debt
repayments.[49] When the coronavirus crashed oil prices, Ecuador's bonds
sold off. From 88 cents on the dollar, the value of bonds coming due in
March 2022 slumped to as little as 24 cents. Faced with the huge cost of
coping with the epidemic, the government simply could not continue debt
service. But to engage in open default on Ecuador's $65 billion foreign debt
would risk being cut off from further credit. In the last week of March,
Quito announced that it had reached agreement with creditors to delay
$800 million in interest payments. On April 17, that was extended for four
months.[50] As one savvy foreign observer remarked, international financial
institutions and creditors were making concessions in the hope that this
would sway the electorate in Ecuador toward a more market-friendly candidate to succeed Lenín Moreno in the elections in 2021.[51]

Neighboring Peru was in far better financial shape than Ecuador.
Thanks to Chinese demand for its copper, its GDP had more than quadru-
pled since 2000. But Peru had similar weaknesses in public health infrastructure and a vulnerable population of 10 million people crowded in the
megalopolis of Lima, to whom Covid posed a mortal threat. Peru's president, Martín Vizcarra, imposed a swift lockdown and backed it up with an
immediate cash payment of $107 to 2.7 million low-income urban families.
Further payments to rural communities followed.[52] Since only 40 percent
of Peruvians have bank accounts, payments were made via mobile phones.[53]

These were imaginative and effective measures. But it was not enough to prevent Lima from becoming a giant incubator. The informal labor force could not remain idle for long. By July, at 289 percent, Lima had the highest excess mortality of any major city in the world. In November, President Vizcarra was removed by parliamentary impeachment vote, and Lima erupted in a month of violent protests. In an effort to calm the protests, the parliament installed a former World Bank technocrat as the interim president until new elections could be held in 2021.

To the north, Colombia tried to prevent the spread of the epidemic by scrambling troops to the mountainous border region with Ecuador. Colombia had one of the most comprehensive health systems in the region. It had introduced universal taxpayer-financed health care in 1993, which secured basic provision for all citizens. But this could not stem the spread of the disease in the *barrios bajos*. As urban unemployment spiraled toward 25 percent, it was not just Colombians who faced impoverishment. Since 2015 a staggering total of 5 million people had flowed across the indistinct boundary between Venezuela and Colombia—the largest refugee movement in the world. The Venezuelans now found themselves adrift. One million were without documents and without work in Colombia. It was testament to their plight that many preferred to return to Venezuela. The movement of return migration spread across the entire region. In the Andes mountains, aid workers rescued Venezuelans who were attempting to trek home from Ecuador, 1,700 kilometers (1,056 miles) away.[54]

For those who did make it back, what awaited them in Venezuela was more misery. The Venezuelan economy was spiraling toward disaster as regular supplies of electricity were interrupted. In the country with the largest oil reserves in the world, 90 percent of the population had no access to petrol. [55] There was serious fear of harvest failure for lack of gasoline on the farms. Clean water was in short supply. The initial response by Maduro's regime to the coronavirus crisis consisted in limiting Covid tests to two government-controlled hospitals.

But it was not just the lower-income countries that struggled. So too did Chile, the poster child of Latin American economic development. Initially, it sought to avoid blanket lockdowns by focusing on sealing off hot spots.

Santiago launched a series of large-scale support packages that added up to more than 10 percent of GDP. Unprecedented though this was, it was not enough to alleviate mass immiseration. In nightly protests, the word *hambre* (hunger) was projected onto the landmark Telefónica tower in the capital. Hoping to forestall a comprehensive social crisis and a resumption of the unrest that had destabilized Chile in 2019, the government in mid-April pushed for a rapid return to the "new normal." It was premature. The disease had not yet peaked. On May 15, a surging wave of infections forced the government to impose a total lockdown on Santiago.[56] In a country that since the days of the Pinochet dictatorship had been a byword for frugality, the deficit in 2020 exploded to 9.6 percent of GDP, the highest in half a century.[57]

But money was not Chile's major problem. To cushion the devaluation of the peso in early 2020, the Chilean central bank spent $20 billion in foreign exchange intervention. To provide it with additional ammunition, Chile joined Peru, Mexico, and Colombia as the first four countries to access a new facility created by the International Monetary Fund, a so-called Flexible Credit Line.[58] The IMF set aside $61 billion for Mexico, $24 billion for Chile, and about $11 billion each for Peru and Colombia. The total of $107 billion ran to a remarkable 10 percent of the IMF's total lending capacity, more than the total funds that the IMF has set aside for Covid support for a hundred smaller countries. Anxious to avoid accusations of high-handed intervention, the IMF provided funding without conditions. In the manner of a gigantic commercial credit line, access depended not on making structural adjustment, but on paying a commitment fee, which, in the case of Mexico's $61 billion facility, came to $163 million in 2020.

As had been the case in 2008–2009, Mexico had the singular distinction of both drawing on an IMF credit line and receiving support direct from the United States by way of a Federal Reserve liquidity swap. There was thus no prospect of Mexico running out of dollars. But despite the level of support it received from the outside, López Obrador's government pursued a remarkably passive response to the coronavirus crisis.[59] It provided virtually no fiscal stimulus to offset the fall in economic activity and exports. All told, emergency spending in 2020 came to a derisory 0.6 percent of GDP.[60] The result was a surge in poverty. The number of Mexicans eking out a living on less than $5.50 per day increased from 33 to 44 million. A similar policy of malign neglect was pursued toward the epidemic itself. For lack of testing, the course of the disease in Mexico is hard to chart with any precision. But the mortality figures tell a tale. By September 26, over 139,000 Mexicans had died of Covid, 1 in 1,000 of the population, second only to Peru.[61] It was Mexico and Brazil, the two giants of Latin America, that would turn the region into the new center of the global pandemic.

With regard to the pandemic, the failure of presidential leadership in Brazil was near total. As the disease spread from the globe-trotting jet set in São Paulo to the rest of Brazilian society, President Bolsonaro continued to deny the seriousness of the situation.[62] It was left up to Brazil's state-level governments—regions the size of European countries—to react. The partial lockdowns that they were able to organize slowed the spread of the disease. But these also caused economic havoc. The virus exposed the huge gap between Brazil's powerhouse global corporations and the millions of small businesses that account for the bulk of employment. Official unemployment, which was already around 12 percent at the beginning of 2020, lurched upward toward 15 percent, and official statistics had little to say about the 40 million informal workers who make up almost half the Brazilian workforce.[63]

The initial impulse of Brazil's Chicago-trained economy minister Paulo Guedes was niggardly. He thought a $1 billion package of emergency measures would suffice. But that did not satisfy the National Congress, where Bolsonaro's opponents were calling for far more generous action. Not wanting to be outflanked, the government threw caution to the wind, declared a "state of calamity," suspended all fiscal rules, and introduced a 600-real-per-month stipend for the 68 million poorest Brazilians.[64] By the end of the year, the bill would run to $57 billion. All in all, the emergency spending of the Bolsonaro government in 2020 came to an impressive $109 billion, or 8.4 percent of GDP, which put Brazil on a par with the UK and Israel.[65] That helped to ensure that the overall contraction of GDP in 2020 was no more than 5 percent, compared to a slump of between 7 and 9 percent in Argentina and Mexico.[66] As in the United States, the scale of the crisis response meant that Brazil actually saw a temporary reduction in poverty and inequality in 2020.

The Latin American countries, which were among the hardest hit by the Covid crisis in 2020, thus rode out the initial impact of the financial shock. And they were even able to access international capital markets. Between March and June, ten Latin American governments, led by Mexico and Brazil, were able to raise a total of more than $24 billion in foreign currency bonds. Rates varied from 5.8 percent for Guatemala to as little as 2.5 percent for Chile. Every issue was several times oversubscribed.[67] Even Peru, in the midst of intense political turmoil, was able to float $1 billion in twelve-year bonds, $2 billion in notes set to mature in 2060, and another $1 billion in century bonds, not repayable until 2120. As investment bankers acknowledged, the "political backdrop" was "challenging." But Peru's growth prospects were good and its existing debt burden was slight. To borrow $1 billion for a century, Peru paid a premium of no more than 1.70 percentage points above U.S. Treasuries, whose current yield was 0.85 percent. As Goldman Sachs's chief Latin American economist remarked, it all came down to the global environment: "we are living in a world with abundant liquidity."[68]

Getting dollars was not the issue. Instead it was the pandemic and the question of economic recovery. Export sectors like Peru's copper mines or Brazilian iron ore offered good prospects for foreign investors. But as for the wider economy, the outlook was grim. In 2020, the IMF predicted that Latin America's gross domestic product would contract by somewhere between 5 and 9 percent, the worst recession on record. Two-thirds of the continent's young workers between the ages of fifteen and twenty-four were furloughed.[69] Allowing for population growth of 1 percent per annum, the continent might not recover to its 2015 level of GDP per capita by 2025. The UN's Economic Commission for Latin America and the Caribbean (ECLAC) warned that the poverty rate across Latin America and the Caribbean was on course to reach 34.7 percent by the end of the year, with the numbers in extreme poverty forecast to rise by 16 million to 83 million.[70] The fear was that 2020 would inaugurate a new lost decade in which the living standards of ordinary people stagnated and the continent was overtaken by more rapidly growing Asian competitors.

And given those underlying conditions, how long would the abundance of financing last? When critics prodded the Mexican government and demanded to know why there had been no substantial stimulus, AMLO's retort was that he had no intention of exposing his policy program, what he dubbed "the fourth transformation," to the kind of creditor pressure that had dogged Mexico in the 1980s and 1990s.[71] His pledge was to preserve Mexico's independence by keeping its debt as a share of GDP well below 50 percent.

Meanwhile, from the opposite end of the political spectrum, Brazil's Paulo Guedes insisted that he would do everything to contain the growth of public debt below 100 percent of GDP.[72] Financial markets were watching the generous social spending of Bolsonaro's government with increasing apprehension. How, they asked, would a populist administration respond to another wave of coronavirus?[73] More and more investors were willing to buy only short-dated Brazilian debt.[74]

The new toolkit for managing the risks of financial globalization allowed low- and middle-income countries to weather the immediate impact of the financial storm of 2020. That was a source of relief for everyone, the lenders as much as the borrowers. With emerging market central banks as high-functioning nodes, the Wall Street consensus was all the more resilient. The avoidance of financial crisis was a huge benefit. But it depended on a world of abundant liquidity and what it could not alleviate, on the ground, was the pandemic.

Part III

A HOT SUMMER

Chapter 9

NEXTGEN EU

In March 2020, the most dangerous debt in the world was neither in the United States nor in an emerging market.[1] It was in Europe. The Italian government owed an enormous 1.7 trillion euros ($1.9 trillion), the fourth largest pile of government obligations in the world, equivalent to 136 percent of Italian GDP.[2] Thanks to the coronavirus crisis, that ratio was predicted to surge to at least 155 percent within the year. That was a higher ratio than in any large advanced economy other than Japan. But what made Italy's debt far harder to handle than that of Japan was the currency it was denominated in. The euro was not exactly a foreign currency, but neither was it a currency that Italy controlled in the way that the U.S. authorities controlled the dollar, or the UK sterling. It was up to European politics to decide how and on what terms Italy's sovereign debt would be supported.

This was not the first time in recent history that Europe's finances had worried the world.[3] Ten years before, Europe's lopsided monetary system had produced an extraordinary crisis. This had been centered on Greece, but it put the entire euro area in peril. For a time in 2011, Italy's debt was rated as more likely to default than that of Zambia and Egypt. The IMF was called in to manage a workout not only in Greece, but in Ireland and Portugal as well. In addition to these individual country programs, under the leadership of its ambitious French managing director Dominique Strauss-Kahn—with the full backing of the Obama administration—the

IMF committed 250 billion euros to support the financial safety net for the euro area as a whole.[4] It was by far the largest intervention ever undertaken by the IMF, and it was deeply incongruous. At a time when the Fund was trying to develop a new twenty-first-century role, it found itself putting out fires in the "old world."

The most dangerous phase of the eurozone crisis was ended in 2012 by the boldness of Mario Draghi's promise that the European Central Bank would do "whatever it takes" to save the single currency. This had calmed the markets, but the ECB had not in fact acted. It did not embark on American- and Japanese-style QE until 2015, and when it did, that provoked a storm of protest from conservative Northern Europeans. In the meantime, consolidation was led by painful fiscal austerity. Anti-EU sentiment surged across much of Southern Europe. As economic growth and inflation slumped, Italy's debt ratio, rather than coming down, edged upward. The question in 2020 was whether the coronavirus crisis would push Italy over the brink and unleash a second and even worse crisis of the euro area. If so, like the first one, it would be more than a European affair.

It was a cruel twist of fate that Italy was in the front line of the pandemic. If the damage had been limited to Italy, that would have been bad enough. But France and Spain were hard hit too. Though they were not in Italy's league of indebtedness, the coronavirus shock would push them above the 100 percent debt-to-GDP ratio that was a psychological threshold for the markets. Most worryingly, there were signs of a doom loop in which fears about sovereign debt became linked to worries about the financial stability of major banks. As the yields on Italian government bonds spiked, so too did the cost of insuring against default the debt of Italy's two major banks—UniCredit and Intesa Sanpaolo.[5] The level of the risk was still judged to be moderate, but the very fact of a linkage was concerning.[6]

If the aim was financial stability for Europe, it was no mystery what needed to be done. The way to stabilize the unstable and unequal debts of the euro area members was to share all or part of them. If the government debts of the euro area had been pooled, in the first quarter of 2020 they would have added up to 86 percent of GDP.[7] That was lower than the debt ratio of the United States, Japan, or the UK. Europe's pooled credit rating, though not quite as good as Germany's, would have been excellent. There would have been no shortage of appetite among global investors. Bumps in the bond markets could be ironed out by the ECB, as other central banks did as a matter of course.

Though these truths were elementary, they were at the same time so contentious in Europe that merely to mention them was to rule oneself out of serious conversation. The distributional issue was everything. Whose debts were higher? Whose lower? Germany's debt-to-GDP ratio in 2019 was just under 60 percent. That of the Netherlands hovered around 50 percent. Europe's fiscal architecture, such as it was, consisted of rules that specified debt targets and constrained fiscal deficits. Those calmed nerves in the north of Europe and bought enough political cover to enable the ECB to engage in bond buying as and when necessary.[8] By way of justification for its interventions, the ECB offered a variety of pretexts, most commonly the need to guard against a threat to the integrity of the euro area that would put in jeopardy its ability to pursue its primary mandate, which was price stability. The ECB was a central bank with one foot in the 1990s and the other in the twenty-first century. It was a makeshift. It was tested at moments of political tension, as in 2015, when a left-wing Greek government came close to the brink of default, and as in 2018, when a self-proclaimed populist government in Italy challenged the patience of the North. Compared to 2020, those were mild tremors. Coronavirus exposed the euro area's institutions as decidedly threadbare.

The first crucial test came in the week beginning March 9. With the markets in New York in turmoil and a worrying gap opening between German and Italian yields, on March 12 the ECB held a press conference. The Fed was already intervening in the Treasury market, struggling to stabilize repo. What could the ECB deliver? President Christine Lagarde had good news for Europe's banks. They would receive an injection of low-cost funding. Lagarde also announced that the ECB would be buying an additional €120 billion in government bonds. This was better than nothing, but divided among the €10 trillion in European sovereign debt, it was far from overwhelming. What would happen if Italy came under serious pressure? Lagarde's answer was bewildering. Dealt a softball question by a German journalist, she sternly replied: "We are not here to close spreads . . . This is not the function or the mission of the ECB. There are other tools for that, and there are other actors to actually deal with those issues."[9]

"Spreads" meant Italy. And what Lagarde seemed to be saying was that Italy was someone else's problem. But if the ECB wasn't going to help Italy, who would? The U.S. Treasury market was in turmoil. The emerging markets were on the rack. Did Europe's central bank expect the member states of the eurozone to string together a fiscal safety net for Italy? Sources from inside the ECB confirmed that Lagarde had taken the line about spreads from Isabel Schnabel, the German member of the six-person executive board.[10] It was the line of the Bundesbank. It was also the line, which when espoused by Lagarde's predecessor but one Jean-Claude Trichet, had helped to precipitate the worst phases of the eurozone crisis. With thousands dying every day, with global financial markets in a state of repressed panic, was the ECB seriously suggesting that it would wait for Berlin, Paris, and Rome to settle their differences before putting out the fire?

For the sovereign debt markets, Lagarde's comment came like a bolt of lightning. The markets slumped, and the price that Italy had to pay to borrow leapt. The spread on Italian ten-year bonds relative to German Bunds surged from 1.25 to 2.75 percent. That may not sound like a big difference, but when applied to a debt mountain the size of Italy's, it raised the interest bill by as much as €14 billion per annum—€2 billion for each of Lagarde's seven words.[11] It was the last thing Italy needed.

Sensing the damage she had done, Lagarde backtracked fast. She went in front of the cameras to promise that the ECB would use the flexibility of its €120 billion program to prevent the fragmentation of the euro area— code for helping Italy. But €120 billion was nowhere near enough to do the job. With panic now gripping both London and New York, the ECB could no longer stand aside. On the evening of Wednesday, March 18, the ECB executive board announced that under a Pandemic Emergency Purchase Programme (PEPP), it would begin by buying €750 billion of government and corporate debt, and if necessary, it would set aside those "self-imposed limits" too.[12] For an institution as hidebound as the ECB, this amounted to a revolution. Self-imposed limits—inflation targets, rules on which European government's debt it could buy and in what quantities—are what the ECB lives by. The Dutch and German central banks continued to put up resistance.[13] In the end, it was the fear in the markets that decided the issue. The ECB needed to send a signal of determination. If Lagarde had fluffed her "whatever it takes" moment, the ECB was now at least promising to do "whatever was necessary."

The ECB's emergency measures bought time. The immediate panic in the markets subsided. But the spread of Italian sovereign bond rates relative to German bonds remained uncomfortably elevated. Coronavirus required a massive response. It was delivered by Europe's member states, but not all European states were under the same strain. Whereas Spain's GDP plunged by 22 percent in the first half of 2020, the contraction in Germany and the Netherlands, though serious, was half as bad. For the duration of the crisis, the EU had lifted all restrictions on national budgets, allowing the crisis-hit countries to spend as much as they needed. It had also lifted all rules on state aid. What would happen in the aftermath? What if the strongest countries powered ahead, compounding the preexisting financial and economic divisions within the euro area? It would drive Europe apart.

For a coalition of nine states led by France, Italy, Spain, and Portugal, the answer was obvious. On March 25 they called for a "common debt instrument" to fund a pan-European crisis response.[14] Predictably, they ran into a wall of resistance. The Dutch and the Germans refused to take any responsibility for common borrowing. A meeting of the European heads of government held remotely on March 26 descended into a shouting match.[15] It turned out that the emotional distance enabled by Zoom was very bad for European politics.

Since the start of the year, as the freshly chosen president of the European Commission, the German centrist conservative Ursula von der Leyen had been doing her best to reset EU politics.[16] Her beguiling new tune was the Green Deal, a nod to America's Green New Deal. The hope in Brussels was that the EU would recover its energy and common purpose around the climate agenda. Now the coronavirus was reopening old wounds, reminding Europeans that since the end of the eurozone crisis in 2012, they had made frustratingly little progress on the key issues of structural reform. There was no fiscal union. There was no banking union. The mood in Spain and Italy was deteriorating. Helpful suggestions from the Dutch and the Germans that Italy should avail itself of the crisis-fighting mechanisms that the euro area already had in place only served to revive bitter memories of the last crisis. Not for nothing President Emmanuel Macron spoke of Europe facing a "moment of truth."[17] And then on May 5, the German constitutional court handed down a judgment that raised tensions in Europe even further.

The case being debated by Germany's top lawyers went back to 2015, when Mario Draghi had launched the ECB's first big round of asset purchases.[18] It had been brought by a motley crew of plaintiffs headed by what passed for the brains trust of Germany's far-right party, the AfD. Faced with the ECB's low interest rate policy, they alleged a failure on the part of the German government to insist on a balancing of interests, particularly those of German savers. The German constitutional court, perhaps the most respected body of its type in the world, is in the habit of taking controversial, politically charged cases.[19] It has carved out a reputation as a defender of national democratic sovereignty. In its previous judgments on ECB matters, it had indicated its growing discomfort with the scope of ECB interventions. It was not a complete surprise, therefore, when the court found in the plaintiffs' favor.[20] But it was nevertheless a rude awakening.

The court ruled that Germany's government had failed in its duty to ensure that the ECB followed the principle of proportionality in its bond-buying interventions. Without that sanction, the ECB's action was ultra vires, done beyond the scope of their legal power or authority. The court's language was lawyerly but stark. Conscious of the impact that it might have, the German chief justice stressed that the ruling did not put in jeopardy the emergency program with which Lagarde and her staff were meeting the coronavirus emergency. But there was no disguising the explosive nature of the question: What was the appropriate level of legal and political oversight over the ECB?

Europe was scandalized. How could a German court claim for national institutions a right to check the European Central Bank? The last thing that Europe needed in the summer of 2020 was a fundamental challenge to the legitimacy of the ECB's support for bond markets. But what the court's ruling exposed was not merely a European question. It was far from obvious that anyone had good answers to the questions that the German justices were posing.[21]

One might not be sympathetic to the plaintiffs or their politics. In financial matters, the justices seemed out of their depth. They took at face value evidence from the most conservative wing of the German economics profession. But for all that, they gave voice to a real historic bewilderment. What were central banks doing? Did they have a mandate? Weren't they supposed to be about inflation control? Why were they lowering interest rates to zero to boost inflation? Who paid? Who benefited? Who was overseeing the central bankers?

Since the massive interventions following the 2008 crisis, these questions had been posed on both sides of the Atlantic. In the United States, the Fed's role was questioned by an array of opinions ranging from paleoconservative proponents of the gold standard, via technocratic advocates of monetary policy rules, to left-wing supporters of Modern Monetary Theory and gung ho advocates of cryptocurrencies.[22] In Europe too, there was an activist community challenging the ECB to define its mandate and justify its complicity with the ratings agencies and market-based finance.[23] Thoughtful central bankers asked these same questions themselves.[24] The ruling by the German constitutional court stated out loud what was undeniable: the vastly expanded role that central banks had taken on since 2008 exploded the paradigm of independent central banking that had been established in the 1990s. Its legitimacy was, indeed, in question.

By the same token, no one wanted to address the issue—not in Europe and not anywhere else either. Yes, independent central banks had taken on a new role. They had done so out of necessity, driven by crisis, and as the events of 2020 had once again demonstrated, that necessity brooked no pause for deliberation or argument. It was the crisis that set the pace. In Germany itself, in May 2020 the crisis was driving a political shift, not in the direction of the court, but away from it, not putting European solidarity in question, but tending, instead, to reinforce it.

As a near-universal experience, the coronavirus pandemic concentrated minds across the world on a single issue, inducing identification, comparison, and sympathy across borders—Chen's convergence, linkage, induction, and amplification effects. European public opinion had been deeply stirred by the nightmarish images from Lombardy of exhausted nurses, overflowing morgues, and lonely funerals. Polls in Germany showed a groundswell of public opinion calling for those countries who were relatively well placed to do more to help.[25] This extended to financial issues as well. The influential weekly newsmagazine *Der Spiegel* declared that "The German government's rejection of eurobonds is selfish, small-minded and cowardly."[26] Berlin was repeating the mistakes it made during the first eurozone crisis. The results had been both economically and politically dysfunctional, leaving a legacy of poverty and resentment across much of Europe.

Angela Merkel had always taken a strong stance against sharing liability for the debt of other European member states. "For as long as I live," she had promised German voters at the height of the eurozone crisis in 2012, there would be no Eurobonds.[27] In April 2020 she resisted the coronavirus bond proposal on those same grounds. But in the second week of May, under intense pressure both from Paris and her coalition partners the SPD, Merkel came around.[28] On a parallel press conference screen with President Macron of France on May 18, she declared Germany's support for a large reconstruction and resiliency fund. There would not be joint coronavirus bonds, but there would be a large new emergency budget for the EU. The budget would be funded by debts issued by the EU itself rather than member states. A large share of the funds would be distributed to distressed countries in the form of grants rather than loans so that it did not add to their already heavy debt burdens. How exactly the debts would be repaid was unclear, but that could be decided later. The debt would surely attract a top rating and interest rates would be at rock bottom. Jumping on the bandwagon, the European Commission promptly doubled down by raising the envisioned recovery fund to 750 billion euros.[29] By the standards of the United States, in relation to eurozone GDP, it was far from overwhelming, but it was nevertheless unprecedented. For the first time, Berlin was joining Paris and Brussels in advocating a substantial debt-funded common fiscal program for Europe.

What had changed Merkel's mind? At moments of crisis, as after the Fukushima Daiichi nuclear accident in 2011 or in 2015 on the refugee question, Merkel had repeatedly shown her willingness to abruptly change course. The constitutional court judgment was one possible trigger. To cut off a nationalist backlash, Merkel needed to make a show of leadership. In Berlin, the case for the deal was strongly argued by the SPD-controlled Finance Ministry, which was determined to avoid sliding back into the trench warfare of the eurozone crisis. Finance Minister Scholz had his own hotline to Paris.[30] But if we are looking for a deeper motivation, it derives from Merkel's appreciation that the coronavirus presented Europe with a new type of challenge, a harbinger of the new era of violent environmental shocks. It was telling that in the pivotal press conference with Macron on May 18, Merkel made the point that Covid was the kind of crisis that demonstrated the obsolescence of the nation-state. "Europe must act together, the nation-state alone has no future."[31] At the time this was greeted with puzzlement. Had not Germany's comparative success in dealing with the first wave of Covid demonstrated the primary importance of competent national government? But Merkel's standard was not basic competence. She was thinking about the bigger strategic question of the European economies and of how such public health crises might be managed in the future, through joint surveillance, countermeasures, and vaccine development. This functionalist logic, the unfashionable common sense of the globalization era, was Merkel's lodestar.[32] It was not a matter of faith or idealistic commitment to liberal internationalism. It was simply realistic. In a world of complex new challenges, European cooperation was more urgent than ever. The centrifugal tendencies amplified by 2020 had to be stopped. Platitudes of globalese morphed into drivers for urgent action.

If Merkel had been hard to win over, her former allies in North Europe were harder still.[33] The Franco-German démarche immediately ran into opposition from the Dutch, who led a grouping that styled themselves as the "frugal four."[34] The final showdown was a classic of EU brinkmanship. Thanks to the summer lull in the pandemic, the Special European Council meeting could take place in person. The marathon began on July 17 and continued for five days. The European Commission's officials combed the files for precedents that justified massive EU borrowing.[35] Teams of sherpas wrote and rewrote the text. Spanish and Italian negotiators suffered through hours of condescension and suspicion. The best that can be said for the Dutch and the Austrian governments is that they gave way in the end.

The result, finally confirmed at the crack of dawn on July 21, was a compromise.[36] It would need to be ratified by the European parliament and then by each of the member states. That would turn out to be a major undertaking. But the core idea was agreed upon. The EU budget for 2021–2027 of 1.074 trillion euros would be supplemented by a 750-billion-euro recovery fund, with 390 billion euros distributed as grants and 360 billion euros as loans. The funds would be raised by issuing a joint debt. Allocating this amount of money was fraught with concerns over corruption and misappropriation. Those would be addressed by rule of law conditionality, the details of which were still to be worked out. To satisfy the austerity hawks, there were checks and balances. Member states would access their allocation of funding by submitting national recovery and resilience plans to the European Commission, which would pass them for approval to the European Council.[37] Those plans were expected to meet the priorities of the Green Deal. The EU would use the crisis to supercharge a program of energy transition. Thirty percent of the combined EU budget and Next Generation EU package, €555 billion over 2021–2027, was to be directed toward climate policy.[38]

For the EU, it marked a moment of relaunch.[39] Since the climax of the eurozone crisis in 2012, the lack of progress on deeper integration had been demoralizing. Merkel had refused to put Germany's weight behind Macron's initiatives. Now suddenly the EU had lurched forward. The unpopular institutional appendices bequeathed by the years of crisis had been sidelined—notably the European Stability Mechanism. Instead, with the UK out of the picture, the powerful mainly Western European members of the euro area had asserted themselves within the EU as a whole. They had established the possibility of EU debt, and on that basis they had given Brussels a meaningful countercyclical fiscal capacity. Skeptics would insist that it was no more than a provisional response to an emergency. Whether any of it would become permanent was an open question, but the precedent had been established. For once, undeniably, the EU had scored a political success. It broke the negative momentum that hung heavy over Europe in the spring. And one place this was strikingly evident was the financial markets.

In the summer of 2020, the EU found itself in the unwonted position of being a darling of investors. Of course, there were political risks, notably in Italy. But as Alessandro Tentori, chief investment officer at AXA Investment Managers, put it, "Investors are hopeful that in 'x' number of years, the EU will be looking like a true fiscal, monetary and political union."[40] The Europeans might be shy about announcing it, but as one London-based fund manager put it, "in times of stress" Europe already had something that amounted to an ad hoc fiscal union. The EU's own newly issued debt would have a credit rating equivalent to the best sovereigns in the world.[41] Potentially, Crédit Agricole gushed, the Europeans were about to create a "massive new pool of high-quality, euro-denominated bonds . . . that could be used by foreign investors to diversify away from [U.S.] Treasuries and the dollar." This was the authentic voice of the people who managed the really big pools of global money. Far from being a dangerous and regrettable liability, good quality public debt was indispensable fuel for private finance.

The vote of confidence from the markets was crucial, because in practical terms, Europe's 2020 plan was just that—a plan. EU-level spending would not start in earnest until 2021 at the earliest.[42] In the meantime, national governments carried the main weight of the crisis response. They were running deficits and issuing debts to the tune of hundreds of billions of euros. It was down to asset purchases by the European Central Bank to ensure that those markets stayed tight, prices stayed high, and interest rates remained low. Above all, it was down to the ECB to ensure that Italy's yields did not rise. Only if the ECB continued to contain the spread was there any realistic probability of Italy recovering from the debt surge of 2020.[43]

A crucial complement to the July fiscal deal, therefore, was the burying of the German constitutional court ruling and a closing of ranks behind the ECB. The ECB refused point-blank to answer to the German court, the German parliament, or any other national political body. It would answer to the European court and the European parliament. If, however, the Bundesbank as a member of the euro system in good standing requested documents pertaining to interest rate decisions, which it in turn chose to share with the German parliament, there could be no objection to that.[44] If that satisfied the German court, so be it. Not having the stomach for a fight, the German justices nodded it through.[45] It was not so much an answer to the challenge as a wet blanket thrown over a political dumpster fire.

Meanwhile, far from being inhibited by the court's ruling, the ECB continued to innovate. Buying government debt was not its only tool. The main flow of credit in the European economy comes from banks. After the 2008 financial crisis, the euro area economy had been dragged down by an implosion in lending as European banks struggled to right their balance sheets. In the long battle to reverse this contraction, the ECB had introduced a system of so-called dual interest rates.[46] In so doing, whether consciously or not, it followed in the footsteps of the People's Bank of China in the 1990s. The idea was to supercharge the incentive for banks to lend by setting the interest rates on deposits and loans independently of each other and widening the gap between them. First the ECB paid banks interest on the funds they held at the central bank. Then it also paid them interest (in the form of negative rates) to borrow money from the ECB to lend on to European business through so-called targeted long-term refinancing operations (TLTRO). This system raised eyebrows because it effectively amounted to a subsidy for the European banking system channeled through the accounts of the ECB.[47] The payoff was that in 2020, unlike after 2008, the flow of credit continued. Not discipline, but ensuring favorable financing conditions for both public and private borrowers, was now the focus of ECB policy.[48]

And the ECB innovated with more than just policy instruments. Like the European Commission, the ECB had joined the green bandwagon. In her confirmation hearings with the European parliament in 2019, Lagarde had emphasized her determination to open the question of the ECB's responsibility with regard to climate change.[49] As the commission began sketching the spending plans for NextGen EU, Lagarde initiated a round of discussions with civil society groups calling for central bank bond buying to be slanted in a green direction.[50] It wasn't just a matter of supporting general government fiscal policy or approving new taxonomies of "green bonds." Key figures in the ECB's leadership indicated that they saw no reason why the bank should maintain "neutrality" in its purchase, for instance, of the bonds of European oil companies, when it was clear that the financial market was not yet fully pricing in the risk of climate catastrophe.[51] The matter was far from settled, but the fact that the idea could even be aired suggested how far the ECB had moved. Central bankers were kicking over the traces.

Many had feared that the coronavirus crisis would distract Europe from the green agenda.[52] It did not have that effect. If the etiology of the coronavirus was not ominous enough, the news in 2020 supplied a constant stream of natural disasters. It turned out that the shocks of the Anthropocene did not arrive in a neat sequence.[53] In 2020 they were arriving all at once. In the Bay of Bengal, Cyclone Amphan was the strongest ever recorded. Gigantic typhoons slammed into the Philippines. Flash flooding submerged large parts of Jakarta. In the Caribbean the relentless hurricane season exhausted the letters of the alphabet. Hurricane Eta had to be given a Greek name. Antarctica's colossal glaciers were breaking apart. In Siberia, the permafrost was thawing. East Africa faced a gigantic locust invasion. A succession of horrifying wildfires consumed tens of millions of acres of bush and forest.[54] California suffered blackouts as air conditioners struggled to meet a sweltering summer. As forests burned, the prison crews on which the Golden State normally relies to fight its fires were quarantined by the Covid lockdown.[55]

Europe was, in fact, spared most of these blows, but opinion polls show that people understood coronavirus as an indication of how seriously to take tail risks.[56] The year 2020 had been billed as one of climate action. The key date was to have been COP26 in Glasgow in November.[57] Five years on from the Paris climate agreement of 2015, it was time to update the so-called Nationally Determined Contributions (NDCs) to decarbonization. If Europe was to maintain its credibility as a climate leader, it needed to do better than the 40 percent cut by 2030 it had promised in 2015.

Though COP26 was postponed, negotiations and planning continued. On March 2, just prior to the shutdowns across Europe, the EC had released a draft climate law that would bind Europe to achieving carbon neutrality by 2050.[58] This received enthusiastic backing from most members of the EU, but Eastern European formerly Communist states, heavily wedded to coal, were far less enthusiastic about the climate agenda. To soften their objections, 17.5 billion euros were earmarked in the July recovery package for a Just Transition Fund with which to pay off Polish miners.[59]

Meanwhile, Europe looked abroad for partners in climate policy. President Trump had declared that America would be exiting the Paris agreement on November 4, one day after the election. By the summer, European relations with the American government were so toxic that Merkel turned down Trump's invitation to a G7 meeting in Washington.[60] Perhaps the U.S. election would bring a new start in the White House, but after the Trump presidency, nothing could be taken for granted. Beijing, not Washington, was the key.

In 2020 China was responsible for more carbon dioxide emissions than the EU and the U.S. put together, but it was also the world leader in solar and wind power, EV cars, and high-speed rail transport. Indeed, since the early 2000s, German and Chinese development in all these areas had been joined at the hip. It was cheap Chinese solar panels that dotted the rooftops of Germany. Germany's world-leading car manufacturers were developing their new electric models in and for China. VW alone had poured $17.5 billion in investment into its EV ventures in China.[61] Would a bold gesture from Europe persuade Beijing to go further? At Paris in 2015, China had accepted the need for all countries, not just the advanced economies, to propose decarbonization plans. Would Xi Jinping commit to a peak for China's emissions and fix a date by which it would achieve carbon neutrality?

Ahead of the Glasgow COP26 meeting, a Sino-European summit had been scheduled for September 2020. Germany was in the chair of the European Council and Merkel threw her weight behind the commission's effort to secure a grand bargain with China. The summit moved online, but the talks went ahead. As a signal of their seriousness on July 23, the European Commission launched a public consultation on the introduction of carbon border adjustments.[62] The year 2023 was envisioned as a possible start date. For emissions from industry and electricity generation, Europe had for the last fifteen years been operating an emissions trading system. Like any other form of quasi money, the value of the emissions allowances depended on the credible commitment to keep the certificates scarce relative to demand. On that score, Europe's record was, to say the least, checkered. But after many false starts, in 2020, the price of emitting a ton of carbon surged to 30 euros, and the outlook was for further increases.[63] This would put Europe's most polluting power plants out of business. By the same token, it also put cost pressure on what was left of Europe's manufacturing industry. To offset that disadvantage, it was essential to impose a carbon border tax on imports manufactured with more polluting power abroad. Given that Europe was China's major export market and that China relied heavily on coal-fired electricity generation, this was an alarming prospect for Beijing. Following the European lead, China was in the process of launching its own carbon pricing system.[64] What the Europeans wanted was a matching commitment from Beijing to decarbonization, thus constituting a climate club led by the number one and number three emitters in the world.[65] Would Beijing take the bait?

Chapter 10

CHINA: MOMENTUM

The Europeans would have loved nothing better than to have staged a historic climate summit with Xi, like the one that Obama had hosted at the White House in September 2015.[1] But 2020 put a crimp in diplomatic style. And that was true even for the biggest event of the year, the UN General Assembly in September. Each leader addressed the world from their own video screen. On September 22, it was the turn of the United States and China. President Trump reprised his usual role as the nationalist and narcissist in chief, boasting of the achievements of his administration in the struggle against "the China virus."[2] He was followed less than an hour later by Xi Jinping. In stark contrast to Trump's, Xi's speech showed a sense of historical occasion. On the seventy-fifth anniversary of World War II, Xi invoked China's "contributions to winning the World Anti-Fascist War." Playing off the foil of Trump's chauvinism, Xi emphasized the need for a common human struggle against Covid. Dividing the world into blocs, "burying one's head in the sand like an ostrich in the face of economic globalization or trying to fight it with Don Quixote's lance goes against the trend of history. Let this be clear," Xi declared. "The world will never return to isolation, and no one can sever the ties between countries." Upping the ante further, he continued: "COVID-19 reminds us that humankind should launch a green revolution and move faster to create a green way of development and life." The Paris Climate Agreement set "the course for the world to transition to green and low-carbon development." And then Xi dropped his bombshell: "China will scale up its Intended Nationally Determined Contributions by adopting more vigorous policies and measures. We aim to have CO_2 emissions peak before 2030 and achieve carbon neutrality before 2060."[3]

China, the greatest fossil fuel economy the world had ever seen, was committing itself to the end of the carbon age within forty years. Behind the scenes, the step had been prepared by a team of climate scientists at the elite Tsinghua University led by veteran climate negotiator Xie Zhenhua.[4] Beijing had dropped hints in talks with the EU over the summer, but Xi's announcement on September 22 came as a surprise. It was disorienting. Climate policy advocates, both in Europe and around the Biden campaign in the United States, had always assumed that they would have to bargain China into a bold move. Now Beijing was preempting and surpassing anything that the Western emitters could offer.

China had unilaterally opened the door to a truly global push for decarbonization. The reaction was skeptical.[5] Delivered from a rostrum bedecked with the paraphernalia of the CCP, Xi's words were easy for Westerners to dismiss. Surely it was a publicity stunt, a feint to distract attention from China's deteriorating relations with the rest of the world?[6] But try as they might, foreign observers could not in the end deny the significance of Xi's announcement. For the first time in thirty years of climate negotiations, the world's leading emitter was committed to radical action.[7] Within weeks, South Korea and Japan had followed China's lead, pledging themselves to neutrality by 2050.[8]

This was to be one of the characteristic ambiguities of 2020. China made a move to set the agenda. The public in much of Asia and Europe reacted with skepticism or outright hostility. The increasing assertiveness of Beijing was unsettling, and its ruthless repression of dissent in any form was alarming. The Trump administration would lead a push against China in 2020 that amounted to a revival of the Cold War, but it wasn't just the United States. According to polls, the mood of public opinion in the rest of the world was more hawkish on China even than in the U.S. In Australia, the share holding a negative view of China surged from 57 percent in 2019 to 81 percent in 2020, compared to 73 percent in the United States. In the UK, the hostile shift was from 55 to 75 percent; in Germany, from 56 to 71 percent.[9] But as suspicious as the public was and as aggressive as U.S. policy would become, there was a powerful countervailing force. China was not suffering the crisis and dislocation the rest of the world was.[10] Any suggestion that coronavirus would rock the legitimacy of the CCP's rule had proven wildly off the mark. China's economy was bouncing back fast. A forecast published by the Organisation for Economic Co-operation and Development (OECD) toward the end of 2020 spoke volumes. By the fourth quarter of 2021, they expected China's recovery to open up a huge gap with all the other major economies of the world. That economic growth exercised a magnetic attraction on powerful interests across the West. Around

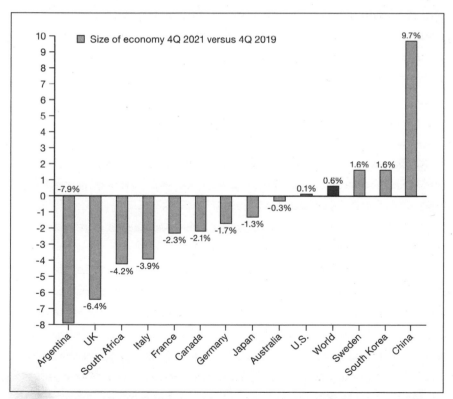

The future as seen from 2020. Most major economies face a long haul, while China powers ahead.

Organisation for Economic Co-operation and Development, December 2020 the world Chinese-manufactured goods and software applications shaped everyday life. In many places Chinese money and technology were reshaping the infrastructure of energy, communication, and transport. Back and forth, China and the rest of the world repelled and attracted each other.

Early in 2020 the symbol of the gap between China and the rest of the world was the face mask. For a brief period, these apparently mundane items were the most sought-after commodity. People around the world took a crash course in textile engineering and thermoplastics to understand what made N95 masks so special.[11]

Prior to the crisis, China had been responsible for half the global production of face masks. Following the Wuhan outbreak in January, the first Chinese reaction was to secure as much as possible of its domestic production and then to buy up all available global supply. On January 30, on a single day, Chinese purchasing agents managed to import 20 million masks. That was a vast number, but hardly enough for a population of 1.4 billion. At the same time, China ramped up its own production, from 10 million masks per day to 115 million by the end of February, still far short of being able to offer its citizens a comfortable supply.[12] And as the pandemic spread, even that huge surge in production was not sufficient to meet global demand. N95 masks remained in desperately short supply. Producer prices for export tripled even as production surged.[13]

What allowed China to overcome its own shortage of PPE was its success in controlling the pandemic. That was a triumph, but turning it into a success for export proved more difficult. China's first efforts in "face mask diplomacy" backfired badly, particularly in Europe. The Serbian prime minister kissed the Chinese flag. The Hungarian government expressed its gratitude to Beijing, as did Czech president Miloš Zeman, who was known already before the pandemic for his pro-Russian and pro-Chinese views.[14] They were the exceptions. As Chinese suppliers chased the boom, reports of quality defects multiplied.[15] Shoddy goods compounded European distaste for the crude propaganda message that accompanied them.[16] Rather than generating warm feelings of solidarity, China's attempt to exercise

soft power triggered calls for self-sufficiency. How could it make sense to
rely on long-range imports for essential medicines and basic hospital supplies? Reshoring became the rage. Japan even allocated $2.2 billion of its
Covid stimulus package to encourage firms to relocate from China.[17]

The pandemic made self-sufficiency seem alluring, but as defenders of
free trade pointed out, the discussion about the global supply of PPE was
based in large part on false premises. China was far from monopolizing
global production.[18] And the idea of a comprehensive reshoring, on account
of Covid, was illusory as well.[19] It was not just costs, but sophisticated networks of suppliers and systems of logistics that made China attractive for
modern manufacturing. Those advantages did not evaporate overnight because of a few substandard masks or defective Covid tests.[20]

Nor should one generalize from the allergic reaction in the West.
Twenty-three million face masks were well received in Russia in March.[21]
In Pakistan, Chinese medical aid, like Chinese investment, was welcomed
enthusiastically.[22] Ethiopia reveled in its role in airlifting Chinese-made
PPE.[23] Latin America, where the epidemic was running wild, needed all the
help it could get. Between March and June, $128 million in aid flowed from
various Chinese agencies to Latin America. That wasn't much, but it was
more than the United States was offering, and Chinese aid did not come
with prescribed batches of President Trump's favorite quack remedy, hy-
droxychloroquine. Most of China's aid went to the disastrous regime of
Nicolás Maduro in Venezuela, but Brazil and Chile also received substantial donations, with individual Brazilian states bypassing Bolsonaro's national government. More important than grants and aid, in any case, was
China's ability to ship volumes of medical equipment, ventilators, and testing equipment. And the partnership was profitable for China also in other
ways. Latin American countries would be partners for China's vaccine development program.[24]

The global politics of the virus drove home the point that the "China
shock" meant something different, depending on where you were in the
world. To Europe and the United States, China appeared as an unwelcome
competitor. For other parts of the world, China's growth might be daunting, but it also opened up spectacular opportunities. Brazil in 2019 exported

twice as much to China as it did to the United States.[25] For the Pacific-facing economies of Peru and Chile, China was even more important.

In China itself, the contrast between Beijing's rapid restoration of control and the shambles in the rest of the world made for an easy propaganda win. Far from retreating, Xi and his clique within the CCP consolidated their grip.[26] When the "two sessions" finally convened on May 21, Xi was paramount. The time had come to make a move on one of the most sensitive areas of China's internal politics—Hong Kong.

Since 1997, when the territory reverted to Chinese rule from British control, the so-called Basic Law had secured for Hong Kong a modus vivendi known as "one country, two systems." It was supposed to last until 2047. Under this arrangement Hong Kong was not a conventional democracy, any more than it had been under British rule. Half the seats on the Legislative Council (LegCo) were reserved for functional groups, like business organizations, chosen on corporatist lines. Nevertheless, Hong Kong tolerated dissent and free speech and the police and judiciary operated with a large measure of independence. With regard to media and travel, the city served as a relatively free interface between China and the West. Even more important was its role in global finance.

After New York and London, Hong Kong was the third most important financial center in the world. In 2019, Hong Kong was competing with Nasdaq and New York for the launch of the biggest initial public offerings of new shares.[27] It was the third-largest dollar trading center, hosting 163 banks and 2,135 asset managers.[28] The city's growth, however, was highly lopsided. In the 1970s and 1980s, Hong Kong had been a manufacturing hub as well as a financial center. The opening up of the Pearl River Delta on Hong Kong's doorstep had subjected the city's light industry to ferocious competitive pressure. Surging real estate prices driven upward by buyers from mainland China and abroad added to a cost of living that left 20 percent of the population living below the official poverty line.[29]

Political and social discontent came together in a groundswell of anti-mainland sentiment, which exploded into open protest, first in the Umbrella Revolution of 2014 and then in a second wave of demonstrations in 2020.[30] Beijing did not want a Tiananmen-style massacre in Hong Kong, but the clock was ticking toward elections to the LegCo in September 2020 and Beijing would not tolerate a strong showing from the opposition. If the coronavirus had not intervened, it is likely that China would have announced new measures in early 2020. By May when the two sessions finally convened in Beijing, it was high time for action. On June 30, China put into force a new national security law criminalizing dissent. In July, the local government barred twelve politicians, including four sitting members of the LegCo, from standing in the elections. Then shortly afterward, with Beijing's hearty approval, the elections were postponed for a year.[31] The pandemic provided the excuse for a crackdown.

It was a unilateral and open repudiation of "one country, two systems." And in the summer of 2020 it presented the Trump administration with a welcome occasion to pick a fight. On July 14, Washington announced sanctions against all those involved in "extinguishing Hong Kong's freedom," as well as on financial firms that did business with them. Henceforth, Hong Kong would no longer be treated as an economic entity distinct from the mainland.[32] The EU, for its part, issued a lukewarm statement expressing "grave concerns." Germany suspended its extradition treaty with China, but the Europeans could not agree on common action.[33] The best that the UK could do was to liberalize access to British passports for Hong Kongers hoping to exit.

The city itself was quiet. Faced with the overwhelming force that Beijing could deploy, many in the opposition were fatalistic. Since any hope of democratization was illusory, continuing involvement in LegCo served only to legitimize what was in fact a puppet parliament.[34] By the end of the year, those campaigners who were not in exile were on trial. January 2021 began with another round of mass arrests of active members of the opposition and their backers. While this repression had overwhelming support on the mainland, many powerful Hong Kongers were also happy to see the backs of the democratic activists. Local interests were not just intimidated. They were bought in.

Hong Kong's economy needed help. The protests of 2019 and then the coronavirus had dealt a blow to confidence. Down to September 2020, Hong Kong's GDP contracted for five straight quarters. Establishment types liked Beijing's promise of stability. After the promulgation of the security law on June 30, the Hang Seng Index surged and the stock market was busier than ever.[35] Huge IPOs by mainland Chinese firms beckoned.[36] If Hong Kong stock prices were beaten down by political uncertainty, mainland Chinese investors scented an opportunity to "buy the dip."[37]

Western banks and law firms with deep roots in Hong Kong went along as well. Finance houses Swire, Jardine Matheson, Standard Chartered, and HSBC all publicly stated their support for the new security law.[38] They did so over the objections both of London and, more important, many of their local Hong Kong staff. The logic was simple. They could not argue with Beijing. The mainland was where the market was. And neither Beijing nor the mainland Chinese staff who increasingly dominated the banks' presence in the region would tolerate anything that smacked of Hong Kong "separatism."

On November 7, 2020, instead of giving her regular report to LegCo, Carrie Lam, Hong Kong's chief executive, and her cabinet traveled to Beijing to meet with Vice Premier Han Zheng to petition for economic assistance. Hong Kong needed help with testing equipment to keep a grip on the virus, and it wanted reassurances on the city's future role as a financial and travel hub.[39] Beijing's vision went well beyond that. Its aim was to merge Guangdong province, Hong Kong, and Macao into a giant economic powerhouse to be known as the Greater Bay Area. When the idea was inaugurated in 2017, the area had a combined population of 71 million and a GDP of $1.6 trillion.[40] That made it the twelfth largest economy in the world, on a par with South Korea. Accounting for 37 percent of China's exports, the Greater Bay Area had spectacular future prospects. Memories of Hong Kong's autonomy would drown in the money to be made in Asia's Silicon Valley.

The Greater Bay Area was exemplary of the vision of streamlined state capitalism that Xi and his team had been pushing since 2013.[41] The core motivation of this project was political. It involved securing for the CCP a strong hold over the most dynamic economy in the world. Across China, party-led committees were planted in tech enterprises and chic private condominiums. The incorporation of Hong Kong was part and parcel of this process. So too was the humbling of Chinese tycoons, whether in Hong Kong or on the mainland. Even global stars like Jack Ma were not immune, as he discovered in November 2020 when the record-breaking IPO of Ant Financial was stopped in its tracks and Ma himself disappeared from public view. There would be no more "expansion of capital without order."

The broader project went beyond direct political control to an effort to tame China's rampaging growth. Key to this was financial regulation and monetary policy to curb excessive credit growth. There would be no recurrence of the near-miss financial crisis of 2015. It was a formidable assertion of Communist Party control, but it went hand in hand with a vista of economic growth and comprehensive prosperity so large that it changed not only Chinese society but the balance of the entire world. In 2019, China accounted for 27 percent of total global economic growth.[42] In the process it overtook the United States to become the largest consumer market in the world.[43] In 2020, it was the only major economy in the world still growing. That was irresistible.

Since the 1990s, American financial interests had led the charge into China, and the repression in Hong Kong in 2020 did not put them off. Indeed, the fondest hope of Wall Street was to break out of the Hong Kong beachhead defined by "one country, two systems" to gain access to the vast market of mainland China. No one was more explicit about this than Ray Dalio, the legendary founder of Bridgewater Associates, the largest hedge fund in the world, with $160 billion under management. "This ain't your grandfather's communism," he told the viewers of Fox Business news from Davos in January 2020. "Some Chinese like capitalism more than Americans do." As the year began, Dalio was worried about the mood back home. Bernie Sanders and Elizabeth Warren, running strong in the Democratic primaries, were stirring an "anticapitalist" mood.[44] And it wasn't only America's socialist tendencies that worried Dalio. Even more concerning was the Federal Reserve. Among American moneymen, Dalio is known for his interest in history. After studying the rise and decline of financial empires over the last five hundred years, Dalio was convinced that a fundamental shift was under way. The United States, he warned, was "creating a lot of debt and printing a lot of money, which in history was a threat to reserve currencies." "The fundamentals are undermining the U.S. dollar." The conclusion could not be dodged: the future belonged to China. As Dalio remarked somewhat defensively, "People have accused me of being biased, naive, and in some cases unpatriotic. I think I'm just being objective."[45]

If Bridgewater's boss was not explicit enough, Karen Karniol-Tambour, the precocious head of investment research at the firm, fleshed out the argument in an interview she gave at the end of the year to *Barron's* magazine, the weekly reading of retail investors and financial advisors across Middle America. China was "a bigger competitor and competitive ecosystem than the U.S. has faced since World War II," she remarked. It was not her responsibility, however, to rally American money to the flag. On the contrary, as she remarked, "unlike during the Cold War with the Soviet Union," in the U.S.-China standoff, "investors can have a stake in both sides." Of course, you could take the patriotic stance, you could say, "I'm sure the U.S. is going to come out on top no matter what, and U.S. technology will be better, and that's where the growth is." But a rational investor, American or not, might also ask: "Why would I take that risk? I would much rather be diversified."[46] It hardly needed saying where Bridgewater had come down.

From one of America's capitalist champions, such talk might be thought outré, but Bridgewater was unusual only in the frankness with which it expressed its views. Though they were not trumpeting the news, 2020 was a banner year in China for the biggest names of Wall Street.[47] JPMorgan was looking forward to taking full control of a futures business in the Chinese markets. Goldman Sachs and Morgan Stanley had taken majorities in their Chinese securities ventures. Citigroup was granted a coveted custodian license to act as a safekeeper of securities. In August, BlackRock was awarded the ultimate prize, a stand-alone, wholly owned mutual fund license that would allow it to compete for the right to manage the c. $27 trillion in financial assets held by Chinese households.[48]

It was the growth of China's wealth that was the basic lure, but as Dalio had pointed out, there were also push factors. The huge central bank interventions in the West in the spring of 2020 were no doubt needed to stabilize the markets, but their negative side effect was that they crushed yields. Even with a Cold War in the air, the most remunerative safe haven for capital in 2020 was Chinese sovereign debt. Offering attractive yields several percentage points above those available in the West, China was the new "hard money capital of the world."[49] By the end of the summer of 2020 the share of foreign investors in Chinese government debt had risen to almost 10 percent.[50] The attraction of the play was doubled by the strength of China's currency. Concerns about "property rights" and "Western values" didn't figure in this investment decision. The worry was not that the PBoC would bare its communist fangs but that it might turn into the Fed and adopt Western-style quantitative easing (QE).[51]

The idea was not farfetched. On May 22, in time for the "two meetings," China's finance ministry announced that the combined fiscal effort of central and provincial government would result in their issuing 8.5 trillion yuan ($1.2 trillion) in new bonds in 2020, nearly twice as many as in 2019. As in the West, the question was how you could issue debt to the tune of 8 percent of GDP without raising interest rates and thus squeezing private borrowing. In late April, Liu Shangxi, head of a think tank linked to the finance ministry, proposed that China should follow the Japanese, Europeans, and Americans and let the People's Bank of China finance the spending by taking new government bonds onto its balance sheet, in effect a direct monetization of the deficit. It was a bold suggestion in light of the fact that in China the memory of inflation dated to as recently as the 1990s.[52]

Reassuringly, for yield-hungry investors, Liu's idea found little favor. Former members of the PBoC's monetary committee, sounding like crotchety German central bankers, warned that QE would undermine confidence in the yuan. Others warned that inflation would show up—if not in consumer prices, then in asset markets. Lou Jiwei, a former finance minister, pointed out that the direct purchase of newly issued government bonds would violate China's central bank law. It might seem odd to invoke legalities in a one-party state, but that was precisely the point. "Deficit moneti-

sation would erase the 'last line of defence' in managing public finances,"
Lou warned.

It was China's monetary conservatives who carried the day. In his remarks to the National People's Congress on May 22, Prime Minister Li
Keqiang insisted that despite the huge surge in new borrowing, China
would find ways to hold interest rates low. But he made no mention of the
PBoC. The extra liquidity would be supplied by reducing the reserves required of private banks.[53] Meanwhile, China's public debt would continue
to offer an attractive spread over its counterparts in the West.[54] What remained unspoken was that China's monetary policy was primarily determined by its exchange rate target. Against the dollar, the yuan was rising,
but against the broader basket of currencies it was now pegged against, it
remained stable. With exports recovering fast, it was an easy balance to strike.

As European diplomats in Beijing remarked not without an element of
pique, the preoccupation with Hong Kong banking and finance was pre-
eminently an Anglo-American concern.[55] For Germany, China was above
all a trading partner, since 2016 its biggest. For the German auto industry,
China's rapid recovery from the pandemic was a lifeline. In 2020 China
saved the bottom line of both Daimler and BMW. What Daimler's CEO
hailed as a "remarkable" V-shaped recovery saw sales surge by 24 percent
year on year.[56] The profits were vital at a time when the European industry
was facing the huge costs of transition to EV. In 2020, after the cancellation
of the Geneva and Detroit auto shows, Beijing played host to the only major
motor exhibition of the year.[57] All the leading manufacturers chose to
showcase their new electric-powered models. It was China's younger and
less hidebound consumers and its ecosystem of battery manufacturers and
makers of electric-powered platforms that would shape the next generation of automobility.

Commodity producers were if anything even more dependent on
China. China was overwhelmingly the largest buyer for internationally
traded iron ore and coal. It was the largest source of market growth for oil.
And China was not just the biggest buyer. Increasingly, it was making the
markets too.

The roller coaster of oil prices was one of the great dramas of 2020. In

April, oil futures prices in the United States had crashed deep into negative territory. Among those worst hurt were Chinese retail investors who had put their savings into highly speculative derivatives-based "crude oil treasures."[58] They would have done better to invest in oil markets at home. In 2018, Shanghai had introduced a new oil futures contract denominated in yuan. With ample storage capacity on hand, in the face of the coronavirus shock it proved far more resilient than the contract priced in dollars. Prices never fell below $30 per barrel.[59] Eager to take advantage of the more robust Chinese prices, tankers were diverted en masse to Chinese ports, helping to absorb the global glut and stabilize prices. Given China's growth prospects, the oil would undoubtedly eventually find a buyer, if not as fuel then as feedstock for the booming plastics industry. In the summer of 2020, the International Energy Agency announced that China would in the foreseeable future overtake the United States as the most important refiner of oil products in the world.[60] The U.S. had held that crown since the dawn of the oil age in the 1850s. Now it was being superseded by China's new fleet of petrochemical refineries. Accounting for half of all growth in the global chemicals industry, China was an irresistible lure for giants like Germany's BASF—once a founding member of the IG Farben conglomerate. Between 2003 and 2019, BASF's total greenfield spending in China came to $27.8 billion, 60 percent of the company's global investment. In the face of the escalating trade war, BASF broke ground in December 2019 on its latest and largest project, a $10 billion plant in Guangdong.[61]

In its early days, China's spectacular economic growth could be hailed as a triumph of market economics and free trade. By 2020, quantitative growth had tipped into qualitative change. Increasingly, global opinion polls showed that China was seen as the world's dominant economy.[62] Under the rule of Xi Jinping, China had also emerged as an assertive superpower. In Asia, this had ominous implications. South Korea, Japan, Taiwan, and Vietnam had centuries of history that testified to China's strategic heft. No more than American bankers, European industrialists, or Arab oil producers could they escape the gravitational force of China's giant growth machine, but they had immediate reason to be concerned about China's aggressive new stance on the South China Sea and its bullying attitude toward weaker trading partners. China's new scale could not be reversed. If it were to be, it would be an economic, a social, and likely a political disaster. The question was how to contain, institutionalize, and frame the new balance of power.

One option had been the negotiations for the Trans-Pacific Partnership (TPP), a giant regional trade and investment treaty that excluded China and was pushed by the Obama administration as a "de facto China containment alliance."[63] This had the backing of Japan, Canada, Mexico, and several Latin American states. But such pacts are complex negotiations. TPP was contentious in Congress. In the course of the 2016 presidential campaign, Hillary Clinton backed away from a deal that she as secretary of state had helped to promote.[64] Under Trump it was a nonstarter. On his first full day in office in January 2017, he canceled American participation. Australia and Japan had invested too much in the negotiations to simply let them drop at the whim of the White House. So the agreement went ahead anyway, renamed as the Comprehensive and Progressive Agreement for Trans-Pacific Partnership (CPTPP). It was a large grouping, ranging from Canada to Chile, Australia, and Singapore, but without the U.S., CPTPP lacked an economic hub. A vacuum was opened in Asian Pacific trade policy that China was only too happy to fill.

Beijing's first move in 2013 was to launch the idea of an Asian Infrastructure Investment Bank (AIIB) that would help to improve the transport networks that linked the economies of the region. Over American objections, the bank went ahead, with Australia, South Korea, and even the UK joining as members.

Most of the major Asian trading nations already had a mesh of bilateral free trade agreements to reduce customs tariffs. But goods would not flow, even with the best infrastructure, if they were hampered by conflicting national regulations and nontariff barriers. Just-in-time supply chains tested the speed and reliability of logistical connections to the limit. In 2012, ASEAN, the Association of Southeast Asian Nations, had begun talks over a trade zone that would facilitate a more efficient circulation of semifinished and intermediate goods.[65] China, given its key role in supply chains, was at the heart of this vision. The negotiations were stop-start, but in 2019 Beijing upped the ante by convening a major trade summit in Beijing. By the summer of 2020 the Regional Comprehensive Economic Partnership (RCEP) was finally ready to be signed. On its official unveiling on Sunday, November 15, 2020, it was hailed as the biggest trade deal in history. The China-centered RCEP had a larger combined GDP than the "China containment" CPTPP, the rebadged U.S.-Canada-Mexico trade bloc, or the EU.

From an economic point of view what was most impressive were the new links forged between China, South Korea, and Japan, which together accounted for 80 percent of the RCEP's combined GDP. Most striking in political terms was the inclusion of Australia. Whereas New Zealand, which was also an RCEP signatory, remained on good terms with Beijing, relations between Australia and China were deteriorating fast.[66] Beijing took umbrage over Australia's assertive stance on Chinese political interference, on the exclusion of Huawei from its telecom network, and on the question of responsibility for the coronavirus. Boatloads of Australian coal were waiting outside Chinese ports under boycott. But Australia could not afford to stand aside from a venture like RCEP. In 2019 a third of Australia's exports went to China, earning a large trade surplus. There were deep vested interests in continuing the export of iron ore and coal. So powerful was the lure of integration with China that the Australian state of Victoria went so far as to sign up as a member of the Belt and Road Initiative, against the expressed wishes of the national government in Canberra.[67] Australia already had bilateral free trade agreements with all the RCEP members. What it gained as a signatory was leverage over the entire bloc.[68] China had wanted RCEP to concentrate exclusively on trade in goods. At the insistence of Canberra and Tokyo, it was extended to foreign investment in health, education, water, energy, telecommunications, finance, and digital trade, sectors that offered the advanced economies lucrative new opportunities for growth.[69]

The one major Asian economy that was missing from RCEP was India. Between 2014 and 2018 India had knocked China off the podium as the fastest-growing economy in the world. There was excited talk about the new role for India as Asia's number one.[70] Riding that wave of optimism, India had been part of the original RCEP talks with ASEAN, but in November 2019 it opted out.

The opening up of the Indian economy since the 1990s had benefited consumers with a flood of cheap imports, mainly from China. But free trade had few friends in Indian politics. The commitment to national economic policy goes back to independence.[71] India's inefficient manufacturing sector had reason to fear Chinese competition. Since 2017, India's growth rate had sharply slowed.[72] Given its huge and growing population, India could ill afford to accelerate the tendency toward deindustrialization. Proponents of the "opening up" strategy argued that India's focus should be on the infrastructure investment and regulatory change necessary to enable its vast low-wage workforce to prosper in the face of global competition. Though the initial shock of surging imports had been severe, China's rising wage costs offered a historic opportunity for India to displace it in global markets. Instead, Modi's government opted out of RCEP and declared a new era of self-reliance, or *atmanirbhar*.[73] Unsurprisingly, India's industrial and agricultural lobbies applauded. They appreciated the promise of protection. Nevertheless, the mounting sense of regional isolation was palpable.

The year 2020 dealt a savage blow to India's pretensions to Asian leadership. Delhi's coronavirus response was botched. Tens of millions were hurled into destitution. India's economic contraction was among the worst in the world. When Indian and Chinese soldiers clashed in the Himalayas in June, in the worst border violence since 1975, it did not end well for the Indians. Dozens were killed and China ended up in control of 600 square miles of extra territory in the disputed Ladakh region.[74] The ensuing patriotic protests led to a boycott of Chinese cell phones and apps like TikTok. But India could not afford a Cold War. For all India's recent growth, Beijing's defense budget was almost four times that of India and its economy six times bigger. China's economic and financial weight was simply too great, and it was making itself felt in India's immediate vicinity. Sri Lanka, Pakistan, and Bangladesh were all clients of China's One Belt One Road program. Those projects were far from trouble free, but they dwarfed any-

thing India could offer. By the autumn of 2020, Delhi was shadowed by
dark fears of strategic encirclement.[75] There was some comfort in the fact
that Washington was pushing "the Quad"—the military relationship between the United States, Japan, Australia, and India—but in that company,
India was far from being number one.[76]

It was not only Asia that lived under the shadow of China's growth. The
shifting balance was felt even on the other side of the Pacific. In purchasing-
power parity terms, allowing for the very different cost of living, China's
economy probably overtook that of the United States in 2013. In current
dollar terms, reflecting purchasing power in global markets, the United
States was still considerably ahead. China was not predicted to become
number one until the mid-2030s. That is, until 2020. The differential impact of the coronavirus crisis forced forecasters to revise their predictions.
By the end of the year China was expected to overtake the U.S. GDP five
years sooner, possibly as early as 2028–29.[77] Certainly, by the 2030s, China
would dominate East Asia. Its economy would be larger than that of Japan
and the United States put together. The longer-term future posed even
more daunting challenges of adjustment. As Larry Summers, Clinton's last
treasury secretary, put it in 2018: "Can the United States imagine a viable
global economic system in 2050 in which its economy is half the size of the
world's largest? Could a political leader acknowledge that reality in a way
that permits negotiation over what such a world would look like? While it
might be unacceptable to the United States to be so greatly surpassed in
economic scale, does it have the means to stop it? Can China be held down
without inviting conflict?"[78] As Summers suggested, it was all too easy for
commercial competition to slide into geopolitical conflict. And the stakes
could hardly be higher.

The year 2020 had started with the Trump administration in a relatively conciliatory mood, celebrating the achievement of the Phase I trade
deal under which China committed itself to raising its imports of goods
and services from the United States by $200 billion. Unlike the sophisti-
cated regulatory bargains of the RCEP and CPTPP, Trump's Phase I was

crude and quota based. Above all, it was a product of Trump's desire to present himself as the dealmaker in chief. Even before coronavirus put Phase I under pressure, it was regarded with skepticism by those who viewed China as a long-term strategic threat. Persuading China to buy more American soybeans did nothing to address that challenge. As the pandemic hit America, Phase I euphoria evaporated. The administration's attacks on China over the virus became ever more vociferous. Ominously from Beijing's point of view, it was the U.S. security policy establishment that was now in the lead. In May 2020, the White House published what it described as the "United States Strategic Approach to the People's Republic of China."[79] This report fleshed out the doctrine promulgated in the National Security Strategy of December 2017. That had first identified the Indo-Pacific as the key arena of great power competition. The 2020 document went further. Every area of government as well as business and civil society was now to be organized in response to the threat posed by Beijing. The question was no longer one of extracting concessions in a trade deal. It was the "rise" of a CCP-controlled China as such that was the problem.

This sweeping reassessment had immediate implications for some of the biggest businesses on both sides of the Pacific. American firms such as Apple and Boeing had huge interests in China. On the Chinese side, telecom provider Huawei found itself in the cross hairs of the U.S. authorities.

In 2020, Huawei was the world's leading supplier of smartphones, with a 20 percent share of the market, ahead of both Apple and Samsung. It was a world leader also in 5G network technology. Huawei was a private firm, but its founder was famously patriotic. It was hard for anyone in the West to believe that Huawei did not ultimately answer to the CCP. Since what was at stake was control of data and personal communications, Huawei's presence in Western telecom networks raised concerns about privacy, and strategic control of information. Already in 2012 the Obama administration had launched an investigation into Huawei and another Chinese telecom firm, ZTE. That resulted in both being banned from U.S. public procurement. ZTE was subject to targeted sanctions. In 2018 the Trump administration reached a settlement with ZTE but dramatically stepped up its pressure on Huawei. Meng Wanzhou, Huawei's CFO and the found-

er's daughter, was arrested in Canada at the behest of the American authorities. The White House issued an executive order banning Huawei
from all U.S. networks, but put the execution of that order on hold. In April
2020 the ban of the purchase of Huawei equipment came into full effect.
Then in May, the U.S. Commerce Department dramatically raised the
stakes by requiring a license for anyone using American equipment to produce chips for sale to Huawei. The leading chip foundries in Asia, South
Korean Samsung and Taiwanese TSMC, would have to choose between
access to state-of-the-art U.S. manufacturing equipment and their giant
markets in China.[80] To go one step further, in September the Commerce
Department widened the sanctions from Huawei to SMIC, China's leading
manufacturer of microchips. At the same time, it exerted pressure on European governments and businesses to cease delivery of essential chip-
making equipment to SMIC.[81] There was an "unacceptable risk," the United
States declared, that equipment would find its way into the hands of the
Chinese military.

The U.S. was striking at China's industrial jugular.[82] Chips are a ubiquitous component not just in electronics, but in everything from cars to
aerospace, domestic appliances, and newfangled energy transmission equipment. The industrial policy offensive came at a considerable price. A quarter of the total revenues of the U.S. semiconductor industry was earned
through sales to China.[83] But commerce was no longer the priority. American firms would have to accept the loss of Chinese markets. The paramount objective was to stop China's advance in this key area of technology.

America was attacking not just Huawei, a national champion, but an
entire pillar of China's industrial economy. Beijing was left with no option
but to rethink its approach to globalization. The new model of economic
development floated at the "two sessions" in May 2020 was "dual circulation."[84] One circuit was the economy of international trade. The other
would be driven by China's national economic development. The idea was
to rebalance the relationship between them and to make the latter independent of the former. This was not a general abandonment of globalization, but a rebalancing away from overdependence both on foreign demand
and on imported inputs that might be vulnerable to U.S. sanctions.

Back in 2015, Beijing had launched the Made in China 2025 program to accelerate the progression up the value chain into more advanced manufacturing. America's aggressive new line gave that program added impetus. In time for the two sessions in May, Beijing announced a giant new technology program with a mandate to spend $1.4 trillion over the next five years.[85] It was focused on strategic areas like data centers, ultra-high-voltage power transmission, AI, and the base stations of the new 5G network. But none of this would matter if America could turn off China's supply of cutting-edge microchips. The year ended with a roll call of seventy-seven Chinse firms added to the sanctions list, including, apart from Huawei and SMIC, DJI, the world's favorite maker of drones.[86]

The Trump administration's declaration of economic war on China was no doubt dismaying for Beijing, but its ramifications spread further. For the United States to be declaring China, the main driver of global growth, to be a national security threat upended one of the basic assumptions of the post–Cold War world. Contrary to the flat-world presumption of globalization, the United States was making the nationality of firms, Chinese or not, fundamental to Washington's willingness to allow them to access American technology. And though it had acted unilaterally and without warning, America clearly expected suppliers in friendly countries to fall into line. Some did so willingly. Australia was ahead of the U.S. in banning Huawei. The UK had long been monitoring the involvement of Huawei in its telecom network.[87] It had found no specific evidence of wrongdoing, but following the U.S. lead, it announced bans on the installation of new Huawei equipment from September 2021.[88] Others were more reluctant and tried to avoid the choice. Germany most notably refused to agree to a blanket ban of Huawei technology.[89] Deutsche Telekom was desperate to gain a slice of the Chinese market. Germany's car firms were too tightly integrated with Chinese communication technology to be able to contemplate a clean break.[90] America's sudden pivot to Cold War mode was at odds with the way in which globalized businesses had been operating in China for three decades. It forced a deeply disconcerting question: Which was the greater threat to the status quo, China or the United States?

In pursuing their new anti-Chinese line, American officials liked to describe themselves as "principled realists."[91] They criticized their predecessors for failing to realize the extent of the China threat. But what exactly was the nature of this American realism? Clearly, China's rise was a world historic event reversing a power asymmetry that had framed the last quarter millennium. The CCP was indeed an ideological antagonist and its ambition was formidable, but was "containing" China a realistic twenty-first-century prospect, or was it a distorted echo of the Cold War with the Soviet Union? Was the aggressive way in which the Trump administration took up this historic challenge in 2020 a reflection of the facts on the ground in Asia, or did it have more to do with the mounting tension within the United States itself?

The anti-China campaign of the Trump administration reached its high point in the summer of 2020 at an extraordinary moment in American public life. Against a backdrop of nationwide protests, sporadic rioting, and curfews across many American cities, senior figures in the Trump administration delivered a blazing denunciation not only of China's communist regime, but of its American fellow travelers, including those in American business. What in Washington was touted as a new realism was in fact the expression of a mounting national crisis in the United States that scrambled the alignment of economic and political forces and put the American Constitution itself in question.

Chapter 11

AMERICA'S NATIONAL CRISIS

In March 2020 the drama of the pandemic onset had temporarily enabled concerted and prompt action by American society, politics, and government. This comity was to prove short-lived. In late April as the medical emergency on the East and West Coasts of the United States eased, agreement on how to meet the pandemic collapsed. Americans blamed one another. They blamed China. Then, as the ugliest legacy of America's national history was once more exposed, they returned to the still-contentious history of slavery and the Civil War, before beginning once again to argue about the crises facing them in 2020. Congress, which had acted so swiftly in March, deadlocked. And rather than resolving the impasse, the election unleashed a spectacular process of political decomposition. As became clear, if one political wing in a contentious democracy departed radically from conventional standards of truth—if it could not agree even on the reality of a pandemic—there was no reason to expect that an election, an act of collective counting, would suffice to settle the question of who governed. In November the election was superseded by a broader and more comprehensive trial of strength. All the powers in the land were summoned onto the national stage—the courts, the military, the media, and business interests—not to address America's public health disaster or the looming social crisis, but to force Donald Trump, and if not Trump himself, then at least the Republican Party, to accept the reality of his defeat.

Meanwhile tension with China escalated, relations with Europe frayed close to the breaking point, and even the great golden calf itself, the national economy, lost its power to organize the national polity.

The struggle started with the argument over reopening. This was contentious all over the world. There were angry antilockdown protests in Britain, Germany, and Italy.[1] But in the United States, the question merged with a broader culture war that was fanned from the very top. Ignoring his own public health experts, Trump called from the White House for economic life to resume. He denounced Democratic governors for their lockdown measures and found an answer among the far-right crowd he had first courted in Charlottesville in 2017. A menacing new chapter was opened when heavily armed Liberty Militia barged their way into the Michigan state capitol. Though the object of contention was, notionally, the economy, big business preferred to do its lobbying from behind the scenes. The "American economy" that the protesters sought to defend was that of tattoo parlors, barbershops, tanning salons, bars, and gyms.[2] Dark money of the Koch brothers played its part from offstage.[3] This was a strange form of class struggle that aligned enraged petty capitalists and right-wing oligarchs against corporate liberalism.

And then a far deeper wound in American society was torn open. On May 25 a police officer in Minneapolis handcuffed a Black man, George Floyd, forced him to the ground, and knelt on his neck until he died.[4] It was not in itself an unusual event. Black men often die at the hands of America's police. But this incident triggered an amplification effect in an extraordinary upsurge in protest across the country. America's Black population suffered disproportionately from the pandemic. Floyd's killing compounded the deep sense of injustice. The mobilization around Black Lives Matter served as a rallying point for an entire coalition of radical and progressive forces. It was by no means confined to the left. By early July, somewhere between 15 and 26 million people are estimated to have taken part in BLM demonstrations of one kind or another.[5] Liberal-minded police chiefs marched with the protesters. The leadership of the Democratic Party donned kente cloth. Jamie Dimon of JPMorgan Chase "took a knee."[6] The bank pledged to put $30 billion over five years into boosting loans to minority families and businesses. Citigroup pledged $1 billion toward addressing the "the racial wealth gap."[7] Allyship was all the rage in corporate America.[8]

For Trump, this was like a red flag to a bull. The more corporate liberals turned woke, the more pugnaciously the administration took up the culture wars, declaring America under threat from subversion. To repress the protests, Trump demanded the use of force. He had the streets around the White House violently cleared so as to stage a Bible-waving photo op alongside America's highest-ranking general dressed in combat fatigues, as if in Kabul or Baghdad. It took interventions by the command chain to stop the deployment of the 82nd Airborne.[9] But even without the declaration of martial law, for a few weeks in June 2020, Americans were subject to a remarkable new regime of discipline. In a bid to contain looting, at least twenty-three major cities across the United States, including New York, Chicago, Los Angeles, and San Francisco, superimposed nightly curfew on the corona lockdown.[10] City dwellers seeking relief from the summer heat were herded into their homes by police bullhorns.

Who was to blame? Among liberals, the opprobrium heaped on Trump reached new heights. He was a fascist or at least an authoritarian. With his grotesque, Mussolini-esque posturing at Mount Rushmore on July 4, he did not even seem to shrink from the accusation.[11] The Trump administration itself blamed enemies foreign and domestic, and increasingly blurred the line between them. Antifa, socialism, and woke antiracism were the threat from within. Elite corporate liberals condoned and encouraged them. And that same group had also been responsible since the era of Clinton for fostering the growth of Communist China, which had now unleashed the coronavirus on America. Senior officials openly espoused conspiratorial views about the spread of the virus. For Trump and leading administration figures, coronavirus was now simply the "Wuhan virus." So insistent were they on this pejorative language that a G7 meeting with Japan and European governments ended without a final communiqué.[12] It stood to reason that international organizations like the WHO were also fronts for the Chinese.[13]

Meanwhile, hawks like Secretary of State Mike Pompeo, National Security Advisor Robert O'Brien, and Attorney General William Barr sketched the ideological agenda of a new Cold War, in which, as the spokespeople of Bridgewater had noted, the cards were distributed in an unfamiliar way.[14] Internal and external threats were melded into a single block. Corporate liberalism, the hawks alleged, was both complicit in appeasement of China and bent on weakening America from within. Attorney General Barr, a lifelong campaigner of the hard right whose career had started amid the anti-Vietnam protests of the 1960s, roundly declared that "the American business community has been a big part of the problem."[15] In their dealings with China, many of America's business leaders were not even interested in the "long-term viability of their companies"; all they were in it for was "short-term profit, so they can get their stock options and move into the golf resort." For Barr, this was not a moment for hedging, but a World War II moment. "We're not speaking German today," he declared, because "American business in the past . . . stood with the United States. And all the privileges and the benefits and the stability and the rule of law and the ability to profit as they do, both as companies and as individuals, comes from the strength of this country."[16] Tech and Hollywood, the two big industries of liberal California, were Barr's particular bugbears. Tech was complicit with China's surveillance state. "Hollywood's actors, producers, and directors pride themselves on celebrating freedom and the human spirit," he scoffed. "And every year at the Academy Awards, Americans are lectured about how this country falls short of Hollywood's ideals of social justice, but Hollywood now regularly censors its own movies to appease the Chinese Communist Party, the world's most powerful violator of human rights."[17] Barr came remarkably close to pronouncing a divorce between his ideal of America and actually existing American capitalism. He even went so far as to threaten that American corporations that spoke out in favor of doing business in China might find themselves falling under the terms of the Foreign Agents Registration Act.[18]

Attorney General Barr was unusual in the capaciousness of his ideological vision, but the tendency to blame China was quite general in the

Trump camp. It anchored the sense that the president was being victimized by a combination of hostile forces: a virus imported from China, the relentless hounding by "fake news," Wall Street liberals, the socialism of Bernie Sanders and "the squad," woke antiracism, liberal governors harassing Trump's loyal following in the small-business community, and a tyranny of public health experts who demanded the wearing of Asian-style face masks.

The opposite of all that was national, virile, and healthy, and if one followed the logic of Barr's remarks, it was blue-collar working-class Americans betrayed by cosmopolitan corporate elites. This in turn meant, in a dizzying inversion of the familiar fronts, that the Republican Party now stood for the working class. It was a theme that Trump had repeatedly struck since the election campaign of 2016. He liked nothing better than to be photographed alongside burly working-class Americans, ideally in work clothes and hard hats. In 2020, the refrain was taken up by leading younger figures in the party, most notably Ted Cruz of Texas and Josh Hawley of Missouri.[19] They combined their right-wing populism with dog whistle attacks on the antiracist politics of Black Lives Matter and vituperative criticism of the CCP in China. As polling showed, their appeal was not without logic.[20] The GOP's base of electoral support was heavily recruited from the white working class. If we take education as a proxy for class, the single best predictor other than race for voting for Trump was the lack of a college degree. The result was a party unified around themes of cultural identity and affect and riven with contradictions when it came to policy.

Trump's GOP was a party of self-proclaimed fiscal conservatives who prioritized tax cuts over budget balance. It was a party of self-reliance that counted on the Fed to juice the stock market. It was a party of working-class voters who supported deregulation for big business.[21] It was a party of small government that loved nothing more than a giant military, mass incarceration, and an oversize muscle-bound police force. It was a party whose base identified passionately with Donald Trump, but whose congressional leadership hesitated to do the obvious thing that would see him reelected: to launch a massive second wave of fiscal stimulus.

———

In Europe and Asia, the summer of 2020 was a period of balancing the imperatives of virus control against the urge to resume ordinary life. As the second and third waves in Europe would show, it was a hard balance to strike. Large parts of the United States, notably Democrat-controlled states on the East Coast, were engaged in the same precarious maneuvering. In New York City, the epicenter of the crisis in the United States in March and April, sustained social distancing succeeded in keeping the virus within manageable limits. The price was the continuing interruption of ordinary public life and social interaction. In many Republican-controlled states, however, and in the White House itself, the attitude was one of outright denial. As the election campaign heated up, the president wanted as little as possible to do with the coronavirus issue. He took to complaining that the real problem was the amount of testing. Close advisors like Larry Kudlow indulged him by referring to the epidemic in the past tense: "It *was* awful. Health and economic impacts *were* tragic, hardship and heartbreak *were* everywhere."[22]

Meanwhile, Trump found his own way back to the future. At the start of the year the economy had been his proudest boast. What that meant for Trump were the jobs numbers and the S&P 500. By the summer of 2020, both had taken a turn for the better. The labor market situation was less dire than in the spring. The stock market was bouncing back. Even the least well-off Americans saw a significant improvement in their situation through to July. In one jaw-dropping press conference, Trump invoked the spirit of the murdered George Floyd, who, he claimed, would have taken satisfaction from the good job numbers.[23] After all it was Black men, historically, who benefited most from lower unemployment.

There were gloomsters and doomsayers. The Trump entourage were once again taking potshots at Jerome Powell and the Fed. "I do think Mr. Powell could lighten up a little when he has these press offerings," ever-loyal Larry Kudlow opined. "You know, a smile now and then, a little bit of optimism. I'll talk with him, and we'll have some media training at some point." Trade policy advisor Peter Navarro was openly contemptuous: "The best strategy for Jay Powell going forward would simply be to . . . let us know where interest rates are going and keep his mouth shut."[24] But "going forward," that telltale phrase, was precisely the issue. How long would the rebound from the recession of March and April last, and how strong would it prove to be?

The evidence from the states most severely affected by the virus over the summer of 2020 was clearer than ever. The problem was not Jerome Powell's gloomy demeanor or the oppressive lockdowns imposed by freedom-hating Democrats. Many of the states that were first to lift the lockdown, true-believing pro-Trump red states, were seeing economic activity relapse. The problem was not the lockdowns but the virus.[25] Until it could be controlled and confidence restored, work life, shopping and socializing, schooling, and childcare could not return to anything like normal. The recovery to date owed much to the scale of the stimulus delivered in the spring, but that was nearing its end. July was the last month for additional federal support for unemployment relief. If millions of households were not to suffer a sudden loss in income, Congress needed to agree to an extension of economic life support.

Among business organizations there was widespread anxiety about the fragile state of the economy. In May, the U.S. Chamber of Commerce and other business lobbies urged Congress to provide support for state and local government.[26] The Democratic majority in the House of Representatives agreed and voted for a $3 trillion stimulus package.[27] Meanwhile, in the Senate, where the Democrats were in the minority, they pushed for an even more ambitious program: extra payments for the unemployed— so-called automatic stabilizers—that would not be at the whim of congressional approval, but would trigger whenever the jobless rate rose above 6 percent.[28] It was no more than a trial balloon, but it highlighted the key weaknesses at the hinge between American society and the economy: the patchwork and exclusionary nature of what passed for a welfare state.

To actually enact a stimulus would require Republican votes, and Republicans were at odds with themselves. A caucus of at least twenty hardline senators wanted no extra spending at all.[29] They backed the optimistic line coming from the White House. The CARES Act could not expire soon enough. Cutting back unemployment benefits would restore the proper "incentives" for work. All this had the ring about it of an employer-friendly policy, but in the summer of 2020, what America's business organizations said they wanted was not less stimulus, but more.

For his part, Mitch McConnell as leader of the Senate opposed any financial support for state and local government, what he dubbed a "blue state bailout" for public sector unions.[30] His hobbyhorse was a liability shield, which would enable an early return to work while protecting employers against lawsuits to do with coronavirus infection. As a license for corporate irresponsibility, this would never pass the Democratic majority in the House.[31] President Trump added noise to the negotiations by insisting on his pet project, a payroll tax cut that no one else was interested in.[32]

When the White House realized that the congressional impasse might leave them with no stimulus at all, they started lobbying for at least a four-month extension of the $600 supplement to the unemployment benefits provided by CARES. But it was too late. The GOP establishment was not in the mood to do favors for a president who was looking more and more like a lame duck.[33] In August the additional support for 30 million unemployed Americans simply lapsed. The best the administration could do was to extend the moratorium on evictions by way of the CDC. It was hardly the normal way to enact a major piece of housing policy; the moratorium was full of loopholes, but it was no doubt true that mass evictions and homelessness would spread the epidemic.[34]

At this point, the initiative passed from McConnell and the Republicans in the Senate to Treasury Secretary Steve Mnuchin, who engaged in almost daily negotiations with Nancy Pelosi and the House Democrats. Whereas McConnell had been willing to consider no more than $500 billion in stimulus, Mnuchin and Pelosi were talking about $1.8 to $2 trillion. The president liked the idea of a really big package with his name on it, but as close as it was to the election, that could be dangerous to both sides. The last thing that the Democrats wanted to do was to hand Trump a last-minute victory. McConnell was concerned that a giant stimulus package would lead to rejection by fiscally conservative voters. He also feared that Pelosi's real interest was in splitting the Republicans precisely at the moment that McConnell was trying to rally them to push through the rapid-fire confirmation of Amy Coney Barrett to the Supreme Court. McConnell let it be known that if Pelosi and the White House did agree to a deal, he would allow it to languish in the Senate until after the election. That would hand a victory to the Democrats, who would paint the Republicans as wreckers. So the best thing, as far as McConnell was concerned, was that there be no deal at all. There were those on the left wing of the Democratic Party who argued that they should take what they could get.[35] But Pelosi was not satisfied with the sums on offer from the White House and gambled that the groundswell of sentiment against Trump would sweep the Democrats into full control of Congress.

Caught in this net of political calculations, even as the second wave of the epidemic began in earnest and the recovery slowed, any hope of a large-scale fiscal response evaporated. In the face of a mounting emergency, America's political system had lost its capacity to assemble a majority for concerted action. What remained of economic policy was left in the hands of the Fed.

After the emergency of March, the Fed had slowed its pace of bond purchases. It had never purchased many of the bonds issued by corporate America or the "municipal" debt issued by states and local government, but the central bank's willingness to offer support, if necessary, put a safety net under Wall Street. In making its promise to buy corporate bonds, at the height of the panic in March, the Fed had crossed one important line, and on August 27, it crossed another.[36] The previous year, the Fed had embarked on a basic review of its monetary policy framework. What was to be done about the repeated failure to meet the inflation target of 2 percent? After a year of deliberation, America's central bank was no closer to an answer. The United States, like all the other advanced economies, had a low-inflation problem. What the Fed could do was to change the way it targeted its policy. Henceforth, rather than committing to keep inflation below 2 percent, it would seek to achieve an average inflation rate of 2 percent. If inflation slipped below that target, as it had done persistently in recent years, the Fed would aim to make up for it. If and when inflation finally did rise above 2 percent, the Fed would not preemptively seek to restrain it, but would allow the economy to "run hot." Amid the economic conditions of 2020, there was little prospect of that actually happening, but it changed the future outlook. Interest rates ticked upward and the hoarding of gold and silver surged.[37] Conservative America was looking for cover, and the political situation only increased their nervousness.

Against the backdrop of the pandemic and the Black Lives Matter mobilization, the electoral contest of 2020 was a lackluster affair. Trump acted out his disregard for the disease by holding mass rallies. When he fell ill, he recovered swiftly, only adding to his bravado. The Democrats had picked the safest candidate in Joe Biden and they got a safe campaign, much of which was conducted from his basement. As a battle over policy, it was grotesquely one-sided. Seeking to unite both wings of the Democratic Party, working with the Sanders campaign, Biden assembled a manifesto that was perhaps the most radical ever offered by a Democratic candidate.[38] It combined the huge scale of the $3 trillion stimulus proposed by the House Democrats with the Green New Deal agenda of the Sanders campaign.

The boldness of the fiscal program was remarkable, as was the emphasis on the climate issue. Once that had been a radical agenda, but in the summer of 2020, the markets were infatuated with Tesla, an electric car company. In August, Exxon, once the dominant player in the fossil fuel industry, was dumped out of the Dow Jones Industrial Average Index.[39] The weight of fossil-fuel energy corporations in the S&P 500, which in 2008 had touched 16 percent, had fallen by 2020 to a mere 2.5 percent. Wall Street was learning to love green capitalism. If the Democrats took Congress as well as the White House, there would be a huge surge in new debt issuance, but with the Fed as the backstop, they would learn to live with that too. More stimulus was overdue. And what, after all, was the alternative? When Trump was put on the spot by a friendly Fox News anchor about what he actually wanted to achieve in a second term, he had no answer. At its national convention the GOP simply did without a manifesto. For them the campaign wasn't about policy. It was about Trump and his personification of a certain vision of America.

This was not a way to win a majority. From the spring, the polls showed a solid margin of victory for Biden, and for all the nail-biting anxiety around the world, that is precisely what America's electorate delivered. What made it close in the electoral college was that Trump did markedly better than the pollsters predicted in most of the key battleground states. Furthermore, Biden's clear win in the presidential race did not translate down ticket into a congressional clean sweep. Control of the Senate was left up for grabs. It would depend on two runoff elections in Georgia on January 5.

The 2020 election translated into politics what were increasingly stark divides in American society along economic, social, regional, and cultural lines.[40] In the election of 2000, George W. Bush had won 2,417 counties that generated 45 percent of the U.S. GDP, while Al Gore won 666 mainly urban counties that generated 55 percent of the national output.[41] By 2020 the split had become far more lopsided. Biden won only 509 counties, but they were home to 60 percent of America's population and generated 71 percent of national output. Trump was left with the rest.[42] In the 2,547 counties that voted for Trump, blue-collar jobs outnumbered white-collar. In Biden's counties, white-collar jobs clearly predominated.[43] Of the hundred counties in the United States with the highest percentage of four-year college degrees, Biden took 84 to Trump's 16. As recently as 2000, Bush had managed 49. Back in 1984, 80 percent of the most educated counties in America had gone for the Republicans.

The irreconcilable clashes in American politics reflected a polarization between those who affirmed the many transformations America has undergone since the tumultuous 1960s and had done well out of those changes and those who hankered after a return to the 1950s, or at least their vision of that bygone era. Trump had satisfied that craving, and though he lost the national vote, red-state America had not repudiated him. He gained more votes than in 2016. Indeed, he gained more votes than any presidential candidate before him in history, other than Biden. And Trump, being Trump, thought he had won. Furthermore, the Republican Party, still contesting the two vital Senate seats in Georgia, refused to break with the president for fear of alienating Trump loyalists. While governments around the world recognized Biden's victory, the incumbent, the leaders of the Republicans in the Senate and the House, and Republican elected officials up and down the country refused to do so.

The likelihood that Trump would accept the election outcome was always slim. He had, after all, disputed the result in 2016, when he did win. If he had defeated Biden, he would no doubt have insisted that the margin of victory was being understated. But the uncertainty in 2020 was of a new quality. Trump's refusal to accept the outcome was not merely a legal tactic. It embraced an alternate reality.[44]

How then did one compel agreement to an outcome? The courts were the obvious route. The Republicans had filled them with their appointees, and the president made no secret of the fact that he expected a quid pro quo. They disappointed him. No court in the land would seriously entertain the cases brought by the Trump campaign. Only in one state, Wisconsin, did they come close to overturning the result.[45]

Could the military be brought in? We know the option was discussed in Trump's circle. The crowd around General Michael Flynn, newly released from jail, called on Trump to "cross the Rubicon" and declare martial law.[46] But senior figures in the command chain pushed back, stating publicly that their oath was to the Constitution, not to the commander in chief. The American army would not involve itself in an election.

As far as corporate America was concerned, 2020 confirmed its unease with the political culture of the GOP, a tension that had first become clear in 2008 with the nomination of Sarah Palin as John McCain's running mate. America's corporate leaders had always been of two minds about Trump. They liked the 2017 tax cuts and his agenda of deregulation. Some maverick billionaires continued their support, but few senior business leaders warmed to Trump's reactionary cultural politics. The owner of a small business might set the tone how he or she pleased. The vast majority of them were solidly pro-Trump. Conversely it was well-nigh unthinkable to run a large corporation in the United States in the summer of 2020 while simultaneously denying the seriousness of the pandemic and the cause of racial justice. What corporate America wanted was not civil war and a Darwinian push for herd immunity, but social peace and an effective containment of the epidemic. The aggressive push against China added fuel to the fire. Partisanship cleaved the national economy.

If the Democrats had swung to the left and picked Sanders as their nominee, things would no doubt have been different. There is little doubt that business interests large and small would have rallied to the Republican cause. Or, as more than one billionaire indicated, they would have mounted a third-party campaign, splitting the anti-Trump vote.[47] That was the blackmail that big business exercised over the Democrats. It was the approval of the wealth lobby, as much as Biden's affable personality, that made him the safe bet.[48]

Biden made no secret of the fact that he was a Democrat of the older school, a throwback to the 1980s. As far as taxation and redistribution were concerned, as he told a group of well-heeled donors at the Carlyle hotel in June 2019, it was time for America's upper class to make concessions. Biden had no intention of "demonizing" wealth, but "you all know, you all know in your gut what has to be done. . . . We can disagree in the margins. But the truth of the matter is, it's all within our wheelhouse and nobody has to be punished. No one's standard of living would change. Nothing would fundamentally change . . . When you have income inequality as large as we have in the United States today, it brews and ferments political discord and basic revolution. It allows demagogues to step in."[49] With Trump, the demagogic nightmare had arrived. If Trump's attorney general had accused American business of selling out democracy to China, now it was the turn of big business to demand that the president and his party abide by America's democratic rules.

Already before the election it was clear that Trump's team intended to make postal voting, necessitated by the epidemic, into a legal issue. In mid-October, a group of fifty prominent business leaders issued a statement calling for every vote to be counted and demanding that media outlets avoid prematurely calling an election that might well be protracted.[50] As the president escalated his campaign against postal voting, an even broader coalition pushed back. On October 27, within hours of Trump declaring that it would be "totally inappropriate" if ballots were still being tallied after election day, eight business organizations, led by the U.S. Chamber of Commerce and the Business Roundtable, took the unusual step of issuing a joint statement, rebutting the president and calling for "peaceful and fair elections," the counting of which might, quite legitimately, extend over "days or even weeks." Jamie Dimon, chairman and chief executive of JP-Morgan Chase, emailed the bank's staff, stressing the "paramount" importance of respecting the democratic process. Two hundred and sixty leading executives signed a statement "warning that the health of the US economy depended on the strength of its democracy." David Barrett of Expensify went all in. Four more years for Trump, he told the ten million users of his software, would damage American democracy to such an extent that he was "obligated on behalf of shareholders to take any action I can to avoid it."[51] For his firm it was an existential question; after all, "not many expense reports get filed during a civil war."[52]

When Trump refused to concede, leading business figures intensified their appeals. Over breakfast on November 6, a regular meeting of CEOs convened by Professor Jeffrey Sonnenfeld of Yale School of Management was regaled with warnings of a "coup d'état" by Timothy Snyder, the Yale historian well-known for his gothic brand of Trump alarmism. As Sonnenfeld admitted, "some thought that was overstating it," but there was no doubt that the C-suite was concerned. Business leaders did not want a "divided nation. They don't want fractured communities. They don't want hostile workplaces."[53]

Come late November, that concern was increasingly practical. How would the continuity of government be secured unless the Trump administration agreed to cooperate in the transition? Yet again, a coalition of senior executives, this one led by Larry Fink and David Solomon, the CEOs of BlackRock and Goldman Sachs, along with 160 others, demanded that the Trump administration should cooperate: "Withholding resources and vital information from an incoming administration puts the public and economic health and security of America at risk . . . every day that an orderly presidential transition process is delayed, our democracy grows weaker in the eyes of our own citizens and the nation's stature on the global stage is diminished."[54]

Finally, in the week of Thanksgiving, something like a normal transition did begin. But the refusal by the GOP leadership to acknowledge Biden's victory continued. The appeals of America's business elite served only to highlight the gulf that separated them from the incumbent in the White House, his supporters in the electorate, and the Trumpian wing of the Republican Party.

Meanwhile, the epidemic roared on. The number of daily fatalities reached a new peak in the early weeks of December. Los Angeles overtook New York City as the metropolis worst affected. And American society became ever more polarized. Those with shares in the stock market ended the year on a high, especially those with shares in Tesla, whose value increased to exceed that of the nine largest car manufacturers worldwide.[55] At the same time, the situation of those dependent on America's fragmenting welfare state was ever more desperate.

By early November 2020, a quarter of out-of-work Americans with children at home had not had enough to eat in the last week. A fifth of the Black population reported going hungry.[56] School closures and the loss of free school meals hit children from poor families hardest. In mid-November, the North Texas Food Bank in Plano, a suburb of Dallas, distributed 300 tons of food to 25,000 people in a single weekend.[57] Lines of cars and trucks stretched as far as the eye could see, and the network of food banks on which the most desperate relied was reaching its limit. The USDA Farmers to Families Food Box program that had been launched with great fanfare by Ivanka Trump was running out of money. In 2020, even America's domestic hunger relief program was hitched to the trade war with China. The Food Purchase and Distribution Program allocated $7.1 billion for purchases from American farmers whose overseas sales had been caught up in the trade war with China. That program ended on December 31, and it had not been renewed. In the final weeks of the year, America's anti-hunger experts warned that food banks across the country would be losing about 50 percent of the food they had hitherto received from the Agriculture Department, even as demand from desperate clients was surging.[58]

Struggling parents who were forced to quit work to look after their children as childcare facilities closed found themselves excluded from unemployment benefits. The granting of food stamps was capricious, and the lines at food banks were interminable.[59] As winter approached and the political system remained in gridlock, the land of the free and the home of the brave was swept by an epidemic of shoplifting for food.

Part IV

INTERREGNUM

Chapter 12

VACCINE RACE

The long-feared second surge of the epidemic hit the United States and Europe in the fall. China and its East Asian neighbors had demonstrated that it was possible to conquer even substantial outbreaks through social distancing and intensive public health measures. Across Europe, Latin America, the United States, and Western Asia, there were differences of degree, but nowhere was suppression achieved. By the winter even the success stories of the spring—Sweden, the East European states, and Germany too—were in trouble. The epidemic was gathering new pace in sub-Saharan Africa, notably in South Africa and Nigeria. Repeated firebreak shutdowns promised to flatten the curve and enable health systems to fight their way through. By November, Britain, Germany, France, Italy, Belgium, and the Czech Republic were all in one or another form of mandatory lockdown. The authorities in each case experimented with tiers and a variety of social distancing restrictions so bewildering that they bamboozled even the officials in charge of defining them. As in the spring, they helped to slow the spread. With more intelligent design the economic damage was less severe. But by this point it was clear: the only way out of the pandemic was going to be with a vaccine.

Arguably, never had more depended on a scientific breakthrough. It is of course a given that modern economies would be impossible without modern technologies. In the economic data, however, the specific impact of particular technologies can be surprisingly hard to pinpoint.[1] An entire scholarly literature is devoted to debating whether the Industrial Revolution would have been possible without the steam engine or the railway. Despite its ubiquity, economists long struggled to measure the impact of IT on productivity.[2] If that was perplexing, the opposite certainty was even less comfortable. By the second half of 2020, there was no escaping the fact that a return to normality depended on mass immunity. The only safe way to achieve that was through comprehensive immunization. Everything hinged on a vaccine.

Financial markets provided a telling barometer of our hopes. Trillions of dollars rose and fell depending on news from the main drug developers. Looking back from September, a study by the Swiss bank UBS found that a quarter of the rebound in the stock market since May, when the publicly funded vaccine race began in earnest, was attributable to vaccine news.[3] In November, on the news of the success of the Pfizer/BioNTech trials, oil prices and shares in airlines surged. Those in food delivery companies and tech slumped. Safe-haven assets in general sold off, led by Treasuries and tech stocks.[4]

The sentiment of relief was overwhelming. Given the dispiriting shambles of pandemic management, it was reassuring to know that in the background some very clever and well-organized people had been at work on a solution. But there was also no hiding from the fact that it is normally desperate dictators in their last-ditch fights who count on miracle weapons for salvation. In 2020, thanks to the failure of our public health policy, that was us. This long-shot gamble on a state-backed technological development program was disconcerting not only because of its historical resonances. It was disconcerting also because it went against the prevailing dogma of economic policy. Since the 1980s, the idea of pursuing an industrial policy based on "picking winners" had been anathematized by advocates of the market revolution in Europe and the United States. It was better, it was argued, to leave research and development priorities to the market. In practice, of course, in many corners of academia and the economy, government-supported research went on. Corporations in aerospace and microelectronics privatized the profits, but it didn't add up to a coherent policy. New challenges, such as the "Made in China 2025" program triggered a resurgence in interest in industrial policy in both the EU and the United States.[5] But the coronavirus crisis was different. We needed a vaccine, not primarily to improve long-run growth, but to overcome the uncertainty and misery of the pandemic. The resumption of trillions of dollars in economic activity and hundreds of millions of jobs depended on it. The question was, who would deliver it and on what terms?

What we were hoping for, if not a miracle, was certainly a biomedical first. There had never been a vaccine for a coronavirus. No vaccine of any type had ever been developed, tested, manufactured, and deployed on the time-table we needed in 2020. And yet it was not blind faith. There were reasons to be hopeful.

In the first decades of the twenty-first century, a cluster of break-throughs were transforming medicine and pharmaceutical development. If it had not been for coronavirus, the headlines in 2020 might have been made by other triumphs. In March, a man in London became the second person in history to be cured of HIV/AIDS. On August 25, after four years without a case, Africa was declared free of the wild polio strain, a dis-ease that had once crippled 75,000 children every year. In November, the computers of a British AI company successfully predicted a protein's 3D shape from its amino acid sequence, promising a huge acceleration in drug development.[6]

These were the fruits, on the one hand, of decades of public health investment and, on the other, of the convergence between molecular biol-ogy and information technology that had reached a first culmination in the sequencing of a single human genome. That project was begun in 1990. It was completed in 2003. The budget for the project as a whole was $2.7 billion. The cost of the sequencing itself was somewhere between $500 million and $1 billion. By 2014 the cost of sequencing a human genome had fallen to $1,000. In 2020, there were two companies—one Chinese, one American—claiming to be able to do it for as little as $100.[7]

The fusion of molecular biology and big data clearly had huge potential.

It also inspired great enthusiasm in financial markets. The biotech revolution was big business. By 2011, global R&D spending from public and private sources on medical research had reached $265 billion.[8] What was less obvious was its efficacy in delivering medicines and treatments for the most prevalent diseases in the world. Standing in the way were patents, the costs and risks of testing, and the fickle nature of medical markets.[9] Nowhere was this more evident than in the scandalously slow response to the HIV/AIDS pandemic, particularly in sub-Saharan Africa. This exposed a fundamental disconnect between science, the capacities of the pharmaceutical business, and the delivery of medicines to those who needed them most.

The sense of outrage generated by the failure to address the AIDS crisis in Africa forced change in the political, economic, and organizational sphere, as much as in medical research.[10] A coalition of civil society groups, NGOs, megadonors, health charities, UN organizations, and a few rich national governments—including the United States—came together to widen and speed up the pipeline of new drugs. Their motives varied from national interest to global justice, economic development, commercial profit, and the comprehensive eradication of dangerous diseases. Eventually even the asset management industry intervened to demand full disclosure of trial data.[11] Not only was the reputation of the pharmaceutical industry at stake— important for its long-term profitability—but a pandemic would clearly pose a global threat to capital accumulation.[12] The push was on to make the public-private model of vaccine development work.

The lead was taken by the Global Alliance for Vaccines and Immunizations (GAVI), launched in January 2000, with US$750 million in funding from the Bill & Melinda Gates Foundation. Its aim was to reverse the downward trend of the 1990s and to rapidly raise the immunization rate of the seventy-four poorest countries.[13] From being a laggard sector relative to other pharmaceuticals, the vaccine business boomed. Global sales surged from $10 billion in 2005 to over $25 billion in 2013.[14] The scientific glory was in projects like Merck's Ebola vaccine. The profits came from vaccines like Shingrix, which protects elderly patients in affluent countries against shingles. Many of the larger pharmaceutical firms preferred to exit the high-cost and high-profile business, but those that remained were now flanked by smaller biotech outfits and low-cost vaccine manufacturers from the developing world, notably India. By the 2010s, two-thirds of the world's children were vaccinated with jabs produced by India's Serum Institute.

The Serum Institute got its start in the early 1970s producing tetanus vaccine from horse serum to replace unaffordable imports.[15] In the 1980s the company positioned itself as one of the mainstays of India's Universal Immunisation Programme, which aims to provide complete coverage each year for the country's giant 27-million-strong birth cohort.[16] As the first developing world manufacturer to obtained prequalified status from the WHO, the Serum Institute in the 1990s became a global supplier. By the 2010s, at 1.3 billion shots per annum, it had the largest manufacturing capacity in the world.

After HIV/AIDS set the ball rolling, every new threat spawned new co-alitions of public health and biomedical activism. One of the most powerful activist coalitions, CEPI, the Coalition for Epidemic Preparedness Innovations, was unveiled in January 2017 at Davos. It focused on developing a vaccination for the highly dangerous MERS-CoV and on building a "rapid response platform" that would enable a quick reaction to the emergence of a hypothetical new pathogen, dubbed "Disease X."[17] Public-private partnerships like CEPI did not end the wrestling match over pricing, IP, and the transparency of contracts, but they did push more money—$706 million—into nineteen vaccine candidates.[18] Ahead of time, 2020 was earmarked as the final year of the first decade-long Global Vaccine Action Plan backed by donors like the Gates Foundation, the Wellcome Trust, the GSK foundation, and CEPI. A number of new vaccines, including those for malaria and HIV, were within sight of the finish line. And then in January 2020 "Disease X" actually arrived.

The scientific community's response to the coronavirus will go down in history as one of humanity's more remarkable collective achievements. After forty hours of nonstop work, on January 5, a team led by Professor Yong-Zhen Zhang at Fudan University in Shanghai was the first to complete sequencing of the virus's genetic code. At that point, the Chinese authorities were still trying to black out the inconvenient news. To break the impasse on Saturday, January 11, one of Zhang's Australian collaborators published the sequence online.[19] Zhang was sanctioned for his indiscipline, but the information was out. Work on what would become the Moderna mRNA vaccine began on January 13. In Germany the Pfizer/BioNTech vaccine was also mapped out within days, as was that being developed at Oxford University.[20]

Well before the outbreak had become a pandemic, scientists had a plan for an antidote on their drawing board. But having a formula and having a vaccine whose efficacy and safety had been legitimately tested and whose production was ramped up to scale were very different things. The drama of the coronavirus vaccine was that for the first time, all three processes—development, testing, ramping up production—were accomplished simultaneously, on a scale intended in due course to cover the entire population of the world, even as the pandemic was still progressing. The researchers got to a solution so fast in part because much of the basic research and preclinical testing on animal models had been done in 2003 in response to the SARS pandemic.[21] The SARS crisis had ebbed before the vaccine development was completed. This time round, the global vaccine race developed a gigantic momentum.

Moderna's trials began on March 16. Pfizer/BioNTech went to trials on May 2. First results were available by mid-July. By the end of the month, both Moderna and Pfizer were pushing into Phase III trials. By the last week of October, 74,000 participants were enrolled. First results from Pfizer/BioNTech emerged by November 9. Moderna's followed a week later, AstraZeneca on November 23.

Attention tends to focus on the Pfizer/BioNTech and Moderna vaccines because they were the first approved in the West and because their technology was so innovative. The announcement of their test results changed the outlook in November 2020, but they were not the only ones. Despite a series of mishaps during testing, AstraZeneca's cheaper and more robust vaccine promised to have greater reach. Around the world, by early January 2021, ninety other vaccines were in various stages of testing.[22] Millions of researchers had turned their laboratories and computers toward the disease. In 2020, around 4 percent of the world's entire published research output was devoted to coronavirus problems.[23]

This mobilization is rightly celebrated as a collective triumph of the human spirit, but it was always also crosscut with competition, rivalry, and the battle for exclusive property rights. Vaccine development was a race, driven not just by scholarly or humanitarian ambition, but by the pursuit of power and profit. In light of the urgency of the collective need for a vaccine, this could seem scandalous. It is in fact the norm. Public health and the modern pharmaceutical industry are zones in which the interests of science and medicine have always intersected those of business and the state.[24]

From the beginning of modern virology and vaccine development, the U.S. military played a leading role in fighting diseases ranging from yellow fever to hepatitis. In 1945, American GIs were the first people in the world to be vaccinated against the flu.[25] In 2020 the largest state-led effort to develop a coronavirus vaccine was the American one. Inspired by the Manhattan Project of World War II, but boasting a title straight out of *Star Trek*, Operation Warp Speed was launched on May 15, 2020. It was a collaboration between biotech, big pharma, and two giant government bureaucracies— the Pentagon and the Department of Health and Human Services. By the end of the year, it had spent $12.4 billion on development and manufacturing deals with six leading pharmaceutical groupings. Three of these were American (Johnson & Johnson, Moderna, and Novavax), two were European (Sanofi/GSK, AstraZeneca-Oxford) and one was a transatlantic collaboration (Pfizer/BioNTech). The initial target was set for October. The leadership paired a venture capitalist, a former director of R&D at GlaxoSmithKline and Moderna board member, with the logistical expertise and political heft of the four-star general who heads the U.S. Army's Matériel Command. In Washington, D.C., Operation Warp Speed had a distinctly military flavor. High on the team's reading list was *Freedom's Forge*, a glowing account of how "American business produced victory in World War II." Not for nothing the same book was also popular with the Green New Deal crowd.[26] The military members of Operation Warp Speed turned up for work in uniform and set a "battle rhythm" of daily meetings.[27]

The flair may have been military, but no one was conscripted on to

Operation Warp Speed. Whether companies joined up was their decision. Merck, one of the giants in the vaccine field, chose to take a backseat.
Johnson & Johnson had already closed a $450 million vaccine deal with the
Trump administration at the end of March.[28] Of the mRNA front-runners,
it was Moderna that most needed help. It was a leader in research, but it
had only 800 employees and had never run a Phase III clinical trial. The
managerial assistance Moderna received from Warp Speed was as important as the $2.5 billion in funding from the U.S. government. Moderna's
team supervisor was a Defense Department official known only as "the
major." His services included rustling up blue-lighted police escorts to
override Covid-19 limitations on interstate trucking and arranging airlifts
of vital manufacturing equipment.[29]

As one of the oldest and largest pharmaceutical firms in the world,
with a fearsome reputation for its competitive practices, Pfizer had less
need for this kind of help. Through its partnership with BioNTech it had
acquired all the scientific know-how it needed. Pfizer was of course happy
to take U.S. government money, signing a $1.95 billion advance contract
for 100 million doses. Otherwise, its outspoken CEO Dr. Albert Bourla
preferred to hold Trump's erratic vaccine politics at arm's length. The most
direct government input to its development process came not from the
United States but from Germany.[30] Berlin put $443 million into BioNTech,
Pfizer's R&D partner. A further $118 million came from the European In-
vestment Bank.[31]

As far as American politics were concerned, Pfizer's concerns were
amply justified. While Trump spent much of the summer bragging about
an imminent vaccine, the overriding concern of the drug firms was the
legitimacy of the drug certification process. The science told them that
they had a remedy that was both safe and effective. The real battle was to
establish these facts beyond reasonable doubt. In the modern medicolegal
environment, that was always a challenge. In the United States in 2020, it
was truly an uphill battle.

In a summer of Black Lives Matter protests, with Black and Latino
patients dying of Covid-related problems at a much higher rate than white
patients, the diversity of the trial populations was a key concern. In late

August, Operation Warp Speed officials realized that the Moderna trial population was far too white. At the last minute, funds had to be mobilized to recruit minority volunteers. That gave Pfizer, which had invested hundreds of millions of dollars in its trials, the edge in the race to the finish line.[32]

What worried Pfizer was the legitimacy of the FDA process itself. When the president began attacking the agency, Bourla decided to draw a line. He contacted his counterpart at Johnson & Johnson, and the two of them recruited further support. In the open letter released on September 8, the nine leading firms of the pharmaceutical industry declared their determination to "unite to stand with science." The FDA guidelines were the gold standard of drug regulation, and they would follow these to the letter.[33] It was a further instance of the refusal of big business to fall into line with Trump's agenda, and this one had immediate practical consequences. As the election approached, Pfizer put its foot on the brake.

In drug trials, a critical variable is the threshold set for significance. Of all the leading contenders, Pfizer had set the most aggressive trial protocol. It would conduct a check of interim results as soon as thirty-two participants in the 42,000-person trial developed Covid-19.[34] This threshold was significantly lower than that set by Moderna. FDA had let it be known that it was unlikely to issue an "emergency use authorization" on such a slender basis. The last thing that Pfizer wanted was to find itself trapped between Trump and the FDA. On October 29, Pfizer asked the FDA for approval to raise the bar to sixty-two cases. This effectively dashed any hope of an announcement before election day. Indeed, Pfizer did not even start testing the samples it had in hand until November 3. If it had started sooner, it feared having to disclose the results to the stock market. It was not until November 9, finally, that the news of the vaccine's 95 percent effectiveness was cleared for public release.

It was on the one hand a vindication of due process and the authority of the science. On the other hand, it was an extraordinary adherence to formal procedures for what were, in the broadest sense of the word, political reasons. Trump of course took that personally, blaming the drug companies for denying him his victory. He was no doubt a risk factor, and few in corporate America mourned the passing of his presidency, but what was really at stake was the legitimacy of the pharmaceutical business and the authority of public science.[35]

By the end of 2020 the first 20 million or so doses of vaccine were beginning to be distributed in the United States and the UK. The next issue was how to ensure that they were used most effectively. In Europe and the U.S., an argument immediately began about who should get the vaccines first. In Europe in the spring of 2021, this would degenerate into bitter arguments between countries, within them, and between the EU and AstraZeneca, which was falling behind in its deliveries. These, however, were the problems of privilege. Sooner or later in 2021, the Europeans would get their jabs. The more basic question was when the billions of people in low-income and middle-income countries at risk from the disease would be immunized. As the saying went, until everyone was safe, no one was safe. From the point of view of conquering the disease, the vaccines needed to be concentrated wherever the hot spots happened to be. It was manifestly unfair for low-risk inhabitants of the UK to receive the shots ahead of frontline medical workers in South Africa or India. It was also a question of political prudence. As Jeremy Farrar of the Wellcome Trust remarked: "If in the first 6 months, Western Europe and the United States are the only regions that are vaccinating people, and other parts of the world are not being vaccinated until the end of 2021, then I think we're going to have a very, very tense global situation."[36]

That was the concern of the G20, when the heads of government convened in November 2020 under Saudi chairmanship. It is what President Macron of France meant when he declared: "We need to avoid at all costs a scenario of a two-speed world where only the richer can protect themselves against the virus and restart normal lives."[37] As far as the G20 were concerned, these were crocodile tears. Between them, the members of this exclusive club had effectively monopolized the world's supply. The richer members of the G20 were several times oversupplied.

The fig leaf of global governance that had been spanned over the

Covid vaccine question was a project known as the Access to COVID-19 Tools Accelerator, and its dedicated vaccine facility, COVAX.[38] These were direct offspring of the global vaccine efforts that had gathered momentum since 2000. COVAX was backstopped by GAVI, the WHO, and CEPI. UNICEF provided logistical support. By the end of 2020, COVAX had enrolled 189 states, representing the vast majority of the world's population. Poor countries joined out of necessity. Rich countries, including rich backers like Germany, Norway, and Japan, joined out of a sense of responsibility, but also as a way of diversifying their portfolio of vaccine options. For reasons known only to itself, the Trump administration chose to denounce COVAX as a WHO-led front for China.[39] In fact, China at first held aloof. It did not join until the autumn, leaving the United States and Russia as the main holdouts.

Their absence was regrettable, but with or without them, COVAX was undersized. Its aim was to provide 2 billion shots by the end of 2021, enough to cover no more than 20 percent of the population of participating countries. By early 2021 it had managed to secure only 1.07 billion doses, and its financial situation was parlous. Altogether, one hundred higher income countries and foundations had made $2 billion in commitments. But little of that money was cash on hand, and a further $5 billion was needed by the end of 2021. On a tight budget of $5 per shot, it had no room for error. At the November 2020 G20 meeting, the EU passed the begging bowl, appealing for contributions to ACT and COVAX.[40] Chancellor Merkel declared that Germany had signed up for €500 million ($592.65 million) and appealed to others to do their part.

It was a revealing discussion. A sum of €500 million was either a lot of money or absurdly parsimonious. If it had chosen to do so, Germany could have borrowed the funds necessary to meet not just the immediate needs of COVAX, but the entire projected cost of vaccinating the world—estimated, as of May 2020, at $25 billion—and it could have done so at negative interest rates. Instead, it chipped in €500 million and waited for others to do their bit.[41] The same logic, of course, applied to every other member of the G20. With the possible exception of Argentina and South Africa, any one of them could have justified the spending needed to end the pandemic and restart the world economy, on grounds of self-interest alone. In truth, even for the big drug companies, the vaccines were not a life-and-death issue. Pfizer had revenues in excess of $50 billion per annum prior to the crisis. The estimated coronavirus vaccine revenue of $14.6 billion it would split with BioNTech in 2021 was an important addition, but by no means decisive to the firm's long-term future.[42] Of greater long-term importance was the mRNA technology.

One of the remarkable things about the vaccine program was the imbalance between the modest costs and the outsize benefits. According to the IMF, rapid and well-targeted immunization of the entire world would add $9 trillion to global GDP by 2025.[43] Nevertheless, no one was willing to make the bold and unilateral gesture necessary to fund a global program. Countries gave a hundred million here and a hundred million there, and the World Health Organization was left to discuss the ways of leveraging its budget through financial engineering. Bruce Aylward, WHO's ACT coordinator, reported that the group had discussed concessional loans and catastrophe bonds as ways of raising the funds. It had hired Citigroup as an advisor to help it manage the risks involved in balancing its fragile balance sheet. As Aylward put it: "Right now financing is what stands between us and getting out of this pandemic as rapidly as possible. It's a real challenge in today's fiscal environment despite the fact that this is the best deal in town."[44]

Precisely how the "fiscal environment" could be a constraint ought to have been a mystery. Most governments around the world were engaged in unprecedented emergency spending that dwarfed the scale of the entire vaccine program. As Aylward pointed out, "This will pay itself off in 36 hours once we get trade and travel moving again." But even in the midst of a ruinous pandemic, costing the world economy trillions of dollars, when it came to making the case for public health spending, global leaders were tongue-tied.

A more compelling constraint than money were the physical bottlenecks in vaccine production. To produce billions of doses of mRNA vaccines taxed obscure supply chains, like that for lipid nanoparticles, the microscopic bubbles of fat that transport the genetic code into the body. Filling billions of vials with serum presented its own challenges.[45] The Trump administration blustered about using its Cold War–era Defense Production Act powers to raise production. Nothing came of it. In Europe critical bottlenecks emerged, especially in AstraZeneca's production system.

To ramp up production, it made sense to expand capacity by involving additional firms.[46] But that required a deal to be struck with the original developers. Despite the public funding that had been provided to them, the intellectual property rights to the first three vaccines remained with the private vaccine makers. For Jamie Love, head of the intellectual property advocacy group Knowledge Ecology International, "The decision not to require the transfer of know-how right from the beginning of vaccine development was a massive global policy failure."[47] When a call for patent pooling was made in the summer of 2020, it found few takers. Moderna, which was dependent on public funds, did offer to share its patents. But that had little practical significance if it was not combined with proprietary manufacturing information. South Africa and India launched an appeal at the WTO calling for all intellectual property protections to be lifted on Covid vaccines and treatments. But they were successfully opposed by a coalition consisting of the U.S., the UK, Canada, and the EU.[48] They supported cooperation, but only on the terms set by the pharmaceutical industry.

As far as the mRNA vaccines were concerned, the difficulty of sharing and expanding production was engineered into the vaccines themselves. They were innovative and expensive. Ramping up their production was always going to be a challenge. The more promising route to achieving a rapid and comprehensive immunization of the world's entire population was to start with a simpler, more traditional vaccine. That was the route taken in the development of the Oxford vaccine, the least glamorous of the three early vaccine contenders in the West. It was inexpensive and tough, making it easy to store. In April, Oxford University's Jenner Institute announced that it would make its vaccine available on an open-license basis, but under pressure from the Gates Foundation, which fervently supports maintaining patents on intellectual property, even for lifesaving drugs, Jenner backtracked. It signed an exclusive deal with AstraZeneca, spinning off a for-profit company, Vaccitech, in which the university and its top scientists owned a majority stake. For the duration of the pandemic, they would supply the vaccine at cost.[49] To expand production capacity, Oxford-AstraZeneca agreed to partnerships with ten manufacturing operations around the world. By far the largest was the Serum Institute in India. It had the capacity to manufacture at least a billion shots per annum and was rapidly preparing to expand production. By early 2021, AstraZeneca was committed to delivering 3.21 billion shots, over half to poor and middle-income countries. That was more than the Pfizer/BioNTech and Moderna vaccines combined, but it was still far from being enough and it depended, of course, on the efficacy and safety of the vaccine.

The narrative of the miraculous mRNA breakthrough of Pfizer/BioNTech and Moderna—*Freedom's Forge* for the twenty-first century—was a Western-centric one. How and when it would become relevant to the rest of the world was, as of the spring of 2021, still an open question. As of the end of March 2021, the United States, which accounted for approximately a quarter of global production, had agreed to export only a few million doses to its neighbors, Canada and Mexico. The EU was less "nationalistic." Up to the spring of 2021, manufacturers in Europe exported 40 percent of their total production. Those deliveries went mainly to rich customers. The first consignment of vaccines from the UN's COVAX facility arrived at Accra, Ghana, on Emirates Flight 787 on the morning of February 24. The shots came from the giant Serum Institute facility in Pune, India, which, as a partner of AstraZeneca, was contracted to produce 86 percent of COVAX's total supply. A month later, not only were there mounting concerns about the AstraZeneca shots, but India, facing a terrifying upsurge in infections, had declared a moratorium on all vaccine exports. Its huge population had its own urgent needs. COVAX, which had hoped to distribute 350 million doses in the first half of 2021, would have to wait for the 90 million doses promised by the Serum Institute for March and April. With Indian production tied up and the rich countries provisioning themselves, the hunt turned elsewhere—to the vaccines developed in Russia and China.

The first officially authorized inoculation against Covid in 2020 did not take place as part of an exquisitely composed mRNA trial in California. It happened in China. On February 29, Major General Chen Wei, a leading virologist in the People's Liberation Army, stood in front of a Chinese Communist Party flag in combat fatigues to receive the first experimental shot. Chen was celebrated as a national hero for her work on Ebola vaccines, her deeds immortalized in the patriotic action flick *Wolf Warrior 2*. She was in Wuhan as part of a joint effort between China's Academy of Medical Military Sciences and the Canadian/Chinese pharmaceutical company CanSino Biologics.[50] Chen and her team volunteered for the shots, not just as a stunt to demonstrate their loyalty to the CCP, though they were no doubt happy to do that. They took the risk because it seemed low. China was developing a vaccine type that was simple but safe and reliable. Starting with military personnel, by the end of 2020, China would vaccinate 4.5 million people, as many as the rest of the world put together. As far as available information allows us to judge, there were no adverse side effects. By the end of March 2021, with over 225 million doses, China was leading the world in overall production and exporting almost half of what it produced.

Russia too adopted a tried-and-tested technology. Rather than starting from scratch and using newfangled mRNA technology, it modified a vaccine type that had been successful against Ebola. This was a route similar to the Oxford-AstraZeneca vaccine, but Russia's Gamaleya's Sputnik V used different adenovirus vectors for the first and second shots, which apparently raised the overall effectiveness to 91.4 percent, well above its Western counterpart. In August, while still in Phase II trials, it became the first vaccine to be licensed anywhere in the world.[51]

With its very name, Sputnik V proclaimed Russia's prowess in science and technology. But the question was, could you trust a vaccine produced in a country where basic information about the seriousness of the epidemic was suppressed? Would you take a shot from a regime that was in the habit of depositing neurotoxins in the underpants of its political opponents, as the FSB did to Alexei Navalny in August 2020? In Russia, as in the U.S., reputable laboratories spoke out to demand that the Sputnik V testing program adhere to the recognized standard for Phase III trials. The heroic model of rushing vaccines into general use after ad hoc testing on brave lab staff was obsolete.[52] Nor was it supported by the Russian population. When asked by *The Moscow Times* in an anonymous poll whether they would take the Sputnik V vaccine, 60 percent of Russians said they would decline.[53]

In 2020 our bodies became the arena of scientific geopolitics. Who would take a Russian vaccine? The answer, it turns out, depended on where you were in the world, how much you were able to pay, and whether you had any alternatives.[54] Gamaleya was offering its Sputnik V vaccine at $10 per shot. By the spring of 2021 it had signed contracts with ten manufacturers worldwide to produce 1.4 billion doses. Twenty-nine countries including EU member Hungary had issued emergency authorization for its use.[55]

Russia's vaccine developers had no problem running Phase III trials at home. The epidemic was rife, and at home, the vaccine rollout was painfully slow. In China, the pandemic was so thoroughly suppressed that Chinese vaccines had to be tested abroad. For China's leading contenders, Sinopharm and Sinovac, it was an opportunity for global expansion. In 2020 they ran trials in fourteen countries on five continents.

On November 3, the week before the Pfizer/BioNTech results were announced, Sheikh Mohammed bin Rashid Al Maktoum, the prime minister of the United Arab Emirates (UAE), staged a photo op for his inoculation with the CNBG/Sinopharm Covid-19 vaccine. The UAE was one of the cornerstones of CNBG's efficacy trials. The cosmopolitan workforce of the UAE enabled it to test its shots on the citizens of 125 different countries simultaneously.[56] Involvement in testing produced buy-in. In January, Peru's interim president, the former World Bank technocrat Francisco Sagasti, announced an initial purchase of 1 million doses of the Sinopharm vaccine. It was affordable, and after helping to run the Phase III trials, Peru's National Institute of Health felt confident in approving its efficacy.[57] By early 2021 Lima had placed orders for 14 million doses from AstraZeneca and 38 million doses from China's Sinopharm.[58] In March 2021, the UAE was selected as the site for a Sinopharm plant capable of producing 200 million doses per annum, enough for the Emirates and many of its neighbors.

CNBG's Chinese rival, Nasdaq-listed Sinovac, looked not to the Gulf but to Brazil for partners. Flouting the hostility of President Bolsonaro, the government of São Paulo state committed $90 million to Sinovac for 46 million doses, a tenth of the price that the U.S. government paid for the mRNA vaccines of Pfizer/BioNTech and Moderna. In addition, Sinovac declared itself open to discussing the transfer of its technology to the Instituto Butantan, a highly reputed public health facility in São Paulo.[59] At the same time, Sinovac was running large-scale trials in Turkey and Indonesia. All three together raised the number of contracted doses to over 120 million. As public health officials in Ankara pointed out, Turkey has "a good infrastructure for the phase III studies," and unlike the United States and much of Europe, it welcomed a Chinese vaccine maker.[60]

Not only was China conducting tests, but it was building a delivery system that would reach the majority of the world's population. In early December, the logistics arm of Chinese internet giant Alibaba, Cainiao, was commissioned as the main delivery agent for Chinese vaccines. To handle the demands of the largest online marketplace in the world, Cainiao had built a giant just-in-time logistics platform. Ethiopian Airlines, which had played a major role in flying PPE out of China earlier in the crisis, was contracted as the airline to carry doses from China. It converted an idle fleet of thirty Airbus and Boeing passenger jets to support the cold chain. A specialized storage facility was established in Addis Ababa and negotiations began to establish a WHO-approved production site in Egypt. Both China's Sinovac and Russia's Sputnik V were under consideration. Until production could begin in Africa, air freight would operate from Shenzhen Airport, where Alibaba was building China's first international cold chain facility.[61] In early March, Ethiopian Airlines made its first delivery, carrying 2.2 million doses provided by COVAX.

By early 2021, as more and more good news came in from Phase III trials around the world, it was clear that it was possible to develop not just one vaccine or one family of vaccines in record quick time, but many. In the development race, America's and Europe's greater wealth bought them an advantage measured not in years, but in weeks and months. They needed it. Other than in Latin America, as 2021 began, it was in the United States and Europe that the second and third waves of infection were at their worst. Within weeks of the first news about the vaccines, mutations were identified in the UK and South Africa that dramatically increased the infectivity of the virus. It was a source of relief that the virus's lethality had not increased, but from a public health point of view, the reproduction rate and the resulting caseload were what mattered. Greater transmissibility was worse than greater lethality because the former is exponential while the latter is linear.

Vaccine makers were optimistic that their jabs would work against the new variations of coronavirus as well, but it would require another round of tests. Before those could be done, the fear at the beginning of 2021 was the same as a year earlier. Health systems would collapse under the load before the vaccine could arrive. Flattening the curve was once again the priority. And the only answer, whether in California, France, the UK, or Germany, was to shut down once more.

Chapter 13

DEBT RELIEF

Facing an alarming surge in infections, unable to wait for the COVAX allocation, South Africa was the first African country to secure a bilateral vaccine deal in January 2021 with AstraZeneca. It was only 1.5 million doses for a population of 58 million, but it would be enough to protect its key health workers.[1] The African Union was working on a deal that would secure 270 million doses from Pfizer, Johnson & Johnson, and the AstraZeneca shot manufactured by the Serum Institute. That wasn't close to enough for the continent's 1.3 billion inhabitants, but it was as much as there was money for. The World Bank and the African Union were haggling over a $5 billion vaccine loan scheme.[2] The money would come from the $12 billion fund set up by the World Bank to fund vaccine purchases by the poorest countries.

New credit helped, but piled on top of existing debt, the burden threatened to become unmanageable. The damage done to the finances of the poorest countries by the 2020 crisis was severe. In exports, remittances, and investments forgone, the lowest income countries would suffer a loss of $150 billion in 2020.[3] For the sake of comparison, the sum total of all overseas development assistance worldwide in 2019 was $152.9 billion.[4] What the most vulnerable countries needed was a package that combined both public health assistance and financial relief.

In November 2020, speaking as both South African president and chair of the African Union, Cyril Ramaphosa called for a multipronged effort to address the financial situation of the hardest-hit African nations.[5] The need was all the greater for the fact that 2020 interrupted what had promised to be an upswing in Africa's fortunes. As Ramaphosa emphasized, failure to take action risked allowing "short-term debt dynamics to derail" Africa's "march towards a green, digitally enabled and globally connected future."[6] Rather than accelerating, in 2020, for the first time since records began, the combined economies of the African continent were contracting.

The African countries were not alone. As United Nations secretary-general António Guterres warned the G20 in November 2020, poor and highly indebted countries, were "on the precipice of financial ruin and escalating poverty, hunger and untold suffering."[7] World Bank president David Malpass, a Trump appointee who could not be accused either of sentimentality or alarmism, doubled down. "Failing to provide more permanent debt relief" to the hardest-hit countries would "lead to increased poverty and a repeat of the disorderly defaults of the 1980s."[8]

But despite the sense of emergency, despite the damage, and despite the scale of action in the advanced economies, the global response to these appeals fell flat. There were piecemeal efforts, most prominently the G20's Debt Service Suspension Initiative. The International Monetary Fund and the World Bank both made loans, but unlike after the 2008 crisis, there was no big G20-led initiative. Proposals to expand the crisis-fighting capacity of the IMF and to embark on large-scale debt relief got nowhere. This was profoundly revealing of how resources and power were distributed in the world economy.

It certainly didn't help that the Trump administration and the conservative wing of the GOP held sway in Washington, D.C. By the summer of 2020 the Trump administration was at war with both the World Trade Organization and the World Health Organization. By comparison they handled the IMF with kid gloves. It helped that relations with the fund were managed by Treasury Secretary Steven Mnuchin, who was the least "Trumpy" of the Trump loyalists. Continuity was one thing, however; large measures to meet the crisis were quite another.

The coalition of European and African leaders that assembled in April to call for large-scale action by the IMF was impressive.[9] The idea of issuing a large allocation of SDRs had appeal across a wide cross section of expert opinion.[10] The benchmark was the initiative launched in London eleven years earlier when the G20 resolved to triple the IMF's regular lending capacity to US$750 billion and expand global liquidity by US$250 billion through a general allocation of SDRs.[11] Eleven years on, the fund was still drawing on the lending capacities created in 2009. For the Trump administration, however, talk of SDRs was a red flag. Though the African-European proposal clearly enjoyed the support of the IMF leadership and a broad coalition of shareholders, the United States killed it. The U.S. jealously guards its veto on the fund's board of governors precisely for moments like this.[12]

The justification offered was practical. The U.S. Treasury insisted that there were more than enough SDRs already in circulation. Some $200 billion remained undrawn from the 2009 allocation. If the Europeans wanted to do something constructive, they could make sure that the existing allowances were made available to those who needed them most.[13] There was some truth to this argument, but it was hardly a reason not to meet the emergency with a further allocation. It was an open secret in Washington that the real reason for Mnuchin's veto was the opposition of Republican hard-liners.

In 2020 Ted Cruz would earn notoriety as one of the most vociferous defenders of Trump in the Senate. Cruz was also a hard-liner on both Russia and China. He had made his mark in 2013, as a freshly elected junior senator from Texas, by doing his best to sabotage a key element of the G20's IMF policy, the quota shift in favor of the emerging markets, led by China. This had been a key part of the deal done at the London G20 to expand the IMF's resources. Cruz set himself to blocking ratification of the agreement that had been signed by the Obama administration.[14] At one point, Christine Lagarde as managing director of the fund offered to do a belly dance if it would win Cruz's approval.[15] Seven years later, Cruz was still leading the charge against China and Russia. In April 2020, in the thick of the coronavirus crisis, no one in the Mnuchin Treasury wanted to stir Cruz into directing his fire once again at the IMF.

It was not until after the U.S. election that Ramaphosa and others renewed their call for SDR issuance.[16] Everything now hinged on the incoming Biden administration and the senatorial runoff election in Georgia. If the GOP retained control, which most thought likely until very late in the year, the only route was for the Biden administration to sidestep Congress. Senate approval was not required if the increase was no larger than the current SDR allocation. That would permit a new issue of about US$650 billion.[17] If combined with a reallocation of SDRs between IMF members, it could provide a serious fillip for the most hard-pressed low-income countries. But it was not the trillion dollars of funding that was necessary to supercharge low income growth and to meet the UN's Sustainable Development Goals.

The veto exercised over world affairs by America's conservative caucus was exasperating and profoundly delegitimizing to institutions like the IMF, but it would be fatuous to attribute the impasse on financial assistance for the developing world to this alone. To see the broader array of forces at work, one only has to look at the one measure of debt relief that the international community did agree on in 2020, the Debt Service Suspension Initiative (DSSI).

The DSSI was launched in April 2020 with a brief that was narrow from the start.[18] It covered only the most impoverished and smallest African and Asian countries. Lower middle-income countries were excluded. It was based on the principle that it should be net present value (NPV) neutral. In other words, though repayment was suspended in the short term, over the life of the loan the lenders would suffer no loss. To compensate them for deferred payments in 2020, they would receive accelerated repayment between 2022 and 2024. Any debtor signing up for DSSI had to weigh carefully the risk of getting into payment difficulties a few years hence. Furthermore, the only debt service payments covered by the initiative were those owed to official bilateral creditors. These were the loans over which the G20 governments had immediate control. But in the new era of developing world debt, they were a diminishing part of the overall problem.

The debt landscape in 2020 reflected earlier rounds of debt relief. The last round had been initiated in 1996 by the Heavily Indebted Poor Countries Initiative and the Jubilee Debt Campaign spearheaded by celebrities like Bono and Bob Geldof. It reached culmination at the 2005 Gleneagles summit of the G8.[19] This slashed the debt-to-GDP ratio of the thirty-five lowest-income countries.[20] In the years after, lending by rich country governments, organized in the Paris Club, moved increasingly into the background.[21] Rather than loans, they provided financial assistance in the form of grants. Thus though the United States remained the largest single source of aid, to the tune of $35 billion, as a bilateral concessionary lender it had dwindled into insignificance. In 2020 India and Brazil, themselves middle-income countries, had more loans outstanding to the poorest countries than did the United States.

The big new bilateral lender on the development finance scene was not an established member of the Paris Club. It was China. The precise scale and nature of China's lending under the banner of the One Belt One Road infrastructure program was much debated, but it was clearly huge. Between 2008 and 2019, according to one particularly meticulous compilation, the China Development Bank and the Export-Import Bank of China

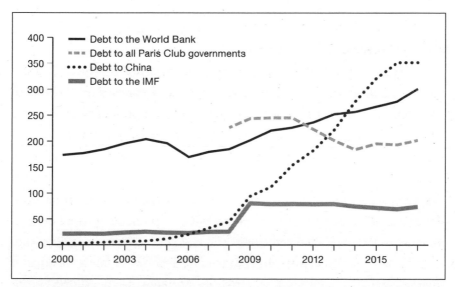

Aggregate external public debt owed to different official creditors (in billion USD). China is the largest official creditor in developing countries.

Based on Horn, Reinhart, and Trebesch, 2019

lent $462 billion to clients all over the world.[22] That was only a hair short of the $467 billion lent by the World Bank over the same period. And the Chinese banks had greater "surge" capacity. At its peak in 2016, lending by the Chinese policy banks not only exceeded that of the World Bank but matched that of all the multilateral development banks—the World Bank, the Asian Development Bank, the Inter-American Development Bank, the European Investment Bank, the European Bank for Reconstruction and Development, and the African Development Bank—put together.[23] Over 40 percent of the $30.5 billion of debt service payments due in 2021 from DSSI-eligible African nations was owed to either Chinese official creditors or China's development banks.[24] The forty-six debtor countries that had actually signed up to participate in DSSI owed China $5.76 billion in repayment, as compared to $1.99 billion owing to the Paris Club members. The largest of those was France, which owed $559 million in payments, followed by Japan, with $481 million in debt service. The United States stood to collect only $155 million, one thirty-seventh of what was due to China.[25]

The banner under which China had grouped its foreign development lending since 2013 was One Belt One Road (OBOR), also known as the Belt and Road Initiative (BRI). These titles were no doubt intended to convey vision and purpose. By the same token, the initiative also attracted international suspicion and accusations of debt imperialism.[26] Rumors circulated of exorbitant Chinese demands that borrowers waive sovereign immunity and put up vital national assets as security.[27] The example of the ill-fated Hambantota port complex in Sri Lanka was widely quoted as an instance of a country falling into a "debt trap."[28] When Sri Lanka defaulted, it forfeited a strategically vital port facility as collateral, or at least so the story went. Whether or not this was a deliberate policy on China's part was hotly debated, as were the exact circumstances of the Hambantota transaction.[29] What was undeniable was that several of China's clients were in deep financial trouble in 2020. Even before coronavirus hit, Venezuela, Pakistan, Angola, and nine other African countries were at risk of falling behind on their payments to China, but Beijing showed no sign of exploiting the coronavirus crisis to gain further leverage. Trump's appointee as president of the World Bank, David Malpass, faulted China for the fact that the China

Development Bank was not included in the DSSI.[30] Beijing insisted that it was a private bank and thus not covered by the terms of the G20 initiative. On its acknowledged official loans, Beijing made concessions to its debtors as large as those offered by all the other lenders put together.

There was no doubt an element of gamesmanship in the exemption of the China Development Bank, but this had less to do with any Chinese grand strategy than with the loopholes created by the exemption of private creditors from the terms of the DSSI. Of the $35 billion in debt service owed by the DSSI eligible countries in 2020, apart from the huge slice due to the Chinese, $13.5 billion was owed to private lenders.[31] About half was owed to banks of various kinds. The rest was due to bondholders. The size of this debt service burden reflected the degree to which, since 2005, private lending had displaced official concessional lending to low-income countries.

In their original appeal for action in April, the EU and African governments had called for the involvement of all lenders to low-income countries, including private creditors. The G20 agreed. The Institute of International Finance, which acts as the lobby group for global finance, duly extended an invitation to its members to participate on a voluntary basis, but by the summer, none had done so. In their defense the IIF added the telling observation that no debtors had asked their members for concessions. What worried the debtor countries was the possible impact on their credit ratings. As much as they might need debt relief, jeopardizing their future access to capital markets was too high a price to pay.[32]

The experience of heavily indebted Cameroon at the hands of the Moody's agency was warning enough. Cameroon's eligibility for the G20 DSSI was confirmed on May 19, 2020, freeing up $276 million in debt service. Eight days later Moody's placed Cameroon on review for downgrade. By way of explanation, Moody's pointed out that the G20 had linked participation in the DSSI to an appeal for similar concessions from private creditors. The appeal alone was enough. Not until August, when it became clear not only that no progress had been made toward enrolling private bondholders in the DSSI, but that it would be up to borrower governments to make a request to their private creditors and that Cameroon had no intention of doing so, did Moody's lift its downgrade threat.[33]

The ratings agencies thus exercised the whip hand over any borrower with substantial private debts. And astonishingly, their sway extended also to the multilateral lenders like the World Bank.

To qualify for the DSSI scheme, countries had first to apply for an IMF program and subject themselves to the fund's supervision. But despite the appeal from the EU and African governments, $12 billion in debt service payments owed to the IMF, World Bank, and other multilateral lenders were exempt from the DSSI. When pushed to explain this anomalous position, Malpass as president of the World Bank pointed to the ratings agencies.

Since 1959 the International Bank for Reconstruction and Development (IBRD), the part of the World Bank organization that makes loans to low- and middle-income countries, had enjoyed a triple-A credit rating. On April 15, 2020, the day of the G20 agreement on the DSSI, the IBRD was in the market raising $8 billion in five-year bonds, at a yield of 0.704 percent. It was the largest and cheapest fundraising exercise ever undertaken by an international financial institution.[34] The reason the World Bank did not join the Debt Service Suspension Initiative was that making concessions to its borrowers, taking a loss on its balance sheet, however small, might have jeopardized the IBRD's triple-A-plus rating and thus put in danger its ability to make low-cost loans to the poorest countries.[35] The World Bank's answer to the crisis was not to suspend or defer existing debt, but to offer $160 billion in new lending capacity through to the summer of 2021.

On the part of the World Bank, it was an extraordinary abdication. Its balance sheet was easily strong enough to absorb the rescheduling of debt payments allowed for under DSSI. It was, after all, NPV neutral. Any losses could have been made up by the shareholders. Alternatively, funds could have been raised by disposing of a small fraction of the IMF's gold holdings, or by issuing SDRs.[36] None of these options was seriously explored in 2020. Beyond the Trump administration's block on SDRs, there was a general failure to summon the political will and resources that would have been necessary to provide substantial financial assistance. The DSSI remained a pale shadow, of which the main beneficiaries were Pakistan and Angola.[37] By the end of the year, the World Bank credited the initiative with

providing $5 billion in relief.[38] As a general solution to the debt problems
of low-income countries, it was a mockery.

Over the summer the UN Conference on Trade and Development
(UNCTAD), one of the more radical UN agencies, pilloried "the stum-
bling efforts by the international community" to provide debt relief. As
UNCTAD said, collective inaction "put a glaring spotlight on the crippling
fragmentation and complexity of existing procedures" for addressing problems concerning international sovereign debt.[39] To restore order and enable a speedy and equitable adjustment of claims, UNCTAD proposed a
"global sovereign debt authority, independent of either (institutional or
private) creditor or debtor interests," which could preside in an evenhanded
and transparent way over restructurings.

The idea had the enthusiastic support of the debt advocacy groups. But
against the entrenched interests of creditors, what coalition had the power to
bring such a supranational agency into being? The IMF, the World Bank, the
G30, and the G20 could hardly deny the inadequacy of current arrangements.
But they had no interest in creating a new global sovereign debt authority.
Instead they relied on moral suasion and earnest appeals to bring all the creditors, including private creditors, to the table. Private sector involvement was
essential to ensuring that restructuring actually provided substantial relief to
debtors. It would eliminate any argument about who was and who was not
involved. It would also legitimate the proceedings on the side of those being
asked to make concessions. As an expert report for the G30, an influential
gathering of former central bank and treasury officials, put it, "An approach
to debt crisis resolution where some creditors effectively finance repayment
to others is politically unsustainable, and is likely to fail. . . . Failure to secure
the participation of all creditors . . . would undermine political support for a
concerted global response to the crisis, and diminish the appetite for official
co-financing in the future."[40] If it was only taxpayer-funded creditors who
offered concessions, they were effectively subsidizing the private creditors.

The appeal of this reform agenda was clear. Ever since the late 1990s
there had been efforts to create a systematic sovereign default regime that

would make the process fair and transparent.[41] Forcing private creditors to share the burden of debt reduction might be arduous and might lead to a temporary exclusion of the debtor countries from bond markets, but in due course, as the G30 experts insisted, one could not escape "economic reality." A country with a lighter debt burden would start with a cleaner sheet. It would be in a better position to embark on new investment and borrowing. The fear of being excluded from bond markets was easily exaggerated. As serial defaulters like Argentina demonstrated, the lenders came back.

To give debtors the leverage they needed to force creditors to the bargaining table, in the autumn of 2020 the International Monetary Fund and the World Bank joined forces to call for the universal introduction of collective action clauses.[42] In the event of a restructuring, these allowed holdout creditors to be outvoted. In the event that credit market stress should escalate into a comprehensive sovereign debt crisis, the IMF floated even more radical proposals. On the one hand, the fund could offer cash or credit enhancements to reluctant private lenders. On the other hand, holdout creditors could be threatened with targeted legislative interventions on the side of distressed low-income borrowers.[43] Belgium had shown the way in 2015 with so-called anti-vulture-fund legislation. If that were to be extended to England and the jurisdiction of New York, where the majority of bond contracts were crafted, it would dramatically shift the balance of power in favor of debtors.[44] That was more than the G20 was likely to stomach, but in November 2020 the G20 did sign off on a "Common Framework for Debt Treatments Beyond the DSSI."[45] This was short of specifics but stated clearly that any debt relief conceded by public lenders should be matched by concessions from private creditors. The question was how to enforce that. Given the key role that American banks, investment funds, and courts play in the world's bond market, this was an issue on which leadership from the United States was essential, but as one report coyly put it, it was not clear, in mid-November, that debt relief for the world's poorest countries was on President Trump's "radar."[46]

It was in the hope of forcing the issue up the agenda following the U.S. election that on November 30, Ramaphosa renewed his appeal for a new issuance of SDR, the extension of DSSI, the enrollment of private creditors, and measures to curb the influence of ratings agencies.[47] He no doubt hoped for a more attentive hearing from the new team being formed around Janet Yellen as the nominee to succeed Steven Mnuchin at the Treasury, but there were also other constituencies that needed winning over. The loudest voice in opposition to the debt-restructuring proposals, somewhat surprisingly, was Vera Songwe, UN under-secretary-general and head of the UN Economic Commission for Africa. As the *Financial Times* reported, in her view, "the last thing developing countries need is enforced private-sector involvement in debt relief." For Songwe, a "common debt framework that confounds public concessional borrowing with commercial market access would undermine Africa's recovery."[48] A balancing of taxpayer against bondholder interests might be a priority for advanced economies, but why should hard-pressed developing countries welcome a coerced day of reckoning with all their creditors at once? What mattered was that in 2020 debt service paid out by developing world governments to creditors exceeded new loans by a total of $167 billion.[49] Reducing debt service might help, but for Africa to recover and to accelerate its development, what was really needed was more investment financed by more loans.

At stake were two different visions of finance and development. The advocates of comprehensive debt restructuring started from a clear idea of what debt was sustainable and called for a clean slate. UNECA didn't deny the need for restructuring in hard cases or the need to enroll private creditors. Despite Songwe's criticism, UNECA's official documents incorporated the G20's "Common Framework." The difference was that UNECA's driving ambition was to generate more, not less, credit.[50] Its model was the so-called blended-finance regime, which relied on close partnership between public agencies and private markets. This conferred power on private lenders and ratings agencies, but as UNECA pointed out, for all the threatening noises, no rating agency had in fact carried out a downgrade of a country participating in DSSI. The overriding need was to multiply credit through every available channel: a new issuance of SDR by the IMF; expanded lending by multilateral development banks; the creation of a liquidity facility that would repo African sovereign bonds, thus making them, like rich-country sovereign bonds, into collateral for further borrowing. In drafting these proposals, UNECA drew on the technical advice of PIMCO, one of the largest private bond managers. What UNECA and PIMCO were calling for was the extension to Africa of the model of public support for private credit prevailing in the advanced economies.[51] Some of this could be done by local financial authorities. Ultimately, it would need to be backstopped by the balance sheets of advanced economy central banks or by the issuance of SDRs, if it should come to that. It was no doubt a precarious construction, but looking around the world, one could find nothing unusual about that. If Italy with debt at 155 percent of GDP could still access markets at 0.2 percent for a five-year bond, courtesy of the support of the ECB, why should African borrowers with far better debt-to-GDP ratios face prohibitive interest rates? It was down to political backing and financial engineering.

The advocates of a rigorous and comprehensive debt restructuring spoke the language of "economic reality" and "debt sustainability," but as the experience of the advanced economies themselves showed, if you borrowed in a currency you controlled, those were negotiable parameters, ultimately at the disposition of central banks. For advocates of a new Africa like Songwe, the governing imperative was the scale of their continent's potential and the immensity of the challenges it faced. The economic reality that dominated UNECA's vision was the drama of Africa's population growth and its urgent need for infrastructure. By 2040, UNECA predicted, Africa would have the largest workforce in the world. It would account for 40 percent of the world's young workers.[52] According to the UN, to meet the Sustainable Development Goals, the continent needed to be spending $1.3 trillion per annum.[53] Not for nothing was "from billions to trillions" the World Bank's motto of 2015.[54] To get there, what was needed was more credit, by practically any means and from any source.

It was the sheer urgency of the investment imperative that gave China such appeal as a lender. In the struggle to make the leap to gigantic scales, China filled a void. One Belt One Road was the springboard. In May 2017, Xi Jinping assembled thirty heads of state and delegates from over 130 countries in Beijing to proclaim "a project of the century." The scale of the Chinese vision was grandiose, but to be talking about trillions of dollars in investment was not hyperbole. On the contrary, this finally was a realistic sense of scale.

The flow of money from China paid for some impressively modern infrastructure. It came with a vision of economic development organized around power generation, transport, and commodity exports, with the promise that this would eventually spill over into the manufacturing supply chains and more high-tech development. The ominous question in 2020, as far as many developing countries were concerned, was not whether they had borrowed too much from China, but whether China was now pulling back.[55] Following the huge surge of lending in 2016, China had applied the brakes. Beijing was worried about capital flight disguised as BRI lending. It was intent on improving the quality of the investment projects and managing the geopolitical fallout. Lending to Africa and Latin America was dialed back.[56] Projects in Pakistan were slowing down as well.[57] By the end of 2020, Chinese lending to BRI countries was down 54 percent, to $47 billion.[58]

If China was indeed retreating, could anyone fill the gap? Could the West muster a strategic response to the giant investment needs of the developing world? What was novel about the years immediately prior to 2020 was that the question was actually being posed.

In January 2017, on taking over the presidency of the G20, Germany proposed the idea of a "Marshall Plan with Africa"—note the "with," not "for"—that would focus on developing private investment.[59] In the same year Canada set up the Development Finance Institute Canada (DFIC), otherwise known as FinDev. In the boilerplate typical of the genre, FinDev was described as "a financial institution that supports inclusive private sector growth and sustainability in developing markets."[60] In 2018, after first proposing to cancel funding for U.S. development finance altogether, the Trump administration threw its weight behind the Better Utilization of Investments Leading to Development Act (or BUILD Act), a bipartisan bill that established the U.S. International Development Finance Corporation (DFC).[61] Subsuming America's existing Overseas Private Investment Corporation, the new finance corporation raised the amount that could be put at risk in support of development lending from $29 billion to $60 billion and extended the terms on which the United States could provide support to include risk-bearing equity.[62] In the summer of 2018, the U.S., Japan, and Australia announced plans to jointly support infrastructure in the Indo-Pacific region.[63] To back that up, in 2019 Australia launched its Infrastructure Financing Facility for the Pacific with a capital of $2 billion.[64] Together, the United States, Japan, and Australia under-wrote the so-called Blue Dot Network to certify infrastructure projects. The aim was to transform the estimated $94 trillion in global infrastructure in-vestments that were so urgently needed in the developing world into "an asset class underpinned by standard contracts," in the manner of commercial real estate projects in the developed world.[65]

The strategic purpose of these ventures was clear. As German devel-opment minister Gerd Müller remarked: "We cannot leave Africa to the Chinese, Russians, and Turks."[66] But what they also had in common was the modesty of the public resources that were committed. The European funds on which the Marshall Plan with Africa was to be based came, alto-gether, to barely 6.5 billion euros. To get to scale, all of these new facilities relied on the magic of leverage and financial engineering to turn billions into, if not trillions, then at least hundreds of billions. In the spirit of the UNECA proposals, they were public-private partnerships. Public institu-tions would absorb designated risks—country risk, project risk, exchange rate risk—so as to multiply private capital flows from rich to poor countries.

However, as novel as was the Western ambition to compete with China, and as intoxicating as the vision of endless market-driven abundance might be, the total amounts of money flowing to the low-income borrowers re-mained inadequate. The overwhelming majority of private funds crowded in by so-called blended finance schemes went to middle-income, not low-income, countries.[67] Even with the support of "derisking" by development banks, capital preferred to go to places that had already demonstrated the capacity to generate sustained and profitable growth. By definition, those were at least middle-income economies. And that ultimately is also why the countries that qualified for the inadequate DSSI were so low down the global policy agenda.

Some 670 million people might live in low-income countries, but they accounted for less than 1 percent of global GDP. Their plight was a human-itarian issue. But it did not pose a systemic risk to the centers of economic and political power in the global north—unless, that is, their misery spilled over into mass migration. As Germany's minister Müller bluntly put it: "Africa's fate is a challenge and an opportunity for Europe. If we do not solve the problems together, they will come to us at some point."[68] That was a future fear. In the short run, the financial difficulties of Zambia or Ghana were a threat to only a tiny part of their creditors' portfolios. And the same was true for the defaults by Ecuador and middle-income debtors like Argentina and Lebanon. Their weight in the world economy was simply too slight, their problems too easily dismissed as idiosyncratic. To actually have forced institutional change on a large scale would have required a far more comprehensive debt crisis than that which arose in 2020, a crisis affecting far larger economies. Something along the lines, perhaps, of the wave of emerging market crises between 1997 and 2001.

In 2020 there was plenty of stress in EM bond markets, but no comprehensive debt crisis had arrived. This was an impressive display of resilience, but was it deceptive? Was 2020 bequeathing a false sense of confidence?

Brazil was far larger and more systemically important than any of the Asian economies had been in the late 1990s. It ended 2021 with public debt standing at 90 percent of GDP, very high for an emerging market.[69] Demand for short-term Brazilian bonds was still strong, but the yields on long-term debt were increasingly exorbitant. In the first four months of 2021, the Brazil Treasury had to roll over $112 billion in debt.[70] This was a huge amount, but given that the vast majority of it was in Brazilian real, given that Brazil's trade balance was strong, its exchange rate flexible, and its central bank actively and effectively managed, there was no immediate crisis driver. Fears, however, were mounting. Bolsonaro's government was opportunistic, his cabinet was as chaotic as ever, and elections were pending in 2022. The markets were not yet in panic mode, but the Brazilian real continued to slide. By April 2021 it was back down to the lowest levels it had reached in the first wave of the crisis. António Guterres, secretary-general of the UN, warned in late March of the ever-shorter maturity of Brazilian borrowing. Above all, the epidemic in Brazil was once again out of control. A new, highly infectious variant was wreaking havoc. Vaccines were arriving far too slowly. In April 2021, daily Covid deaths surged to four thousand and the total surpassed four hundred thousand. As Guterres insisted, in a crisis, everything would become interlinked—health, poverty, finances.[71]

If a general financial crisis was pending, South Africa was even more vulnerable than Brazil. Its growth record was worse. Even before the 2020 crisis, unemployment was close to 30 percent. South Africa's export potential was less dynamic than that of its Latin American counterparts. As the South African Reserve Bank admitted, the quantity of domestic public debt held by South Africa's banks and pension funds created a dangerous link between public and private balance sheets.[72] A downgrade of sovereign debt would hit the balance sheets of banks and pension funds. And the same logic operated in reverse. The South Africa government had backstopped the bonds of its bankrupt power utility Eskom.[73] If those guarantees were called, it would raise South Africa's public debt at a stroke from 2.62 trillion to close to 3 trillion rand. But South Africa had mastered the new EM toolkit. Though the public debts were substantial, they were not yet at worrying levels. The exchange rate fell in early 2020 but then rebounded. By the end of 2020, South Africa's foreign exchange reserves were larger than they had been at the beginning of the year. Given the depressed state of the economy, the South African Reserve Bank held its line. It would not raise rates until absolutely necessary.

In 2020 the most dramatic test of market power and EM resilience was in Turkey. In November, strong man President Erdoğan bowed to market pressure, forced the resignation of his son-in-law from his position at the head of Turkey's economic policy, and performed a U-turn on interest rates.[74] It was a surrender. But what had it taken for Turkey to reach this point? For years Erdoğan had scorned and threatened the global financial markets. He had bullied and fired two central bank chiefs. He pursued an extraordinarily aggressive foreign policy, making enemies of all of Turkey's neighbors, including its main trading partner, the EU.[75] Added to which, under the leadership of Erdoğan's unqualified son-in-law, Turkey violated one of the basic rules in the new EM toolkit. When the lira came under pressure in 2019, rather than employing a delaying action, the Turkish authorities stood their ground and burned more than $140 billion in reserves in a vain effort to prevent devaluation of the lira. With inflation surging, the lira in free fall, and unemployment on the rise, in September 2020 Erdoğan involved Turkey on Azerbaijan's side in its war with Armenia. At that point, according to the best estimates of foreign bankers, Turkey's foreign exchange reserves had disappeared. Short-term borrowing outweighed any assets still on the balance sheet, so the overall balance of reserves was negative.[76] As if to block any recourse to outside help, Erdoğan invited U.S. sanctions by taking delivery of Russian antiaircraft missiles. He refused point-blank to consider an IMF program, since that would be a throwback to Turkey's last major financial crisis in 2001, the crisis that had launched Erdoğan's career.[77] Accepting even the mere suggestion of IMF conditionality was out of the question. Ankara's only remaining source of external support were the Qataris. They chipped in a $15 billion swap line, but Qatar itself was under blockade by the Saudis and the UAE.[78] Biden's victory on November 3 didn't help. Trump was one of Erdoğan's last friends in Washington. Over the weekend of November 7–8, facing pressure from within his own ruling party, Erdoğan pulled the emergency brake and installed a conservative team at the central bank and finance ministry.

The autonomy enjoyed by the big emerging markets was not absolute. The risk of reaching the edge of the cliff was real. The Turkish economy would pay the price for Erdoğan's brinkmanship in tough interest rates for years to come.[79] It was no doubt humbling for Ankara to change its tune toward foreign investors. But Erdoğan was no victim. He was a gambler. He had tested the patience of the markets to the limit and then pulled back at the last minute. Investors were surprisingly forgiving. The panic created the opportunity to make profit on the rebound. With its low-cost base on the border of Europe, Turkey had huge potential. As soon as interest rates were raised, capital moved back in and the lira strengthened.[80] Peace, it seemed, had broken out. But that was to reckon without the mercurial Turkish president. Without warning, on Saturday, March 20, 2021, Erdoğan fired the head of the central bank and then his deputy. It was almost as if Ankara was setting out to provoke a crisis. Behind the scenes, to stop the drain of both domestic and foreign funds, the central bank resorted to capital controls by stealth, limiting the capacity of investors to exit their lira positions.[81]

The hierarchy of the world economy has many tiers and at every level trials of strength were played out. To reassure bondholders and stabilize the growth in its debt short of 100 percent of GDP, South Africa was preparing to undertake painful efforts at budget consolidation.[82] In 2021, Brazil would face the choice as to whether to continue the subsidy to low-income households that had made such a difference during the first wave of the coronavirus crisis. But compared to the options facing Zambia or Ecuador following their defaults, those were good problems to have. The gap between the low-income countries enrolled in DSSI and the likes of Brazil or Turkey was huge. To make that leap was precisely what ambitious elites in countries like Tanzania or Ethiopia aspired to.[83] For all of the damage done by the coronavirus shock, that dream remained very much alive, and as 2020 ended, for elites in emerging markets and developing economies around the world, global financial markets still appeared to offer the best available ladder.

If 2020 started with foreign funds hemorrhaging out of the emerging markets, the year ended with a record inflow. In late November, weeks after Peru floated its century bond, Côte d'Ivoire issued a twelve-year EUR1 billion Eurobond. Despite offering a record-low yield of 5 percent, it was five times oversubscribed. In 2021, rating agency Fitch predicted that Namibia, Nigeria, and South Africa would roll over old debt. Côte d'Ivoire, Ghana, and Kenya might embark on new issues. Benin, 158 in 2019 out of 189 on the Human Development Index, was on the list of those expected to return to the market.[84] The countries in question urgently needed the money and were willing to pay, but what was pushing money out even to the most impoverished corners of the world economy was the huge abundance of dollar liquidity. It was the stance of the U.S. Federal Reserve that gave the global credit system the extraordinary elasticity it exhibited in the face of the coronavirus crisis. The abundance of dollars underwrote the market-based system of global credit and deferred the kind of crisis that might force a general reckoning. Only a tightening of U.S. monetary policy would expose the real constraints on low-income borrowers. That would be decided not in Côte d'Ivoire or Kenya, but in the United States, between Wall Street and Washington, D.C.

Chapter 14

ADVANCED ECONOMIES: TAPS ON

Imagining future crises in Argentina, Turkey, or Brazil came relatively easily. In living memory, they had been through deep financial turmoil and regime change. That was what defined them as "emerging" markets. Advanced economies were credited with more stability and solidly established institutions. All the more remarkable that in the final days of 2020 the country most haunted by talk of coups was not in Latin America, Africa, the Middle East, or Asia. Instead it was the United States.

Populists love drama. They love drama so much that both leaders and led can find it difficult to distinguish what is real from what is not.[1] The line between rhetoric and actually enacting political change blurs. Their outrages tempt their opponents to a response in kind, which risks its own loss of reality. The best way to respond may be simply to ignore the histrionics. That was the path chosen by the Biden transition team, ignoring the increasingly manic attempts by Trump and his entourage to deny their defeat. The result in the final months of 2020 was that the U.S. political system was thrown into an acute state of cognitive dissonance. President-elect Biden and his team went ahead with the transition. They prepared coronavirus responses, climate policies, and plans for a stimulus. Meanwhile, a substantial caucus within the GOP continued to pander to the defeated incumbent and thus to validate his alternate reality.

The grotesquerie reached its height on January 6 with the mob invasion of the Capitol incited by the president, his entourage, and several Republican members of Congress. In the wave of collective indignation that followed, talk of coups and fascism reached its height.[2] That was always a stretch, at least if one regards fascism not as an attitude, but as an articulation of social forces. The U.S. military refused to have anything to do with the Trumpists and there was no real socioeconomic antagonism motivating his movement. To see the force of that point, imagine the level of tension in the United States on January 6, 2021, if it had been Bernie Sanders whose victory the GOP was contesting. That would have been a true test of constitutional fidelity for the powers that be. Between Donald Trump and Joe Biden, it wasn't even a choice. For all the furor over the transition, in the weeks prior to January 6, America's political class had already reached a basic compromise to stave off the actual threat of the moment—the looming collapse of the country's fragile welfare system.

The initial fallout from the shutdowns had been contained by the largesse of the CARES Act, but by early December, time and money were running out. The across-the-board $600 supplement to unemployment insurance had expired in July. The supplemental schemes to cover the self-employed and backstop state funds were due to end within weeks. According to estimates by the Century Foundation, unless Congress acted, 13.5 million out-of-work Americans would lose all benefits the day after Christmas.[3] To make matters worse, the eviction moratorium declared by the Centers for Disease Control and Prevention was also due to expire at the end of the year. Millions faced eviction in the midst of a resurgent pandemic.[4] Even if they remained housed, according to Moody's Analytics, by January 2021, 10 million tenants would owe more than $57 billion in rent arrears.[5]

Despite the urgency of this impending crisis, in the weeks following the election, stimulus talks were stalled. On aid for states and an employer liability shield, the two sides were irreconcilable. Desperate to break the deadlock, a bipartisan group of centrists worked out a compromise to the tune of $900 billion that excluded the most contentious issues on both sides. It was not to the liking of the House Democrats who had voted for a far bigger stimulus, but it would at least avert the looming disaster. The transition team decided to support the proposal. Biden's nightmare was to take office with an economy in free fall.[6]

At this point, the decision hung on McConnell and the Senate GOP. Throughout November, McConnell had stuck by the president. But after the electoral college votes on December 14 confirmed Biden's victory, McConnell made a shift that would turn out to be decisive for the subsequent course of events. He recognized Biden's victory and threw his weight onto the side of those preparing for the transition. For McConnell, of course, that meant not preparing for cooperation, but preparing to obstruct the Biden administration. Holding the Republican seats in Georgia would secure his hold on the Senate and give the GOP a veto over any legislative move by the Biden administration. To have any chance in Georgia, the GOP needed not to look like the chief obstacle to a stimulus. So McConnell dropped his objections to the $900 billion bill.

Even that, however, did not seal the deal. As soon as a compromise seemed possible, other interests mobilized around the stimulus. Bernie Sanders on the left and Josh Hawley on the right joined forces to demand much larger stimulus payments than the $600 checks that had emerged from the first weeks of negotiations. Then conservative Senator Pat Toomey raised a more fundamental issue, the Fed.

Since the late summer Toomey had been waging a campaign to restrict the extraordinary expansion of Fed activism.[7] And this campaign acquired an even sharper edge as the wrestling match over the stimulus intensified. For the event that the Republicans retained control of the Senate, one option suggested to the Biden team was to use the funds remaining in the Fed's CARES Act allocations to launch more adventurous lending programs.[8] In the weeks after the election, Treasury Secretary Mnuchin moved to cut off this option.[9] He instructed the Fed to "return" to the Treasury the unused sums allocated in the March stimulus package. It was an accounting exercise, money moving from one government account to another, but it was an accounting exercise with sharp political teeth. The point was to ensure that the Republican majority in the Senate retained a whip hand over economic policy. Given the dug-in positions in Congress, the implications of Mnuchin's intervention were so serious that they triggered a rare act of open dissent on the part of Jerome Powell. Mnuchin went ahead regardless, nor was that the end of the saga. Seizing his chance in the delicately balanced stimulus negotiations in December, Toomey pounced. In a last-minute amendment, he called for a bar on any further Fed lending programs that used the already-appropriated resources, or in future, any programs similar to those approved during the panic in March 2020.[10] This attack on Fed autonomy was enough to summon Ben Bernanke out of retirement.[11] In the superheated partisan atmosphere, it was an alarming prospect that one of the last functioning organs of American government might be checkmated. Only after protracted negotiations with Chuck Schumer was Toomey willing to back down. With some anodyne language about not cloning the March programs, the package passed.

It was, after CARES, the second largest stimulus ever delivered. And it was, even by the standards of modern American legislation, a mammoth bill. Baked together with the annual appropriation bill, it came to 5,600 pages. Hastily run off the presses by the Government Publishing Office, it was airlifted to Florida for Trump's signature. One of the banquet halls at Mar-a-Lago was decked out for the occasion. The timetable was short. If the president did not sign by December 26, benefits would expire. The worst-off Americans would lose billions in welfare checks. If he held out until January 3, the 116th Congress would reach its statutory end and the elaborate compromise would vanish into thin air.[12] At every stage in the negotiations, Treasury Secretary Mnuchin insisted that Trump had been kept in the loop, but the president now decided otherwise. On December 23 he denounced the bill as a "disgrace," demanding that it should be garnished with $2,000 stimulus checks, presumably with his name on them.

It was Trump's last act of real power. While the president golfed, the benefits on which millions of Americans depended were cut off, the government faced shutdown, defense spending was in limbo, and the fragile stimulus compromise began to disintegrate. Reverting to the House Democrats' more ambitious agenda, Pelosi piled in behind those calling for bigger checks. Meanwhile, the high priest of Clinton-era centrism Larry Summers took to the airwaves to declare that stimulus checks to the tune of $2,000 would likely cause the economy to overheat.[13] Anything on which Trump, Sanders, and Hawley could agree was bound to be a bad idea. Then, on December 27, having made his final mark, Trump signed the original bill into law.

It was a temporary deal. Benefits would expire again in March. As things stood on December 27, with the Georgia Senate seats still in play, the Democrats faced the prospect of further knife-edge negotiations with a hostile Senate majority. But the immediate social crisis had been averted and the Fed's scope for action had been preserved. While the House Republicans continued in their state of denial, the GOP's leadership in the Senate, where they had the responsibility of being in the majority, accommodated itself to the reality of the transition. Fighting to retain that majority involved acknowledging concern for the economy as one thing all Americans had in common. A polity that could agree on practically nothing else did in the end agree on people's need for money.[14]

The December 2020 stimulus deal reasserted the key role of budgetary politics in America's response to the crisis. This was driven by domestic politics. It was necessitated by the inadequate system of welfare that left millions at dire risk of poverty. It served as a trading ground between Washington's warring political camps. The result was that through 2020 and beyond, the United States was committed to running the world's largest fiscal stimulus. That had implications far beyond the United States.

This was good not only for America. With its generous budget deficits, the U.S. pumped demand into the world economy. The overall effect was in sharp contrast to 2008–2009. Then too the government budget deficit had exploded, but under the impact of the financial crisis, both households and businesses had tightened their belts. The private savings rate shot up, and this substantially offset the government deficit. The U.S. current account deficit was cut in half, sucking purchasing power out of world markets. In 2020 too there was a huge surge in household saving, but thanks to the stabilization policies of March, the corporate sectoral balance sheet remained steady and the federal government deficit imparted a giant positive

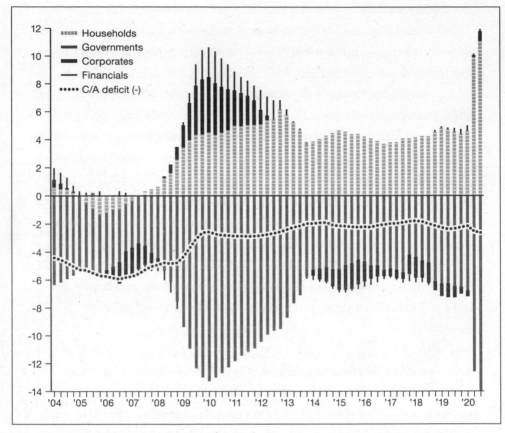

United States as the engine of world demand as seen in saving-investment balance
by sector, in %GDP
(4qma) last data point Q3 2020
IIF

boost. At a time when trade all over the world was imploding, the U.S. current account widened slightly.

For all the sound and fury of Trump's trade wars, America's net imports from China actually increased in 2020. Chinese manufacturers could
barely keep up with export demand.[15] Factories outbid each other for workers. In Shanghai, port container freight rates shot up.[16]

The vertiginous thing about America's economic policy at the end of
2020, as was true for so many other aspects of American public life, was
how fragile its political foundations were. After the swift passage of the
CARES Act in the spring, it had taken months of intense negotiation to

finally put together the second stimulus deal in December 2020, and then it all hung on Trump's signature. On the Democratic side, the main reason to get the second stimulus deal done sooner rather than later was the expectation that as soon as Biden was inaugurated, the GOP would pivot. The party that under Trump had happily voted for huge deficits would rediscover fiscal rectitude and insist on budget balance. They would sabotage Biden as they had done Obama. If the Republicans held the majority in the Senate, fiscal policy would be paralyzed and the entire onus of economic policy would fall on the Fed.

The Fed's instruments were powerful, but they were blunt. The most powerful effect of quantitative easing was through asset markets. Big monetary policy interventions inflated the stock market, benefiting the small minority with substantial equity holdings. If in 2021 monetary policy was left unassisted by redistributive fiscal policy, it was a surefire recipe for progressively increasing inequality. As 2021 began, with equity prices surging, stock markets appeared to be entering a true bubble scenario. Pundits warned of a vicious spiral in which widening social differences stoked resentment that further inflamed the populist anti-elite backlash.[17]

A lopsided reliance on the Fed would also have implications for the world at large. Whereas U.S. fiscal policy tended to stoke demand for imports, benefiting countries like Germany or China, a Fed with the throttle stuck open had a rather different effect. It weakened the dollar and eased monetary policy throughout the world economy, pushing down interest rates. Econometric testing done since the advent of the QE era showed that this had a strongly positive spillover effect.[18] It eased credit and reduced the local currency price of the many commodities that were traded in dollars.[19] But the effect was not equally positive in all economies worldwide. Whereas the commodity exports of Brazil tended to be priced in dollars and thus benefited from a devaluation, for Asian and European manufactured exports, the opposite was the case. If countries wanted to resist the appreciation of their currencies against the dollar, as several emerging market competitors did in 2020, they were forced to adopt countermeasures. They could, for instance, buy dollars and accumulate foreign exchange reserves.[20] The risk was that it would trigger a hostile reaction on the part of the

United States. At the end of 2020 the odd couple of Switzerland and Vietnam were singled out by Washington as currency manipulators.[21]

Two very different scenarios both for the United States and the world economy hinged on the balance of power in Congress, which was finally settled on January 6 with the announcement of the result of the Georgia runoffs. This statewide election was one of the most expensive contests in history. In total, the two sides would spend a staggering $937 million on the campaign.[22] The result hung, in the end, on the fallout from Trump's antics, a sustained electoral mobilization by Democratic Party activists led by Stacey Abrams, and a few hundred thousand votes in the suburbs of Atlanta. With the Democrats gaining their two majority-confirming seats and the GOP deeply riven over Trump's disgraceful behavior, the balance of power and with it the direction of economic policy had finally been decided.

It was this that accounted for the jarring juxtaposition on January 6. Even as the mob cavorted in the congressional chambers on live TV, the S&P 500 surged. As Rana Foroohar of the *Financial Times* commented, "Normally when a financial market rises amid a coup or extreme political instability, it is because the leftists are out and the animal spirits of business have been released."[23] What boosted the markets on January 6 was the knowledge that even if Nancy Pelosi and her colleagues were sheltering for safety under armed guard, one thing was now clear: the fiscal taps were staying open.

Between November 2020 and January 2021, the United States lived through a profound national political crisis. The only other Western nation to experience anything similar was the UK. Brexit and Trump's presidency were born together in 2016. There was a painful symmetry about their ending together too.

In the manner of the entire Brexit psychodrama, the negotiations with the EU were taken to the very edge. On Christmas Eve, a deal was done.[24] What had emerged from the talks was a very "hard" Brexit, far harder than most had imagined or voted for. The British had imagined that the path to an advantageous deal would lie in splitting the Europeans along economic lines, pitting German car exporters against the French, but that turned out to be misguided. Preserving the integrity of the single market, the fundamental driver of the EU, which Margaret Thatcher's government in the 1980s had done more than any member state to set in motion, turned out to be the overriding interest of the EU. In the end it was the UK, not the EU, that needed the deal more, and as the pandemic surged once more, the UK needed it very badly.

The shock suffered by the UK economy in 2020 was spectacular. The fastidiousness of British statisticians may somewhat exaggerate the impact of the downturn by painting the decline in the public service contribution to GDP in particularly grim terms.[25] However, the fall in household consumption was real, and the prospects for 2021 were grim. It was, according to the Bank of England, the worst recession in three hundred years.[26]

Brexit entailed a morass of delays and paperwork. That became obvious almost immediately. In early 2021, trade with the EU and with Germany in particular plunged. The longer-term implications for investment were unforeseeable but were likely bad. And for all that, the impact of the coronavirus was vastly greater. As the new virus strain ran rampant through London, much of the UK shut down, in some cases for the third time. In Britain too, the essential policy response to avoid an immediate social and economic catastrophe was a further fiscal boost.

In their relentless pursuit of Brexit, the Tories, like the Republicans in the United States, had let go of their traditional affiliation with UK business. The City of London had been sidelined in the Brexit talks. Symbolic issues like fishing rights took center stage. The only interests the government seemed reliably to serve were its crony networks.[27] Unlike the Republicans, however, the Tories did boast a track record of imposing fiscal discipline on their own watch. Austerity had been the signature policy of David Cameron's government between 2010 and 2016. Following the surprise outcome of the Brexit referendum, there had been a change. Theresa May had talked in terms of a new national welfarism.[28] Much was made of Tory gains in working-class northern constituencies in 2019. And to meet the crisis in March, the comprehensive furlough measures the government adopted did have an incongruously "European" flavor.[29] Initially, they were declared to be temporary, but as the October cliff edge approached, the government performed a U-turn and extended the scheme into 2021.

In truth, amid the chaos of 2020, it was hard to discern any clear pattern. Johnson and his crew appeared panic-stricken and opportunistic, a campaign team rather than a government. About the fiscal balance, however, there was little ambiguity. For the budget year 2020–2021, rather than the £55 billion in borrowing expected in March 2020, the final total came to a total of £300 billion. This was unprecedented in peacetime. As 2021 began, there was talk around Westminster of the need to "restore order" to public finances and return to true Tory fiscal principles.[30] In an effort to economize, public sector wages, including those for nurses, were frozen and the UK's foreign aid budget was slashed. The sheer mean-spiritedness of the measures awakened memories of the turn to austerity in 2010, with its combination of public spending cuts and giveaways for corporations. But when the budget was announced to Parliament in March 2021, it offered the reverse. Though there was no new stimulus, the key pillars of the Covid crisis response remained in place at least until September. With the vaccine campaign rolling out and a summer reopening in sight, the Treasury estimated that the UK's total crisis spending would come to a massive 16 percent of GDP.[31] When taxes rose, it would be corporations that would be hit first and hardest. And there was another key thing missing in 2020 from the austerity scenario: any talk of bond market panic. In 2010, against the backdrop of the Greek crisis, it had been easy to conjure up the specter of bond market vigilantes. In 2020, one might have thought that the outsize deficits and the knife-edge Brexit talks would have spooked financial markets, but nothing of the sort. The giant borrowing drive was flanked by an openhanded monetary policy courtesy of the Bank of England. The bank steadfastly denied that its pattern of bond purchases had anything to do with fiscal policy. Central bankers' eyes, they insisted, were fixed on ensuring that Britain did not slide into deflation. If they were buying bonds, it was to keep interest rates in check. No one in the markets cared. The bank was underpinning debt issuance, and none of the key players in the gilt market saw anything wrong with that.[32] With the world awash with liquidity, in January 2021, the UK Treasury was selling gilts at negative yields.

The coronavirus crisis confirmed what had already been clear four years earlier at the time of the 2016 referendum. One of the ironies of the belligerent Brexiteer slogan "Take Back Control" was that it appeared at a moment when due to the giant liquidity of capital and money markets, advanced economies like the UK were under less external financial constraint than at any previous moment in modern history. The challenge was not, as the slogan suggested, to throw off external fetters. The challenge was to make the best of the ample options that were available.

Of the many miscalculations made by the Brexiteers in their dealings with Brussels, the most basic was to assume that the UK was ever the first item of business, either in Brussels or Berlin. It was not. Not in 2016, when the EU was recovering from its "polycrisis" over Ukraine, Greece, and the surge of refugees from Syria, and not in December 2020, as the moment of Brexit truth arrived. As 2020 ground to an end, the main preoccupations of the EU were the pandemic, the unfinished business of the July compromise, and the uncertainty surrounding relations with China and the United States.

The EU's political investment in the NextGen EU fiscal package of July 2020 was huge. The compromise, even if it remained on paper, had turned the political narrative and calmed the markets. Before it could be implemented, it needed to be ratified by the increasingly assertive European Parliament. In the parliament, a coalition of forces ranging from the center right to the left were alarmed at the thought of tens of billions of euros going to the governments of Poland and Hungary, countries that had undercut the independence of their judiciary, challenged the freedom of expression, attacked the civil rights of minorities, curtailed reproductive rights, and resisted the Green Deal. On top of that, Viktor Orbán's regime in Hungary was developing into a notorious kleptocracy. As a safeguard, the parliament insisted on adding rule of law provisions to the July compromise.[33] Not surprisingly, the nationalists in Warsaw and Budapest took umbrage.[34] They wrapped themselves in the flag of resistance, accusing their opponents of undermining traditional Western values and using the EU to wage law-fare against legitimately elected national governments. Poland and Hungary had joined the EU to escape their bitter history of foreign domination. Now they would unfurl the banner of national resistance once more.

Months of negotiations were fruitless. The much-hailed NextGen EU package remained in suspense. By early December, the EU was beginning to resemble the United States not just in regard to the virus numbers. On both sides of the Atlantic, nationalist populism was paralyzing the economic policy response to the crisis. Fortunately for the EU, Trump's analogues in Europe were in a weak position. Hungary and Poland needed the EU's money. In the European Council they were isolated and outgunned. As the decisive meeting of the heads of government approached on December 10, Angela Merkel offered them a deal they could not refuse.[35] The parliament's rule of law provisions would come into force, but only after their opponents had had a chance to challenge them in the European Court of Justice. It was face-saving and convenient.[36] For Orbán, crucially, the provisions would only take effect after Hungary's next general election. In the meantime, European money would continue to flow.[37]

A less ambitious meeting might have ended there and then, early on the evening of December 10, but the German presidency had other items on its agenda. After the bold climate change announcement from Beijing, the EU needed to raise its carbon commitments for 2030. Once again, this ran into opposition from Eastern Europe. No one was more wedded to coal than the Poles. Coal was more than a fuel; the nationalists had turned it into a patriotic fetish.[38] Once again Poland's prime minister, Mateusz Mora-wiecki, dug in. If he went home having surrendered on both the rule of law and coal, he warned his European counterparts, his government would be overthrown by his even more right-wing coalition partners. At 2:30 a.m., an EU diplomat sent the *Politico* news service a text that consisted of a single emoji: an exploding head.[39] As Merkel reminded the meeting, for the EU to fail to raise its Paris commitments would be a "disaster."[40] Eventually, early in the morning of December 11, Poland got what it wanted—more money to close down coal. The details would have to wait for further talks, but a deal was done, simultaneously on all three fronts: finance, rule of law, and climate.

EU officials themselves were surprised. "It's completely different than ten years ago," one commission official remarked, "and I don't think it's because we're better policymakers but because the world has changed completely." [41] The accumulation of science, a generation of youth protest, the changing economics, and the coronavirus had shifted the Overton window. As Spain's chief climate negotiator Teresa Ribera reflected, "Coming at this pivot point, the coronavirus forced the world to face the 'contradictions' in its economy." Or as one senior official summed it up, in the characteristically broken English of the EU: "Frankly, without the pandemic, I don't know if we had [sic] solved it."[42]

Politically, it may have been impressive, but as a macroeconomic intervention the EU's budget deal was less so. The EU's fiscal effort was still far short of the U.S. government stimulus. And it showed.

As the Organisation for Economic Co-operation and Development reviewed the growth record of 2020, the results were sobering. In 2020, euro area GDP fell by 7.6 percent. That was a far worse contraction than Europe had suffered in 2008–2009 or in the worst years of the eurozone crisis. It was also worse than in the United States, where GDP contracted in 2020 by 3.5 percent. Gross fixed capital formation in the euro area fell by more than 10 percent, versus a fall of only 1.7 percent in the U.S. To put that in round figures, the European Commission and the European Investment Bank estimated that the shortfall in private investment would come to €831 billion in 2020 and 2021, more than the entire recovery package.[43] Most worryingly, the impact was worst in Southern Europe, which has been suffering from chronically low investment since 2010.

In 2021, it would continue to be national budgets that carried the main weight of the crisis-fighting in Europe.[44] The unemployment problem that the Europeans had successfully managed through short-time working schemes would loom large, and growth prospects were dismal. On current fiscal settings, the outlook for the European economy was nothing short of depressing. According to the OECD, at the end of 2021, euro area GDP

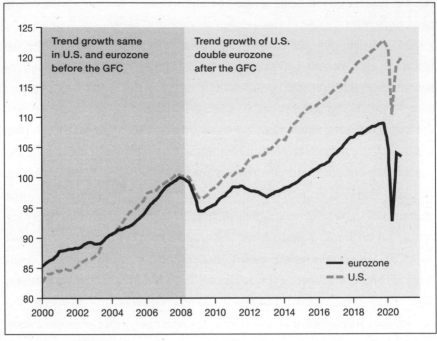

Divergence in growth trends between the United States and the eurozone before and after the GFC (GDP, 2008=100)

IIF

would still be 3 percent down from where it had been at the end of 2019. By contrast, by the end of 2021, the United States was expected to have fully recovered. China would be 10 percent ahead of where it was at the end of 2019.[45] The euro area as a whole was not expected to regain its 2019 level until 2022. The much-ballyhooed NextGen EU program would, according to the IMF's calculations, raise the growth path by at most 1.5 percent of GDP and more likely half that.[46] Furthermore, recovery would be worryingly uneven. Whereas Germany, the European champion, was by 2022 expected to be 1.5 percent ahead of where it was at the end of 2019, the OECD expected Spain's GDP to be 3 percent down on its pre-crisis level, even in 2022.

A comparison with 2000 makes a stark divide apparent. Up to 2008 the United States and the euro area had grown in parallel. Since then, their trajectories had diverged. Europe had never made good the losses of the double-dip recession after 2008. The deep 2020 recession and Europe's modest fiscal response to the coronavirus crisis were set to compound the growing divide. As 2021 began, while America was delivering another round of fiscal stimulus, Europe was adopting ever-tighter lockdown measures. A second recession was imminent.

What preserved the veneer of complacency in Europe was the calm in the bond markets. Throughout the autumn the European Central Bank had watched national government spending plans closely. On December 10, the day of the showdown with Poland and Hungary at the European Council, the ECB announced that it was increasing its emergency debt-buying program by 37 percent to 1.85 trillion euros. Even if, as some economists predicted, EU bond issuance in 2021 ran to as much as 1.25 trillion euros ($1.5 trillion), the ECB would have buying capacity to spare. By the end of 2021, the ECB was on track to hold 40 percent or more of both German and Italian debt. That was enough to pin benchmark German ten-year rates safely in negative territory and create unprecedentedly easy funding conditions for the rest of Europe. The EU would be issuing 225 billion euros in green bonds, the largest amount ever sold. But there was no risk of this flooding the market. The Dutch government was notorious for its penny-pinching approach to European finance, but as Elvira Eurlings, the director of the Dutch State Treasury Agency, remarked: "Appetite for AAA paper is enormous, and supply is way below demand."[47]

As 2021 began, the U.S., the UK, and the governments of the EU were all running huge deficits. Their economies were ailing. The political situation was tense—in the case of the U.S. and the UK, at times, unbearably so. This was democratic politics and intergovernmental diplomacy in the raw. It was a constellation one might have expected to light up the currency or bond markets, but they barely flickered. From the financial record, you would not have known that anything of any note was going on. Conversely, there was little financial turmoil to compound the political battles of December and January.

That is not to say that democratic politics was free from the power of money. Crucially, in all three cases there was no left-wing option on the table. The battle was between right populists and centrists, and the centrists had the stronger hand. It was disconcerting, no doubt, to hear Senator Hawley railing about a corporate elite conspiracy to steal the election. No British prime minister of any party, let alone a Tory, had ever before told British business to "fuck" off.[48] But disagreeable as right-wing populism might be, it was not the same as facing a militant Bernie Sanders bent on bringing social democracy to America, or a radical Labour government determined to turn Brexit into Lexit.

Even allowing for the defeat of the left, however, the stakes were huge, the economic and financial situation was bad, and the financial markets nevertheless remained calm. The combination of massive global liquidity injections led by the Fed and the obvious willingness of all the central banks to stabilize bond markets if they did become unstable simply removed the constraint of bond market pressure. As the new year began and the anniversary of the pandemic approached, the problem was not money. The problem was how to use it.

The biggest recipient of the EU's NextGen recovery fund was Italy. It needed to be. It had been hard-hit by the virus. Its debt had been driven to even more worrying levels. Its economy had been on a downgrade for more than a decade. The year 2020 knocked Italy back even further. As things stood at the end of 2020, Italy's GDP was 10 percent below where it had been at the beginning of 2008.[49] To meet this prolonged malaise, the EU had allocated 200 billion euros in funding to Italy—10 percent of Italian GDP over five years—80 billion euros of it in grants.[50] It was potentially a historic opportunity to revive investment. To unlock the funding, Rome had to write a national recovery plan for submission to the commission and the suspicious North European governments in the council.[51] For Italy's political class, it was a spectacular challenge, one it struggled to meet. In December, as Berlin and Brussels wrestled with Hungary and Poland, the coalition underpinning Prime Minister Conte's government came apart. Led by former Prime Minister Matteo Renzi, critics attacked the government for failing to focus spending squarely on education and health.[52] Confindustria, the powerful Italian business lobby, demanded "reforms," starting with the pension system. Hoping to clarify the fronts and capitalize on his personal popularity, Prime Minister Conte resigned, but no new majority emerged.[53] New elections were a nightmare not only because of the pandemic but because of the upsurge of right-wing support, not for Silvio Berlusconi or even Matteo Salvini of the League, but the openly postfascist Fratelli d'Italia. On February 3, 2021, Italian president Sergio Mattarella turned to the safest pair of hands in Italy: Mr. "whatever it takes," Mario Draghi—formerly of Italian Treasury, Goldman Sachs, the Banca d'Italia, and the ECB. It was on the one hand a confirmation of the emblematic role of central bankers as the technocrats of the modern age and on the other hand a crash test of that model. Neither Italian politics nor the Italian economy would respond to Draghi's strong words as bond markets once had. As the skeptical North European countries watched, it was a test not only for Italy, but for the entire project of the EU. If Italy botched the NextGen program, the argument for deepening fiscal union would be set back, perhaps irretrievably.[54] And as 2021 began, Italy was not even the most urgent problem facing Europe.

The question preoccupying governments across the rich world was not how to spend hundreds of billions or how to plan for the decades hence, but how to get shots, each of which cost no more than a restaurant meal, into as many vulnerable arms as quickly as possible. The vaccines were rolling out of the labs, but the virus was mutating and it was clearly crucial to immunize billions of people as quickly as possible. The rich countries had monopolized the vast majority of supply. In early 2021 the question was, could they use it?

In the UK and the U.S., rollout began in December. There was a gradual ramp up, but by the end of January both were achieving an accelerating pace of vaccination. By contrast, in Europe the vaccines were not arriving. The EU had been ambitious. National rivalry would have been a disaster for the union. As in the development of the NextGen Recovery package, the emphasis had been on unity. The EU was the only part of the world where money did not dictate national rates of immunization. Bulgaria and Germany each received their rations. This was a remarkable achievement, but it was not matched by similar energy with regard to either securing orders or managing delivery. Approval for vaccines was also slow. On cost grounds, EU purchasing had favored AstraZeneca, which turned out to have difficulties both in testing and in production. Brussels did not force the pace, but neither did national governments. Ursula von der Leyen and the rest of the commission tried to correct the narrative. As they pointed out, unlike the United States or the United Kingdom, the EU was a large net exporter of vaccines. One of Mario Draghi's early actions in office was to stop shipments of Italian-manufactured vaccine to Australia, where the virus was largely suppressed. Despite its slow start, the European program was accelerating. By the summer the vulnerable population would be immunized. But as every major city across the continent again shut down and families were once again confronted with the stresses of school closures and confinement, these protestations cut little ice. On the anniversary of the public health disaster of the spring of 2020, Europe's governmental machine was again failing the coronavirus test. In light of this shambles, John Maynard Keynes's emancipatory exclamation that we can afford anything we can actually do began to take on an increasingly bitter taste.

Conclusion

In democracies, the handover of power is a delicate business. In many countries it is handled matter-of-factly—a handshake in the parliament chamber, a round of applause, a removal truck to take away the personal effects. In the United States, the transition is agonizingly protracted and culminates in the pomp and ceremony of what amounts to a democratic coronation. It is always a show, but no inauguration has ever been more anxiously awaited than that of Joseph Biden as 46th President of the United States on January 20, 2021.

In his first speech as president, Biden presented his ascent to power as the outcome of a perennial battle between the "American ideal that we are all created equal" and the "harsh, ugly reality that racism, nativism, fear, and demonization have long torn us apart."[1] His victory, he promised, confirmed the fact that "history, faith, and reason show the way." He quoted Abraham Lincoln on the occasion of the Emancipation Proclamation on New Year's Day 1863. He evoked the suffragettes of 1919 and Martin Luther King Jr. He also paraphrased, without attribution, Bill Clinton's clarion call for Barack Obama's presidency: America should lead "not merely by the example of our power but by the power of our example."[2]

But what example did America have to offer?[3] Biden spoke to a spare socially distanced audience, shielded by barbed wire and 25,000 troops against the threat of violence by Americans against Americans. And which

America did Joe Biden represent? Born in 1942, Biden was among the teen-
agers who heard John F. Kennedy declare that the "torch" had passed to a
"new generation." That was in 1961. Biden's first run for president was in
1988. At the inauguration in 2021, the age gap between Biden and his vice
president, Kamala Harris, was so large that it was hard not to think of the
presidential and vice presidential couples as a family group—adult children and spry elderly parents. A consoling image for those Americans who
voted for them, but also atavistic, an echo of the Trump, Clinton, and Bush
clans.

The question of how his administration would react to the immediate
challenges facing America entered into Biden's inaugural speech only par-
enthetically. The answer came in the well-prepared volleys of executive
orders delivered by the White House in the days that followed—on the
pandemic, on climate, on housing, on the environment, on immigration.[4]
On the campaign trail, Biden had repeatedly evoked four converging or
overlapping crises—his version of the polycrisis—the pandemic, the economy, the call for racial justice, and the climate.[5] In his inaugural, he added
"America's standing in the world." While the rituals of America's civic re-
ligion continued to be performed, the magic was wearing thin. The model
of American-led globalization that Biden and his predecessors had shaped
was in deep trouble, and it had been for some time.

It was in Biden's first term as vice president between 2008 and 2012
that an existential financial crisis coincided with and compounded a splin-
tering of conventional norms in democratic politics on both sides of the
Atlantic. The same moment saw a sudden surge in geopolitical tension with
Russia. After four years of frantic firefighting on both sides of the Atlantic,
there was a brief period of stabilization between 2012 and 2014, demar-
cated by Draghi's "whatever it takes," Obama's reelection, and the run-up
to the Paris climate accords. But this stabilization proved short-lived. Between 2014 and 2016 the status quo was rocked by the Ukraine crisis, the
commodity price collapse, the Syrian refugee crisis, Greece's near default,
China's near-miss financial meltdown, Bernie Sanders's unexpectedly strong
challenge to Hillary Clinton, Brexit, Trump's victory, and the Gilets Jaunes
explosion in France. Given the extraordinary relief of the arrival of the

vaccines and the departure of the Trump presidency, it was tempting to think of January 2021 as a moment of culmination. The Biden team themselves knew different. They had not just inherited a train wreck but were in the middle of one.

The immediate priorities of the administration were controlling the pandemic and addressing the economic crisis. From Trump, the Biden administration inherited both an out-of-control epidemic and a vaccine program that was about to take off. To its credit, the Biden team made the best of the situation. It doubled down on social distancing and forced the vaccine rollout at top speed. It also consistently enforced the provisions of the Defense Production Act, which ensured that America's orders for vaccines were met first. Through May 2021, until vaccines were freely available for all Americans, the United States exported virtually no vaccines to the rest of the world. Moderna and Pfizer supported this policy because they wanted to avoid liability for any safety issues that might arise with the newfangled mRNA vaccines outside the U.S. It was a policy of "America First," to make Donald Trump proud, all the more effective for the fact that the Biden administration avoided nationalist bluster. Instead, the administration proclaimed itself the "arsenal of vaccines," but only once America's own needs had been fully met.

As far as the economy was concerned, the Biden team showed every sign of being determined not to repeat the mistakes of 2009. They had read the postmortems on the Obama administration. They would go large. They would hold out no hope of cooperation from the Republicans. They would start with the $1.9 trillion American Rescue Plan and follow that with a $2.3 trillion infrastructure program and the American Families Plan, costed out at $1.8 trillion. On top of the $3.6 trillion stimulus delivered in 2020, this level of government spending was unprecedented in peacetime. Unlikes CARES in March 2020, the $1.9 trillion Rescue Plan was squarely focused on middle-class and low-income Americans and small businesses, providing a minimum of pork for big business and the wealthy. Expert opinion divided, but the stimulus from the $1.9 trillion Rescue Plan alone exceeded the amount of economic slack, the so-called output gap, by a considerable margin.[6] It implied deliberately running the economy hot.

Unsurprisingly, this bold approach to fiscal policy ran up against criticism. The Republicans forced the Democrats to go around them in the Senate, and the plan was also attacked from the center by voices like Larry Summers and economists of international repute like Olivier Blanchard.[7] They considered it excessive and ill targeted, lacking a focus on investment. It was, Summers griped, the most irresponsible fiscal policy in forty years, a product of the perverse interaction between Republican intransigence and the veto power of the left wing of the Democratic Party. Significantly, one place from which there was little if any opposition was Wall Street.[8] The business lobby did have one demand: drop the $15 national minimum wage. Once that was gone, the nation's CEOs fell readily into line. So too did the Fed.

It was hard to credit, but it seemed that finally, after decades of quiescence in the labor market, the Fed was wakening up to the implications of the historic defeat of organized labor in the 1980s and the dawning of a new era of globalization. This meant that it could afford to run the economy hot without fear of a runaway wage-price spiral. Of course, if the economy picked up steam, so too would prices, but that was nothing to fear. When asked at a press conference on January 27, 2021, whether he considered inflation a risk, Powell gave a remarkable answer. "Frankly, we welcome slightly higher inflation. . . . The kind of troubling inflation that people like me grew up with seems, seems far away and unlikely in both domestic and global context that we've been in for some time."[9] Of course, investors might sell bonds, as they adjusted their portfolios for more rapid growth over the coming years. The debt issuance of the Treasury was imposing, especially as it would need to tap the longer end of the market, which it had largely avoided in 2020. But as everyone was only too well aware, the Fed could if necessary ramp up its own asset purchases. There might be a tug-of-war, but the implication of the Fed's reframed policy targets of August 2020 was that it was now committed to tolerating inflation above 2 percent, at least for a while. It was time for the markets to adjust to that.

The outcome of this tug-of-war would be critical not just for the United States. The balance of the world economy depends on the quadrilateral that links the U.S. labor market, the U.S. bond market, fiscal policy, and Fed interventions. If the American economy ran hot and U.S. interest rates went up sharply, that would apply the squeeze that foreign borrowers of dollars had long dreaded. It would be a true test of the new toolkit for managing the risks of global financialization.

In the emerging markets, memories were still fresh of the taper tantrum of 2013, when Bernanke's announcement that the Fed might be ending its easing had triggered a sustained period of pressure. Though Bernanke had pulled back, for many emerging markets the taper tantrum marked the end of the good years. At the time, Jay Powell had been in his first year as a member of the Fed board and Janet Yellen had been Bernanke's vice-chair. The question of how safely to raise rates dominated both their periods of office. In September 2015 it was Yellen's turn to pull back from tightening when China seemed to be on the brink of crisis. She would be accompanied for years afterward by the rumor that the Fed and the PBoC had struck a secret "Shanghai Accord."[10] When the Fed did finally raise rates in December 2015, the economy was slowing faster than expected and Yellen earned fierce criticism from Bernie Sanders. After 2017, Jerome Powell attempted to continue interest rate "normalization" but soon found himself on the brink of all-out war with Trump's White House. In 2019, rather than raising rates, the Fed cut them three times. The year 2020 ended talk of normalization for the foreseeable future. As managers of the global dollar system, America's central bankers were walking a tightrope, and as it turned out, this tightrope had no end.

The Fed's predicament concentrated in distilled form the situation facing governments more generally in the wake of 2020. None of the forces that had come together to make 2020 a moment of global crisis had exhausted themselves. Far from it.

Environmental historians speak of the "great acceleration" that has been driving the radical transformation in humanity's relationship with our natural habitat.[11] They date the moment of takeoff to 1945, with a further acceleration in the 1970s. Despite the signs of a return to something like normality in 2021, the great acceleration is the right historical frame within which to situate the 2020 moment: an exceptional and transient crisis, no doubt, but also a way station on an ascending curve of radical change.[12]

Borrowing from environmental history seems all the more apt, because it was a biological shock that dominated the events of 2020. Though it had long been foreshadowed, the coronavirus cruelly exposed the deep incapacity of most modern societies to cope with the kinds of challenges that the era of the Anthropocene will throw up with ever-greater force. As the fumbling efforts to contain the second wave of the virus demonstrated, this was every bit as true of Europe as it was of the United States and Latin America. In the spring of 2021, the epidemic was accelerating alarmingly in Brazil and India. The huge caseload in both countries raised fears of dangerous new mutations that would put stabilization being achieved elsewhere at risk.

Given the limitation of our social, cultural, and political coping capacities, we depend ultimately on technoscientific fixes. Generating those depends on our willingness and ability actually to mobilize the scientific and technical resources at our disposal. What is striking about the experience of 2020 in this regard is not just the success in developing the vaccine, but the disproportion between the scale of the crisis and the scale of the means used to resolve it. Tens of trillions in damage. Tens of billions on the vaccines. Even less to ensure their efficient deployment and fair distribution.

The future challenge laid down by 2020 seems clear. Either we find ways to turn the billions invested in research and development and futuristic technologies into trillions, either we take seriously the need to build more sustainable and resilient economies and societies and equip ourselves with the standing capacities necessary to meet fast-moving and unpredictable crises, or we will be overwhelmed by the blowback from our natural environment. These are the kinds of demands easily dismissed as unrealistic. But after the shock of 2020, how much more evidence do we need? What needs adjusting is our common understanding of the reality that we are actually in. It was those who have for decades warned of systemic megarisks who have been crushingly vindicated. Like it or not, we are in what Ulrich Beck already in the 1980s dubbed "second modernity," a world comprehensively convulsed and transformed by our own activities.[13] To meet the environmental challenges ahead, we have to take the innovative potential of science and technology revealed by the first centuries of modernization and actually unlock and fully mobilize it at a global level. Otherwise, there is every reason to think that 2020 will be only the first of an increasingly unmanageable series of global disasters. Either way, for better and for worse there is no escaping the fact that "big things" are going to happen. The continuation of the status quo is the one option we do not have.

The significance of central banking as a domain of modern government is that it is one arena in which the authorities have been forced to grasp the scale of the challenges facing us. The level of policy response in 2020 puts even that of 2008 in the shade. But in other respects, it is also a warning. What drove those massive interventions was the fragile and inegalitarian dynamic of debt-fueled economic growth. What has made central bankers into the exemplar of modern crisis-fighting is the vacuum created by the evisceration of organized labor, the absence of inflationary pressure, and more broadly, the lack of antisystemic challenge. The interventions can be as large as they are because though they have huge material consequences, and though the bond market itself has a real-world presence in the form of traders and computers and legal documents, central bank asset purchases are the equivalent of waving a digital wand. The monetary spell cast in 2020 was as dramatic as it was because the crisis put at risk the most important market of all, the market for safe Treasury assets. What threatened was an avalanche even greater than that triggered by Lehman. It turned out that in the world of market-based finance, no asset is truly safe unless it is provided with the ultimate backstop.

The scale of government interventions was so large in 2020 as to prompt comparisons to models of war finance. Central bank bond buying was the functional twin of fiscal policy. But as tempting as the idea may be, we cannot travel back in time to the days of postwar Keynesianism. And that is certainly not the ambition of twenty-first-century central bankers, who are far from revolutionary. Their practice is that of Bismarckian conservatives in the second half of the nineteenth century: "Everything must change so that everything remains the same."[14] In 2020, at least as far as the financial system is concerned, managerialism once again prevailed, but it was less an exercise in all-powerful technocratic manipulation than a scrambling effort to preserve a dangerous status quo. "Too big to fail" has become a total systemic imperative. The effect is to underwrite successive rounds of escalating debt-fueled speculation and growth. Can it go on? There is no fundamental macroeconomic limit that anyone can discern. The question rather is whether technocratic governance can keep up and whether society and politics can handle it. Can it be democratized? If not, can it at least be legitimated? And can we find ways to absorb or offset the inequalities that this growth model produces? The full force of those questions was first recognized after 2008. After 2020, they still awaited an answer.

Thanks to the prevalence of the dollar as the de facto global currency, the credit expansion is global in scope. The dollars flushed out into the world economy in 2020 enabled a remarkable display of autonomy on the part of the better-placed emerging markets. This confirms one of the tendencies that was already evident in 2008: the emergence of emerging market states as key nodes in the global system of dollar finance. Today the global economy is stabilized at many points. Increasingly, it is decentered from the West. This creates a problem of perspective. What to observers in the West may seem like fundamental roadblocks to further globalization— the increasing difficulty of brokering trade deals, for instance—may have no more than local significance. In the most important growth nodes, trade and investment are continuing apace. If this rebalancing was not already apparent before 2020, the huge East-West gradient in dealing with the coronavirus crisis drove it home. Largely as a result of the recovery in Asia, world trade in 2020 contracted far less than the WTO had predicted in its earlier apocalyptic forecasts. For the year as a whole, the volume of merchandise trade in 2020 was down by no more than 5.3 percent. But this new, multipolar world economy is still in one fundamental respect at least attached to the old world. It remains a dollar-based system. A severe tightening in U.S. monetary policy or even a full-fledged taper tantrum would put global resilience to a stern test. So too would a violent escalation of geopolitical tension in one of the major regions of the world economy.

The new era of globalization is generating a centrifugal multipolarity. Major regional powers proliferate, ally and conflict with each other, then thrive or fade. In 2008 the main driver of conflict was the resurgence of Putin's Russia clashing with the NATO powers. In 2020, the most violent of these force fields was in the wider Middle East—the augmentation of the Saudi versus Iran axis by the UAE on the one hand and Qatar and Turkey on the other. Their wars and proxy wars, spiraling out of the wreckage of U.S. and European policy in the region, have brought misery to tens of millions of people in Libya, Syria, Iraq, and Yemen. They sit astride the key fossil fuel reservoirs. In 2020, however, the global consequences of that multicentered regional conflict remained contained. The regional oligarchs felt the pressure of the oil price collapse. Europe and the United States were preoccupied. China is not (yet) heavily engaged. Faced with the very real risk of financial crisis, Erdoğan played cat and mouse with the markets.

By far the most significant shift produced by this combined and uneven process of global economic growth is the ascent of China. Its growth is of an order of magnitude never seen before. As is true with other emerging market economies, China's economic development has taken place within a global monetary field set by the United States, but Beijing's homegrown crisis-fighting capacities are like no one else's. The aggressiveness of its domestic regulatory interventions far exceeds that in either Europe or the U.S. China's size is such that it puts American preeminence in question. This prospect was not lost on U.S. planners already in the 1990s. After he left office, Bill Clinton sagely remarked that it was the key task for American policy to "create a world we would like to live in when we are no longer the world's only superpower."[15] The unipolar moment came and went. Even at the height of its power, the idea that the United States could reshape the world to its liking was always hubristic. In 2020, the world that the United States found itself living in seemed not to be to the liking of American strategists at all. In Trump's final year, unease about China's rise tipped into what amounted to a declaration of economic war. In its early stages, the Biden administration shows every sign of continuing this campaign. In his first press conference as president on March 25, 2021, Biden roundly declared: "China has an overall goal, and I don't criticize them for the goal, but they have an overall goal to become the leading country in the world, the wealthiest country in the world, and the most powerful country in the world. That's not going to happen on my watch because the United States are going to continue to grow and expand."[16]

Biden did not just state his flat refusal to accept the likely consequences of compound economic growth, he backed it up with a vision of domestic policy couched in terms redolent of the era of the Sputnik shock and the space race. Biden's infrastructure program with spending on everything from bridges and roads to green energy and elder care explicitly evoked America's "great projects of the past." Like them, the American Jobs Plan as laid out on March 31, 2021, was designed to "unify and mobilize the country to meet the great challenges of our time: the climate crisis and the ambitions of an autocratic China."[17]

Would the rest of the world follow America back to the future? Facing the Trump administration's escalation of tension with China, in 2019 the EU had set out on a different path. In the March 2019 strategy paper on EU-China relations, the EU had for the first time designated China as a systemic rival, but at the same time it had also recognized China as a conventional economic competitor, a partner to negotiate with and a partner to cooperate with.[18] Sensibly, the EU had refrained from posing the question of primacy, let alone announcing a struggle to sustain Western preeminence in the face of Asia's rise. It was fully in keeping with this multipronged strategy that Brussels and Beijing ended 2020 by announcing on December 30 the EU-China Comprehensive Agreement on Investment (CAI), which aimed to boost foreign direct investment to levels that were more commensurate with the size of the two economic blocs.[19] For Beijing, following the conclusion of RCEP with its Asian neighbors, the CAI was a coup. In Washington, the deal was taken as an affront. The announcement came on the very day that the UK—one of America's keenest new allies in the confrontation with China—finalized its exit from the EU.[20] American advocates of an antitotalitarian line evoked dark fantasies of a neutralized, amoral Europe, drifting between the blocs.[21] Others dismissed the Sino-EU agreement as a last hurrah of an era of China appeasement that, with Angela Merkel, was fading from the scene.[22] Biden's transition team let it be known that they were not best pleased. And in truth the CAI ran against the tide of public opinion in Europe too. For Berlin, Paris, and Brussels, however, what had priority was to work out the terms of a mutually advantageous modus vivendi.[23] Economic integration with China was already far too deep to be reversed, and would likely get even more so. China was pivotal to the new technologies of the green energy transition. Far from marking a moment of decoupling, thanks to the slump in the West and China's continued growth, 2020 was the first year in which China overtook all its rivals to become the world's favorite destination for foreign direct investment.[24]

The logic of the EU's multipronged strategy, however, cut both ways. As clear as the imperative for bargained agreement on the CAI might be, no less obvious was the need for it to be balanced by other considerations. Yes, China was a partner with whom one could negotiate, but it was also a profoundly alien and inimical regime. The most immediate question, it turned out, was not whether the Biden administration could live with the EU's policy of balancing, but whether Beijing could.

The CAI would have to be ratified by the European parliament, and there was well-justified indignation there about the ongoing repression in Xinjiang and China's tightening grip on Hong Kong. When European governments, in a coordinated action with the United States, imposed sanctions on a handful of relatively junior Chinese officials responsible for the repressive regime in Xinjiang, Beijing might have brushed it aside as a triviality of no strategic significance. Instead, China responded by imposing sanctions on some of its leading critics in the European parliament, as well as Germany's Mercator Institute for China Studies and a Danish NGO. The result was to hurl EU-China relations into the deep freeze, to put the CAI on hold, and to push Europe toward the United States. Meanwhile, Western analysts were left to wonder what was driving Beijing's escalation. Was the Chinese leadership reckless and naive, or was it trapped in a nationalist propaganda narrative of its own making? Or was Beijing's reaction indicative of something more sinister? Was Beijing convinced that America and Europe's decline was entering a terminal stage? Following the fiasco of the Western response to Covid, was now the moment for Beijing to press home its advantage and demand acceptance and respect for its ruthlessly effective regime?[25]

In the summer of 2021, the CCP celebrated its hundredth anniversary. It did so in style. On November 24, 2020, the last remaining counties had been removed from China's list of poor regions.[26] On December 4, Xi announced that the party had accomplished its goal of ending "absolute and regional" poverty in China.[27] In an eight-year campaign involving the mobilization of 2.9 million party cadres and an investment of RMB 1.5 trillion, 99 million severely poor rural Chinese had been lifted above the basic poverty line.[28] Western critics pointed out that China's poverty standard set the bar too low.[29] The focus on getting the basics to the countryside distracted from the intractable problem of integrating the vast army of urban migrant workers into a modern social safety net.[30] Beijing didn't let that muddy its message. In a year in which according to the World Bank, around 100 million people worldwide were hurled back into abject poverty, no other state could boast of any similar achievement.

As Xi put it to a full meeting of the Politburo Standing Committee in January 2021, "time and momentum" were on China's side.[31] Any idea of convergence with liberal norms once touted by Western modernization theory was clearly obsolete. Advocates of the middle-income trap—a negative version of modernization theory that highlights the great difficulties facing middle-income countries in making the leap to advanced economy status— might cling to their doxa.[32] But as the Chinese like to point out, if social science is a matter of data, China's modernization, through its sheer scale, generates more data points than any previous episode of economic growth. It is the greatest social experiment of all time. That is the materialist foundation of what Beijing calls twenty-first-century Marxism.[33] The point is not that modernization theory is wrong, but only when it incorporates China's transformation will it actually come into its own. This does not mean that managing China development is without risk. What 2020 demonstrated were the stresses generated by China's astonishing growth, the flaws in the Chinese apparatus of power, and its resilience, potency, and ambition.[34] Beijing too is walking a tightrope without an end.[35]

In any case, it was not in China that 2020 brought a moment of profound national crisis. It was in the United States. It is tempting to say, in fact, that it is really in the United States that simple liberal visions of modernization have most conclusively come to grief. In a world of unevenness, it is in the U.S. that the disharmony between politics and economic and social development is at its most extreme and consequential.[36]

Twenty-first-century America is a country in which political power is shared between two parties, one of which, the Republican Party, has been for decades committed to blocking the construction of a state apparatus befitting of an advanced society and dismantling it where it does exist. Furthermore, as 2008 demonstrated and 2020 confirmed, in moments of national crisis, the GOP is no longer a party with a vision of government either in the long or even the short term. It has revealed itself as a vehicle for the undisciplined pursuit of particular interests and the expression of affect rather than considered national policy.

There are, of course, massive, modernizing forces at work in the United States. For better and for worse, they are aligned increasingly unambiguously with the Democratic Party. As they have demonstrated in successive presidential elections, the Democrats are majoritarian, but thanks to America's eighteenth-century Constitution and the GOP's rearguard action in gerrymandering and voter suppression, the grip on power of this modernizing coalition is frustratingly weak. The Biden administration's spending programs in its first hundred days suggests an effort to overcome this impasse. They suggest the outline of a plan to consolidate a national coalition around modest overall social rebalancing, targeted interventions to address the urgent demand for racial justice, green modernization, and systemic competition with China. This is not the Green New Deal or the social democratic vision offered by Bernie Sanders. Dropping the minimum wage from the American Rescue Plan was significant. As for Biden's infrastructure and Families Plan, their rhetoric is radical. The headline spending figures are impressive. But unlike CARES in 2020 or the Rescue Plan of March 2020, which disbursed trillions in a matter of months, these are long-term programs stretching out over a horizon of eight to ten years.

Aspirationally, before haggling with Congress began, they amounted to roughly 2 percent of American GDP per annum. Spread across priorities ranging from childcare to the energy transition, that was far too little to effect a transformation of American society or to put the United States on course to climate stabilization. Especially with regard to the energy transition, they appeared to rest on optimistic assumptions about the private investment that would be triggered by modest public stimulus combined with regulatory change. When it came to long-term policy, Bidenomics was a continuation of the public-private, blended finance, Frankenstein policies that had been so typical of the crisis-fighting in 2020.

Why were the spending programs not larger? Congressional support was the rate-limiting factor. In the hope of winning support from Democratic Party centrists, the infrastructure plan and Families Plan were linked to "pay fors." To please the left wing of the party, those were focused on corporate taxes and capital gains earned by the wealthiest. This met the dual agendas of fiscal stabilization and social justice, but the overall effect was to stunt the program. The absolute priority was to sustain political momentum. The nightmare of the Biden administration is a repeat of the devastating midterm setbacks suffered by Obama in 2010 and Clinton in 1994. Even without a majority, the Republicans can be counted on to deploy all the checks and balances of America's Constitution to their full effect. As is increasingly apparent, their political future depends on resisting the logic of majority rule by all means necessary. Given their inability to formulate a political vision that could encompass a majority of the American electorate, their best bet is to consolidate the kind of rigged constitutional settlement more commonly associated with the nineteenth century.

But the inherited political structures of the American Constitution also produce another effect. Government in the United States is built on division, and when under pressure, it can continue to function in a divided way. This is what we saw in 2020: the United States functioning as a disarticulated state. The circus of Trump's politics and McConnell's struggle to keep his grip on the Senate were patched together with fiscal compromises. They were backed up by the Fed's buying of America's own debt on a huge scale. In 2020, as in 2008, the Treasury and Fed collaborated with the

Democrats in Congress to keep the show on the road, bypassing large parts of the congressional GOP and even, at times, the White House. Meanwhile, erratic foreign policy statements issued from the Trump entourage, while the U.S. military did its best to ignore the commander in chief.[37]

The Biden presidency's first order of business is to attempt to restore coherence. That is a tall order, and, given the lack of guardrails, the precarious balance of party politics, and the uncertain future of the GOP, it is a gamble. With Trump as president, pluralism and incoherence were a saving grace. In light of the experience of 2020, it is not obvious whether America and the world have more to fear from a unified American government subject to risk of capture by the nationalist right, or a more incoherent American regime in which key levers of power remain the purview of functional elites, globalized interests, and modernizing coalitions in key centers like New York and Silicon Valley. The polite way of framing this, for instance when conversation turns to the latest impasse in American climate policy, is to argue that a progressive future for the United States depends on the dynamism of "subnational actors."[38] For all the enthusiasm surrounding the early months of the Biden administration, the haunting question remains: Is the United States as a nation-state capable of responding in a coherent and long-term fashion to the challenges of the great acceleration?

Any of these vectors of global change—environmental, economic, political, geopolitical—by themselves would suggest that far from being a culmination, 2020 is merely a moment in a process of escalation. Taken together, they form a dynamic parallelogram that makes de-escalation hard if not impossible to imagine. The great acceleration continues.

In an earlier period of history this sort of diagnosis might have been coupled with the forecast of revolution. If anything is unrealistic today, that prediction surely is. Indeed, radical reform is a stretch. The year 2020 was not a moment of victory for the left. The chief countervailing force to the escalation of global tension in political, economic, and ecological realms is therefore crisis management on an ever-larger scale, crisis-driven and ad hoc. This may lack the grandeur or ambition of transformative politics, but it is not without historical consciousness or consequence. It is the choice between the third- and the fourth-best options, and as such, it really matters.

The place where this new era of ad hockery has been spelled out most clearly and with least inhibition is with regard to the toolkit of economic policy developed by the emerging markets. And no lesser authority than the IMF has put its seal on this development by publishing in 2020 what it called an "Integrated Policy Framework." Abandoning any doctrinaire commitment to freedom of capital movement or freely floating exchange rates, the IMF outlined a tactical view of policy that acknowledged the need for pragmatic intervention. The challenge is to map and rationalize a path between "one size fits all" and "anything goes."[39]

The condition of the freedom of maneuver enjoyed by the emerging markets in 2020 was the gigantic deluge of money unleashed by the advanced economies. That too was the result of learning. The memory of the 1930s overshadowed the crisis response of the U.S. authorities in 2008. The memory of the Obama administration shadowed the incoming Biden administration in 2021. Even more spectacular was the effect of learning in the EU. Europe's failure in the years after 2010 was of historic dimensions. The year 2020 could have been the same. It was not. In a conscious determination to avoid a disastrous repetition, Europe's political class defined the 2020 crisis as new. The least that you can say for them is that they found new ways to fail. They took on the task of a common vaccine policy and turned its launch into a legitimation crisis. They constructed a new fiscal capacity that was undersized for the job. Another intervention by the German constitutional court, this time on the legality of the joint financing of the NextGen EU fund, served notice that the legal foundation of Europe's federal institutions remained unsteady. Meanwhile, not only was the United States rolling out an effective vaccination program, but Biden's Rescue Plan promised to catapult America's economic growth far into the lead. Europe faced the prospect of having to relaunch its relaunch.

It is a Sisyphean labor. And, if the evidence of recent decades is anything to go by, the latest round of crisis-management is a formula for yet more to come.

Crisis-fighting is both relentless and hectic. It is driven by the urgency of the immediate situation. It is caught in a tangled web of interests and must make up its instruments as it goes along. It is also, however, guided by reflection on past crisis-fighting. Whether in the form of books, articles, or "folk narratives," contemporary history is part of that process of collective learning. History-writing is part and parcel of history-making.

The historical account laid out in this book is critical in intent. But it would be foolish to deny that it is entangled with and indeed complicit with its subject matter—the efforts of elites around the world to master the crisis. This is a matter of personal politics, biography, institutional attachment, and social identity. The force of those factors should not be denied by any self-aware writer. In a pandemic, this entanglement takes on a more material quality. How each of us came through the crisis was defined in large part by the events and decisions described in this book. I and my immediate family were all early beneficiaries of President Trump's Operation Warp Speed and the efforts of American officials at every level to roll out mass immunization. *De te fabula narratur*—the tale is told of you. For us, the lucky ones, the fear of the pandemic lifted early in 2021.

But beyond such material conditions, which define the writing and reception of any book, a historical narrative of this type is entangled at a deeper intellectual level with the exercise of power. This is because, in modernity, power and knowledge are constituted together. None of the shocks of 2020—the pandemic itself, the turmoil in the repo market that threatened the global hegemony of U.S. Treasuries, the crises of the EU, or the limitations of the G20's DSSI, or the possibilities of Sino-EU climate diplomacy—would be comprehensible without recourse to technical expertise generated from within the apparatus of power and money. This inside knowledge cannot simply be taken at face value. It does not suffice. But it is indispensable. A critical history of modern power must find a way into the thickets of analysis, information, and knowledge produced day by day from inside the apparatus as its protagonists struggle to cope with the radical outcomes that their systems are producing.[40]

The frontier of this technical knowledge is not just dauntingly complex and opaque but constantly evolving. To keep up with it, we have to run to stand still. Like it or not, we are in medias res.[41] We can, to a degree, choose how we relate to this condition. There are many different frames with which we may situate our immediate experience and our immersion in the technical fields of power. We may stay close to the daily action and its protagonists, we may construct for ourselves a detached and superior watchtower, we may pose as cartographers mapping history's grand contours, we may imagine an Archimedean lever and a historical agent to move it, but all of these intellectual self-positionings should be seen for the stylized gestures that they are—all of them are conditioned by our situation in the here and now, by our history in the "before times," by our expectation of the future to come. All this applies to this book, and the concepts and narrative framings that it employs, when, for instance, it evokes the idea of the great acceleration or the epoch of neoliberalism. Each such move implies a history and a politics that must to a degree be presupposed—we have to start somewhere—but must, by the same token, be open to criticism and debate. If 2020 taught us anything, it is how ready we must be to revise our world view. The Green New Deal was brilliantly on point, but it imagined climate as the most urgent threat of the Anthropocene. It too was overrun by the pandemic. Such revisions do not imply a lack of intellectual or political principle. They are simply the openness commensurate with the times we live in.

So this is the project of *Shutdown*, as it was of my earlier books: to wrestle with power and knowledge in time. Uncovering arcane expertise, situating and interpreting it, unpicking concepts and rearranging the narratives that power incessantly spins about itself, recognizing and turning to critical purposes the innovations that power-knowledge produces.

This book like the others is cast as "grand narrative." I hope thereby to do justice to the momentousness and complexity of the shocks and transformations we are living through and to the importance of the stakes involved. For all that, each historical picture, each arrangement of the pieces, is provisional, heuristic, experimental. If we are not beyond the end of history, that is what writing history involves. Not definitive pronouncement, but writing to be overwritten.

———

I graduated from college in 1989. You could feel the Iron Curtain shaking. It was the summer of Fukuyama and of Tiananmen. My first historical research—on German economists and statisticians amid the violent turmoil of the Weimar Republic and the Third Reich—was done in the archive of the recently deceased GDR, housed in a run-down barracks in Potsdam half-occupied by the Red Army. I faced that archive, like generations of apprentice historians before me, with pencil, pen, and filing cards. Thirty years later, in Manhattan, grounded by lockdown and curfew but free to roam the world on the laptop that never leaves my side, I stumbled on the analysis of the "six effects" by one of Xi Jinping's closest advisors. This book begins by referencing Chen Yixin's pronouncements not simply for the sake of their inherent interest, but to make a larger point. The fact that Chen's map of convergent crises was so apt, that it was more illuminating than the EU's talk of polycrisis or America's solipsistic preoccupation with its national narrative, should give us pause. The intellectuals of the Chinese regime are loyal to their party's political project. They are at work on their own version of history. In that history, whether we like it or not, we are all enrolled. And in that respect too, as the Covid crisis brought home, we are just at the beginning.

If our first reaction to 2020 was disbelief, our watchword in facing the future should be: "We ain't seen nothing yet."

Notes

INTRODUCTION

1. IMF, *World Economic Outlook Update*, June 2020; www.imf.org/en/Publications/WEO/Issues/2020/06/24/WEOUpdateJune2020.
2. O. D. Westad, "The Sources of Chinese Conduct: Are Washington and Beijing Fighting a New Cold War?" *Foreign Affairs* 98, no.5 (2019): 86.
3. IMF, *World Economic Outlook*, January 2020; www.imf.org/en/Publications/WEO/Issues/2020/01/20/weo-update-january2020.
4. J. Londono, S. Ma, and B. A. Wilson, "Quantifying the Impact of Foreign Economic Uncertainty on the U.S. Economy," FED Notes, *Board of Governors of the Federal Reserve System*, October 8, 2019.
5. P. Commins, "Uncertainty Remains as Long as Trump Tweets," *Financial Review*, October 14, 2019.
6. "Veranstaltungsbericht 'Westlessness'—Die Münchner Sicherheitskonferenz 2020," https://securityconference.org/news/meldung/westlessness-die-muenchner-sicherheitskonferenz-2020.
7. A. Fotiadis, "Greece's Refugee Plan Is Inhumane and Doomed to Fail. The EU Must Step In," *Guardian*, February 16, 2020.
8. Strategy, Policy, & Review Department, World Bank, "The Evolution of Public Debt Vulnerabilities in Lower Income Economies," International Monetary Fund, February 10, 2020.
9. A. Tooze, "The Fierce Urgency of COP26," *Social Europe*, January 20, 2020.
10. B. Milanovic, *Capitalism, Alone: The Future of the System That Rules the World* (Harvard University Press, 2019).
11. M. Kelly, "The 1992 Campaign: The Democrats—Clinton and Bush Compete to Be Champion of Change; Democrat Fights Perception of Bush Gain," *New York Times*, October 31, 1992.
12. T. Blair, "Tony Blair's Conference Speech 2005," *Guardian*, September 27, 2005.
13. A. Tooze, *Crashed: How a Decade of Financial Crises Changed the World* (Viking, 2018).
14. See, for instance, Janet Yellen in February 2020: S. Lane, "Yellen Pins Rise of Populism, Trade Skepticism on Economic Inequality," *The Hill*, February 4, 2020.
15. B. Latour, *Down to Earth: Politics in the New Climatic Regime* (Polity, 2018).
16. M. Wucker, *The Gray Rhino: How to Recognize and Act on Obvious Dangers We Ignore* (St. Martin's Press, 2016).
17. "The Hunt for the Origins of SARS-COV-2 Will Look Beyond China," *Economist*, July 25, 2020.
18. D. H. Autor, D. Dorn, and G. H. Hanson, "The China Shock: Learning from Labor-Market Adjustment to Large Changes in Trade," *Annual Review of Economics* 8, no. 1 (2016): 205–40.

19. ILO, "COVID-19 and the World of Work," Fifth Edition, *International Labour Organization*, June 30, 2020.
20. V. Strauss, "1.5 Billion Children Around Globe Affected by School Closure. What Countries Are Doing to Keep Kids Learning During the Pandemic," *Washington Post*, March 27, 2020.
21. "COVID-19 Could Lead to Permanent Loss in Learning and Trillions of Dollars in Lost Earnings," *World Bank*, June 18, 2020.
22. H. Else, "How a Torrent of COVID Science Changed Research Publishing—in Seven Charts," *Nature*, December 16, 2020; www.nature.com/articles/d41586-020-03564-y.
23. For a brilliant example of the genre, see G. Packer, "We Are Living in a Failed State," *Atlantic*, June 2020.
24. J. Konyndyk, "Exceptionalism Is Killing Americans: An Insular Political Culture Failed the Test of the Pandemic," *Foreign Affairs*, June 8, 2020.
25. E. Morin, *Homeland Earth: A Manifesto for the New Millennium (Advances in Systems Theory, Complexity and the Human Sciences)*, trans. A. B. Kern (Hampton Press, 1999).
26. J.-C. Juncker, "Speech at the Annual General Meeting of the Hellenic Federation of Enterprises," June 21, 2016; ec.europa.eu/commission/presscorner/detail/en/SPEECH_16_2293.
27. For a classic analysis that brilliantly unpicks an earlier moment of crisis, see S. Hall, C. Critcher, T. Jefferson, J. Clarke, and B. Roberts, *Policing the Crisis: Mugging, the State and Law and Order* (Red Globe Press, 2013).
28. W. Wo-Lap Lam, "Xi Jinping Warns Against the 'Black Swans' and 'Gray Rhinos' of a Possible Color Revolution," *Jamestown Foundation*, February 20, 2019.
29. M. Hart and J. Link, "Chinese President Xi Jinping's Philosophy on Risk Management," *Center for American Progress*, February 20, 2020.
30. J. Cai, "Beijing Pins Hopes on 'Guy with the Emperor's Sword' to Restore Order in Coronavirus-Hit Hubei," *South China Morning Post*, February 12, 2020.
31. Hart and Link, "Chinese President Xi Jinping's Philosophy on Risk Management."
32. For a remarkable map, see https://www.creosotemaps.com/blm2020.
33. M. Wolf, "What the World Can Learn from the COVID-19 Pandemic," *Financial Times*, November 24, 2020.
34. M. Stott and G. Long, "'This Is a Real World War': Ecuador's President on the Virus," *Financial Times*, June 15, 2020.
35. "The Vocabularist: Where Did the Word 'Crisis' Come From?" *BBC*, September 15, 2020. R. Koselleck; trans. M. W. Richter, "Crisis," *Journal of the History of Ideas* 67, no. 2 (2006): 357–400; *JSTOR*, www.jstor.org/stable/30141882.
36. G. George, "Covid-19 and the Tussle Between Coercion and Compliance," *Daily Maverick*, May 4, 2020.
37. B. G. Rivas, "The OAS Must Condemn Repressive Measures Taken to Combat the Pandemic," *Amnesty*, September 7, 2020.
38. U. Beck, *Risk Society: Towards a New Modernity* (SAGE Publications, 1992).
39. On the agnotocene, see "agnotology," C. Bonneuil and J.-B. Fernbach, *The Shock of the Anthropocene: The Earth, History and Us* (Verso, 2016).
40. A. Tooze, "The Sociologist Who Could Save Us from Coronavirus," *Foreign Policy*, August 1, 2020.
41. L. Lenel, "Geschichte ohne Libretto," *H-Soz-Kult*, May 12, 2020. L. Lenel, "Public and Scientific Uncertainty in the Time of COVID-19," *History of Knowledge*, May 13, 2020.
42. A. Roberts, *The Logic of Discipline: Global Capitalism and the Architecture of Government* (Oxford University Press, 2011).
43. Paradigmatically G. R. Krippner, *Capitalizing on Crisis: The Political Origins of the Rise of Finance* (Harvard University Press, 2011).
44. A. Kapczynski and G. Gonsalves, "Alone Against the Virus," *Boston Review*, March 13, 2020.
45. FT Series, The New Social Contract, www.ft.com/content/774f3aef-aded-47f9-8abb-a523191f1c19.
46. A. Pettifor, *The Case for the Green New Deal* (Verso, 2020); K. Aronoff, A. Battistoni, D. A. Cohen, and T. Riofrancos, *A Planet to Win: Why We Need a Green New Deal* (Verso, 2019).
47. Popularized in 2020 by S. Kelton, *The Deficit Myth: Modern Monetary Theory and the Birth of the People's Economy* (PublicAffairs, 2020).
48. J. M. Keynes, 1942 BBC Address *(Collected Works XXVII)*.
49. BIS Annual Economic Report 30 June 2019; www.bis.org/publ/arpdf/ar2019e2.htm.
50. S. Hannan, K. Honjo, and M. Raissi, "Mexico Needs a Fiscal Twist: Response to Covid-19 and Beyond," IMF Working Papers, October 13, 2020.

51. A. Doherty, "Has the Coronavirus Crisis Killed Neoliberalism? Don't Bet on It," *Guardian*, May 16, 2020. C. Crouch, *The Strange Non-Death of Neoliberalism* (Polity, 2011). P. Mason, "Day One of UK's Suppression Strategy," *The Waves*, March 17, 2020.

52. D. Harvey, *A Brief History of Neoliberalism* (Oxford University Press, 2007).

53. As tracked in exemplary fashion by D. Gabor, "Three Myths About EU's Economic Response to the COVID-19 Pandemic," *Critical Macro Finance*, June 15, 2020.

54. D. Gabor, "The Wall Street Consensus," *SocArXiv*, 2 July 2020.

55. D. Gabor, "Revolution Without Revolutionaries: Interrogating the Return of Monetary Financing," *Transformative Responses to the Crisis*, 2020; https://transformative-responses.org/wp-content/uploads/2021/01/TR_Report_Gabor_FINAL.pdf.

56. Following a logic brilliantly sketched out by D. Gabor, "Critical Macro-Finance: A Theoretical Lens," *Finance and Society* 6, no. 1 (2020): 45–55.

57. I am indebted to conversations with Barnaby Raine for bringing home this point.

58. Rudi Dornbusch Essays 1998/2001, web.mit.edu/15.018/attach/Dornbusch,%20R.%20Essays%201998-2001.pdf.

59. R. Picket, "U.S. Household Net Worth Surged in Closing Months of 2020," *Bloomberg*, March 11, 2021.

60. J. Henley, "European Elections: Triumphant Greens Demand More Radical Climate Action," *Guardian*, May 21, 2019.

61. Associated Press, "Japan Adopts Green Growth Plan to Go Carbon Free by 2050," *Politico*, December 25, 2020. For the Biden campaign, see: joebiden.com/build-back-better/. ec.europa.eu/info/strategy/priorities-2019-2024/european-green-deal_en.

62. Y. Yang and C. Shepherd, "WHO Investigators Probe Wuhan Virology Lab," *Financial Times*, February 3, 2021.

63. G. G. Chang, "China Deliberately Spread the Coronavirus: What Are the Strategic Consequences?" *Hoover Institution*, December 9, 2020.

64. By J. C. Hernández and J. Gorman, "On W.H.O. Trip, China Refused to Hand Over Important Data," *New York Times*, February 12, 2021.

65. "Fact Sheet: Advancing the Rebalance to Asia and the Pacific," the White House, Office of the Press Secretary, November 16, 2015; obamawhitehouse.archives.gov/the-press-office/2015/11/16/fact-sheet-advancing-rebalance-asia-and-pacific. Remarks by B. Obama, "Remarks by President Obama to the Australian Parliament," the White House, Office of the Press Secretary, November 17, 2011.

66. National Security Strategy of the United States of America, December 17, 2020; trumpwhitehouse.archives.gov/wp-content/uploads/2017/12/NSS-Final-12-18-2017-0905.pdf.

67. "EU-China—A Strategic Outlook," European Commission, March 12, 2019, ec.europa.eu/info/sites/info/files/communication-eu-china-a-strategic-outlook.pdf.

68. France: www.diplomatie.gouv.fr/en/country-files/asia-and-oceania/the-indo-pacific-region-a-priority-for-france/ Germany: www.auswaertiges-amt.de/blob/2380514/f9784f7e3b3fa1bd7c5446d274a4169e/200901-indo-pazifik-leitlinien—1—data.pdf. For a comparison see: M. Duchâtel and G. Mohan, "Franco-German Divergences in the Indo-Pacific: The Risk of Strategic Dilution," *Institut Montaigne*, October 30, 2020.

69. On the pivot of the City of London toward China: J. Green, "The City's Pivot to China in a Post-Brexit World: A Uniquely Vulnerable Policy," London School of Economics, June 15, 2018. On the pivot of UK defense planning against China in 2020, see H. Warrell, "Britain's Armed Forces Pivot East to Face Growing China Threat," *Financial Times*, July 3, 2020.

70. G. Yu, "Beijing Observation: Xi Jinping the Man," *China Change*, January 26, 2013; T. Greer, "Xi Jinping in Translation: China's Guiding Ideology," *Palladium*, May 31, 2019.

71. USTR, "Investigation: Technology Transfer, Intellectual Property, and Innovation"; ustr.gov/issue-areas/enforcement/section-301-investigations/section-301-china/investigation.

72. K. Mattson, *"What the Heck Are You Up To, Mr. President?": Jimmy Carter, America's "Malaise," and the Speech That Should Have Changed the Country* (Bloomsbury USA, 2010).

73. D. Kurtzleben, "Rep. Alexandria Ocasio-Cortez Releases Green New Deal Outline," *All Things Considered*, NPR, February 7, 2019.

74. R. O. Paxton, "I've Hesitated to Call Donald Trump a Fascist, Until Now," *Newsweek*, January 11, 2021.

75. J. A. Russell, "America's Forever Wars Have Finally Come Home," *Responsible Statecraft*, June 4, 2020.

76. J. Iadarola, "What if Bernie Has Already Won This Thing?" *The Hill*, February 23, 2020. S. Hamid, "The Coronavirus Killed the Revolution," *Atlantic*, March 25, 2020.

77. G. Ip, "Businesses Fret Over Potential Bernie Sanders Presidency," *Wall Street Journal*, March 1, 2020. B. Schwartz, "Mike Bloomberg Prepares Media Onslaught Against Democratic Front-Runner Bernie Sanders," *CNBC*, February 24, 2020.
78. A. Tooze, "'We Are Living Through the First Economic Crisis of the Anthropocene,'" *Guardian*, May 7, 2020.
79. The best compact introduction is C. Bonneuil and J.-B. Fressoz, trans. D. Fernbach, *The Shock of the Anthropocene: The Earth, History and Us* (Verso, 2016).
80. B. Croce, *History: Its Theory and Practice* (Russell & Russell, 1960).

CHAPTER 1. ORGANIZED IRRESPONSIBILITY

1. Institute for Health Metrics and Evaluation, *Financing Global Health 2019: Tracking Health Spending in a Time of Crisis* (IHME, 2020); www.healthdata.org/sites/default/files/files/policy_report/FGH/2020/FGH_2019_Interior_Final_Online_2020.09.18.pdf.
2. "Soziale Unterschiede in Deutschland: Mortalität und Lebenserwartung," Robert Koch Institute; www.rki.de/DE/Content/Service/Presse/Pressemitteilungen/2019/03_2019.html.
3. A. Lövenich, "Lebenserwartung PKV-GKV versichert," August 6, 2018; www.hcconsultingag.de/lebenserwartung-pkv-gkv-versichert.
4. A. Wilper et al., "Health Insurance and Mortality in US Adults," *American Journal of Public Health* 99, no. 12 (2009): 2289–95.
5. J. L. Hadler, K. Yousey-Hindes, A. Pérez et al., "Influenza-Related Hospitalizations and Poverty Levels—United States, 2010–2012," *Morbidity and Mortality Weekly Report* 65, no. 5 (2016): 101–105.
6. "Relative Share of Deaths in the United States, 1999 to 2016," Our World in Data; ourworldindata.org/grapher/relative-share-of-deaths-in-usa.
7. R. W. Fogel, *The Escape from Hunger and Premature Death, 1700–2100: Europe, America, and the Third World* (Cambridge University Press, 2004).
8. W. D. Nordhaus, "The Health of Nations: The Contribution of Improved Health to Living Standards," February 2020; cowles.yale.edu/sites/default/files/files/pub/d13/d1355.pdf.
9. A. R. Omran, "The Epidemiologic Transition. A Theory of the Epidemiology of Population Change," *Milbank Memorial Fund Quarterly* 49 (1971): 509–38; www.ncbi.nlm.nih.gov/pmc/articles/PMC2690264/.
10. M. A. Brazelton, *Mass Vaccination: Citizens' Bodies and State Power in Modern China* (Cornell University Press, 2019).
11. M. Davis, *The Monster at Our Door: The Global Threat of Avian Flu* (Macmillan, 2006).
12. J. Iliffe, *The African AIDS Epidemic: A History* (Ohio University Press, 2005).
13. UNAIDS, "Global HIV & AIDS Statistics—2020 Fact Sheet," www.unaids.org/en/resources/fact-sheet.
14. S. S. Morse, "Regulating Viral Traffic," *Issues in Science and Technology* 7, no. 1 (Fall 1990): 81–84.
15. W. Anderson, "Natural Histories of Infectious Disease: Ecological Vision in Twentieth-Century Biomedical Science," *Osiris* 19 (2004): 39–61. N. B. King, "Security, Disease, Commerce: Ideologies of Postcolonial Global Health," *Social Studies of Science* 32, no. 5–6 (2002): 763–789. C. E. Rosenberg, "Pathologies of Progress: The Idea of Civilization as Risk," *Bulletin of the History of Medicine* 72, no. 4 (Winter 1998), 714–30.
16. J. R. Rohr, C. B. Barrett, D. J. Civitello, et al., "Emerging Human Infectious Diseases and the Links to Global Food Production," *Nature Sustainability* 2 (2019): 445–56.
17. Davis, *The Monster at Our Door*.
18. WHO, Programme Budget 2020–21; www.who.int/publications/i/item/programme-budget-2020-2021. S. K. Reddy, S. Mazhar, and R. Lencucha, "The Financial Sustainability of the World Health Organization and the Political Economy of Global Health Governance: A Review of Funding Proposals," *Globalization and Health* 14, no. 1 (2018): 1–11.
19. M. Liverani and R. Coker, "Protecting Europe from Diseases: From the International Sanitary Conferences to the ECDC," *Journal of Health Politics, Policy and Law* 37, no. 6 (2012): 915–34.
20. S. Gebrekidan, K. Bennhold, M. Apuzzo, and D. D. Kirkpatrick, "Ski, Party, Seed a Pandemic: The Travel Rules That Let Covid-19 Take Flight," *New York Times*, September 30, 2020.
21. T. Neale, "World Health Organization Scientists Linked to Swine Flu Vaccine Makers," *ABC News*, June 4, 2020.
22. J. Farrar, "All Is Not Well at the World Health Organization," *Wall Street Journal*, January 22, 2015.

23. A. Benjamin, "Stern: Climate Change a 'Market Failure,'" *Guardian*, November 29, 2007.
24. A. Toscano, "Beyond the Plague State," *Socialist Project*, May 14, 2020.
25. A. Lakoff, *Unprepared: Global Health in a Time of Emergency* (University of California Press, 2017).
26. "Pandemic Influences Preparedness in WHO Member States," *World Health Organization*, June 2019.
27. U. Beck, *Gegengifte: Die Organisierte Unverantwortlichkeit* (Edition Suhrkamp, 1988).
28. A. Desanctis, "How Much Is a Human Life Worth?" *National Review*, May 7, 2020.
29. A. Mische, "Projects and Possibilities: Researching Futures in Action," *Sociological Forum* 24 (2009): 694–704.
30. B. Adam and C. Groves, *Future Matters: Action, Knowledge, Ethics* (Brill, 2007).
31. D. A. Harvey, "Fortune-Tellers in the French Courts: Antidivination Prosecutions in France in the Nineteenth and Twentieth Centuries," *French Historical Studies* 28, no. 1 (2005): 131–57. C. Corcos, "Seeing It Coming Since 1945: State Bans and Regulations of Crafty Sciences Speech and Activity," *Louisiana State University Law Center*, 2014; digitalcommons.law.lsu.edu/cgi/viewcontent.cgi?article =1407&context=faculty_scholarship.
32. D. Adam, "Special Report: The Simulations Driving the World's Response to COVID-19," *Nature*, April 2, 2020; www.nature.com/articles/d41586-020-01003-6.
33. D. Cutler and L. Summers, "The COVID-19 Pandemic and the $16 Trillion Virus," *JAMA* 324, no. 15 (2020): 1495–96.
34. W. K. Viscusi and C. J. Masterman, "Income Elasticities and Global Values of a Statistical Life," *Journal of Benefit-Cost Analysis* 8, no. 2 (2017): 226–50; law.vanderbilt.edu/phd/faculty/w-kip-viscusi /355_Income_Elasticities_and_Global_VSL.pdf.
35. L. A. Robinson, "COVID-19 and Uncertainties in the Value Per Statistical Life," *The Regulatory Review*, August 5, 2020; www.theregreview.org/2020/08/05/robinson-covid-19-uncertainties-value -statistical-life/.
36. C. Landwehr, "Depoliticization and Politicization in the Allocation of Health Care: Decision-Making Procedures in International Comparison"; ecpr.eu/Filestore/PaperProposal/0dac228d-63fb -45c6-8384-21d764abaf6a.pdf.
37. A. Folley, "Texas Lt Gov: 'Grandparents "Don't Want the Whole Country Sacrificed" Amid Coronavirus Closures,'" *The Hill*, March 23, 2020.
38. C. Landwehr, "Deciding How to Decide: The Case of Health Care Rationing," *Public Administration* 87, no. 3 (2009): 586–603.
39. Calder, *The Myth of the Blitz* (Random House, 1992); D. Edgerton, "When It Comes to National Emergencies, Britain Has a Tradition of Cold Calculation," *Guardian*, March 17, 2020.
40. S. Roberts, "Flattening the Coronavirus Curve," *New York Times*, March 27, 2020.
41. S. Kaufman, *And a Time to Die: How American Hospitals Shape the End of Life* (University of Chicago Press, 2006).
42. M. Foucault, trans. A. Sheridan, *Discipline and Punish: The Birth of the Prison* (Penguin, 1977).
43. On the history of the economy, see A. Desrosières, *The Politics of Large Numbers: A History of Statistical Reasoning* (Harvard University Press, 1998). J. A. Tooze, *Statistics and the German State, 1900–1945: The Making of Modern Economic Knowledge* (Cambridge University Press, 2001). T. Mitchell, *Rule of Experts: Egypt, Techno-Politics, Modernity* (University of California Press, 2002). M. Goswami, *Producing India: From Colonial Economy to National Space* (University of Chicago Press, 2004).
44. M. Gorsky, M. Vilar-Rodríguez, and J. Pons-Pons, *The Political Economy of the Hospital in History* (University of Huddersfield Press, 2020).
45. G. Winant, *The Next Shift: The Fall of Industry and the Rise of Health Care in Rust Belt America* (Harvard University Press, 2021).
46. L. Spinney, *Pale Rider: The Spanish Flu of 1918 and How It Changed the World* (PublicAffairs, 2017); J. M. Barry, *The Great Influenza* (Penguin Books, 2005), 37.
47. R. Peckham, "Viral Surveillance and the 1968 Hong Kong Flu Pandemic," *Journal of Global History* 15, no. 3 (2020): 444–58. J. Fox, "Solving the Mystery of the 1957 and 1968 Flu Pandemics," *Bloomberg*, March 11, 2021.
48. D. J. Sencer and J. D. Millar, "Reflections on the 1976 Swine Flu Vaccine Program," *Emerging Infectious Diseases* 12, no. 1 (2006): 29–33. R. E. Neustadt and H. V. Fineberg, *The Swine Flu Affair: Decision-Making on a Slippery Disease* (National Academies Press, 1978).
49. C. McInnes and A. Roemer-Mahler, "From Security to Risk: Reframing Global Health Threats," *International Affairs* 93 no. 6 (2017): 1313–37.

50. C. McInnes, "Crisis! What Crisis? Global Health and the 2014–15 West African Ebola Outbreak," *Third World Quarterly* 37, no. 3 (2016): 380–400.
51. K. Mason, *Infectious Change: Reinventing Chinese Public Health After an Epidemic* (Stanford University Press, 2016).
52. F. Keck, *Avian Reservoirs: Virus Hunters and Birdwatchers in Chinese Sentinel Posts* (Duke University Press, 2020).
53. S. H. Lim and K. Sziarto, "When the Illiberal and the Neoliberal Meet Around Infectious Diseases: An Examination of the MERS Response in South Korea," *Territory, Politics, Governance* 8, no. 1 (2020): 60–76.
54. S. Lee, "Steering the Private Sector in COVID-19 Diagnostic Test Kit Development in South Korea," *Frontiers in Public Health* 8 (2020): 563525.
55. J. H. Wang, T.-Y. Chen, and C.-J. Tsai, "In Search of an Innovative State: The Development of the Biopharmaceutical Industry in Taiwan, South Korea and China," *Development and Change* 43, no. 2 (2012): 481–503.
56. J. C. Kile, R. Ren, L. Liu, et al., "Update: Increase in Human Infections with Novel Asian Lineage Avian Influenza A(H7N9) Viruses During the Fifth Epidemic—China, October 1, 2016–August 7, 2017," *Morbidity and Mortality Weekly Report* 66, no. 35 (2017): 928–32.
57. M. M. Kavanagh, H. Thirumurthy, R. Katz, et al., "Ending Pandemics: U.S. Foreign Policy to Mitigate Today's Major Killers, Tomorrow's Outbreaks, and the Health Impacts of Climate Change," *Journal of International Affairs* 73, no. 1 (2019): 49–68.
58. S. Harman and S. Davies, "President Donald Trump as Global Health's Displacement Activity," *Review of International Studies* 45, no. 3 (2018): 491–501.

CHAPTER 2. WUHAN, NOT CHERNOBYL

1. T. Mitchell, C. Shepherd, R. Harding, et al., "China's Xi Jinping Knew of Coronavirus Earlier Than First Thought," *Financial Times*, February 16, 2020.
2. C. Buckley, D. D. Kirkpatrick, A. Qin, and J. C. Hernández, "25 Days That Changed the World: How Covid-19 Slipped China's Grasp," *New York Times*, December 30, 2020.
3. "China Didn't Warn Public of Likely Pandemic for 6 Key Days," *CNBC*, April 15, 2020.
4. G. Shih, "In Coronavirus Outbreak, China's Leaders Scramble to Avert a Chernobyl Moment," *Washington Post*, January 29, 2020. J. Anderlini, "Xi Jinping Faces China's Chernobyl Moment," *Financial Times*, February 10, 2020. "Coronavirus 'Cover-up' Is China's Chernobyl—White House Advisor," *Reuters*, May 24, 2020.
5. J. Li, "Chinese People Are Using 'Chernobyl' to Channel Their Anger About the Coronavirus Outbreak," *Quartz*, January 27, 2020.
6. J. Mai and M. Lau, "Chinese Scholar Blames Xi Jinping, Communist Party for Not Controlling Coronavirus Outbreak," *South China Morning Post*, February 6, 2020.
7. L. Zhou and K. Elmer, "China Coronavirus: Thousands Left Wuhan for Hong Kong, Bangkok or Tokyo Before Lockdown," *South China Morning Post*, January 27, 2020.
8. K. Nakazawa, "Party's Half-Baked Admission Misses Xi's Biggest Problem," *Nikkei Asia*, February 6, 2020.
9. J. Mai, "Beijing Braced for 2020 of Managing Risks, with Xi Jinping's Feared 'Swans and Rhinos' Yet to Disperse," *South China Morning Post*, January 1, 2020.
10. C. Buckley, "Xi Jinping Assuming New Status as China's 'Core' Leader," *New York Times*, February 4, 2016.
11. P. M. Thornton, "Crisis and Governance: SARS and the Resilience of the Chinese Body Politic," *The China Journal* 61 (2009): 23–48.
12. M. Levinson, "Scale of China's Wuhan Shutdown Is Believed to Be Without Precedent," *New York Times*, January 22, 2020.
13. J. Page, W. Fan, and N. Khan, "How It All Started: China's Early Coronavirus Missteps," *Wall Street Journal*, March 6, 2020.
14. J. Kynge, S. Yu, and T. Hancock, "Coronavirus: The Cost of China's Public Health Cover-up," *Financial Times*, February 6, 2020.
15. M. Levinson, "Scale of China's Wuhan Shutdown Is Believed to Be Without Precedent," *New York Times*, January 22, 2020.
16. R. McGregor, "China's Deep State: The Communist Party and the Coronavirus," *Lowy Institute*, July 23, 2020.

17. T. Heberer, "The Chinese 'Developmental State 3.0' and the Resilience of Authoritarianism," *Journal of Chinese Governance* 1, no. 4 (2016): 611–32.
18. "China Declares 'People's War' on COVID-19," *All Things Considered*, NPR, February 13, 2020.
19. D. Weinland, "Chinese Developers Hit by Coronavirus Sales Ban," *Financial Times*, February 15, 2020.
20. A. J. He, Y. Shi, and H. Liu, "Crisis Governance, Chinese Style: Distinctive Features of China's Response to the Covid-19 Pandemic," *Policy Design and Practice* 3, no. 3 (2020): 242–58.
21. R. Zhong and P. Mozur, "To Tame Coronavirus, Mao-Style Social Control Blankets China," *New York Times*, February 15, 2020.
22. R. McGregor, "China's Deep State: The Communist Party and the Coronavirus," *Lowy Institute*, July 23, 2020.
23. D. Weinland, "Chinese Villages Build Barricades to Keep Coronavirus at Bay," *Financial Times*, February 7, 2020.
24. T. Mitchell, D. Weinland, and B. Greeley, "China: An Economy in Coronavirus Quarantine," *Financial Times*, February 14, 2020.
25. L. Yutong, B. Yujie, and Z. Xuan, "Railway Passenger Volumes Plummet More Than 70% Amid Coronavirus Outbreak," *Caixin*, February 1, 2020.
26. W. Jing and D. Jia, "Coronavirus Costs China's Service Sector $144 Billion in a Week," *Caixin*, February 1, 2020.
27. "Carmakers Brace for Crisis as Virus Wreaks Havoc in China," *Caixin*, February 1, 2020.
28. H. Lockett, J. Rennison, and P. Georgiadis, "Coronavirus Fears Rattle Shares and Oil Market," *Financial Times*, January 27, 2020.
29. K. Bradsher, "'Like Europe in Medieval Times': Virus Slows China's Economy," *New York Times*, February 10, 2020. L. Che, H. Du, and K. W. Chan, "Unequal Pain: A Sketch of the Impact of the Covid-19 Pandemic on Migrants' Employment in China," *Eurasian Geography and Economics* 61, no. 4–5 (2020): 448–63.
30. "Xi Chairs Leadership Meeting on Epidemic Control," *Xinhua*, February 3, 2020.
31. H. Lockett and S. Yu, "How the Invisible Hand of the State Works in Chinese Stocks," *Financial Times*, February 4, 2020.
32. M. Mackenzie, "A Dicey Period for Risk Sentiment," *Financial Times*, February 3, 2020.
33. H. Lockett, N. Liu, and S. Yu, "Chinese Stocks Suffer Worst Day Since 2015 on Coronavirus Fears," *Financial Times*, February 3, 2020.
34. X. Hui, B. Zhiming, C. Lijin, and M. Walsh, "Intensive Care Doctor Tells of a Hospital Teetering on Collapse in Wuhan," *Caixin*, February 14, 2020.
35. J. Kynge and N. Liu, "Coronavirus Whistleblower Doctor Dies in Wuhan Hospital," *Financial Times*, February 6, 2020.
36. S. Yu, "Coronavirus Death Toll Tops Sars as Public Backlash Grows," *Financial Times*, February 9, 2020.
37. V. Yu and E. Graham-Harrison, "'This May Be the Last Piece I Write': Prominent Xi Critic Has Internet Cut After House Arrest," *Guardian*, February 16, 2020.
38. M. Zanin et al., "The Public Health Response to the COVID-19 Outbreak in Mainland China: A Narrative Review," *Journal of Thoracic Disease* 12, no. 8 (2020): 4434–49.
39. F. Tang, "Coronavirus Prompts Beijing Residential Lockdown as Millions Return to Work," *South China Morning Post*, February 10, 2020.
40. R. McMorrow, C. Shepherd, and T. Mitchell, "China Struggles to Return to Work After Coronavirus Shutdown," *Financial Times*, February 10, 2020.
41. Bradsher, "'Like Europe in Medieval Times': Virus Slows China's Economy."
42. "Editorial: Coronavirus Epidemic Poses Test for Rule of Law," *Caixin*, February 18, 2020.
43. "Editorial: Coronavirus Epidemic Poses Test for Rule of Law."
44. Che, Du, and Chan, "Unequal Pain: A Sketch of the Impact of the Covid-19 Pandemic on Migrants' Employment in China."
45. R. McMorrow and N. Liu, "Chinese Shun People from Centre of Coronavirus Outbreak," *Financial Times*, February 12, 2020.
46. S. Fan and F. Yingzhe, "Fewer Than a Third of China's Nearly 300 Million Migrant Laborers Have Returned to Work," *Caixin*, February 18, 2020.
47. M. Funke and A. Tsang, "The People's Bank of China's Response to the Coronavirus Pandemic: A Quantitative Assessment," *Economic Modeling* 93 (2020): 465–73.
48. T. Mitchell, D. Weinland, and B. Greeley, "China: An Economy in Coronavirus Quarantine," *Financial Times*, February 14, 2020.

49. F. Tang, "Coronavirus: China's Firms Face Grim Reality as Help from Beijing Could Take Too Long to Trickle Down," *South China Morning Post*, February 11, 2020.
50. T. Mitchell, D. Weinland, and B. Greeley, "China: An Economy in Coronavirus Quarantine," *Financial Times*, February 14, 2020.
51. R. McMurrow, K. Hille, and T. Mitchell, "Foxconn Recalls Workers in Phases Following Coronavirus Shutdown," *Financial Times*, February 11, 2020.
52. J. Mai, "China Postpones Year's Biggest Political Gathering Amid Coronavirus Outbreak," *South China Morning Post*, February 17, 2020.
53. R. McMurrow, K. Hille, and N. Liu, "Coronavirus Hits Return to Work at Apple's Biggest iPhone Plant," *Financial Times*, February 18, 2020.
54. T. Ng, Z. Xin, and F. Tang, "Help China's Key Manufacturers Plug Back Into Global Supply Chain, Xi Jinping Says," *South China Morning Post*, February 21, 2020.
55. D. Yi and H. Shujing, "Foxconn Allows Henan Workers to Return to Its Zhengzhou Complex," *Caixin*, February 21, 2020.
56. Y. Ruiyang and L. Yutong, "China's Roads to Be Toll-Free Until Epidemic Ends," *Caixin*, February 17, 2020.
57. "Coronavirus Wednesday Update: China Gradually Gets Back to Work in Face of Worker, Material Shortages," *Caixin*, February 19, 2020.
58. W. Zheng, "Coronavirus Is China's Fastest-Spreading Health Crisis, Xi Jinping Says," *Politico*, February 23, 2020.
59. "With Its Epidemic Slowing, China Tries to Get Back to Work," *Economist*, February 27, 2020.
60. "Xinhua Headlines: Xi Stresses Unremitting Efforts in COVID-19 Control, Coordination on Economic, Social Development," *Xinhua*, February 24, 2020.
61. "WHO Director-General Opening Remarks at the Media Briefing on COVID-19," *World Health Organization*, February 23, 2020.
62. F. Tang, "Coronavirus: Xi Jinping Rings Alarm on China Economy as Country Shifts Priority to Maintaining Growth," *South China Morning Post*, February 24, 2020.
63. R. McMorrow, N. Liu, and K. Hille, "China Eases Quarantine and Lays On Transport to Get People Back to Work," *Financial Times*, February 25, 2020.
64. N. Sun, "Virus Hits China's Economic Heart—Its Small Businesses," *Nikkei Asia*, February 21, 2020.
65. F. Tang, "Coronavirus: China Grants Banks Extra Funding to Spur Loans to Hard Hit Small Businesses," *South China Morning Post*, February 26, 2020.
66. E. Barrett, "The Mystery of China's Unemployment Rate," *Fortune*, May 24, 2020.
67. C. Deng and J. Cheng, "Some Economists Question Strength of China's Labor Market," *Wall Street Journal*, June 7, 2020.
68. Che, Du, and Chan, "Unequal Pain: A Sketch of the Impact of the Covid-19 Pandemic on Migrants' Employment in China."
69. F. Tang, "Coronavirus: Small Business Sentiment Sinks to an All-Time Low as Outbreak Knocks China's Economy, Survey Shows," *South China Morning Post*, February 27, 2020.
70. C. Zhang, "Covid-19 in China: From 'Chernobyl Moment' to Impetus to Nationalism," *Made in China Journal*, May 4, 2020.
71. Later summarized as "Fighting COVID-19: China in Action," June 7, 2020; www.xinhuanet.com/english/2020-06/07/c_139120424.htm.

CHAPTER 3. FEBRUARY: WASTING TIME

1. A. Wilkinson, "The 2011 Film *Contagion* Is Even More Relevant in 2020, and Not Just Because of Coronavirus," *Vox*, February 4, 2020.
2. D. M. Herszenhorn and S. Wheaton, "How Europe Failed the Coronavirus Test," *Politico*, April 7, 2020.
3. D. MacKenzie, *COVID-19: The Pandemic That Never Should Have Happened and How to Stop the Next One* (Hachette, 2020).
4. S. Sen, "How China Locked Down Internally for COVID-19, but Pushed Foreign Travel," *Financial Times*, April 30, 2020.
5. S. Nebehay, "WHO Chief Says Widespread Travel Bans Not Needed to Beat China Virus," *Reuters*, February 3, 2020.

6. C. Shepherd, "Coronavirus: Chinese Carmakers Struggle with Disruption," *Financial Times*, February 24, 2020.
7. W. Boston, "The Company That Fought the Coronavirus and Won," *Wall Street Journal*, March 6, 2020.
8. D. Sheppard, "Why Coronavirus Is Pushing Down the Oil Price," *Financial Times*, January 23, 2020.
9. A. Woodhouse, P. Wells, M. Rocco, et al., "Coronavirus: WHO Warns of 'Concerning' Transmissions in Europe—As It Happened," *Financial Times*, February 10, 2020.
10. B. Elder, "Markets Not Live, Monday 24th February 2020," *Financial Times*, February 24, 2020.
11. S. LaFraniere, K. Thomas, N. Weiland, et al., "Politics, Science and the Remarkable Race for a Coronavirus Vaccine," *New York Times*, November 21, 2020.
12. J. Cohen, "China's Vaccine Gambit," *Science* 370, no. 6522 (2020): 1263–67.
13. "The New Virus Was Crowned in the Kremlin," *Kommersant*, January 30, 2020.
14. Peter Navarro, "Memorandum to the Task Force," February 9, 2020; www.sciencemag.org/sites /default/files/manhattan%20project%20bright%20exhibit%2021.pdf.
15. R. Morin, "Trump Aide Peter Navarro Warned 'As Many as 1.2 Million Souls' Could Be Lost to Coronavirus: Report," *USA Today*, April 7, 2020.
16. S. Geimann, "Trump Aide Accuses China of Using Travelers to 'Seed' Virus," *Bloomberg*, May 17, 2020.
17. M. Ward, "15 Times Trump Praised China as Coronavirus Was Spreading Across the Globe," *Politico*, April 15, 2020.
18. G. Sherman, "Inside Donald Trump's and Jared Kushner's Two Months of Magical Thinking," *Vanity Fair*, April 28, 2020.
19. R. Siegel, "Commerce Secretary Wilbur Ross Says China's Coronavirus 'Will Help' Bring Jobs Back to U.S.," *Washington Post*, January 30, 2020.
20. M. Fletcher, "Britain and Covid-19: A Chronicle of Incompetence," *New Statesman*, July 1, 2020.
21. S. Grey and A. MacAskill, "Special Report: Johnson Listened to His Scientists About Coronavirus—But They Were Slow to Sound the Alarm," *Reuters*, April 7, 2020.
22. Speech by B. Johnson, "PM Speech in Greenwich: 3 February 2020," February 3, 2020; www.gov.uk /government/speeches/pm-speech-in-greenwich-3-february-2020. F. O'Toole, "The Fatal Delusions of Boris Johnson," *New Statesman*, July 1, 2020.
23. Speech by B. Johnson, "PM Speech in Greenwich: 3 February 2020."
24. M. Liverani and R. Coker, "Protecting Europe from Diseases: From the International Sanitary Conferences to the ECDC," *Journal of Health Politics, Policy and Law* 37, no. 6 (2012): 915–34.
25. Herszenhorn and Wheaton, "How Europe Failed the Coronavirus Test."
26. B. Riegert and J. C. Gonzalez, "Coronavirus Containment in Europe Working 'So Far,' Says Germany's Spahn," *DW*, February 13, 2020.
27. M. Birnbaum, J. Hudson, and L. Morris, "At Munich Security Conference, an Atlantic Divide: U.S. Boasting and European Unease," *Washington Post*, February 15, 2020.
28. K. Martin, "Markets Face Fresh Jolt of Coronavirus Nerves," *Financial Times*, February 24, 2020.
29. S. Donnan, J. Randow, W. Horobin, et al., "Committee to Save World Is a No-Show, Pushing Economy to Brink," *Bloomberg*, March 13, 2020.
30. "Coronavirus: Iran Cover-up of Deaths Revealed by Data Leak," *BBC*, August 3, 2020.
31. J. Horowitz, "The Lost Days That Made Bergamo a Coronavirus Tragedy," *New York Times*, November 29, 2020.
32. M. Johnson, "Italy Quarantines Northern Towns in Coronavirus Outbreak," *Financial Times*, February 23, 2020.
33. Herszenhorn and Wheaton, "How Europe Failed the Coronavirus Test."
34. Elder, "Markets Not Live, Monday 24th February 2020."
35. Martin, "Markets Face Fresh Jolt of Coronavirus Nerves."
36. C. Smith and C. Henderson, "US 10-Year Treasury Yield Nears Record Low," *Financial Times*, February 24, 2020.
37. M. MacKenzie, "In No Mood for Catching a Falling Knife," *Financial Times*, February 25, 2020.
38. R. Wigglesworth, K. Martin, and T. Stubbington, "How the Coronavirus Shattered Market Complacency," *Financial Times*, February 28, 2020.
39. MacKenzie, "In No Mood for Catching a Falling Knife."
40. S. Johnson, "Global Inventories at 7-Year Low Prior to Coronavirus Hit," *Financial Times*, February 24, 2020.

41. L. Du, "Tourism Hotspot Locks Down as Japan's Hokkaido Fights Virus," *Bloomberg*, February 28, 2020.

42. C. Terhune, D. Levine, H. Jin, J. L. Lee, "Special Report: How Korea Trounced U.S. in Race to Test People for Coronavirus," *Reuters*, March 18, 2020.

43. J. Cohen, "The United States Badly Bungled Coronavirus Testing—But Things May Soon Improve," *Science*, February 28, 2020.

44. E. Lipton, A. Goodnough, M. D. Shear, M. Twohey, A. Mandavilli, S. Fink, and M. Walker, "The C.D.C. Waited 'Its Entire Existence for This Moment.' What Went Wrong?" *New York Times*, June 3, 2020.

45. G. Lee, "South Korea Approves First Four COVID-19 Test Kits Under Urgent-Use License," *Bio-World*, March 17, 2020. D. Lee and J. Lee, "Testing on the Move: South Korea's Rapid Response to the COVID-19 Pandemic," *Transportation Research Interdisciplinary Perspectives* 5 (2020): 100111.

46. Herszenhorn and Wheaton, "How Europe Failed the Coronavirus Test."

47. L. Kudlow and K. Evans, *CNBC* interview transcript, February 25, 2020; www.cnbc.com/2020/02 /25/first-on-cnbc-cnbc-transcript-national-economic-council-director-larry-kudlow-speaks -cnbcs-kelly-evans-on-cnbcs-the-exchange-today.html.

48. E. Luce, "Inside Trump's Coronavirus Meltdown," *Financial Times*, May 14, 2020.

49. S. Donnan, J. Randow, W. Horobin, and A. Speciale, "Committee to Save World Is a No-Show, Pushing Economy to the Brink," *Bloomberg*, March 13, 2020.

50. Martin, "Markets Face Fresh Jolt of Coronavirus Nerves."

51. C. Henderson, C. Smith, and P. Georgiadis, "Markets Tumble as Fed Rate Cut Fails to Ease Fears," *Financial Times*, March 3, 2020.

52. "Transcript: Donald Trump Visits CDC, Calls Jay Inslee a 'Snake,'" *Rev*, March 6, 2020.

53. D. Agren, "Mexican Governor Prompts Outrage with Claim Poor Are Immune to Coronavirus," *Guardian*, March 26, 2020.

54. "Mexico: Mexicans Need Accurate COVID-19 Information," *Human Rights Watch*, March 26, 2020.

55. F. Ng'wanakilala, "Tanzanian President Under Fire for Worship Meetings Aid Virus," *Bloomberg*, March 22, 2020.

56. L. Lenel, "Public and Scientific Uncertainty in the Time of COVID-19," *History of Knowledge*, May 13, 2020.

57. Grey and MacAskill, "Special Report: Johnson Listened to His Scientists About Coronavirus—But They Were Slow to Sound the Alarm." M. Fletcher, "Britain and Covid-19: A Chronicle of Incompetence," *New Statesman*, July 1, 2020.

58. J. Horowitz, "The Lost Days That Made Bergamo a Coronavirus Tragedy," *New York Times*, November 29, 2020.

CHAPTER 4. MARCH: GLOBAL LOCKDOWN

1. P. Smith, "An Overview and Market Size of Tradable Commodities," *The Tradable*.

2. IEA, Oil Market Report—February 2020, IEA, Paris; www.iea.org/reports/oil-market-report-february -2020.

3. A. Ward, "The Saudi Arabia-Russia Oil War Sparked by Coronavirus, Explained," *Vox*, March 6, 2020. J. Yaffa, "How the Russian-Saudi Oil War Went Awry—For Putin Most of All," *New Yorker*, April 15, 2020.

4. C. Ballentine and V. Hajric, "U.S. Stocks Plunge Most Since Financial Crisis: Markets Wrap," *Bloomberg*, March 9, 2020.

5. R. Costa, J. Dawsey, J. Stein, and A. Parker, "Trump Urged Mnuchin to Pressure Fed's Powell on Economic Stimulus in Explosive Tirade About Coronavirus," *Washington Post*, March 11, 2020.

6. "WHO Director-General's Opening Remarks at the Media Briefing on COVID-19," *World Health Organization*, March 11, 2020.

7. J. Sexton and J. Sapien, "Two Coasts. One Virus. How New York Suffered Nearly 10 Times the Number of Deaths as California," *ProPublica*, May 16, 2020.

8. B. Woodward, *Rage* (Simon & Schuster, 2020), 277.

9. "France Pledges Support for State-Backed Firms, Sees Virus Fallout Costing Billions," *Reuters*, March 13, 2020.

10. S. Donnan, J. Randow, W. Horobin, and A. Speciale, "Committee to Save World Is a No-Show, Pushing Economy to the Brink," *Bloomberg*, March 13, 2020.
11. H. Stewart, K. Proctor, and H. Siddique, "Johnson: Many More People Will Lose Loved Ones to Coronavirus," *Guardian*, March 12, 2020.
12. M. Fletcher, "Britain and Covid-19: A Chronicle of Incompetence," *New Statesman*, July 1, 2020.
13. S. Jones, "How Coronavirus Took Just Weeks to Overwhelm Spain," *Guardian*, March 25, 2020. L. Mannering, "Spain's Right Wing Sees Coronavirus as Opportunity," *Foreign Policy*, May 29, 2020.
14. Fletcher, "Britain and Covid-19: A Chronicle of Incompetence," *New Statesman*, July 1, 2020.
15. F. O'Toole, "The Fatal Delusions of Boris Johnson," *New Statesman*, July 1, 2020.
16. SPI-B Insights on Public Gatherings, March 12, 2020; assets.publishing.service.gov.uk/government /uploads/system/uploads/attachment_data/file/874289/13-spi-b-insights-on-public-gatherings-1 .pdf. L. Freedman, "The Real Reason the UK Government Pursued 'Herd Immunity'—And Why It Was Abandoned," *New Statesman*, April 1, 2020.
17. S. Grey and A. MacAskill, "Special Report: Johnson Listened to His Scientists About Coronavirus— But They Were Slow to Sound the Alarm," *Reuters*, April 7, 2020.
18. J. Macías, "School Meals: A Reflection of Growing Poverty in LA," *Cal Matters*, October 8, 2020.
19. Sexton and Sapien, "Two Coasts. One Virus. How New York Suffered Nearly 10 Times the Number of Deaths as California."
20. C. Pietralunga and A. Lemarié, "Coronavirus: l'exécutif réfléchit au confinement des Français," *Le Monde*, March 16, 2020.
21. C. Pietralunga and A. Lemarié, "'Nous sommes en guerre': face au coronavirus, Emmanuel Macron sonne la 'mobilisation Générale,'" *Le Monde*, March 17, 2020. F. Rousseaux, "Coronavirus: 35 millions de Français devant l'allocution de Macron, un record d'audience absolu," *Le Parisien*, March 17, 2020.
22. N. Aspinwall, "Coronavirus Lockdown Launches Manila Into Pandemonium," *Foreign Policy*, March 14, 2020.
23. K. Varagur, "Indonesia's Government Was Slow to Lock Down, So Its People Took Charge," *National Geographic*, May 13, 2020.
24. M. Afzal, "Pakistan Teeters on the Edge of Potential Disaster with the Coronavirus," *Brookings*, March 27, 2020.
25. M. Mourad and A. Lewis, "Egypt Declares Two-Week Curfew to Counter Coronavirus," *Reuters*, March 24, 2020.
26. D. Pilling, "No Lockdown, Few Ventilators, but Ethiopia Is Beating Covid-19," *Financial Times*, May 27, 2020.
27. V. Mallet and R. Khalaf, "FT Interview: Emmanuel Macron Says It Is Time to Think the Unthinkable," *Financial Times*, April 16, 2020.
28. V. Strauss, "1.5 Billion Children Around Globe Affected by School Closure. What Countries Are Doing to Keep Their Kids Learning During Pandemic," *Washington Post*, March 27, 2020.
29. N. Ferguson, D. Laydon, et al., "Report 9: Impact of Non-Pharmaceutical Interventions (NPIs) to Reduce COVID-19 Mortality and Healthcare Demand," Imperial College Response Team, March 16, 2020.
30. M. Claeson and S. Hanson, "COVID-19 and the Swedish Enigma," *Lancet* 397, no. 10271 (2021): 259–261. G. Vogel, "'It's Been So, So Surreal.' Critics of Sweden's Lax Pandemic Policies Face Fierce Backlash," *Science*, October 6, 2020.
31. Grey and MacAskill, "Special Report: Johnson Listened to His Scientists About Coronavirus—But They Were Slow to Sound the Alarm."
32. M. Fletcher, "Britain and Covid-19: A Chronicle of Incompetence," *New Statesman*, July 1, 2020.
33. E. Luce, "Inside Trump's Coronavirus Meltdown," *Financial Times*, May 14, 2020.
34. M. McGraw and C. Oprysko, "Inside the White House During '15 Days to Slow the Spread,'" *Politico*, March 29, 2020.
35. J. White, "Temporary Work Stoppage at Fiat Chrysler's Warren Truck Plant as Wildcat Strikes Spread in Global Auto Industry," *World Socialist Web Site*, March 17, 2020.
36. D. DiMaggio, "Organizing Around the World for PTO: Pandemic Time Off," *Labor Notes*, March 16, 2020.
37. G. Coppola, D. Welch, K. Naughton, and D. Hull, "Detroit Carmakers Close Plants While Musk Keeps Tesla Open," *Bloomberg*, March 18, 2020.

38. A. Wilen and D. Hipwell, "European Retail Braces for Slump as Epicenter Shifts from China," *Bloomberg*, March 16, 2020.
39. J. Emont, "Retailers Cancel Orders from Asian Factories, Threatening Millions of Jobs," *Wall Street Journal*, March 25, 2020.
40. D. Biller and D. Rodrigues, "Rio's Christ Statue Closes and State of Emergency Decreed," *ABC News*, March 18, 2020.
41. J. L. Anderson, "In Brazil, Jair Bolsonaro, Trump's Close Ally, Dangerously Downplays the Coronavirus Risk," *New Yorker*, April 1, 2020. P. Asmann, "What Does Coronavirus Mean for Criminal Governance in Latin America," *InSight Crime*, March 31, 2020.
42. McGraw and Oprysko, "Inside the White House During '15 Days to Slow the Spread.'"
43. V. Chandrashekhar, "1.3 Billion People. A 21-Day Lockdown. Can India Curb the Coronavirus?" *Science*, March 31, 2020.
44. Chandrashekhar, "1.3 Billion People. A 21-Day Lockdown. Can India Curb the Coronavirus?"
45. K. Komireddi, "Modi's India Isn't Prepared for the Coronavirus," *Foreign Policy*, April 10, 2020.
46. P. Sinha, Twitter, March 20, 2020.
47. R. Venkataramakrishnan, "Coronavirus: Did India Rush into a Lockdown? Or Is This a Difficult but Needed Move to Fight Covid?" *Scroll.in*, March 24, 2020.
48. International Labour Organization, "ILO Monitor, COVID-19 and the World of Work. Third edition," April 29, 2020; www.ilo.org/wcmsp5/groups/public/—-dgreports/—-dcomm/documents/briefing note/wcms_743146.pdf.
49. Giorgio Agamben's essays from the crisis are collected in *Where Are We Now? The Epidemic as Politics*, eris.press/Where-Are-We-Now.
50. F. O'Toole, "The Fatal Delusions of Boris Johnson," *New Statesman*, July 1, 2020.
51. M. Margolis, "China Laps U.S. in Latin America with Covid-19 Diplomacy," *Bloomberg*, June 24, 2020.
52. L. Paraguassu and J. McGeever, "Brazil Government Ad Rejects Coronavirus Lockdown, Saying #BrazilCannotStop," *Reuters*, March 27, 2020.
53. "Federal Judge Bans Bolsonaro's 'Brazil Cannot Stop' Campaign," *teleSUR*, March 28, 2020.
54. D. Agren, "Mexican Governor Prompts Outrage with Claim Poor Are Immune to Coronavirus," *Guardian*, March 26, 2020.
55. "'Escuchen al presidente, yo nunca los voy a engañar': López Obrador pidió confianza ante amenaza de coronavirus en México," *infobae*, March 20, 2020.
56. Morning Conference with A. M. López Obrador, "Versión estenográfica de la conferencia de prensa matutina," March 11, 2020.
57. T. Phillips, "Mexican President Ignores Coronavirus Restrictions to Greet El Chapo's Mother," *Guardian*, March 30, 2020.
58. R. Costa and P. Rucker, "Inside Trump's Risky Push to Reopen the Country amid the Coronavirus Crisis," *Washington Post*, March 28, 2020.
59. R. Costa, L. Vozzella, and J. Dawsey, "Inslee Clashes with Trump over His Leadership on Coronavirus Aid: 'We Need a Tom Brady,'" *Washington Post*, March 26, 2020.
60. P. Rucker, J. Dawsey, Y. Abutaleb, R. Costa, and L. H. Sun, "34 Days of Pandemic: Inside Trump's Desperate Attempts to Reopen America," *Washington Post*, May 2, 2020.
61. J. Lemire, J. Colvin, and Z. Miller, "What Changed Trump's Mind About Reopening on Easter?" *York Dispatch*, March 30, 2020.
62. M. D. Shear, M. Crowley, and J. Glanz, "Coronavirus Death Toll May Reach 100,000 to 240,000 in U.S., Officials Say," *New York Times*, March 31, 2020.

CHAPTER 5. FREE FALL

1. D. Chronopoulos, M. Lukas, and J. Wilson, "Real-Time Consumer Spending Responses to COVID-19 Crisis and Lockdown," *VoxEU*, May 6, 2020.
2. V. Carvalho, J. R. García, et al., "Tracking the COVID-19 Crisis Through the Lens of 1.4 Billion Transactions," *VoxEU*, April 27, 2020.
3. IMF, World Economic Outlook Reports, "World Economic Outlook, October 2020: A Long and Difficult Ascent," October 2020.
4. P. Brinca, J. B. Duarte, and M. F. Castro, "Is the COVID-19 Pandemic a Supply or a Demand Shock?" Economic Research, Federal Reserve Bank of St. Louis, *Economic Synopses* No. 31, 2020.
5. L. Kilian, "Not All Oil Price Shocks Are Alike: Disentangling Demand and Supply Shocks in the Crude Oil Market," *American Economic Review* 99, no. 3 (2009): 1053–69.

6. K. Schive, "How Safe Is Air Travel?" *MIT Medical*, July 23, 2020.
7. S. Hodge, "Private Jet Use Skyrockets During Coronavirus Pandemic—Luxury No Longer Seen as a Splurge," *Paper City*.
8. "Industry Losses to Top $84 Billion in 2020," *IATA*, June 9, 2020. "What if Aviation Doesn't Recover from Covid-19?" *Economist*, July 2, 2020.
9. "Air Travel's Sudden Collapse Will Reshape a Trillion-Dollar Industry," *Economist*, August 1, 2020.
10. E. Balibar, "Mi-temps de la crise expériences, questions, anticipations (1ère partie)," 2020; aoc .media/opinion/2020/07/14/ce-que-devient-le-politique-mi-temps-de-la-crise-1-3/.
11. C. Flaherty, "Women Are Falling Behind," *Inside Higher Ed*, October 20, 2020.
12. NYC Health also endorsed glory holes as a safe sex option. See NYC Health, "Safer Sex and Covid-19," www1.nyc.gov/assets/doh/downloads/pdf/imm/covid-sex-guidance.pdf.
13. Statista, "Number of Fixed Broadband Internet Subscriptions Worldwide from 2005 to 2019," www.statista.com/statistics/268673/number-of-broadband-internet-subscriptions.
14. S. Vibert, "Children Without Internet Access During Lockdown," *Children's Commissioner*, August 18, 2020.
15. "Two Thirds of the World's School-Age Children Have No Internet Access at Home, New UNICEF-ITU Report Says," *UNICEF*, November 30, 2020.
16. K. Purohit, "Coronavirus: India's Outsourcing Firms Struggle to Serve US, British Companies amid Lockdown," *South China Morning Post*, March 31, 2020. S. Phartiyal and S. Ravikumar, "India's Huge Outsourcing Industry Struggles with Work-from-Home Scenario," *Reuters*, March 25, 2020. L. Frayer and S. Pathak, "India's Lockdown Puts Strain on Call Centers," *NPR*, April 24, 2020.
17. A. Tanzi, "Half the Labor Force in Major U.S. Cities Is Working from Home," *Bloomberg*, November 24, 2020. K. Weise, "Pushed by Pandemic, Amazon Goes on a Hiring Spree Without Equal," *New York Times*, November 27, 2020. "FedEx Tries to Think Beyond the Pandemic," *Economist*, July 2, 2020.
18. A. Wilkinson, "How the Coronavirus Outbreak Is Roiling the Film and Entertainment Industries," *VoxEU*, September 23, 2020. A. Barker and A. Nicolaou, "The Unhinged Bet to Jump-Start the Movie Business," *Financial Times*, June 16, 2020. A. Kaul, "The Six Sigma to Rescue 1 Million COVID-Affected Film Industry Workers," *Exchange4Media*, May 2, 2020. A. Chopra, "How the Pandemic Hit Bollywood," *New York Times*, May 15, 2020. A. Dhillon, "India's Bollywood Cuts Kissing Scenes, Epic Dance Routines Under New Coronavirus Rules," *South China Morning Post*, June 4, 2020.
19. E. Schwartzel, "Covid-19 Derails China's Push to Be Biggest Movie Market," *Wall Street Journal*, July 6, 2020.
20. P. Fronstin and S. A. Woodbury, "How Many Americans Have Lost Jobs with Employer Health Coverage During the Pandemic?" *Commonwealth Fund*, October 7, 2020.
21. H. Meyers-Belkin, "'Today Is Wonderful': Relief in Lagos as Nigeria Emerges from Covid-19 Lockdown," *France24*, May 5, 2020.
22. E. Akinwotu, "'People Are More Scared of Hunger': Coronavirus Is Just One More Threat in Nigeria," *Guardian*, May 15, 2020.
23. O. Sunday, "Gangs Terrorised Africa's Largest City in Coronavirus Lockdown. Vigilantes Responded," *South China Morning Post*, May 18, 2020. N. Orjinmo and A. Ulohotse, "Lagos Unrest: The Mystery of Nigeria's Fake Gangster Attacks," *BBC*, April 15, 2020.
24. S. Maheshwari, "With Department Stores Disappearing, Malls Could Be Next," *New York Times*, July 5, 2020. M. Bain, "The US Shopping Mall Was Already in Trouble—Then Came Covid-19," *Quartz*, May 26, 2020.
25. R. Clough and J. Hill, "Brooks Brothers Goes Bust with Business Clothes Losing Favor," *Bloomberg*, July 8, 2020.
26. L. Abboud and D. Keohane, "Parisian Retail Stalwart Tati Bites the Dust," *Financial Times*, July 10, 2020.
27. L. Abboud, "Troubles of Famed Paris Bookshop Expose French Retail Shift," *Financial Times*, December 2, 2020.
28. "A Wave of Bankruptcies Is Coming in Europe," *Economist*, May 16, 2020.
29. H. Ziady, "25,000 Jobs at Risk as Debenhams Closure Follows Topshop Collapse," *CNN*, December 1, 2020.
30. H. Gupta, "Why Some Women Call This Recession a 'Shecession,'" *New York Times*, May 9, 2020.
31. R. Siegal, "Women Outnumber Men in the American Workforce for Only the Second Time," *Washington Post*, January 10, 2020.

32. T. Alon, M. Doepke, J. Olmstead-Rumsey, and M. Tertilt, "The Shecession (She-Recession) of 2020: Causes and Consequences," *VoxEU*, September 22, 2020.
33. J. Hurley, "COVID-19: A Tale of Two Service Sectors," *Eurofound*, February 3, 2021.
34. A. Olson and C. Bussewitz, "Child Care Crisis Pushes US Mothers Out of the Labor Force," *AP News*, September 4, 2020.
35. M. Paxton, "The Coronavirus Threat to Wildlife Tourism and Conservation," *United Nations Development Programme*, April 21, 2020. "Global Wildlife Tourism Generates Five Times More Revenue Than Illegal Wildlife Trade Annually," *World Travel and Tourism Council*, December 8, 2019.
36. "Share of GDP Generated by the Travel and Tourism Industry Worldwide from 2000 to 2019," *Statista*, February 4, 2021.
37. Paxton, "The Coronavirus Threat to Wildlife Tourism and Conservation."
38. J. K. Elliot, "Thailand's 'Monkey City' Overrun by Gangs of Hungry, Horny Macaques," *Global News*, June 24, 2020.
39. D. Jones, "The Coronavirus Pandemic Has Halted Tourism, and Animals Are Benefiting from It," *Washington Post*, April 3, 2020.
40. M. Toyana, "Jobs Gone, Investments Wasted: Africa's Deserted Safaris Leave Mounting Toll," *Reuters*, June 11, 2020.
41. Conversation with D. Mogajane, "South Africa Looks Toward Inclusive Recovery to Stabilize Debt," *International Monetary Fund*, August 3, 2020.
42. L. Frayer, "For Bangladesh's Struggling Garment Workers, Hunger Is a Bigger Worry Than Pandemic," *NPR*, June 5, 2020.
43. J. Emont, "Developing World Loses Billions in Money from Migrant Workers," *Wall Street Journal*, July 5, 2020.
44. L. Frayer, "1 Million Bangladeshi Garment Workers Lose Jobs Amid COVID-19 Economic Fallout," *NPR*, April 3, 2020. A. Becker, "Coronavirus Disruptions Deal Severe Blow to Bangladesh's Garment Industry," *DW News*, June 23, 2020.
45. FAO and WFP, "FAO-WFP Early Warning Analysis of Acute Food Insecurity Hotspots," July 17, 2020; www.wfp.org/publications/fao-wfp-early-warning-analysis-acute food-insecurity-hotspots.
46. K. Hearst, "COVID-19 and the Garment Industry's Invisible Hands," *Open Democracy*, July 20, 2020; www.opendemocracy.net/en/oureconomy/covid-19-and-the-garment-industrys-invisible-hands/.
47. Z. Ebrahim, "'Moving Mountains': How Pakistan's 'Invisible' Women Won Workers' Rights," *Guardian*, December 1, 2020.
48. G. Flynn and M. Dara, "Garment Workers Cornered by Job Loss, Virus Fears and Looming Debt," *VOD*, April 16, 2020.
49. K. Brenke, U. Rinne, and K. F. Zimmermann, "Short-Time Work: The German Answer to the Great Recession," *International Labour Review* 152, no. 2 (2013): 287–305.
50. EIB, Investment Report 2020; www.eib.org/attachments/efs/eib_investment_report_advance_copy.pdf.
51. OECD Economic Outlook, Volume 2020; https://www.oecd-ilibrary.org/economics/oecd-economic-outlook_16097408.
52. R. Carroll, S. Jones, L. Tondo, K. Connolly, and K. Gillet, "Covid-19 Crisis Stokes European Tensions over Migrant Labour," *Guardian*, May 11, 2020. M. Andriescu, "Under Lockdown Amid COVID-19 Pandemic, Europe Feels the Pinch from Slowed Intra-EU Labor Mobility," *Migration Policy Institute*, May 1, 2020.
53. M. Weisskircher, J. Rone, and M. S. Mendes, "The Only Frequent Flyers Left: Migrant Workers in the EU in Times of Covid-19," *Open Democracy*, April 20, 2020.
54. S. Jha, "Migrant Workers Head Home in Coronavirus Lockdown, Exposed and Vulnerable," *Business Standard*, March 26, 2020.
55. A. K. B. Basu, and J. M. Tapia, "The Complexity of Managing COVID-19: How Important Is Good Governance?" *Brookings*, November 17, 2020.
56. "21 Days and Counting: COVID-19 Lockdown, Migrant Workers, and the Inadequacy of Welfare Measures in India," *Stranded Workers Action Network*, April 15, 2020.
57. "The Jobs Bloodbath of April 2020," *Centre for Monitoring Indian Economy*, May 5, 2020.
58. "Policy Basics: How Many Weeks of Unemployment Compensation Are Available?" *Center on Budget and Policy Priorities*, February 1, 2021.
59. M. Haag, "To Reach a Single A.T.M., a Line of Unemployed Stretches a Block," *New York Times*, July 7, 2020.
60. V. Stracqualursi and A. Kurtz, "Trump Administration Asking States to Delay Release of Unemployment Numbers," *CNN*, March 20, 2020.

61. G. Iacurci, "Job Losses Remain 'Enormous': Coronavirus Unemployment Claims Are Worst in History," *CNBC*, July 9, 2020.
62. "2020: Charts from a Year Like No Other," *Financial Times*, December 29, 2020.
63. S. Matthews, "U.S. Jobless Rate May Soar to 30%, Fed's Bullard Says," *Bloomberg*, March 22, 2020.
64. Remarks by D. G. Azevêdo, "Trade Set to Plunge as COVID-19 Pandemic Upends Global Economy," *World Trade Organization*, April 8, 2020.
65. H. Tan, "Thousands of Seafarers Are Stranded as Coronavirus Shuts Down Borders—That Could Hurt Trade," *CNBC*, June 24, 2020.
66. "Why the Philippines Is a Magnet for Idled Cruise Ships," *Economist*, May 23, 2020.
67. "Cargo-Ship Crews Are Stuck at Sea," *Economist*, June 20, 2020. J. Emont, "Developing World Loses Billions in Money from Migrant Workers," *Wall Street Journal*, July 15, 2020.
68. N. Ghani and G. Platten, "Shopping on Black Friday? Remember the Stranded Seafarers Who Made It Possible," *Guardian*, November 27, 2020.
69. "Is the World Economy Recovering?" *Economist*, September 19, 2020.

CHAPTER 6. "WHATEVER IT TAKES," AGAIN

1. A. Samson, P. Georgiadis, et al., "US Stocks Fall 10% in Worst Day Since 1987 Crash," *Financial Times*, March 12, 2020.
2. Z. He and A. Krishnamurthy, "Are US Treasury Bonds Still a Safe Haven?" *National Bureau of Economic Research, The Reporter*, October 2020. P. Mehrling, "Financialization and Its Discontents," *Finance and Society* 3 (2017): 1–10.
3. D. Duffie, "Still the World's Safe Haven? Redesigning the U.S. Treasury Market After the Covid-19 Crisis," *Brookings*, June 22, 2020.
4. "Holistic Review of the March Market Turmoil," *Financial Stability Board,* November 17, 2020.
5. A. Samson, R. Wigglesworth, C. Smith, and J. Rennison, "Strains in US Government Bond Market Rattle Investors," *Financial Times*, March 12, 2020.
6. L. Norton, "How the Pandemic Will Change Financial Markets Forever," *Barron's*, July 22, 2020.
7. A. Tooze, *Crashed: How a Decade of Financial Crises Changed the World* (Viking, 2018). A. Mian and Amir Sufi, *House of Debt: How They (and You) Caused the Great Recession, and How We Can Prevent It from Happening Again* (University of Chicago Press, 2015).
8. J. Harper, "Global Housing Markets 'Overheating' amid Pandemic Stimulus?" *DW*, November 15, 2020.
9. "Global Financial Stability Report: Markets in the Time of COVID-19," *International Monetary Fund,* April 2020. "Financial Stability Report," *Board of Governors of the Federal Reserve System*, November 2020.
10. "How Resilient Are the Banks?" *Economist*, July 2, 2020.
11. "Financial Stability Review," *European Central Bank*, May 2020.
12. "Navigating Monetary Policy Challenges and Managing Risks," *International Monetary Fund*, April 2015. "Market Fragility and Interconnectedness in the Asset Management Industry," speech by S. W. Bauguess, acting director and acting chief economist, DERA, *U.S. Securities and Exchange Commission*, June 20, 2017.
13. S. Avdjiev, P. McGuire, and G. von Peter, "International Dimensions of EME Corporate Debt," *BIS*, June 3, 2020.
14. The best accounts of the repo system are D. Gabor, "The (Impossible) Repo Trinity: The Political Economy of Repo Markets," *Review of International Political Economy* 23, no. 6 (2016): 967–1000, and C. Sissoko, "The Collateral Supply Effect on Central Bank Policy," August 21, 2020. Available at SSRN: ssrn.com/abstract=3545546 or dx.doi.org/10.2139/ssrn.3545546.
15. G. B. Gorton and A. Metrick, "Securitized Banking and the Run on Repo," *NBER Working Paper 15223,* August 2009.
16. D. Duffie, "Still the World's Safe Haven? Redesigning the U.S. Treasury Market After the COVID-19 Crisis" (Brookings, 2020); www.brookings.edu/research/still-the-worlds-safe-haven.
17. "Holistic Review of the March Market Turmoil," *FSB*.
18. A. Etra, "2020 UST March Madness," *Money: Inside and Out*, January 13, 2021.
19. A. Samson, R. Wigglesworth, et al., "Strains in US Government Bond Market Rattle Investors," *Financial Times*, March 12, 2020.
20. D. Beckworth, "Carolyn Sissoko on the Collateral Supply Effect and Other Concerns in the Money Market," *Mercatus Center*, George Mason University, September 21, 2020.

21. K. Brettell and K. Pierog, "Treasury Liquidity Worsens, Worries Build About Broad Selling Pressures," *Reuters*, March 12, 2020.

22. "Financial Stability Review," *European Central Bank*, May 2020.

23. A. Hauser, "From Lender of Last Resort to Market Maker of Last Resort via the Dash for Cash: Why Central Banks Need New Tools for Dealing with Market Dysfunction" (London: Bank of England, 2021); www.bankofengland.co.uk/-/media/boe/files/speech/2021/january/why-central-banks -need-new-tools-for-dealing-with-market-dysfunction-speech-by-andrew-hauser.pdf.

24. R. Costa, J. Dawsey, J. Stein, and A. Parker, "Trump Urged Mnuchin to Pressure Fed's Powell on Economic Stimulus in Explosive Tirade About Coronavirus," *Washington Post*, March 11, 2020.

25. "Trump Presses 'Pathetic' Fed to Cut Rates More Aggressively," *Reuters*, March 10, 2020.

26. S. Donnan, J. Randow, W. Horobin, and A. Speciale, "Committee to Save the World Is a No-Show, Pushing Economy to Brink," *Bloomberg*, March 13, 2020.

27. S. O'Grady, "Janet Yellen: The Treasury Secretary Who Trump Thought Was 'Too Political'—And 'Too Short,'" *Independent*, February 1, 2020.

28. D. Borak, "How Jerome Powell Stopped a US Default—in 2011," *CNN*, July 19, 2019.

29. On Powell: T. L. Hogan, "Can the Fed Reduce Inequality?," American Institute for Economic Research, August 18, 2020. J. L. Yellen, "Perspectives on Inequality and Opportunity from the Survey of Consumer Finances," *Board of Governors of the Federal Reserve System*, October 17, 2014. On the ambiguities of Yellen's position: see R. V. Reeves, "Janet Yellen's Inequality Speech Revealed a 'Closet Conservative,'" *Brookings*, October 14, 2014.

30. N. Timiraos, "New York Fed Names New Leadership for Top Markets Jobs," *Wall Street Journal*, December 19, 2019.

31. R. Kuttner, "Liberalish: The Complex Odyssey of Lael Brainard," *American Prospect*, September 23, 2020.

32. C. Torres and L. McCormick, "Fed Dissent and Bond Volatility Are in Powell's Taper Future," *Bloomberg*, February 2, 2021.

33. J. Cox, "Fed Boosts Money It's Providing to Banks in Overnight Repo Lending to $175 Billion," CNBC, March 11, 2020.

34. "Federal Reserve Issues FOMC Statement," Federal Reserve press release, March 15, 2020.

35. C. Jones, "Why the Dollar Crunch Is (Mostly) a Rich World Problem," *Financial Times*, March 24, 2020. I. Kaminska, "Why FX Swap Lines Are Back," *Financial Times*, March 17, 2020. "The Successes of the Fed's Dollar-Swap Lines," *Economist*, June 20, 2020. B. W. Setser, "How Asia's Life Insurers Could 'Shelter-in-Place,'" *Council on Foreign Relations*, March 22, 2020.

36. A. Tooze, "This Is the One Thing That Might Save the World from Financial Collapse," *New York Times*, March 20, 2020.

37. P. LeBlanc, "Trump Congratulates Federal Reserve for Slashing Interest Rates: 'It Makes Me Very Happy,'" *CNN*, March 15, 2020.

38. Y. Li, "Plunging Stocks Triggered a Key Market 'Circuit Breaker.' Here's What That Means," *CNBC*, March 16, 2020.

39. H. Lambert, "The Adults in the Room," *New Statesman*, July 15, 2020.

40. A. Debnath, M. Hunter, and S. Barton, "Currency Liquidity Vanishes on Mounting Fears of London Hub Slamming Shut," *Bloomberg*, March 18, 2020.

41. J. Surane, P. Seligson, A. Harris, and L. McCormick, "Key Source of Corporate Cash Seizing Up Amid Credit Market Rout," *Bloomberg*, March 15, 2020.

42. N. Kumar, "Bridgewater Makes $14 Billion Short Against European Stocks," *Bloomberg*, March 16, 2020.

43. S. Potter and J. Lee, "Diary of a Crisis: Inside Wall Street's Most Volatile Week Ever," *Bloomberg*, March 20, 2020.

44. Potter and Lee, "Diary of a Crisis: Inside Wall Street's Most Volatile Week Ever."

45. T. Stubbington and C. Smith, "Investment Veterans Try to Get to Grips with 'Broken' Markets," *Financial Times*, March 20, 2020.

46. C. Giles, "BoE Compelled to Act as Coronavirus Pummels Economy," *Financial Times*, March 19, 2020.

47. E. Conway, "Coronavirus: Bank of England Rescued Government, Reveals Governor," *Sky News*, June 22, 2020.

48. Lambert, "The Adults in the Room."

49. Lambert, "The Adults in the Room."

50. Potter and Lee, "Diary of a Crisis: Inside Wall Street's Most Volatile Week Ever."

51. "COVID-19 and Global Capital Flows," *Organisation for Economic Development and Co-operation (OEDC)*, July 3, 2020.
52. C. Torres, "Meet Fed's Nine New Offspring, Each with Different Market Role," *Bloomberg*, April 16, 2020.
53. "VW Urges ECB to Buy Short-Term Debt to Stabilise Markets," *Reuters*, March 27, 2020.
54. M. J. Lee and T. Hasegawa, "BOJ Becomes Biggest Japan Stock Owner with $434 Billion Hoard," *Bloomberg*, December 6, 2020.
55. "Federal Reserve Issues FOMC Statement," Federal Reserve Press Release, March 15, 2020.
56. Beckworth, "Carolyn Sissoko on the Collateral Supply Effect and Other Concerns in the Money Market."
57. C. Peterson-Withorn, "The World's Billionaires Have Gotten $1.9 Trillion Richer in 2020," *Forbes*, December 16, 2020.

CHAPTER 7. ECONOMY ON LIFE SUPPORT

1. C. Hulse and E. Cochrane, "As Coronavirus Spread, Largest Stimulus in History United a Polarized Senate," *New York Times*, March 26, 2020.
2. B. Battersby, W. R. Lam, and E. Ture, "Tracking the $9 Trillion Global Fiscal Support to Fight COVID-19," *International Monetary Fund*, May 20, 2020. V. Gaspar, P. Medas, J. Ralyea, and E. Ture, "Fiscal Policy for an Unprecedented Crisis," *International Monetary Fund*, October 14, 2020. IMF Fiscal Monitor, January 2021, Update.
3. A. Martin and J. Younger, "War Finance and Bank Leverage: Lessons from History," Yale School of Management, September 8, 2020.
4. C. Giles, "Central Bankers Have Been Relegated to Second Division of Policymakers," *Financial Times*, October 1, 2020.
5. For this essential insight, see D. Gabor, "Revolution Without Revolutionaries: Interrogating the Return of Monetary Financing," *Transformative Responses to the Crisis*, 2020.
6. IMF Fiscal Monitor, October 2020, Figure 1.1.
7. CEPAL, "Addressing the Growing Impact of COVID-19 with a View to Reactivation with Equality: New Projections," July 15, 2020; repositorio.cepal.org/bitstream/handle/11362/45784/1/S2000470_en.pdf.
8. O. Sunday, "Gangs Terrorised Africa's Largest City in Coronavirus Lockdown. Vigilantes Responded," *South China Morning Post*, May 18, 2020.
9. S. Dixit, Y. K. Ogundeji, and O. Onwujekwe, "How Well Has Nigeria Responded to COVID-19?" *Brookings*, July 2, 2020.
10. A. Rettman, "Merkel Defends EU Legacy on Refugees and Austerity," *EU Observer*, May 16, 2019.
11. OECD Economic Outlook, Volume 2020, Issue 1.
12. M. Schieritz, "Was traut er sich?" *Die Zeit*, November 13, 2019.
13. M. Ashworth, "Germany's 'Black Zero' Rule May Be Gone Forever," *Bloomberg*, February 26, 2020.
14. M. Nienaber, "German Parliament Suspends Debt Brake to Fight Coronavirus Outbreak," *Reuters*, March 25, 2020.
15. G. Chazan, "Scholz Insists Record German Borrowing Manageable," *Financial Times*, June 17, 2020. "Germany Opens the Money Tap," *Economist*, June 13, 2020.
16. D. Adler and J. Roos, "If Coronavirus Sinks the Eurozone, the 'Frugal Four' Will Be to Blame," *Guardian*, March 31, 2020. H. Von Der Burchard, I. Oliveira, and E. Schaart, "Dutch Try to Calm North-South Economic Storm over Coronavirus," *Politico*, March 27, 2020.
17. D. Gutensohn, "Kliniken schließen—wenn sie am nötigsten gebraucht werden," *Die Zeit*, April 7, 2020.
18. B. Tanjangco, Y. Cao, R. Nadin, L. Calabrese, and O. Borodyna, "Pulse 1: Covid-19 and Economic Crisis—China's Recovery and International Response," *ODI Economic Pulse* series, November 2020.
19. J. Sipalan, "Malaysia Announces $58-Billion Stimulus Package to Cushion Impact of Coronavirus," *Reuters*, March 27, 2020.
20. J. Follain, "Italian Leader Takes to Basement to Plot How to Fight Virus," *Bloomberg*, March 9, 2020.
21. J. Ford, "The New Wartime Economy in the Era of Coronavirus," *Financial Times*, March 25, 2020. "How to Battle the Coronavirus and Win: A Historians' Roundtable," www.bloomberg.com/opinion/articles/2020-03-29/history-s-coronavirus-lessons-going-to-war-against-covid-19.
22. E. Levitz, "This Recession Is a Bigger Housing Crisis Than 2008," *Intelligencer*, July 13, 2020.
23. M. Konczal, "Our Political System Is Hostile to Real Reform," *Dissent*, March 26, 2020.

24. A. Tooze, *Crashed: How a Decade of Financial Crises Changed the World* (Viking, 2018) and A. Mian and A. Sufi, *House of Debt: How They (and You) Caused the Great Recession, and How We Can Prevent It from Happening Again* (University of Chicago Press, 2015).

25. J. Politi, "US Heads for Fiscal Cliff as Stimulus Fades," *Financial Times*, July 11, 2020.

26. R. Chetty, J. N. Friedman, N. Hendren, M. Stepner, and the Opportunity Insights Team, "The Economic Impacts of Covid-19: Evidence from a New Public Database Built Using Private Sector Data," *National Bureau of Economic Research Working Paper 27431*, November 2020.

27. U.S. Bureau of Economic Analysis, Personal Saving Rate [PSAVERT], retrieved from FRED, Federal Reserve Bank of St. Louis; fred.stlouisfed.org/series/PSAVERT, February 10, 2021.

28. A. Madgavkar, T. Tacke, S. Smit, and J. Manyika, "COVID-19 Has Revived the Social Contract in Advanced Economies—For Now. What Will Stick Once the Crisis Abates?" McKinsey Global Institute, December 10, 2020.

29. Madgavkar et al., "COVID-19 Has Revived the Social Contract in Advanced Economies—For Now. What Will Stick Once the Crisis Abates?"

30. "Job Retention Schemes During the COVID-19 Lockdown and Beyond," *OECD*, October 12, 2020.

31. M. Konczal, "Unemployment Insurance Is a Vital Part of Economic Freedom," *The Nation*, June 15/22, 2020.

32. "Income Has Risen Through the COVID Recession but That May Soon Change," *Committee for a Responsible Federal Budget*, July 20, 2020.

33. A. Jäger and D. Zamora, "'Welfare Without the Welfare State': The Death of the Postwar Welfarist Consensus," *New Statesman*, February 9, 2021.

34. P. Baldwin, *The Politics of Social Solidarity: Class Bases of the European Welfare State, 1875–1975* (Cambridge University Press, 1990).

35. "State Aid: Commission Adopts Temporary Framework to Enable Member States to Further Support the Economy in the COVID-19 Outbreak," *European Commission*, March 19, 2020. D. Boffey, "Von der Leyen Warns State Aid 'Unlevelling the Playing Field' in Europe," *Guardian*, May 13, 2020.

36. OECD Economic Outlook, Volume 2020, Issue 1.

37. D. Autor, D. Cho, L. Crane, et al., "An Evaluation of the Paycheck Protection Program Using Administrative Payroll Microdata," *MIT Department of Economics*, July 22, 2020.

38. G. Hubbard and M. R. Strain, "Has the Paycheck Protection Program Succeeded?" *Brookings Papers on Economic Activity*, September 23, 2020.

39. L. Schalatek, "Urgently Wanted: A US Stimulus Package in Which More Than the Dollar Bills Are Green," *Heinrich Böll Stiftung*, July 2, 2020.

40. T. Healey, S. B. Herman, T. J. Lynes, and B. J. Seifarth, "COVID-19 Update: US Senate Passes $61 Billion Relief Package for Aviation Industry," *National Law Review* 11, no. 72 (March 26, 2020).

41. "COVID-19 and the Aviation Industry: Impact and Policy Responses," *OECD*, October 15, 2020.

42. J. Drucker, "The Tax-Break Bonanza Inside the Economic Rescue Package," *New York Times*, April 24, 2020.

43. C. Giles, "The Expensive Promise of England's Covid Test and Trace," *Financial Times*, October 15, 2020.

44. J. Bradley, S. Gebrekidan, and A. McCann, "Waste, Negligence and Cronyism: Inside Britain's Pandemic Spending," *New York Times*, December 17, 2020.

45. "Sovereign Borrowing Outlook for OECD Countries 2020," *Organisation for Economic Co-Operation and Development*, 2020.

46. "Sovereign Borrowing Outlook for OECD Countries 2020," OECD, "Sovereign Borrowing Outlook for OECD Countries 2021."

47. K. Seibel and H. Zschäpitz, "11,6 Milliarden Euro—Bund macht Rekordgewinn mit neuen Schulden," *Welt*, December 7, 2020.

48. Moody's Analytics, "Financial Markets Have Largely Priced-In 2021's Positive Outlook," www.moodysanalytics.com/-/media/article/2020/weekly-market-outlook-financial-markets-have-largely-priced-in-2021s-positive-outlook.pdf.

49. L. H. Summers, "Why Stagnation Might Prove to Be the New Normal," December 15, 2013. J. Furman and L. Summers, "A Reconsideration of Fiscal Policy in the Era of Low Interest Rates," November 30, 2020; www.brookings.edu/wp-content/uploads/2020/11/furman-summers-fiscal-reconsideration-discussion-draft.pdf.

50. O. Blanchard, "Public Debt and Low Interest Rates," *American Economic Review* 109, no. 4 (2019): 1197–229.

51. O. Blanchard, "Italian Debt Is Sustainable," *Peterson Institute for International Economics*, March 18, 2020.

52. Indeed, the Treasury itself built up a cash hoard in the process: L. McCormick, E. Barrett, and K. Greifeld, "American Investors Are Plugging the U.S.'s Record Budget Deficit," *Bloomberg*, July 12, 2020.

53. T. Stubbington and C. Giles, "Investors Sceptical over Bank of England's QE Programme," *Financial Times*, January 4, 2021.

54. B. Holland, L. McCormick, and J. Ainger, "Coronavirus Bills Are So Big, Only Money-Printing Can Pay Them," *Bloomberg*, May 15, 2020.

55. A. P. Lerner, "Functional Finance and the Federal Debt," *Social Research* 10, no. 1 (1943): 38–51.

56. For contrasting takes, see S. Kelton, *The Deficit Myth: Modern Monetary Theory and the Birth of the People's Economy* (PublicAffairs, 2020) and G. Selgin, *The Menace of Fiscal QE* (Cato Institute, 2020).

57. F. Coppola, *The Case for People's Quantitative Easing* (Wiley, 2019).

58. B. Bernanke, "What Tools Does the Fed Have Left? Part 3: Helicopter Money," *Brookings*, April 11, 2016.

59. E. Bartsch, J. Boivin, S. Fischer, and P. Hildebrand, "Dealing with the Next Downturn: From Unconventional Monetary Policy to Unprecedented Policy Coordination," *SUERF*, October 2019.

60. A. Yablon, "Wall Street Has Always Been Progressives' 'Big Bad.' But a New Generation in the Finance Industry Is Starting to Sound More Like Allies Than Enemies," *Insider*, December 6, 2020.

61. C. Goodhart and M. Pradhan, "The Great Demographic Reversal: Ageing Societies, Waning Inequality, and an Inflation Revival"; www.suerf.org/policynotes/17385/the-great-demographic-reversal -ageing-societies-waning-inequality-and-an-inflation-revival.

62. Stubbington and Giles, "Investors Sceptical over Bank of England's QE Programme."

63. Speech by I. Schnabel, "The Shadow of Fiscal Dominance: Misconceptions, Perceptions and Perspectives," *European Central Bank*, September 11, 2020.

64. Stubbington and Giles, "Investors Sceptical over Bank of England's QE Programme."

65. Bank of England, "Quantitative Easing"; www.bankofengland.co.uk/monetary-policy/quantitative -easing.

66. B. Braun, "Central Banking and the Infrastructural Power of Finance: The Case of ECB Support for Repo and Securitization Markets," *Socio-Economic Review* 18, no. 2 (2020): 395–418.

67. On Lerner's incomplete revolution, see M. Buchanan and Richard E. Wagner, *Democracy in Deficit: The Political Legacy of Lord Keynes* (Liberty Fund, 2000).

68. Speech by A. Haldane, "What Has Central Bank Independence Ever Done for Us?" *Bank of England*, November 28, 2020.

69. Tooze, *Crashed: How a Decade of Financial Crises Changed the World*.

70. B. Dudley, "When the Fed Tapers, the Market Will Have a Tantrum," *Bloomberg*, January 21, 2021. "Raghuram Rajan Says Another 'Taper Tantrum' Possible. What Is It?" *CNBC*, January 22, 2021.

71. J. Smialek, "How the Fed's Magic Machine Will Turn $454 Billion Into $4 Trillion," *New York Times*, March 27, 2020.

72. J. B. Bolzani, "Has the CARES Act Expanded the Red's Legal Mandate," *The FinReg Blog*, October 26, 2020. G. Selgin, "The Constitutional Case for the Fed's Treasury Backstops," *Cato Institute*, April 13, 2020.

73. G. Robb, "Fed Will Make Up to $4 Trillion in Loans to Businesses to Rescue the U.S. Economy, Mnuchin Says," *Market Watch*, March 28, 2020.

74. L. DePillis, J. Elliott, and P. Kiel, "The Big Corporate Rescue and the America That's Too Small to Save," *ProPublica*, September 12, 2020.

75. J. Rennison, "US Credit Market off to a Record Start in 2021," *Financial Times*, January 6, 2021.

76. "Companies Have Raised More Capital in 2020 Than Ever Before," *Economist*, December 10, 2020.

77. A. Tangel and D. Cameron, "Boeing Asks for $60 Billion in Aid for U.S. Aerospace Industry," *Wall Street Journal*, March 17, 2020.

78. Y. Torbati and A. Gregg, "How a $17 Billion Bailout Fund Intended for Boeing Ended Up in Very Different Hands," *Washington Post*, November 25, 2020.

79. K. Duguid, J. Franklin, and D. Shepardson, "How Boeing Went from Appealing for Government Aid to Snubbing It," *Reuters*, May 1, 2020.

80. D. Gates, "Boeing to Cut Thousands More Employees as Losses Mount," *Seattle Times*, October 28, 2020.

81. Periodic Report: Update on Outstanding Lending Facilities Authorized by the Board Under Section 13(3) of the Federal Reserve Act September 7, 2020, www.federalreserve.gov/publications

/files/pdcf-mmlf-cpff-pmccf-smccf-talf-mlf-ppplf-msnlf-mself-mslpf-nonlf-noelf-9-8-20.pdf
#page=3.

82. D. Scigliuzzo, S. Bakewell, and G. Gurumurthy, "Carnival Boosts Bond Sale After 12% Yield At-
    tracts $17 Billion," *Bloomberg*, April 1, 2020.

83. N. Randewich, "Big Tech Drives S&P 500 to Record High in Coronavirus Rally," *Reuters*, August
    18, 2020.

84. M. Rubinstein, "The Stock Market as Entertainment," *Net Interest*, June 5, 2020.

85. M. Fitzgerald, "Many Americans Used Part of Their Coronavirus Stimulus Check to Trade Stocks,"
    CNBC, May 21, 2020.

86. E. Wolff-Mann, "43% of Retail Investors Are Trading with Leverage," *Yahoo!*, September 9, 2020.

CHAPTER 8. THE TOOLKIT

1. J. Wheatley and A. Schipani, "Bolsonaro, Brazil and the Coronavirus Crisis in Emerging Markets,"
   Financial Times, April 19, 2020. "COVID-19 and Global Capital Flows," *Organisation for Economic
   Co-operation and Development*, July 3, 2020.

2. http://www.worldgovernmentbonds.com/cds-historical-data/brazil/5-years/.

3. Wheatley and Schipani, "Bolsonaro, Brazil and the Coronavirus Crisis in Emerging Markets."

4. "Global Financial Stability Report," *International Monetary Fund*, October 2019.

5. D. Gabor, "The Wall Street Consensus," *SocArXiv*, July 2, 2020.

6. H. Rey, "Dilemma Not Trilemma: The Global Financial Cycle and Monetary Policy Independence,"
   National Bureau of Economic Research Working Paper 21162, 2015.

7. International Monetary Fund press release, "The IMF Executive Board Discusses 'The Evolution of
   Public Debt Vulnerabilities in Lower Income Economics'"; www.imf.org/~/media/Files/Publications
   /PP/2020/English/PPEA2020003.ashx.

8. I. Grabel, *When Things Don't Fall Apart* (MIT Press, 2017), 197.

9. "Just in Case," *Economist*, October 10, 2013.

10. The following section is based on BIS Annual Economic Report, "Monetary Policy Frameworks in
    EMEs: Inflation Targeting, the Exchange Rate and Financial Stability," *Bank for International Set-
    tlements*, June 30, 2019.

11. G. Benigno, J. Hartley, et al., "Credible Emerging Market Central Banks Could Embrace Quantita-
    tive Easing to Fight COVID-19," *VoxEU*, June 29, 2020.

12. International Monetary Fund, World Bank Group, Staff Note for the International Financial Ar-
    chitecture Working Group, "Recent Developments on Local Currency Bond Markets in Emerging
    Economies," January 27, 2020; documents1.worldbank.org/curated/en/129961580334830825/pdf
    /Staff-Note-for-the-G20-International-Financial-Architecture-Working-Group-IFAWG-Recent
    -Developments-On-Local-Currency-Bond-Markets-In-Emerging-Economies.pdf.

13. A. Carstens and H. S. Shin, "Emerging Markets Aren't Safe Yet," *Foreign Affairs*, March 15, 2019.

14. L. Borodovsky, "Stock Valuation Metrics Look Increasingly Stretched," *Daily Shot*, January 12,
    2021.

15. O. Negus, "The Chiang Mai Initiative Multilateralization (CMIM): If Not Now, Then When?,"
    Center for Strategic and International Studies, September 1, 2020. W. N. Kring and W. W. Grimes,
    "Leaving the Nest: The Rise of Regional Financial Arrangements and the Future of Global Gover-
    nance," *Development and Change* 50, no. 1 (2019): 72–95.

16. B. Steil, "Central Bank Currency Swaps Tracker," *Council on Foreign Relations*, November 5, 2019.

17. J. Frost, H. Ito, and R. van Stralen, "The Effectiveness of Macroprudential Policies and Capital
    Controls Against Volatile Capital Inflows," *BIS Working Papers*, June 2, 2020.

18. I. Grabel, "The Rebranding of Capital Controls in an Era of Productive Incoherence," *Review of
    International Political Economy* 22, no. 1 (2015): 7–43. I. Grabel, "Capital Controls in a Time of
    Crisis," in G. A. Epstein, ed., *The Political Economy of International Finance in an Age of Inequality*
    (Edward Elgar Publishing, 2018), 69–105.

19. BIS Annual Economic Report, "Monetary Policy Frameworks in EMEs: Inflation Targeting, the
    Exchange Rate and Financial Stability," *Bank for International Settlements*, June 30, 2019.

20. Grabel, "The Rebranding of Capital Controls in an Era of Productive Incoherence."

21. FAO, IFAD, UNICEF, WFP, and WHO, *The State of Food Security and Nutrition in the World 2020.
    Transforming Food Systems for Affordable Healthy Diets*, 2020.

22. "Transcript of IMF Press Briefing," *International Monetary Fund*, May 21, 2020.

23. Extraordinary G2 Leaders' Summit: Statement on COVID-19, March 26, 2020; www.g20.utoronto .ca/2020/2020-g20-statement-0326.html.

24. "The Great Lockdown: Worst Economic Downturn Since the Great Depression," *International Monetary Fund*, March 23, 2020.

25. "Only Victory in Africa Can End the Pandemic Everywhere," *Financial Times*, April 14, 2020.

26. K. Georgieva, "Statement on the United States Congress Move to Strengthen the IMF's Resources," *International Monetary Fund*, March 27, 2020.

27. OECD Economic Outlook, Volume 2020, Issue 1.

28. Table 3: I. Fresnillo, "Shadow Report on the Limitations of the G20 Debt Service Suspension Initiative: Draining Out the Titanic with a Bucket?," *Eurodad*, October 14, 2020.

29. Georgieva, "Statement on the United States Congress Move to Strengthen the IMF's Resources."

30. P. Bolton, L. Buchheit, P.-O. Gourinchas, et al., "Born Out of Necessity: A Debt Standstill for COVID-19," *Centre for Economic Policy Research*, April 2020.

31. T. Stubbs, W. Kring, C. Laskaridis, et al., "Whatever It Takes? The Global Financial Safety Net, Covid-19, and Developing Countries," *World Development* 137 (2021): 105171.

32. D. Munevar, "Arrested Development: International Monetary Fund Lending and Austerity Post Covid-19," *Eurodad*, October 26, 2020. S. Ambrose, "In the Midst of the Pandemic, Why Is the IMF Still Pushing Austerity on the Global South?" *Open Democracy*, October 13, 2020.

33. Y. Arslan, M. Drehmann, and B. Hofmann, "Central Bank Bond Purchases in Emerging Market Economies," *BIS Bulletin*, June 2, 2020. "Emerging Markets' Experiments with QE Have Not Turned Out Too Badly," *Economist*, October 29, 2020.

34. G. Beningo, J. Hartley, et al., "Credible Emerging Market Central Banks Could Embrace Quantitative Easing to Fight COVID-19," *VoxEU*, June 29, 2020.

35. OECD Policy Responses to Coronavirus (COVID-19), "COVID-19 and Global Capital Flows," July 3, 2020.

36. OECD, "COVID-19 and Global Capital Flows."

37. A. W. Akhlas, "Bank Indonesia in Talks with US, China on Currency Swaps," *Jakarta Post*, April 2, 2020. "Indonesia Central Bank Says in Talks with U.S. Fed, China on Swap Lines," *Reuters*, April 2, 2020. K. Salna and T. Sipahutar, "Indonesia Says New York Fed Offers $60 Billion Credit Line," *Bloomberg*, April 7, 2020.

38. www.worldgovernmentbonds.com/cds-historical-data/indonesia/5-years/.

39. C. Goko, "Africa's Junk Bonds Among Hottest Investments with Big Yields," *Bloomberg*, June 4, 2020.

40. P. Naidoo, "After More Than 25 Years S. Africa Is Now Junk with Moody's Too," *Bloomberg*, March 27, 2020.

41. "South Africa Borrows from the IMF for the First Time Since Apartheid," *Economist*, August 1, 2020.

42. International Monetary Fund African Dept., "Regional Economic Outlook, October 2020, Sub-Saharan Africa: A Difficult Road to Recovery," *IMF*, October 22, 2020.

43. *Eurodad*, "A Debt Pandemic," Briefing Paper March 2021.

44. G. Long, "Ecuador's Virus-Hit Guayaquil Is Grim Warning for Region," *Financial Times*, April 5, 2020.

45. R. Dube and J. de Córdoba, "Ecuador City Beat One of World's Worst Outbreaks of Covid-19," *Wall Street Journal*, June 30, 2020.

46. K. Brown, "Coronavirus Pandemic Exposes Inequality in Ecuador's Guayaquil," *Al Jazeera*, May 27, 2020.

47. "Latin America's Health Systems Brace for a Battering," *Economist*, April 11, 2020.

48. G. Long, "Peru Tries to Emerge from Shadow of Corruption Scandal," *Financial Times*, March 12, 2020.

49. G. Long, "Ecuadorean Bonds Drop as Government Calls for Time," *Financial Times*, March 24, 2020.

50. G. Long and C. Smith, "Ecuador Reaches Deal to Postpone Debt Repayments Until August," *Financial Times*, April 17, 2020.

51. G. Long, "Ecuador Takes Far-Reaching Measures to Save Economy," *Financial Times*, May 20, 2020.

52. M. Stott, "Coronavirus Set to Push 29m Latin Americans into Poverty," *Financial Times*, April 27, 2020.

53. "Peru Is Heading Towards a Dangerous New Populism," *Economist*, July 25, 2020.
54. G. Long, "Venezuelan Migrants Face Tough Choices as Virus Spreads," *Financial Times*, April 23, 2020.
55. Long, "Venezuelan Migrants Face Tough Choices as Virus Spreads."
56. "Covid-19 Hastens Changes to Chile's Market-Led Economic Model," *Economist*, July 18, 2020.
57. "Covid-19 Hastens Changes to Chile's Market-Led Economic Model." M. Stott and A. Schipani, "Fears Mount of a Fresh Latin American Debt Crisis," *Financial Times*, July 21, 2020.
58. E. Martin, "IMF Builds a $107 Billion Safety Net Under Key Latin Economies," *Bloomberg*, June 19, 2020.
59. M. B. Sheridan, "Mexico's Pandemic Policy: No Police. No Curfews. No Fines. No Regrets," *Washington Post*, January 26, 2021.
60. S. Pérez and A. Harrup, "Mexico's Leftist President Becomes Fiscal Hawk in Midst of Pandemic," *Wall Street Journal*, December 2, 2020.
61. O. Dyer, "Covid-19: Mexico Acknowledges 50,000 More Deaths Than Official Figures Show," *BMJ* 2020; 371: m4182.
62. L. Nassif-Pires, L. Carvalho, and E. Rawet, "Multidimensional Inequality and Covid-19 in Brazil," *Levy Economics Institute of Bard College*, Public Policy Brief No. 153, September 2020.
63. B. Harris and A. Schipani, "Virus Compounds Brazil's Prolonged Economic Slump," *Financial Times*, June 17, 2020.
64. "Brazil Faces Hard Spending Choices in 2021," *Economist*, December 16, 2020.
65. M. Viotti Beck and A. Rosati, "Brazil's Coronavirus Splurge Is Sparking a Rebellion in Markets," *Bloomberg*, October 27, 2020.
66. B. Harris, "Brazil's Economy Rebounds in Third Quarter," *Financial Times*, December 3, 2020.
67. ECLAC Special Report No. 5, "Addressing the Growing Impact of COVID-19 with a View to Reactivation with Equality: New Projections," July 15, 2020; repositorio.cepal.org/bitstream/handle/11362/45784/1/S2000470_en.pdf.
68. C. Smith and G. Long, "Peru Joins Select Group of Nations Selling Century Bonds," *Financial Times*, November 23, 2020.
69. M. Margolis, "Covid-19's Toll Will Rewrite Latin America's Future," *Bloomberg*, July 1, 2020.
70. Stott, "Coronavirus Set to Push 29m Latin Americans Into Poverty."
71. Pérez and A. Harrup, "Mexico's Leftist President Becomes Fiscal Hawk in Midst of Pandemic."
72. M. Viotti Beck, "Brazil Economy Chief Vows Fiscal Control If Virus Hits Again," *Bloomberg*, November 10, 2020.
73. Harris, "Brazil's Economy Rebounds in Third Quarter."
74. M. Sergio Lima and C. Lucchesi, "Fraga Warns 'Combustible' Situation Brewing in Brazilian Markets," *Bloomberg*, October 15, 2020.

CHAPTER 9. NEXTGEN EU

1. R. J. Samuelson, "Opinion: Why Italy's Debt Matters for Everybody," *Washington Post*, May 24, 2020.
2. M. Ashworth, "Italy's Debt Is Less Terrifying Than It Looks," *Bloomberg*, April 9, 2020.
3. A. Tooze, *Crashed: How a Decade of Financial Crises Changed the World* (Viking, 2018).
4. R. Olivares-Caminal, "The New EU Architecture to Avert a Sovereign Debt Crisis: EFSM, EFSF & ESM," October 2011; www.oecd.org/daf/fin/48887542.pdf.
5. J. Detrixhe, "Europe's 'Doom Loop' of Government Debt Is Alive and Well," *Quartz*, May 13, 2020.
6. "Financial Stability Review," *European Central Bank*, May 2020.
7. Eurostat, "First Quarter of 2020 Compared with Fourth Quarter of 2019," ec.europa.eu/eurostat/documents/2995521/11129607/2-22072020-AP-EN.pdf/ab6cd4ff-ec57-d984-e85a-41a351df1ffd.
8. L. van Middelaar, *Alarums and Excursions: Improvising Politics on the European Stage* (Agenda Publishing, 2019).
9. ECB Press Conference March 12, 2020; www.ecb.europa.eu/press/pressconf/2020/html/ecb.is200312~f857a21b6c.en.html.
10. J. Randow and P. Skolimowski, "Christine Lagarde's $810 Billion U-Turn Came in Just Four Weeks," *Bloomberg*, April 6, 2020.
11. "Loose Lips Cost Ships: Lagarde's Language and Italy's EUR14 Billion Bill," *General Theorist*, May 15, 2020; thegeneraltheorist.com/category/lagarde.

12. "ECB Announces €750 Billion Pandemic Emergency Purchase Programme (PEPP)," press release, *European Central Bank*, March 18, 2020.
13. F. Canepa and B. Koranyi, "Exclusive: ECB's Lagarde Overruled German and Dutch Resistance to 'No-Limits' Pledge—Sources," *Reuters*, March 19, 2020.
14. D. Dombey, G. Chazan, and J. Brunsden, "Nine Eurozone Countries Issue Call for 'Coronabonds,'" *Financial Times*, March 15, 2020.
15. D. M. Herszenhorn, J. Barigazzi, and R. Momtaz, "Virtual Summit, Real Acrimony: EU Leaders Clash Over 'Corona Bonds,'" *Politico*, March 27, 2020.
16. M. Karnitschnig, "The Inconvenient Truth About Ursula von der Leyen," *Politico*, July 2, 2019. B. Judah, "The Rise of Mrs Europe," *Critic*, October 2020.
17. Interview with E. Macron, "Macron: Coronavirus Is Europe's 'Moment of Truth,'" *Financial Times*, April 16, 2020; https://www.ft.com/video/96240572-7e35-4fcd-aecb-8f503d529354.
18. N. de Boer and J. van 't Klooster, "The ECB, the Courts and the Issue of Democratic Legitimacy After Weiss," *Common Market Law Review* 57, no. 6 (2020): 1689–724.
19. J. Collings, *Democracy's Guardians* (Oxford University Press, 2015).
20. D. Grimm, "A Long Time Coming," *German Law Journal* 21, no. 5 (2020): 944–49.
21. A. Tooze, "The Death of the Central Bank Myth," *Foreign Policy*, May 13, 2020.
22. J. Goldstein, "A Gold Bug's Moment in the Political Sun," *Planet Money*, NPR, January 23, 2012. R. Paul, *End the Fed* (Grand Central Publishing, 2009). R. Sharma, "Will Bitcoin End the Dollar's Reign?" *Financial Times*, December 9, 2020. M. Stoller, "How the Federal Reserve Fights," *Naked Capitalism*, December 12, 2011.
23. Two leading examples are www.positivemoney.eu/ and dezernatzukunft.org/en/category/monetarypolicy/.
24. P. Tucker, *Unelected Power: The Quest for Legitimacy in Central Banking and the Regulatory State* (Princeton University Press, 2018).
25. S. Kinkartz, "Corona-krise: Was haben die deutschen gegen Eurobonds?" *DW*, April 22, 2020.
26. S. Klusmann, "Germany Must Abandon Its Rejection of Eurobonds," *Der Spiegel*, April 4, 2020.
27. "Merkel: Keine Eurobonds, 'solange ich lebe,'" *Der Tagesspiegel*, June 26, 2012.
28. B. Pancevski and L. Norman, "How Angela Merkel's Change of Heart Drove Historic EU Rescue Plan," *Wall Street Journal*, July 21, 2020.
29. S. Amaro, "EU Unveils Plan to Borrow 750 Billion Euros to Aid Economic Recovery," *CNBC*, May 27, 2020.
30. G. Chazan, S. Fleming, V. Mallet, and J. Brunsden, "Coronavirus Crisis Revives Franco-German Relations," *Financial Times*, April 13, 2020.
31. A. Tooze, "It's a New Europe—If You Can Keep It," *Foreign Policy*, August 7, 2020.
32. C. Pazzanese, "Angela Merkel, the Scientist Who Became a World Leader," *Harvard Gazette*, May 28, 2019.
33. H. von der Burchard and E. Schaart, "Dutch Face Friendly Fire as Corona Bond Bad Cops," *Politico*, March 30, 2020.
34. "EU 'Frugals' Formally Oppose Merkel-Macron Plan for Coronavirus Grants," *CNBC*, May 23, 2020.
35. D. Herszenhorn, L. Bayer, and R. Momtaz, "The Coronavirus Plan That von der Leyen built," *Politico*, July 15, 2020.
36. D. Herszenhorn and L. Bayer, "EU Leaders Agree on €1.82T Budget and Coronavirus Package," *Politico*, July 21, 2020.
37. EU Commission, Recovery and Resilience Facility, ec.europa.eu/info/business-economy-euro/recovery-coronavirus/recovery-and-resilience-facility_en.
38. European Council Conclusions July 17–21, 2020; www.consilium.europa.eu/en/press/press-releases/2020/07/21/european-council-conclusions-17-21-july-2020. G. Claeys and S. Tagliapietra, "Is the EU Council Agreement Aligned with the Green Deal Ambitions?" *Bruegel Blog*, July 23, 2020.
39. L. Guttenberg, J. Hemker, and S. Tordoir, "Everything Will Be Different: How the Pandemic Is Changing EU Economic Governance," *Hertie School, Jacques Delors Centre*, February 11, 2021.
40. O. Konotey-Ahulu and J. Ainger, "Big Bond Traders Double Down on Their Bet on Europe," *Bloomberg*, August 4, 2020.
41. O. Konotey-Ahulu and N. Jagadeesh, "Euro Skeptics Are Now Believers and It's Driving Markets Higher," *Bloomberg*, July 24, 2020.
42. Z. Darvas, "Next Generation EU Payments Across Countries and Years," *Bruegel Blog*, November 12, 2020.

43. A. Consiglio and S. Zenios, "Growth Uncertainty, European Central Bank Intervention and the Italian Debt," *Bruegel Blog*, October 28, 2020.

44. M. Huertas, H. Schelling, and C. von Berg, "Resolving Karlsruhe—What's Happened Since?" *JD Supra*, July 7, 2020.

45. K. Hempel, "Anleihekäufe erneut Thema in Karlsruhe," *Tagesschau*, May 8, 2020. C. Siedenbiedel, "Ultimatum abgelaufen—die EZB scheint aus dem Schneider," *Frankfurter Allgemeine Zeitung*, May 8, 2020.

46. E. Lonergan, "European Central Bank Has One Item Left in Its Toolkit: Dual Rates," *Financial Times*, January 1, 2020.

47. J. Sindreu, "In Europe, Monetary Policy Is All About Giving Banks Free Money," *Wall Street Journal*, December 10, 2020.

48. www.ecb.europa.eu/press/key/date/2021/html/ecb.sp210325~e424a7f6cf.en.html).

49. L. Alderman, "Lagarde Vows to Put Climate Change on the E.C.B.'s Agenda," *New York Times*, September 4, 2019.

50. "Christine Lagarde Meets with Positive Money Europe," *Positive Money Europe*, December 4, 2019. M. Arnold, "ECB to Consider Using Climate Risk to Steer Bond Purchases," *Financial Times*, October 14, 2020.

51. C. Look, "Lagarde Says ECB Needs to Question Market Neutrality on Climate," *Bloomberg*, October 14, 2020.

52. K. Oroschakoff and K. Mathiesen, "How the EU's Green Deal Survived the Coronavirus Pandemic," *Politico*, December 17, 2020.

53. The best running guide to this mayhem in 2020 for many years has been twitter.com/70sBachchan.

54. A. Thompson, "A Running List of Record-Breaking Natural Disasters in 2020," *Scientific American*, December 22, 2020.

55. T. Fuller, "Coronavirus Limits California's Efforts to Fight Fires with Prison Labor," *New York Times*, August 22, 2020.

56. J. Poushter and C. Huang, "Despite Pandemic, Many Europeans Still See Climate Change as Greatest Threat to Their Countries," *Pew Research Center*, September 9, 2020.

57. A. Tooze, "The Fierce Urgency of COP26," *Social Europe*, January 20, 2020.

58. European Commission, Regulation of the European Parliament and of the Council establishing the framework for achieving climate neutrality, eur-lex.europa.eu/legal-content/EN/TXT/?uri=CELEX:52020PC0080.

59. C. Farand, "Poland Bails Out Coal, Yet Wins Access to EU Climate Funds," *Climate Change News*, July 21, 2020.

60. M. Karnitschnig, D. M. Herszenhorn, J. Barigazzi, and A. Gray, "Merkel Rebuffs Trump Invitation to G7 Summit," *Politico*, May 29, 2020.

61. "VW to Put $17.5bn into China's Electric Cars," *Asia Times*, September 28, 2020.

62. C. Early, "The EU Can Expect Heavy Pushback on Its Carbon Border Tax," *China Dialogue*, September 1, 2020. "Commission Launches Public Consultations on Energy Taxation and a Carbon Border Adjustment Mechanism," *European Commission*, July 23, 2020.

63. D. Sheppard, "Price of Polluting in EU Rises as Carbon Price Hits Record High," *Financial Times*, December 11, 2020.

64. "China Eyes Launch of National Emissions Trade Scheme Within Five Years," *Reuters*, October 28, 2020. H. Slater, "Despite Headwinds, China Prepares for World's Largest Carbon Market," *Lowy Institute*, May 5, 2020. ec.europa.eu/clima/policies/ets/markets_en. K. Appunn, "Emission Reduction Panacea or Recipe for Trade War? The EU's Carbon Border Tax Debate," *Clean Energy Wire*, November 30, 2020. E. Krukowska and J. Shankleman, "Carbon Border Tax: Europe May Not Need a Climate Levy as Biden Targets Pollution," *Bloomberg*, November 16, 2020.

65. F. Simon, "MEP Canfin: EU's Carbon Border Adjustment Mechanism 'Is Not a Tax,'" *Euractiv*, December 17, 2020.

CHAPTER 10. CHINA: MOMENTUM

1. "U.S.-China Joint Presidential Statement on Climate Change," September 25, 2015; obamawhitehouse.archives.gov/the-press-office/2015/09/25/us-china-joint-presidential-statement-climate-change.

2. Remarks by President Trump to the 75th Session of the United Nations General Assembly, September 22, 2020; it.usembassy.gov/remarks-by-president-trump-to-the-75th-session-of-the-united-nations-general-assembly-september-22-2020.

3. "Statement by H.E. Xi Jinping President of the People's Republic of China at the General Debate of the 75th Session of the United Nations General Assembly," September 22, 2020; www.fmprc.gov.cn/mfa_eng/zxxx_662805/t1817098.shtml.

4. "The Secret Origins of China's 40-Year Plan to End Carbon Emissions," *Bloomberg Green*, November 22, 2020.

5. A. Weeden and S. Yang, "China's Carbon Neutral by 2060 Pledge Has Wowed Some, but Where Is the Detail?" *ABC News*, September 24, 2020.

6. H. Spross, "China: An Unpopular Winner in the Year of the Coronavirus," *DW*, October 27, 2020.

7. T. Nordhaus and S. Wang, "China Breaks Decades of Climate Gridlock," *Foreign Policy*, January 11, 2021.

8. J. McCurry, "South Korea Vows to Go Carbon Neutral by 2050 to Fight Climate Emergency," *Guardian*, October 28, 2020.

9. L. Silver, K. Devlin, and C. Huang, "Unfavorable Views of China Reach Historic Highs in Many Countries," *Pew Research Center*, October 6, 2020.

10. S. L. Myers, K. Bradsher, S.-L. Wee, and C. Buckley, "Power, Patriotism and 1.4 Billion People: How China Beat the Virus and Roared Back," *New York Times*, February 5, 2021.

11. M. Wilson, "The Untold Origin Story of the N95 Mask," *Fast Company*, March 24, 2020.

12. K. Bradsher and L. Alderman, "The World Needs Masks. China Makes Them, but Has Been Hoarding Them," *New York Times*, March 13, 2020.

13. H. Mowbray, "Trending in China: Wholesale Mask Prices Fall Over 90% and Raw Materials Fall to Fraction of Peak Price," *CX Tech*, July 15, 2020.

14. D. Stojanovic, "China's 'Mask Diplomacy' Wins Support in Eastern Europe," *AP News*, April 14, 2020.

15. A. Lo, "Beijing Loses Face with 'Face-Mask Diplomacy,'" *South China Morning Post*, April 23, 2020.

16. A. Frachon, "Dissecting China's Failed Experiment at Face Mask Diplomacy," *Worldcrunch*, April 7, 2020. L. Jacinto, "Can the Unmasking of China's Covid-19 'Mask Diplomacy' Stem Beijing's Global Power Grab?" *France 24*, January 5, 2020.

17. S. Denyer, "Japan Pays 87 Companies to Break from China After Pandemic Exposed Overreliance," *Washington Post*, July 21, 2020.

18. R. Baldwin and S. Evenett, "COVID-19 and Trade Policy: Why Turning Inward Won't Work," *VoxEU*, April 29, 2020.

19. A. Beattie, "Coronavirus-Induced 'Reshoring' Is Not Happening," *Financial Times*, September 30, 2020.

20. "Is a Wave of Supply-Chain Reshoring Around the Corner," *Economist*, December 16, 2020.

21. Vyacheslav Polovinko, "Russia Feeds China," *Novaya Gazeta*, March 27, 2020.

22. H. Le Thu, "Vietnam: A Successful Battle Against the Virus," Council on Foreign Relations, April 30, 2020.

23. L. Schlein, "UN Begins Airlift to Help Africa Fight Coronavirus," *Voice of America*, April 14, 2020.

24. C. Sanborn, "Latin America and China in Times of COVID-19," *Wilson Center*, 2020.

25. M. Paarlberg, "China Was Already Winning over the US's Neighbors. Trump's COVID-19 Response Just Makes Beijing's Job Easier," *Business Insider*, August 27, 2020.

26. G. Wu, "Continuous Purges: Xi's Control of the Public Security Apparatus and the Changing Dynamics of CCP Elite Politics," *China Leadership Monitor*, December 1, 2020.

27. "Ant Group Announces Plans to List in Shanghai and Hong Kong," *Economist*, July 25, 2020.

28. N. Somasundaram and N. Sun, "China Inc.'s Role in Hong Kong Grows After Security Law," *Nikkei*, November 18, 2020.

29. "Government Should Increase Recurrent Expenditure by HK$36.7B," *Oxfam*, September 25, 2018; www.oxfam.org.hk/en/news-and-publication/inequality-alarming-as-city-s-richest-earn-44-times-more-than-poorest.

30. P. Ngai, "Reflecting on Hong Kong Protests in 2019–2020," *HAU: Journal of Ethnographic Theory* 10, no. 2 (Autumn 2020). "The Turmoil in Hong Kong Stems in Part from Its Unaffordable Housing," *Economist*, August 24, 2019.

31. S. Tiezzi, "Hong Kong's Elections Were Already Rigged. Now They Won't Happen," *Diplomat*, August 1, 2020.

32. "Why Business in Hong Kong Should Be Worried," *Economist*, July 18, 2020.
33. "Nathan Law Says the Battle Is Not Over in Hong Kong," *Economist*, November 17, 2020.
34. "Leaving in Despair—Hong Kong's Legislature Has Been Stripped of a Vocal Opposition," *Economist*, November 12, 2020.
35. "Why Business in Hong Kong Should Be Worried," *Economist*.
36. P. Riordan, "Hong Kong's Bourse Reaps Benefits of China Homecomings," *Financial Times*, July 7, 2020.
37. H. Lockett, "Chinese Investors Flood Hong Kong's Bruised Stock Market with Cash," *Financial Times*, January 12, 2021.
38. P. Riordan, "HSBC and StanChart Publicly Back China's Hong Kong Security Law," *Financial Times*, June 3, 2020.
39. T. Kihara, "Hong Kong Tilts Further Toward Beijing with Carrie Lam's Trip," *Nikkei*, November 7, 2020.
40. T. Summers, "China's Greater Bay Area Has Real Economic Power," *Chatham House*, September 20, 2018.
41. "Xi Jinping Is Trying to Remake the Chinese Economy," *Economist*, August 15, 2020.
42. "China Rises to Top Engine of Global Economic Growth in 70 Years," *Xinhua*, August 29, 2020.
43. Jingshan Report, 2020, "Release China's New Advantage of the Super-Large Market"; new.cf40.org .cn/uploads/2020_Jingshan_Report.pdf.
44. J. Garber, "Ray Dalio on China: 'This Ain't Your Grandfather's Communism,'" *Fox Business*, January 22, 2020.
45. "Bridgewater's Dalio Supports Ant IPO Suspension, Bullish on China," *Reuters*, November 11, 2020.
46. R. Kapadia, "The Biggest Investment Opportunity for Americans Is China, Bridgewater's Karen Karniol-Tambour Says," *Barron's*, December 4, 2020.
47. "Is Wall Street Winning in China?" *Economist*, September 5, 2020.
48. L. Wei, B. Davis, and D. Lim, "China Has One Powerful Friend Left in the U.S.: Wall Street," *Wall Street Journal*, December 2, 2020.
49. G. Wilson, "China's Digital Currency Is a Game Changer (Part 1)," *Money: Inside and Out*, January 3, 2021.
50. A. Galbraith, "Explainer: Foreign Access to China's $16 Trillion Bond Market," *Reuters*, September 23, 2020.
51. Y. Hairong, Z. Yuzhe, and D. Jia, "In Depth: Should China's Central Bank Buy Treasury Bonds?," *Caixin*, May 25, 2020.
52. "China's Economists Debate Deficit Monetization," *Economist*, May 30, 2020.
53. "China's Economists Debate Deficit Monetization."
54. "China's Economists Debate Deficit Monetization."
55. "China's Rulers Will Pay a High Price for Repression in Hong Kong," *Economist*, August 22, 2020.
56. J. Miller, "Daimler Chief Hails 'V-Shaped' Recovery in China Car Sales," *Financial Times*, December 3, 2020.
57. A. Pandey, "Auto China 2020: German Carmakers Look to Switch Gears," *DW*, September 25, 2020.
58. X. Yu, F. Yoon, and J. Yang, "When Oil Prices Went Negative, Investors in China Took a Hit," *Wall Street Journal*, April 23, 2020.
59. H. Sanderson, "China Aims for More Sway over Copper Prices with Future Launch," *Financial Times*, November 18, 2020.
60. S. Sundria, G. Freitas Jr., and R. Graham, "China to Take Oil-Refining Crown Held by U.S. Since 19th Century," *Bloomberg*, November 21, 2020.
61. S. Shehadi, "BASF's $10bn China Plant Followed 'Market Logic Not Trade War,'" *FDI Intelligence*, January 8, 2019. J. Zhu, "BASF Kicks Off China Megaproject," *FDI Intelligence*, December 16, 2019.
62. Silver, Devlin, and Huang, "Unfavorable Views of China Reach Historic Highs in Many Countries."
63. M. Landler, *Alter Egos: Hillary Clinton, Barack Obama, and the Twilight Struggle Over American Power* (Random House, 2016).
64. D. Palmer, "Clinton Raved About Trans-Pacific Partnership Before She Rejected It," *Politico*, October 8, 2016.
65. S. Baliño, "With RCEP Agreement Signed, Eyes Turn to Interactions Among Trade Deals in the Asia-Pacific Region," *IISD*, November 25, 2020; sdg.iisd.org/commentary/policy-briefs/with-rcep -agreement-signed-eyes-turn-to-interactions-among-trade-deals-in-the-asia-pacific-region/.
66. M. Ryan, "China-Australia Clash: How It Started and How It's Going," *Nikkei Asia*, December 9, 2020.

67. J. Varano, "Most Read of 2020: The State of Victoria and China's Belt and Road Initiative: Where Does It Leave Victorians?" *Australian Institute of International Affairs*, January 6, 2021.

68. P. Ranald, "We've Just Signed the World's Biggest Trade Deal, but What Exactly Is the RCEP?," *The Conversation*, November 16, 2020.

69. R. Intan, "What RCEP Can Tell Us About Geopolitics in Asia," *The Interpreter*, December 1, 2020.

70. N. Blarel, "Rising India: Status and Power," *International Affairs* 95, no. 4 (2019): 957–58.

71. M. Goswani, *Producing India: From Colonial Economy to National Space* (University of Chicago Press, 2004).

72. C. Jaffrelot, "From Slowdown to Lockdown, India's Economy and the COVID-19 Shock," *Institut Montaigne*, June 11, 2020.

73. S. Gupta and S. Ganguly, "Why India Refused to Join the RCEP, the World's Biggest Trading Bloc," *Foreign Policy*, November 23, 2020. S. Chatterjee, "India's Inward (Re)Turn: Is It Warranted? Will It Work?" *Ashoka Centre for Economic Policy*, October 2020.

74. S. Singh, "Why China Is Winning Against India," *Foreign Policy*, January 1, 2021.

75. M. Billah, "Is Bangladesh Growing Closer to China at the Expense of Its Relations with India?," *The Diplomat*, September 23, 2020.

76. C. R. Mohan, "India's Growing Strategic and Economic Interests in the Quad," December 1, 2020; valdaiclub.com/a/highlights/india-s-growing-strategic-and-economic-interests.

77. "China to Overtake US as Largest Global Economy by 2028: Report," *DW*, December 26, 2020; p.dw.com/p/3nE83.

78. L. Summers, "Can Anything Hold Back China's Economy?," December 5, 2018; larrysummers.com /2018/12/05/can-anything-hold-back-chinas-economy.

79. United States Strategic Approach to the People's Republic of China, May 20, 2020; www.defense .gov/Newsroom/Releases/Release/Article/2193725/united-states-strategic-approach-to-the -peoples-republic-of-china.

80. C. Bown, "How Trump's Export Curbs on Semiconductors and Equipment Hurt the US Technology Sector," Peterson Institute for International Economics, September 28, 2020; www.piie.com /blogs/trade-and-investment-policy-watch/how-trumps-export-curbs-semiconductors-and -equipment-hurt-us.

81. A. Kharpal, "U.S. Sanctions on Chipmaker SMIC Hit at the Very Heart of China's Tech Ambitions," *CNBC*, September 28, 2020.

82. C. Bown, "How the United States Marched the Semiconductor Industry into Its Trade War with China," Peterson Institute for International Economics, December 2020; www.piie.com/sites/default /files/documents/wp20-16.pdf.

83. Bown, "How Trump's Export Curbs on Semiconductors and Equipment Hurt the US Technology Sector."

84. J. Crabtree, "China's Radical New Vision of Globalization," *Noema*, December 10, 2020.

85. "China's Got a New Plan to Overtake the U.S. in Tech," *Bloomberg*, May 20, 2020.

86. www.federalregister.gov/documents/2020/12/22/2020-28031/addition-of-entities-to-the-entity -list-revision-of-entry-on-the-entity-list-and-removal-of-entities.

87. "Britain Lets Huawei into Part of Its 5G Networks," *Economist*, April 24, 2019.

88. A. Timsit, "The UK Will Ban Huawei from Its 5G Network Earlier Than Expected," *Quartz*, November 27, 2020.

89. W. Boston and S. Woo, "Huawei Gets Conditional Green Light in Germany as Government Approves Security Bill," *Wall Street Journal*, December 16, 2020.

90. K. Bennhold and J. Ewing, "In Huawei Battle, China Threatens Germany 'Where It Hurts': Automakers," *New York Times*, January 16, 2020.

91. United States Strategic Approach to the People's Republic of China, May 20, 2020.

CHAPTER 11. AMERICA'S NATIONAL CRISIS

1. K. Bennhold, "Germany's Coronavirus Protests Anti-Vaxxers, Anticapitalists, Neo-Nazis," *New York Times*, May 18, 2020. "Protests Against Coronavirus Lockdown Measures Spread in the UK and Across Europe," *ABC News*, May 16, 2020. W. Callison and Q. Slobodian, "Coronapolitics from the Reichstag to the Capitol," *Boston Review*, January 12, 2021.

2. A. Abad-Santos, "How Hair Became a Culture War in Quarantine," *Vox*, June 10, 2020.

3. L. Graves, "Who's Behind the 'Reopen' Protests?" *New York Times*, April 22, 2020.

4. E. Levitz, "Is This What a Recovery Looks Like?," *Intelligencer*, June 6, 2020.

5. L. Buchanan, Q. Bui, and J. K. Patel, "Black Lives Matter May Be the Largest Movement in U.S. History," *New York Times*, July 3, 2020.

6. T. McErney, "Jamie Dimon Drops Into Mt. Kisco Chase Branch, Takes a Knee with Staff," *New York Post*, June 5, 2020.

7. "Serious Help May Be on the Way for America's Black Entrepreneurs," *Economist*, December 10, 2020.

8. E. Levitz, "Corporate America Loves Increasing Racial Inequality," *Intelligencer*, June 16, 2020.

9. L. Seligman, "Esper Orders Hundreds of Troops from 82nd Airborne Home from D.C. Area," *Politico*, June 4, 2020.

10. A. Nally, "The Curfews in Place in US Cities and States After the Death of Black Man George Floyd," *ABC News*, June 2, 2020.

11. F. Finchelstein, "Trump's Mount Rushmore Speech Is the Closest He's Come to Fascism," *Foreign Policy*, July 8, 2020.

12. D. Choi, "G7 Countries Fail to Deliver a Joint Statement Because US Insists on Saying 'Wuhan Virus' for the Coronavirus," *Insider*, March 25, 2020.

13. D. J. Lynch and E. Rauhala, "Trump Says U.S. to Withdraw from World Health Organization and Announces New Broadsides Against Beijing," *Washington Post*, May 29, 2020.

14. G. Schmitt, "Pompeo's China Speech at Odds with Trump's 'America First' Foreign Policy," *The Hill*, July 25, 2020.

15. L. Green, "America's Top Cop Is a Rightwing Culture Warrior Who Hates Disorder. What Could Go Wrong?," *Guardian*, June 6, 2020.

16. T. Czuczka, "Barr Says U.S. Businesses 'Part of Problem' in Battling China," *Bloomberg*, June 21, 2020.

17. AG William Barr China Policy Speech Transcript, July 16, 2020; www.rev.com/blog/transcripts/ag-william-barr-china-policy-speech-transcript-july-16.

18. A. Viswanatha and W. Maudlin, "Barr Warns Company Executives on Pushing Policies at Behest of China," *Wall Street Journal*, July 16, 2020.

19. E. Green, "Josh Hawley's Vision for the Post-Trump GOP," *Atlantic*, November 24, 2019.

20. E. Levitz, "The GOP Coalition Is Getting More Working-Class. Its Agenda Isn't," *Intelligencer*, July 18, 2020.

21. Levitz, "The GOP Coalition Is Getting More Working-Class. Its Agenda Isn't."

22. E. Levitz, "On Night Two, the RNC Went on Offense Against Reality," *Intelligencer*, August 26, 2020.

23. K. Rogers, "Trump Says Jobs Report Made It a 'Great Day' for George Floyd, Stepping on Message," *New York Times*, June 5, 2020.

24. E. Levitz, "White House: Stocks Are Plunging Because Jerome Powell Doesn't Smile," *Intelligencer*, June 11, 2020.

25. J. Valentino-DeVries, E. Koeze, and S. Maheshwari, "Virus Alters Where People Open Their Wallets, Hinting at a Halting Recovery," *New York Times*, August 18, 2020.

26. S. Hansen, "Business Leaders Urge Congress to Send $1 Trillion in Relief to States and Local Governments," *Forbes*, May 19, 2020.

27. E. Werner, "House Democrats Pass $3 Trillion Coronavirus Relief Bill Despite Trump's Veto Threat," *Washington Post*, May 15, 2020.

28. E. Levitz, "GOP Hopes to Revive Economy by Making Life Harder for Unemployed," *Intelligencer*, July 1, 2020.

29. E. Levitz, "The GOP's Procrastination on COVID Relief Is Inexcusable," *Intelligencer*, July 25, 2020.

30. "The Fiction of Mitch McConnell's 'Blue State Bailout,'" *Chicago Sun-Times*, April 27, 2020.

31. E. Levitz, "Send Money to the States Already," *Intelligencer*, June 18, 2020.

32. E. Levitz, "Trump Calls for Limiting COVID Relief to Less Needy," *Intelligencer*, July 16, 2020.

33. E. Levitz, "Trump and the GOP Establishment Are Falling Out of Love," *Intelligencer*, August 1, 2020.

34. C. Arnold, "Why the CDC Eviction Ban Isn't Really a Ban: 'I Have Nowhere to Go,'" *The Coronavirus Crisis*, NPR, December 20, 2020.

35. E. Levitz, "3 Reasons Pelosi Should Take Trump's $1.8 Trillion Stimulus Deal," *Intelligencer*, October 13, 2020.

36. Speech by J. H. Powell, "New Economic Challenges and the Fed's Monetary Policy Review," *Board of Governors of the Federal Reserve*, August 27, 2020.

37. J. Dizard, "Don't Bet on the Silver Boom," *Financial Times*, July 3, 2020.

38. S. Detrow, "Democratic Task Forces Deliver Biden a Blueprint for a Progressive Presidency," *Morning Edition*, NPR, July 8, 2020.

39. P. Stevens, "Exxon Mobil Replaced by a Software Stock After 92 Years in the Dow Is a 'Sign of the Times,'" *CNBC*, August 8, 2020.

40. A. I. Abramowitz, *The Great Alignment: Race, Party Transformation, and the Rise of Donald Trump* (Yale University Press, 2018).

41. A. Van Dam and H. Long, "Biden Won Places That Are Thriving. Trump Won Ones That Are Hurting," *Washington Post*, November 15, 2020.

42. M. Muro, E. Byerly Duke, Y. You, and R. Maxim, "Biden-Voting Counties Equal 70% of America's Economy. What Does This Mean for the Nation's Political-Economic Divide?" *Brookings*, November 10, 2020.

43. A. Zitner and D. Chinni, "How the 2020 Election Deepened America's White-Collar/Blue-Collar Split," *Wall Street Journal*, November 24, 2020.

44. *Axios*, "Off the Rails" Series; www.axios.com/off-the-rails-episodes-cf6da824-83ac-45a6-a33c-ed8b00094e39.html.

45. E. Kilgore, "Wisconsin Supreme Court Was Close to Flipping State to Trump," *Intelligencer*, December 15, 2020.

46. K. Wehle, "No, Flynn's Martial Law Plot Isn't Sedition. But It's Not Necessarily Legal Either," *Politico*, December 24, 2020.

47. E. Luce, "The Audacity of America's Oligarchy," *Financial Times*, January 31, 2019.

48. E. Levitz, "Biden 2020: Change That Wall Street Liberals Can Believe In?," *Intelligencer*, September 8, 2020.

49. J. Epstein, "Biden Tells Elite Donors He Doesn't Want to 'Demonize' the Rich," *Bloomberg*, June 18, 2019.

50. A. Edgecliffe-Johnson, "US Business Leaders Warn of Disruption in Event of Disputed Election," *Financial Times*, October 14, 2020.

51. A. Edgecliffe-Johnson, "US Business Lobby Groups for Patience over Election Result," *Financial Times*, October 27, 2020.

52. C. Cutter, "Expensify CEO Urges Customers to Vote Against Trump," *Wall Street Journal*, October 23, 2020.

53. A. Edgecliffe-Johnson and M. Vandevelde, "Stephen Schwarzman Defended Donald Trump at CEO Meeting on Election Results," *Financial Times*, November 14, 2020.

54. A. Edgecliffe-Johnson, "US Business Leaders Press Donald Trump to Start Transition to Joe Biden," *Financial Times*, November 23, 2020.

55. M. Wayland and L. Kolodny, "Tesla's Market Cap Tops the 9 Largest Automakers Combined—Experts Disagree About if That Can Last," *CNBC*, December 14, 2020.

56. T. Frankel, B. Martin, A. Van Dam, and A. Fowers, "A Growing Number of Americans Are Growing Hungry," *Washington Post*, November 25, 2020.

57. M. Alonso and S. Cullinane, "Thousands of Cars Form Lines to Collect Food in Texas," *CNN*, November 16, 2020.

58. L. Reiley and G. Jaffe, "A $4.5 Billion Trump Food Program Is Running Out of Money Early, Leaving Families Hungry and Food Assistance Charities Scrambling," *Washington Post*, December 8, 2020.

59. A. Bhattarai and H. Denham, "Stealing to Survive: More Americans Are Shoplifting Food as Aid Runs Out During the Pandemic," *Washington Post*, December 10, 2020.

CHAPTER 12. VACCINE RACE

1. P. A. David, "The Dynamo and the Computer: An Historical Perspective on the Modern Productivity Paradox," *American Economic Review* 80, no. 2 (1990): 355–61.

2. R. Solow, "We'd Better Watch Out," *New York Times Book Review*, July 12, 1987, 36.

3. L. Light, "Good Vaccine News Has Immediate Impact on the Stock Market," *Chief Investment Officer*, September 2, 2020.

4. A. Scaggs, "High-Yield Bonds Are Surging While Treasuries Slump on Vaccine News," *Barron's*, November 2, 2020. G. Campbell and J. Turner, "How Has the News of a Vaccine Affected World Stock Markets?," *Economics Observatory*, November 13, 2020.

5. M. Mazzucato, *The Entrepreneurial State: Debunking Public vs. Private Sector Myths* (PublicAffairs, 2015).

6. "Triumph of Science Is Cause for Festive Cheer," *Financial Times*, December 24, 2020.
7. "The Cost of Sequencing a Human Genome," *National Human Genome Research Institute*, December 7, 2020.
8. H. Moses III, D. Matheson, and S. Cairns-Smith, et al., "The Anatomy of Medical Research: US and International Comparisons," *JAMA* 313, no. 2 (2015): 174–89.
9. A. S. Rutschman, "The Vaccine Race in the 21st Century," *Arizona Law Review* 61, no. 4 (2019): 729.
10. T. Bollyky and C. Bown, "Vaccine Nationalism Will Prolong the Pandemic," *Foreign Affairs*, December 29, 2020.
11. E. Silverman, "Funds Join Campaign to Pressure Pharma to Disclose Trial Data," *Wall Street Journal*, July 22, 2015.
12. "Institutional Investors Tell Big Pharma to Cooperate on Coronavirus," *Reuters*, April 7, 2020.
13. R. Brugha, M. Starling, and G. Walt, "GAVI, the First Steps: Lessons for the Global Fund," *Lancet* 359, no. 9304 (2002): 435–38.
14. R. G. Douglas and V. B. Samant, "The Vaccine Industry," in *Plotkin's Vaccines* (Elsevier, 2018).
15. M. Balachandran, "Serum Institute: How an Indian Horse Breeder Built Asia's Largest Vaccine Company," *Quartz India*, September 22, 2015.
16. S. H. E. Kaufmann, "Highly Affordable Vaccines Are Critical for Our Continued Efforts to Reduce Global Childhood Mortality," *Human Vaccines & Immunotherapeutics* 15, no. 11 (2019): 2660–65.
17. "CEPI Survey Assesses Potential COVID-19 Vaccine Manufacturing Capacity," *CEPI*, August 5, 2020.
18. B. Hunneycut, N. Lurie, S. Rotenberg, et al., "Finding Equipoise: CEPI Revises Its Equitable Access Policy," *Science Direct*, February 24, 2020.
19. I. Sample, "The Great Project: How Covi Changed Science Forever," *Guardian*, December 15, 2020.
20. A. Bastani, "The Rapid Development of Covid Vaccines Shows How Healthcare Will Completely Change. But Who Will Benefit?," Novara Media, December 28, 2020.
21. D. Wallace-Wells, "We Had the Vaccine the Whole Time," *Intelligencer*, December 7, 2020.
22. Sample, "The Great Project: How Covi Changed Science Forever." C. Zimmer, J. Corum, and S-L. Wee, "Covid-19 Vaccine Tracker Updates: The Latest," *New York Times*, January 30, 2020.
23. H. Else, "How a Torrent of COVID Science Changed Research Publishing—in Seven Charts," *Nature*, December 16, 2020.
24. M. Wadman, *The Vaccine Race: Science, Politics, and the Human Costs of Defeating Disease* (Penguin, 2017). Rutschman, "The Vaccine Race in the 21st Century."
25. S. Ratto-Kim, I-K. Yoon, R. M. Paris, et al., "The US Military Commitment to Vaccine Development: A Century of Successes and Challenges," *Frontiers in Immunology*, June 21, 2018; doi.org/10.3389/fimmu.2018.01397.
26. P. Mason, "Alexandria Ocasio-Cortez's Green New Deal Is Radical but It Needs to Be Credible Too," *New Statesman*, February 13, 2019.
27. S. LaFraniere, K. Thomas, N. Weiland, D. Gelles, S. G. Stolberg, and D. Grady, "Politics, Science and the Remarkable Race for a Coronavirus Vaccine," *New York Times*, November 21, 2020.
28. D. Diamond, "The Crash Landing of 'Operation Warp Speed,'" *Politico*, January 17, 2021.
29. LaFraniere et al., "Politics, Science and the Remarkable Race for a Coronavirus Vaccine."
30. B. Pancevski, "Germany Boosts Investment in Covid-19 Vaccine Research," *Wall Street Journal*, September 15, 2020.
31. "Germany: Investment Plan for Europe—EIB to Provide BioNTech with Up to €100 Million in Debt Financing for COVID-19 Vaccine Development and Manufacturing," *European Investment Bank*, June 11, 2020.
32. LaFraniere et al., "Politics, Science and the Remarkable Race for a Coronavirus Vaccine."
33. L. Facher, "Amid Broad Mistrust of FDA and Trump Administration, Drug Companies Seek to Reassure Public About Covid-19 Vaccine Safety," *Stat*, September 8, 2020.
34. M. Herper, "No News on Pfizer's Covid-19 Vaccine Is Good News—and Bad News," *Stat*, October 27, 2020.
35. D. Wallace-Wells, "We Had the Vaccine the Whole Time," *Intelligencer*, December 7, 2020.
36. J. Cohen and K. Kupferschmidt, "As Vaccines Emerge, a Global Waiting Game Begins," *Science* 370, no. 6523 (2020): 1385–87.
37. R. Jalabi, R. Woo, and A. Shalal, "G20 Leaders Seek to Help Poorest Nations in Post-COVID World," *Reuters*, November 20, 2020.
38. "More Than 150 Countries Engaged in COVID-19 Vaccine Global Access Facility," *World Health Organization*, July 15, 2020.

39. J. H. Tanne, "Covid-19: US Will Not Join WHO in Developing Vaccine," *BMJ* 370 (20202): m3396.
40. Jalabi, Woo, and Shalal, "G20 Leaders Seek to Help Poorest Nations in Post-COVID World." A. Mullard, "How COVID Vaccines Are Being Divvied Up Around the World," *Nature*, November 30, 2020. Cohen and K. Kupferschmidt, "As Vaccines Emerge, a Global Waiting Game Begins." H. Dempsey and T. Wilson, "WHO Head Warns of Global 'Moral Failure' on Vaccines," *Financial Times*, January 18, 2021.
41. M. Peel and A. Jack, "Cost of Vaccinating Billions Against Covid-19 Put at More Than $20bn," *Financial Times*, May 3, 2020.
42. "Where Do Covid-19 Vaccine Stocks Go from Here?" *Wall Street Journal*; www.wsj.com/graphics /covid19-vaccine-stocks.
43. "$9 Trillion: The Potential Income Boost from Coronavirus Vaccine," *Al Jazeera*, October 16, 2020.
44. S. Nebehay and E. Farge, "New Kinds of Loans and Bonds Could Fill $28 Billion COVID Funding Gap," *Reuters*, December 15, 2020. F. Guarascio, "Exclusive—WHO Vaccine Scheme Risks Failure, Leaving Poor Countries with No COVID Shots Until 2024," *Reuters*, December 16, 2020.
45. H. Kuchler, J. Miller, and K. Stacey, "US Offers to Help Increase Production of Pfizer/BioNTech Covid Vaccine," *Financial Times*, December 11, 2020.
46. A. Acharya and S. Reddy, "It's Time to Use Eminent Domain on the Coronavirus Vaccines," *Foreign Policy*, December 29, 2020.
47. A. Beattie, "The Struggle to Defuse the Global Vaccine Conflict," *Financial Times*, January 28, 2020.
48. A. Beattie, "Impending Row over Covid Vaccine Patents at WHO," *Financial Times*, October 8, 2020. "Pfizer and Moderna Vaccines Can Only Be Scaled Up Globally if Many More Suppliers Can Produce," *ReliefWeb*, December 8, 2020. M. Rathod and K. Barot, "India and South Africa's COVID Vaccine Proposal to the WTO: Why Patent Waiver Must Be Considered Over Compulsory Licensing," *IP Watchdog*, January 2, 2021.
49. J. Hancock, "They Pledged to Donate Rights to Their COVID Vaccine, Then Sold Them to Pharma," *Kaiser Health News*, August 25, 2020. J. Strasburg, "If Oxford's Covid-19 Vaccine Succeeds, Layers of Private Investors Could Profit," *Wall Street Journal*, August 2, 2020.
50. J. Cohen, "China's Vaccine Gambit," *Science* 370, no. 6522 (2020): 1263–67. G. Chazan, S. Neville, and L. Abboud, "European Leaders Under Pressure to Speed Up Mass Vaccination," *Financial Times*, January 1, 2021.
51. C. Shepherd and M. Seddon, "Chinese and Russian Vaccines in High Demand as World Scrambles for Doses," *Financial Times*, January 18, 2020.
52. "Pharmaceutical Companies Urged the Ministry of Health to Postpone Registration of Vaccine Against COVID-19," RBC, August 10, 2020; www.rbc.ru/society/10/08/2020/5f3120959a79472536b da2db.
53. C. Baraniuk, "Covid-19: What Do We Know About Sputnik V and Other Russian Vaccines?," *BMJ* 2021; 372:n743.
54. R. Dube and G. Kantchev, "Argentina Is a Testing Ground for Moscow's Global Vaccine Drive," *Wall Street Journal*, January 18, 2021.
55. Baraniuk, "Covid-19: What Do We Know About Sputnik V and Other Russian Vaccines?"
56. Cohen, "China's Vaccine Gambit."
57. "Peru Inks Deal with Sinopharm for COVID-19 Vaccines," *Xinhua*, January 7, 2021.
58. J. Wheatley, "Lower-Income Countries Fall Behind in Race for Vaccines," *Financial Times*, January 20, 2021.
59. Cohen, "China's Vaccine Gambit."
60. J. Mardell, "China's Vaccine Diplomacy Assumes Geopolitical Importance," *Mercator Institute for China Studies*, November 24, 2020. C. Tan and E. Maulia, "Red Pill? Behind China's COVID-19 Vaccine Diplomacy," *Nikkei Asia*, November 4, 2020.
61. R. Liao, "Alibaba and Ethiopian Airlines to Launch Cold Chain Exporting China's COVID Vaccines," *TechCrunch*, December 3, 2020.

CHAPTER 13. DEBT RELIEF

1. A. Winning, "South Africa to Pay $5.25 a Dose for AstraZeneca Vaccine from India's SII," *Reuters*, January 21, 2021.
2. H. Dempsey and T. Wilson, "WHO Head Warns of Global 'Moral Failure' on Vaccines," *Financial Times*, January 18, 2021.

3. "Sovereign Debt and Financing for Recovery," *Group of Thirty*, October 2020; group30.org/images /uploads/publications/G30_Sovereign_Debt_and_Financing_for_Recovery_after_the_COVID -19_Shock_1.pdf.

4. OECD, "Official Development Assistance," www.oecd.org/dac/financing-sustainable-development /development-finance-standards/official-development-assistance.htm.

5. C. Ramaphosa, "Global Response Is Needed to Prevent a Debt Crisis in Africa," *Financial Times*, November 30, 2020.

6. Ramaphosa, "Global Response Is Needed to Prevent a Debt Crisis in Africa."

7. R. Jalabi, R. Woo, and A. Shalal, "G20 Leaders Seek to Help Poorest Nations in Post-COVID World," *Reuters*, November 20, 2020.

8. Jalabi, Woo, and Shalal, "G20 Leaders Seek to Help Poorest Nations in Post-COVID World."

9. "Only Victory in Africa Can End the Pandemic Everywhere," *Financial Times*, April 14, 2020.

10. A. Nye, "The G20's Impasse on Special Drawing Rights (SDRs)," Yale School of Management, August 11, 2020.

11. IMF Annual Report 2009.

12. Tooze, "The IMF Was Organizing a Global Pandemic Bailout—Until the Trump Administration Stopped It," *Foreign Policy*, April 17, 2020.

13. "U.S. Treasury Secretary Steven T. Mnuchin's Joint IMFC and Development Committee Statement," *U.S. Department of the Treasury*, April 16, 2020.

14. M. Lewis, "How Ted Cruz Killed IMF Expansion: A Timeline," *Daily Caller*, March 26, 2014. C. Hooks, "Ted Cruz Tanks a Major Diplomatic Effort," *Texas Observer*, April 3, 2014.

15. J. Trindle, "Lagarde Pushes U.S. Lawmakers to Pass IMF Reforms," *Foreign Policy*, October 29, 2014.

16. Ramaphosa, "Global Response Is Needed to Prevent a Debt Crisis in Africa."

17. K. Gallagher, J. A. Ocampo, and U. Volz, "Special Drawing Rights: International Monetary Support for Developing Countries in Times of the COVID-19 Crisis," *De Gruyter*, August 17, 2020.

18. Table 5 in I. Fresnillo, "Shadow Report on the Limitations of the G20 Debt Service Suspension Initiative: Draining Out the Titanic with a Bucket?" *Eurodad*, October 14, 2020.

19. A. Payne, "Blair, Brown and the Gleneagles Agenda: Making Poverty History, or Confronting the Global Politics of Unequal Development?," *International Affairs* 82, no. 5 (2006): 917–35. E. Helleiner and G. Cameron, "Another World Order? The Bush Administration and HIPC Debt Cancellation," *New Political Economy* 11, no. 1 (2006): 125–40.

20. M. Arnone and A. F. Presbitero, *Debt Relief Initiatives: Policy Design and Outcomes* (Routledge, 2016). C. A. Primo Braga and D. Dömeland, *Debt Relief and Beyond: Lessons Learned and Challenges Ahead* (World Bank, 2009).

21. "After Gleneagles What Role for Loans in ODA?," www.oecd-ilibrary.org/development/after -gleneagles_186548656812.

22. R. Ray and B. A. Simmons, "Tracking China's Overseas Development Finance," *Boston University Global Development Policy Center*, December 7, 2020.

23. J. Kynge and J. Wheatley, "China Pulls Back from the World: Rethinking Xi's 'Project of the Century,'" *Financial Times*, December 11, 2020.

24. K. Strohecker and J. Bavier, "As New Debt Crisis Looms, Africa Needs More Than World Is Offering," *Reuters*, November 19, 2020.

25. P. Fabricius, "How to Get Africa Out of Debt," *South African Institute of International Affairs*, November 25, 2020.

26. B. Chellaney, "China's Debt-Trap Diplomacy," *The Strategist*, January 24, 2017.

27. D. Brautigam and W. Kidane, "China, Africa, and Debt Distress: Fact and Fiction About Asset Seizures," *SAIS China-Africa Research Initiative*, June 2020.

28. U. Moramudali, "The Hambantota Port Deal: Myths and Realities," *The Diplomat*, January 1, 2020.

29. L. Jones and S. Hameiri, "Debunking the Myth of 'Debt-Trap Diplomacy,'" *Chatham House*, August 2020.

30. "Confronting the Economic and Financial Challenges of Covid-19: A Conversation with World Bank Group President David Malpass," *World Bank*, December 14, 2020.

31. Nye and J. Rhee, "The Limits of the G20's Debt Service Suspension Initiative," *Yale Program on Financial Stability*, May 18, 2020.

32. Fabricius, "How to Get Africa Out of Debt."

33. "Rating Action: Moody's Places Cameroon's B2 Rating on Review for Downgrade," *Moody's*, May 27, 2020. "Rating Action: Moody's Confirms Cameroon's Rating, Outlook Stable," *Moody's*, August 7,

2020. Fresnillo, "Shadow Report on the Limitations of the G20 Debt Service Suspension Initiative: Draining Out the Titanic with a Bucket?"

34. "World Bank Raises Record-Breaking USD8 Billion from Global Investors to Support Its Member Countries," *World Bank*, April 15, 2020.

35. World Bank, "World Bank Group President David Malpass: Remarks to G20 Finance Ministers," Statement, April 15, 2020.

36. Fresnillo, "Shadow Report on the Limitations of the G20 Debt Service Suspension Initiative: Draining Out the Titanic with a Bucket?"

37. "Sovereign Debt and Financing for Recovery," *Group of Thirty*, October 2020.

38. "COVID 19: Debt Service Suspension Initiative," *World Bank*, January 12, 2021.

39. "Trade and Development Report 2020," *United Nations*, 2020.

40. "Sovereign Debt and Financing for Recovery," *Group of Thirty*, October 2020.

41. Address by Anne Krueger, "A New Approach to Sovereign Debt Restructuring," *International Monetary Fund*, November 26, 2001.

42. Fresnillo, "Shadow Report on the Limitations of the G20 Debt Service Suspension Initiative: Draining Out the Titanic with a Bucket?"

43. International Monetary Fund, "The International Architecture for Resolving Sovereign Debt Involving Private-Sector Creditors—Recent Developments, Challenges, and Reform Options," *International Monetary Fund*, October 1, 2020.

44. K. Pistor, *The Code of Capital: How the Law Creates Wealth and Inequality* (Princeton University Press, 2019).

45. "Statement Extraordinary G20 Finance Ministers and Central Bank Governors' Meeting November 13, 2020; www.sciencespo.fr/psia/sovereign-debt/wp-content/uploads/2020/11/English _Extraordinary-G20-FMCBG-Statement_November-13.pdf.

46. A. Karni and A. Rappeport, "G20 Summit Closes with Little Progress and Big Gaps Between Trump and Allies," *New York Times*, November 22, 2020.

47. Ramaphosa, "Global Response Is Needed to Prevent a Debt Crisis in Africa."

48. J. Wheatley, "Why the Developing World Needs a Bigger Pandemic Response," *Financial Times*, November 19, 2020.

49. UNDAD, "A Debt Pandemic," Briefing Paper March 2021.

50. United Nations, "Innovative Finance for Private Sector Development in Africa," *United Nations Economic Commission for Africa*, 2020.

51. D. Gabor, "The Wall Street Consensus," *SocArXiv*, December 22, 2020.

52. UNECA, "Building Forward Together"; www.uneca.org/archive/sites/default/files/PublicationFiles /building_forward_together.pdf.

53. United Nations, Economic Commission for Africa, "Economic Report on Africa 2020: Innovative Finance for Private Sector Development in Africa"; repository.uneca.org/handle/10855/43834.

54. *From Billions to Trillions: MDB Contributions to Financing for Development (English)*. World Bank Group. documents.worldbank.org/curated/en/602761467999349576/From-billions-to-trillions -MDB-contributions-to-financing-for-development.

55. J. Kynge and J. Wheatley, "China Pulls Back from the World, Rethinking Xi's 'Project of the Century,'" *Financial Times*, December 11, 2020.

56. B. Tangjanco, Y. Cao, et al., "Pulse 1: Covid-19 and Economic Crisis—China's Recovery and International Response," *ODI Economic Pulse*, November 2020.

57. F. M. Shakil, "China Slowly Retreating from Pakistan's Belt and Road," *Asia Times*, December 26, 2020.

58. C. Shepherd, "China Pours Money into Green Belt and Road Projects," *Financial Times*, January 26, 2021.

59. J. P. Pham, "Germany's 'Marshall Plan' for Africa," *Atlantic Council*, January 23, 2017.

60. www.findevcanada.ca/en.

61. D. F. Runde and R. Bandura, "The BUILD Act Has Passed: What's Next?" *Center for Strategic and International Studies*, October 12, 2018.

62. "BUILD Act: Frequently Asked Questions About the New U.S. International Development Finance Corporation," *CRS Report*, January 15, 2019.

63. OPIC, "U.S.-Japan-Australia Announce Trilateral Partnership for Indo-Pacific Infrastructure Investment," July 30, 2018, press release.

64. S. Hameiri, "Debunking the Myth of China's 'Debt-Trap Diplomacy,'" *Interpreter*, September 9, 2020.

65. M. P. Goodman, D. F. Runde, and J. E. Hillman, "Connecting the Blue Dots," *Center for Strategic and International Studies*, February 26, 2020.
66. Pham, "Germany's 'Marshall Plan' for Africa."
67. S. Attridge and L. Engen, "Blended Finance in the Poorest Countries," *Overseas Development Institute*, April 2019.
68. Pham, "Germany's 'Marshall Plan' for Africa."
69. B. Harris, "Brazil's Economic Dilemma: Public Debt Restraint or Sluggish Recovery," *Financial Times*, January 28, 2021.
70. J. McGeever, "Analysis: Brazil Faces $112 Billion Refinancing Cliff in Early 2021," *Reuters*, November 24, 2020.
71. J. Wheatley, "UN Chief Warns of Coming Debt Crisis for Developing World," *Financial Times*, March 29, 2021.
72. R. Henderson and P. Naidoo, "S. Africa's Rising Debt Is 'Major' Threat to Finance Sector," *Bloomberg*, November 24, 2020.
73. A. Sguazzin, R. Naidoo, and L. Pronina, "Eskom Bailout Emerging as Equity Swap by Biggest Bondholder," *Bloomberg*, December 16, 2020.
74. L. Pitel, "Scale of Turkey's Economic Crisis Triggered Erdogan Family Implosion," *Financial Times*, November 13, 2020.
75. L. Pitel, "Erdogan's Great Game: Soldiers, Spies and Turkey's Quest for Power," *Financial Times*, January 12, 2021.
76. L. Pitel, "Turkey's Lira Sinks to 8 Against US Dollar for First Time," *Financial Times*, October 26, 2020. B. W. Setser, "The Changing Nature of Turkey's Balance Sheet Risks," *Council on Foreign Relations*, October 23, 2020. L. Pitel, "Erdogan Gambles on Fast Recovery as Turkey Burns Through Reserves," *Financial Times*, August 3, 2020.
77. B. Ghosh, "Erdogan Should Break His IMF Taboo," *Bloomberg*, April 19, 2020. A. Erdemier and J. A. Lechner, "Why Erdogan Won't Ask the IMF for Help," *Foreign Policy*, June 1, 2020.
78. A. Kucukgocmen and O. Coskun, "Qatar Offers Turkey Relief by Tripling FX Swap Line to $15 Billion," *Reuters*, May 20, 2020.
79. L. Pitel, "Turkey Raises Interest Rates Again in Bid to Rebuild Credibility," *Financial Times*, December 24, 2020.
80. C. Ostorff, "Turkish Markets Bounce Back as Foreign Investors Return," *Wall Street Journal*, January 6, 2021. "Investors Back in Turkey for Short Term Only as Erdogan Record Questioned," *Ahval*, January 7, 2021.
81. "Investors Left Shocked After Erdogan Upends Turkey's Markets," *Financial Times*, March 25, 2021.
82. P. Naidoo, "South Africa Treasury Denies That Budget Cuts Will Stifle Growth," *Bloomberg*, November 6, 2020.
83. J. Ott, "Tanzanians Debate the Meaning of New 'Lower-Middle-Income' World Bank Status," *Global Voices*, July 13, 2020.
84. "Debt Markets Re-Open for Sub-Saharan Issuers," *Fitch Ratings*, November 29, 2020.

CHAPTER 14. ADVANCED ECONOMIES: TAPS ON

1. B. McClendon, "Lost Lost Causes," *n+1*, January 9, 2021.
2. T. Snyder, "The American Abyss," *New York Times*, January 9, 2021.
3. H. Shierholz, "Unemployment Claims Hit Highest Level in Months: Millions More Jobs Will Be Lost if Congress Doesn't Act," *Economic Policy Institute*, December 10, 2020.
4. R. Rainey and E. Mueller, "'We're Already Too Late': Unemployment Lifeline to Lapse Even with an Aid Deal," *Politico*, December 11, 2020.
5. J. Parrott and M. Zandi, "Averting an Eviction Crisis," *Urban Institute*, January 2021.
6. Contrasting accounts of how the congressional deal was done were offered by *The Washington Post* and *The New York Times*. J. Stein and M. DeBonis, "How Moonshine, Multi-Hour Zooms and a Deadly Pandemic Pushed Congress to Approve New Stimulus," *Washington Post*, December 22, 2020. C. Hulse, "Coronavirus Stimulus Bolsters Biden, Shows Potential Path for Agenda," *New York Times*, December 21, 2020.
7. www.youtube.com/watch?v=qOOPzkHF6yc. N. Rummell, "Intercession of Fed Brings Some Calm to Rocky Markets," *Courthouse News*, June 16, 2020.

8. M. C. Klein, "Divided Government May Push the Fed to Go Bigger. Here's What That Might Look Like," *Barron's*, November 9, 2020.

9. J. Smialek and A. Rappeport, "Mnuchin to End Key Fed Emergency Programs, Limiting Biden," *New York Times*, November 19, 2020.

10. E. Cochrane and J. Smialek, "Lawmakers Resolve Fed Dispute as They Race to Close Stimulus Deal," *New York Times*, December 19, 2020.

11. "Stimulus Talks Bogged Down on Fed Lending Powers," *FR 24 News*, December 20, 2020; www .fr24news.com/a/2020/12/stimulus-talks-bogged-down-on-fed-lending-powers.html.

12. E. Cochrane and L. Broadwater, "Answering Trump, Democrats Try and Fail to Jam $2,000 Payments Through House," *New York Times*, December 24, 2020.

13. L. H. Summer, "Trump's $2,000 Stimulus Checks Are a Big Mistake," *Bloomberg*, December 27, 2020.

14. Paraphrasing the brilliant article by A. Jäger and D. Zamora, "'Welfare Without the Welfare State': The Death of the Postwar Welfarist Consensus," *New Statesman*, February 9, 2021.

15. "China's Manufacturers Are Forced to Up Wages to US$1,500 a Month, with Workers Unwilling to Return Ahead of Lunar New Year," *South China Morning Post*, December 21, 2020.

16. W. Richter, "Holy-Cow Spikes in China-US Container Freight Rates & US Consumer Spending on Goods Trigger Mad, Possibly Illegal Scramble for Empties. US Framers Twist in the Wind," *Wolf Street*, December 20, 2020.

17. E. Luce, "America's Dangerous Reliance on the Fed," *Financial Times*, January 3, 2021.

18. B. Erik, M. J. Lombardi, D. Mihaljek, and H. S. Shin, "The Dollar, Bank Leverage and Real Economic Activity: An Evolving Relationship," *BIS Working Papers* No. 847, March 17, 2020.

19. G. Gopinath, E. Boz, C. Casas, F. J. Díez, P.-O. Gourinchas, and M. Plagborg-Møller, "Dominant Currency Paradigm," *American Economic Review* 110, no. 3 (2020): 677–719.

20. B. W. Setser, "Weaker Dollar Means More Dollar Reserves," *Council on Foreign Relations*, August 12, 2020.

21. M. Sobel, "US Treasury's Vietnam Problem," *OMFIF*, August 27, 2020. M. Sobel, "Treasury FXR Struggles with Realities of Manipulation," *OMFIF*, December 17, 2020.

22. C. Joyner, "Record Fundraising in Georgia Senate Races the New Norm, Experts Say," *Atlanta Journal-Constitution*, February 5, 2021.

23. R. Foroohar, "Why Investors Shrugged Off the Capitol Riots," *Financial Times*, January 10, 2021.

24. G. Parker, P. Foster, S. Fleming, and J. Brunsden, "Inside the Brexit Deal: The Agreement and the Aftermath," *Financial Times*, January 22, 2021.

25. M. Haynes, "Is Economic Output an Accurate Measure of the Covid-19 Impact?" *UK in a Changing Europe*, August 25, 2020.

26. S. P. Chan, "Bank of England Warns of Sharpest Recession on Record," *BBC News*, May 7, 2020. W. Park, "Is There Such a Thing as a 'Good' or 'Bad' Recession?" *BBC News*, August 11, 2020.

27. D. Edgerton, "The Tories Aren't Incompetent on the Economy," *Guardian*, September 11, 2020.

28. R. Espiet-Kilty, "Cameron and Big Society. May and Shared Society. Same Party: Two Visions?," *Observatoire de la société britannique* 21 (2018): 213–33.

29. M. Sandbu, "Shock Therapy: How the Pandemic Is Resetting Britain's Whole Free Market Model," *Prospect*, December 6, 2020.

30. G. Parker and C. Giles, "Sunak Tells Tory MPs There Is No 'Magic Money Tree,'" *Financial Times*, January 21, 2021.

31. C. Giles, "Sunak Goes Big and Bold in Bid to Repair UK Public Finances," *Financial Times*, March 3, 2021.

32. T. Stubbington and C. Giles, "Investors Sceptical over Bank of England's QE Programme," *Financial Times*, January 4, 2021.

33. M. Khan, M. Peel, and V. Hopkins, "EU Reaches Deal to Suspend Funds to Member States That Breach Rule of Law," *Financial Times*, November 5, 2020.

34. M. de la Baume, H. von der Burchard, and D. M. Herszenhorn, "Poland Joins Hungary in Threatening to Block EU's Budget and Coronavirus Recovery Package," *Politico*, September 18, 2020.

35. L. Bayer, "EU Leaders Back Deal to End Budget Blockade by Hungary and Poland," *Politico*, December 10, 2020.

36. M. Pardavi, "After the Crisis, Before the Crisis: The Rule of Law Headache That Won't Go Away," *Heinrich Böll Stiftung*, December 18, 2020.

37. M. Karnitschnig, "Angela Merkel's Rule-of-Law Legacy: A Divided Europe," *Politico*, December 18, 2020.

38. Piotr Żuk, Paweł Żuk, and Przemysław Pluciński, "Coal Basin in Upper Silesia and Energy Transition in Poland in the Context of Pandemic: The Socio-Political Diversity of Preferences in Energy and Environmental Policy," *Resources Policy* 71 (2021): 101987.

39. D. M. Herszenhorn, "At Summit, EU Leaders Dial Back to Edge Forward," *Politico*, December 11, 2020.

40. M. Khan and D. Hindley, "EU Leaders Strike Deal on 2030 Climate Target After All-Night Talks," *Financial Times*, December 11, 2020.

41. K. Oroschakoff and K. Mathiesen, "How the EU's Green Deal Survived the Coronavirus Pandemic," *Politico*, December 17, 2020.

42. Oroschakoff and Mathiesen, "How the EU's Green Deal Survived the Coronavirus Pandemic."

43. "Investment Report 2020/2021," *European Investment Bank*, 2020; www.eib.org/attachments/efs /economic_investment_report_2020_2021_en.pdf. ec.europa.eu/info/sites/info/files/economy-finance /assessment_of_economic_and_investment_needs.pdf.

44. S. Haroutunian, S. Hauptmeier, and S. Osterloh, "Draft Budgetary Plans for 2021: A Review in Times of the Covid-19 Crisis," *ECB Economic Bulletin*, August 2020.

45. OECD, *OECD Economic Outlook,* Volume 2020, Issue 2.

46. "Euro Area Policies: 2020 Consultation on Common Euro Area Policies-Press Release; Staff Report; and Statement by the Executive Director for Member Countries," *International Monetary Fund, European Dept.*, December 22, 2020.

47. J. Hirai, "Bond-Guzzling ECB Will Shield the Market from the Next Debt Tsunami," *Bloomberg*, December 31, 2020.

48. "Boris Johnson Challenged over Brexit Business 'Expletive,'" *BBC*, June 26, 2018.

49. @RobinBrooksIIF tweet January 23, 2021, twitter.com/RobinBrooksIIF/status/1352999427334660096 ?s=20.

50. M. Johnson and S. Fleming, "Italy Crisis Raises Concerns About EU Recovery Spending," *Financial Times*, January 28, 2021.

51. M. Khan, D. Ghiglione, and I. Mount, "EU Recovery Plan Faces Bottleneck, Economists Warn," *Financial Times*, January 5, 2021.

52. M. Khan, "'Demolition Man' Renzi Roils Rome," *Financial Times*, January 14, 2021.

53. M. Johnson, "Italy's PM Conte Resigns as Government Crisis Intensifies," *Financial Times*, January 26, 2021.

54. J. Pisani-Ferry, "Europe's Recovery Gamble," September 25, 2020; www.bruegel.org/2020/09/europes -recovery-gamble.

CONCLUSION

1. J. R. Biden, Jr., "Inaugural Address by President Joseph R. Biden, Jr." (Speech, Washington, D.C., January 20, 2021); www.whitehouse.gov/briefing-room/speeches-remarks/2021/01/20/inaugural -address-by-president-joseph-r-biden jr.

2. B. Clinton, "'Transcript: Bill Clinton's Prime-Time Speech," *NPR*, August 27, 2008.

3. J. Kirshner, "Gone but Not Forgotten," *Foreign Affairs*, March/April 2021.

4. See the list of Presidential Actions at the White House website, www.whitehouse.gov/briefing -room/presidential-actions.

5. G. Korte, "Biden Plans 10 Days of Action on Four 'Overlapping' Crises," *Bloomberg*, January 16, 2021. R. Beitsch, "Biden Calls Climate Change One of America's Four Major Crises," *The Hill*, August 21, 2020.

6. "How Much Would the American Rescue Plan Overshoot the Output Gap?" *Committee for a Responsible Federal Budget*, February 3, 2021.

7. L. H. Summers, "Opinion: The Biden Stimulus Is Admirably Ambitious. But It Brings Some Big Risks, Too," *Washington Post*, February 4, 2021. N. Irwin, "The Clash of Liberal Wonks That Could Shape the Economy, Explained," *New York Times*, February 8, 2021. L. H. Summers, "Opinion: My Column on the Stimulus Sparked a Lot of Questions. Here Are MY ANSWERS," *Washington Post*, February 7, 2021.

8. J. Mackintosh, "Markets Don't Think Biden's $1.9 Trillion Covid Relief Is Too Much," *Wall Street Journal*, February 9, 2021.

9. "Transcript of Chair Powell's Press Conference," January 27, 2021; www.federalreserve.gov/medi acenter/files/FOMCpresconf20210127.pdf.

10. S. Sjolin, "Did Central Bankers Make a Secret Deal to Drive Markets? This Rumor Says Yes," *Market Watch*, March 21, 2016. "Janet Yellen on Monetary Policy, Currencies, and Manipulation," *Dollar and Sense Podcast*, Brookings Institution, February 19, 2019; www.brookings.edu/wp-content /uploads/2019/02/Janet-Yellen-on-monetary-policy-currencies-and-manipulation.pdf.

11. J. R. McNeil, *The Great Acceleration: An Environmental History of the Anthropocene Since 1945* (Belknap Press of Harvard University Press, 2014).

12. M. E. Mann, *The Hockey Stick and the Climate Wars: Dispatches from the Front Lines* (Columbia University Press, 2013).

13. U. Beck and C. Lau, "Second Modernity as a Research Agenda: Theoretical and Empirical Explorations in the 'Meta-Change' of Modern Society," *British Journal of Sociology* 56, no. 4 (2005): 525–57. B. Latour, "Is *Re*-modernization Occurring? And if So, How to Prove It? A Commentary on Ulrich Beck," *Theory, Culture & Society* 20, no. 2 (2003): 35–48.

14. H. A. Kissinger, "The White Revolutionary: Reflections on Bismarck," *Daedalus* 97, no. 3 (1968): 888–924.

15. D. H. Chollet and J. Goldgeier, *America Between the Wars: From 11/9 to 9/11; The Misunderstood Years Between the Fall of the Berlin Wall and the Start of the War on Terror* (Public Affairs, 2008), 318.

16. Remarks by President Biden in Press Conference, March 25, 2021; www.whitehouse.gov/briefing -room/speeches-remarks/2021/03/25/remarks-by-president biden-in-press-conference/.

17. "Fact Sheet: The American Jobs Plan, March 31, 2021," www.whitehouse.gov/briefing-room /statements-releases/2021/03/31/fact-sheet-the-american-jobs-plan/.

18. European Commission, "EU-China—A Strategic Outlook," March 12, 2019; ec.europa.eu/info /sites/info/files/communication-eu-china-a-strategic-outlook.pdf.

19. "Key Elements of the EU-China Comprehensive Agreement on Investment," *European Commission*, December 30, 2020.

20. K. Nakazawa, "Analysis: China Splits Atlantic with Game-Changing EU Investment Deal," *Nikkei Asia*, January 7, 2021.

21. M. Karnitschnig, "Europe Gives Biden a One-Finger Salute," *Politico*, January 29, 2020.

22. E. Solomon and G. Chazan, "'We Need a Real Policy for China': Germany Ponders Post-Merkel Shift," *Financial Times*, January 5, 2021.

23. H. Thompson, "The New EU China Trade Deal Is Driven by a Commercial Realpolitik—And the World Knows It," *New Statesman*, January 27, 2021.

24. "China Was Largest Recipient of FDI in 2020: Report," *Reuters*, January 24, 2021.

25. "China Is Betting That the West Is in Irreversible Decline," *The Economist*, April 3, 2021; www .economist.com/china/2021/04/03/china-is-betting-that-the-west-is-in-irreversible-decline.

26. "China Announces Eradication of Extreme Poverty in Last Poor Countries," *Reuters*, November 24, 2020.

27. A. Lee, "China's Xi Jinping Declares Victory on Poverty Alleviation, but Warns of 'Unbalanced' Development," *South China Morning Post*, December 4, 2020.

28. K. Looney, "The Blunt Force of China's Mobilisation Campaigns," *Financial Times*, January 26, 2020. For a critical evaluation, see T. Sicular, "Will China Eliminate Poverty in 2020?," *China Leadership Monitor*, December 1, 2020.

29. I. Gill, "Deep-Sixing Poverty in China," *Brookings*, January 25, 2021.

30. J. Richardson, "China's Policy Dilemma: Raising Local Demand While Protecting Exports," *ICIS*, September 13, 2020.

31. K. Lo and K. Huang, "Xi Jinping Says 'Time and Momentum on China's Side' as He Sets Out Communist Party Vision," *South China Morning Post*, January 12, 2021.

32. T. Taylor, "Will China Be Caught in the Middle-Income Trap?" *Conversable Economist*, October 26, 2020.

33. Jiang Shigong, "Philosophy and History: Interpreting the 'Xi Jinping Era' Through Xi's Report to the Nineteenth National Congress of the CCP." Introduction by David Ownby and Timothy Cheek; www.readingthechinadream.com/jiang-shigong-philosophy-and-history.html.

34. Looney, "The Blunt Force of China's Mobilisation Campaigns."

35. Michael Pettis has been the most consistent critic of these imbalances: M. Pettis, "China's Economy Can Only Grow with More State Control Not Less," *Financial Times*, April 26, 2020. M. Pettis, "Xi's Aim to Double China's Economy Is a Fantasy," *Financial Times*, November 22, 2020.

36. A. Tooze, *The Deluge: The Great War, America and the Remaking of the Global Order, 1916–1931* (Penguin Books, 2015).

37. H. Cooper, "Top General Declines to Endorse Trump's Afghan Withdrawal Timeline," *New York Times*, October 12, 2020.

38. N. Hultman and S. Gross, "How the United States Can Return to Credible Climate Leadership," March 1, 2021; www.brookings.edu/research/us-action-is-the-lynchpin-for-successful-international -climate-policy-in-2021/.

39. "Toward an Integrated Policy Framework," *International Monetary Fund*, October 8, 2020.

40. Three exemplary analysts working in this mode are Daniela Gabor, Nathan Tankus, and Carolyn Sissoko, all interviewed by D. Beckworth, "Daniela Gabor on Financial Globalization, Capital Controls, and the Critical Macrofinance Framework," Mercatus original podcast, June 22, 2020. D. Beckworth, "Nathan Tankus on Public Finance in the COVID-19 Crisis: A Consolidated Budget Balance View and Its Implications for Policy," *Macro Musings with David Beckworth*, podcast, May 11, 2020. D. Beckworth, "Carolyn Sissoko on the Collateral Supply Effect and Other Concerns in the Money Market," *Macro Musings with David Beckworth*, podcast, September 21, 2020.

41. P. Anderson, "Situationalism à l'envers?," *New Left Review* 119 (September/October 2019).

Index

Note: Page numbers in *italics* indicate tables and charts.